FORM AND THOUGHT
IN
HERODOTUS

PHILOLOGICAL MONOGRAPHS

PUBLISHED BY THE
AMERICAN PHILOLOGICAL ASSOCIATION

NUMBER XXIII

Edited by

WALTON MORRIS
College of Charleston

FORM AND THOUGHT
IN
HERODOTUS

By

HENRY R. IMMERWAHR
The University of North Carolina

PUBLISHED FOR

THE AMERICAN PHILOLOGICAL ASSOCIATION·

BY THE

PRESS OF WESTERN RESERVE UNIVERSITY
Cleveland, Ohio 44106

1966

Library of Congress Catalog Number: 66–25319

Composed in Great Britain by
William Clowes and Sons, Limited, London and Beccles

Lithoprinted and bound in the United States by
Cushing-Malloy, Incorporated, Ann Arbor and Grand Rapids

TO MY PARENTS

Nur alle Menschen machen die Menschheit aus, nur alle Kräfte zusammengenommen die Welt. Diese sind unter sich oft im Widerstreit, und indem sie sich zu zerstören suchen, hält sie die Natur zusammen und bringt sie wieder hervor.

Goethe, *Wilhelm Meisters Lehrjahre.*

PREFACE

This study is intended to serve two purposes. Insofar as it presents a survey of the text of Herodotus, it is hoped that it may be useful as a companion and guide to the work. For this purpose, Chapter I furnishes a general survey of the *Histories*, and Chapters III and VI provide a more detailed analysis. The index of passages at the end can be used as a chart of the overall structure of the work.

Beyond this, however, the book is an argument for the unity of style, organization, and indeed the historical vision found in the *Histories* of Herodotus. This argument is inherent in each chapter, but especially in Chapters II (which deals with style), IV and V (which analyze aspects of Herodotus' historical philosophy), and the Conclusion. As Professor Walter Marg has recently reminded us (*Herodot* 2), Herodotus is a difficult author. His simplicity, charm, and apparent directness are often taken for naiveté by readers who fail to perceive the interrelation of his stories and the complexity of his thought. My aim has been to select those features of his work which show most clearly its inner connections, and to construct, on the basis of this evidence, the philosophy of history which really unifies the work. I am aware of the inadequacy of this procedure in the eyes of those who would want to see Herodotus whole, and to whom a basic distinction between form and thought is false, as indeed it ultimately must be. But the reader should consider this dichotomy simply a device for constructing a base for future, more comprehensive interpretations of the work. Since my several chapters establish different kinds of connections between parts of the narrative, some repetition has been unavoidable; I have tried to remedy this by frequent cross references between the chapters, as well as by references to my earlier articles, which are often summarized or expanded here.

The first draft of this book was written in 1955-56 in Cambridge, England, during my tenure of a Morse Fellowship from Yale University. I wish to thank the Morse Committee at Yale, the University Librarian, Cambridge, and in particular Professor

D. L. Page, Dr. F. H. Stubbings, and Mr. G. S. Kirk, for helping me in many personal ways. Professor Kenneth J. Reckford has read the manuscript, and I am indebted to him for a number of valuable suggestions. A referee of the American Philological Association has helped me greatly with certain specific criticisms. Mr. Theodore Crane, Jr. and Miss Judith Wright have assisted me in the preparation of the manuscript. Special thanks are due my wife, who has typed it and has helped me in many details. Mrs. Vance P. Packard has read much of the proof and has prepared the Index of Passages. I am very much obliged to Professor Walton Morris for having corrected my style in many places and edited the book with the greatest circumspection and care.

Chapel Hill, North Carolina   H.R.I.
Christmas 1964.

CONTENTS

ABBREVIATED REFERENCES

AAlt	*Anzeiger für die Altertumswissenschaft*
AAntHung	*Acta antiqua Academiae Scientiarum Hungaricae*
AHR	*American Historical Review*
AJA	*American Journal of Archaeology*
AJP	*American Journal of Philology*
Aly, *Volksmärchen*	Aly, W. *Volksmärchen, Sage und Novelle bei Herodot und seinen Zeitgenossen* (Göttingen 1921).
Aly, *Formprobleme*	Aly, W. *Formprobleme der frühen griechischen Prosa. Philologus*, Supplementband 21, Heft 3 (Leipzig 1929).
A&R	*Atene e Roma*
ASGW	*Abhandlungen der Sächsischen Gesellschaft der Wissenschaften*
ATL	Meritt, B. D., H. T. Wade-Gery, and M. F. McGregor, *The Athenian Tribute Lists* (Cambridge [Mass.] and Princeton 1939-1953), Vols. 1-4.
BCO	*Bibliotheca classica orientalis*
Bischoff, *Warner*	Bischoff, H. *Der Warner bei Herodot* (Diss. Marburg 1932).
BSA	*Annual of the British School at Athens*
CAH 4	Bury, J. B., et al., eds. *The Cambridge Ancient History.* Vol. 4: *The Persian Empire and the West* (Cambridge 1926; corr. repr. 1960).
CalCA	*University of California Publications in Classical Archaeology*
CalCP	*University of California Publications in Classical Philology*
CJ	*The Classical Journal*
C&M	*Classica et mediaevalia*
CP	*Classical Philology*
CQ	*The Classical Quarterly*
CR	*The Classical Review*
Crahay, *Litt. orac.*	Crahay, R. *La Littérature oraculaire chez Hérodote. Bibliothèque de la Faculté de Philosophie et*

Lettres de l'Université de Liège. Fasc. 138 (Paris 1956).

CW — *The Classical Weekly* (*The Classical World*)

Daniels, *Rel.-hist. Studie* — Daniels, G. C. J. *Religieus-historische Studie over Herodotus* (Antwerp 1946).

EC — *Études classiques*

EClás — *Estudios clásicos*

Egermann, *Geschichtswerk* — Egermann, F. "Das Geschichtswerk des Herodot. Sein Plan," *Neue Jahrbücher für Antike und deutsche Bildung* 1 (1938) 191-97 and 239-54.

Fränkel, *Stileigenheit* — Fränkel, Hermann. "Eine Stileigenheit der frühgriechischen Literatur," *Göttingische gelehrte Nachrichten* (1924) 63-127 (= *Wege und Formen frühgriechischen Denkens* ² [Munich 1960] 40-96). Cited after the new edition.

Fränkel, *Dichtung und Philosophie* — Fränkel, Hermann. *Dichtung und Philosophie des frühen Griechentums* ² (Munich 1962).

GHI — Tod, Marcus N., ed. *A Selection of Greek Historical Inscriptions.* 1 ² (Oxford 1946), 2 (Oxford 1948).

GM — *Giornale di metafisica*

Van Groningen, *Paratact. Comp.* — Van Groningen, B. A. "Paratactische Compositie in de oudste grieksche Literatuur," *Mededeelingen der Kon. Akademie van Wetenschappen,* Afd. Letterkunde, Deel 83, Serie A, No. 3 (Amsterdam 1937).

Van Groningen, *Comp. litt.* — Van Groningen, B. A. *La Composition littéraire archaïque grecque. Verhandelingen der Kon. Nederlandse Akademie van Wetenschappen,* Afd. Letterkunde, nieuwe Reeks, Deel 65, No. 2 (Amsterdam 1960).

Grundy, *Great Pers. War* — Grundy, G. B. *The Great Persian War and its Preliminaries* (London 1901).

Hammond, *Hist. Greece* — Hammond, N. G. L. *A History of Greece to 322 B.C.* (Oxford 1959).

Hauvette, *Hérodote* — Hauvette, A. *Hérodote: Historien des guerres médiques* (Paris 1894).

Hellmann, *Kroisos-Logos* — Hellmann, F. *Herodots Kroisos-Logos* (Berlin 1934). Neue philologische Untersuchungen 9.

How and Wells — How, W. W., and J. Wells. *A Commentary on Herodotus, with Introduction and Appendices.* 2 vols. (Oxford, corr. repr. 1928).

HSCP   *Harvard Studies in Classical Philology*

Hude   Hude, Carl, ed. *Herodoti Historiae*³. 2 vols.
                             (Oxford 1927). Oxford Classical Texts.

HZ   *Historische Zeitschrift*

[Immerwahr,] *Action*   Immerwahr, H. R. "Historical Action in
                             Herodotus," *TAPA* 85 (1954) 14–45.

[——————] *Causation*   Immerwahr, H. R. "Aspects of Historical
                             Causation in Herodotus," *TAPA* 87 (1956)
                             241-80 (Supplementary Paper).

[——————] *Samian*   Immerwahr, H. R. "The Samian Stories of
   Stories   Herodotus," *CJ* 52 (1956-57) 312-22.

[——————] *Rev.*   Immerwahr, H. R., review of Crahay, *Litt. orac.*
   Crahay   in *Gnomon* 31 (1959) 204-10.

[——————] *Ergon*   Immerwahr, H. R. "*Ergon*: History as a
                             Monument in Herodotus and Thucydides,"
                             AJP 81 (1960) 261-90.

[——————] *Tat und*   Immerwahr, H. R. "Tat und Geschichte bei
   Geschichte   Herodot," in Marg, *Herodot* 497–540. Cited
                             only where it differs from [Immerwahr,]
                             Action.

Jacoby, *Entwicklung*   Jacoby, F. "Ueber die Entwicklung der
                             griechischen Historiographie und den Plan
                             einer neuen Sammlung der griechischen
                             Historikerfragmente," *Klio* 9 (1909) 80-123.

Jacoby, *RE* Suppl. 2   Jacoby, F. Article "Herodotus" in *RE*,
                             Supplementband 2 (Stuttgart 1913) 205-520
                             (=*Griechische Historiker* [Stuttgart 1956]
                             7-164).

Jacoby, *FGrH* I   Jacoby, F. *Die Fragmente der griechischen Histo-
                             riker*. Vol. 1: *Genealogie und Mythographie* ²
                             (Leiden 1957), Parts A and a.

JHI   *Journal of the History of Ideas*

JHS   *Journal of Hellenic Studies*

Lang, *Biogr.*   Lang, Mabel. *Biographical Patterns of Folklore*
   Patterns   *and Morality in Herodotus' History* (Diss. Bryn
                             Mawr 1944). University Microfilms.

Legrand, Budé;   Legrand, Ph.-E. *Hérodote: Histoires*. Books 1-9
   Legrand, *Index*   and *Index analytique*. 10 vols. (Paris 1956 and
                             ff.). Collection . . . Guillaume Budé.

Legrand, *Introduction*   Legrand, Ph.-E. *Hérodote: Introduction* ² (Paris
                             1955). Collection . . . Guillaume Budé.

LSJ	Liddell, Scott, Jones, McKenzie. *A Greek-English Lexicon* [9] (Oxford 1940).
Macan, *IV-VI*	Macan, R. W. *Herodotus: The Fourth, Fifth, and Sixth Books, with Introduction, Notes*, etc. 2 vols. (London 1895).
Macan, *VII-IX*	Macan, R. W. *Herodotus: The Seventh, Eighth, and Ninth Books, with Introduction*, etc. 2 vols. in 3 parts (London 1908).
Marg, *Herodot*	Marg, W., ed. *Herodot: Eine Auswahl aus der neueren Forschung* (Munich 1962).
Meyer, *Forschungen*	Meyer, Eduard. "Herodots Geschichtswerk," in *Forschungen zur alten Geschichte*. Vol. 2 (Halle/S 1899) 196-268.
MH	*Museum Helveticum*
Myres, *Herodotus*	Myres, John L. *Herodotus, Father of History* (Oxford 1953).
NGG	*Nachrichten von der Gesellschaft der Wissenschaften zu Göttingen*
NJbb	*Neue Jahrbücher für das klassische Altertum*
Oliver, *Demokratia*	Oliver, James H. *Demokratia, the Gods and the Free World* (Baltimore 1961).
Olmstead, *Hist. Pers.*	Olmstead, A. T. *History of the Persian Empire* (Chicago 1948).
Van Otterlo, *Ringkomposition*	Van Otterlo, W. A. A. "Untersuchungen über Begriff, Anwendung und Entstehung der griechischen Ringkomposition," *Mededeelingen der Kon. Nederlandse Akademie van Wetenschappen*, Afd. Letterkunde, nieuwe Reeks, Deel 7, No. 3 (Amsterdam 1944).
Pagel, *Aitiol. Moment*	Pagel, K.-A. *Die Bedeutung des aitiologischen Momentes für Herodots Geschichtschreibung* (Diss. Berlin 1927).
PCPS	*Proceedings of the Cambridge Philological Society*
Platon	Πλάτων. Δελτίον τῆς Ἑταιρείας Ἑλλήνων Φιλολόγων
Pohlenz, *Herodot*	Pohlenz, M. *Herodot der erste Geschichtschreiber des Abendlandes* (Leipzig 1937). *Neue Wege zur Antike* II, 7-8.
Powell, *Lexicon*	Powell, J. Enoch. *A Lexicon to Herodotus* (Cambridge 1938).
Powell, *Hist. Herodotus*	Powell, J. Enoch. *The History of Herodotus* (Cambridge 1939). *Cambridge Classical Studies* 4.

Powell, *Translation*   Powell, J. Enoch, trans. *Herodotus.* 2 vols. (Oxford 1949).

PP   *La Parola del passato*

RAL   *Rendiconti della Classe di Scienze morali, storiche e filologiche dell'Accademia dei Lincei*

RBP   *Revue Belge de philologie et d'histoire*

RE   Pauly, Wissowa, Kroll, Mittelhaus, Ziegler, eds. *Realencyclopädie der classischen Altertumswissenschaft.*

REA   *Revue des études anciennes*

REG   *Revue des études grecques*

Regenbogen, *Werk*   Regenbogen, Otto. "Herodot und sein Werk," *Die Antike* 6 (1930) 202–48 (= *Kleine Schriften* [Munich 1960] 57-100 and Marg, *Herodot* 57-108).

RFIC   *Rivista di filologia e d'istruzione classica*

Schmid-Stählin 1.2   Schmid, Wilhelm, and Otto Stählin. *Geschichte der griechischen Literatur.* Part I, Vol. 2: *Die griechische Literatur in der Zeit der attischen Hegemonie vor dem Eingreifen der Sophistik* (Munich 1934).

Sieveking, *Herodot*   Sieveking, W. "Herodot, 1928–36," in *Jahresbericht über die Fortschritte der klassischen Altertumswissenschaft*, ed. by C. Bursian and A. Thierfelder. 263 (1939) 100-160.

SIFC   *Studi italiani di filologia classica*

SO   *Symbolae Osloenses*

Stein, *ed. maior*   Stein, Heinrich, ed. *Herodoti Historiae.* 2 vols. (Berlin 1869 and 1871).

Stein   Stein, Heinrich. *Herodotos.* 5 vols., various editions (Berlin 1893-1908).

TAPA   *Transactions and Proceedings of the American Philological Association*

Trüdinger, *Studien*   Trüdinger, K. *Studien zur Geschichte der griechischrömischen Ethnographie* (Diss. Basel 1918).

Wells, *Studies*   Wells, J. *Studies in Herodotus* (Oxford 1923).

WS   *Wiener Studien*

*   *   *

The following books appeared too late to be given more than cursory attention:

Burn, A. R. *Persia and the Greeks: The Defence of the West, c. 546-478 B.C.* (London 1962).
Frye, R. N. *The Heritage of Persia* (Cleveland 1963).
Hignett, C. *Xerxes' Invasion of Greece* (Oxford 1963).
Huxley, G. L. *Early Sparta* (Cambridge [Mass.] 1962).
Maronitis, D. N. *Ἔρευνες στὸ ὕφος τοῦ Ἡροδότου* (Salonica 1962).
Maronitis, D. N. *Εἰσαγωγὴ στὸν Ἡρόδοτον* (Athens 1964).

INTRODUCTION

I

When the work of Herodotus was finally published, probably after the author's death during the early years of the Peloponnesian War, so radical were the changes that had taken place in the intellectual climate of the day that both the form of this work and its underlying philosophy must have seemed strange to contemporaries. The sophistic movement, already active in Herodotus' earlier years, had begun to win the day. Among the tragedians, Euripides was questioning established views regarding the relations of gods and men, as well as the relation of man and the state. Critias and others used lyric poetry for novel ends. Most important for us, technical prose writings were appearing in quantity, among them works on physical science, medicine, geography, and, in particular, history itself, as we see from the chronological treatises of Hellanicus and Hippias. At the same time, both tragedy and rhetoric were beginning to change the Greek sense of style. These were the years in which Thucydides, by his own testimony, was contemplating a new kind of history under the stimulus of the sophists, rhetoricians, and the new tragedians.

If Herodotus' work nevertheless made a profound and lasting impression, this was due not so much to his style or to his philosophy, but to the patriotic importance of its subject matter and to the fact that it preserved so much oral material. Though Thucydides recognized Herodotus as his great predecessor, yet his own style, and his philosophy, came to differ vastly from those of the earlier historian. Xenophon, who imitates Herodotus' style to a degree, is far removed from him in thought. One cannot help feeling that in the late fifth century, and in the fourth, Herodotus' *Histories* were read primarily for their content, an impression confirmed by certain local histories and geographical tracts which supplement, and sometimes correct, his work.[1]

---

[1] Jacoby, *Entwicklung* 118; *RE* Suppl. 2.506-508; *Atthis* (Oxford 1949) 149 ff. and 221; Lionel Pearson, *The Local Historians of Attica* (Lancaster [Pa.] 1942), index s.v. Herodotus. Cf. the *testimonia* in Stein's *editio maior* (1869 and 1871).

For the relation between Sophocles and Herodotus (their affinity goes back to the

Only much later did Hellenistic and Roman rhetoricians return to Herodotus as a model of style.

A similar fate has befallen Herodotus in modern times, although for somewhat different reasons. Nineteenth-century scholarship, pursuing the notion of scientific history, believed itself to have found a kindred spirit in Thucydides, who appeared to subscribe to the doctrine that the historian must construct his own inter-pretation of events on the basis of facts analyzed according to strict method. By contrast, Herodotus seemed the victim of the traditions he followed so closely, and his work appeared a con-fused and rather untrustworthy collection of tales. However, in the period following the First World War, contemporary ideas of history, its methods and meaning, have changed so radically that the superiority of Thucydides over Herodotus (considered as thinkers rather than as sources) no longer obtains. Contemporary scholarship is thus better able to understand, and sympathize with, the very different presuppositions of the two greatest of ancient historians.[2] The increased interest in recent and contem-porary history, caused by the events of the last fifty years, has brought about a change in historical methodology, with the result that the strict methods of the classic nineteenth-century historians, based on the impartial analysis of old written records, can no longer be a model for all the types of history that need to be written. At the same time, there has been a great deal of investi-gation into the meaning of history itself, particularly in England, Germany, and the United States. The result has been a serious questioning of the so-called scientific aspects of historiography, and the further development of the social sciences so dear to Herodotus' heart. Some present-day works on recent history resemble his *Histories* a good deal more than they do Thucydides.

Critical judgment on the merits of Herodotus in the last fifty years has kept pace with these changes in historical outlook. About the turn of the century, the first steps were taken to show

---

forties of the fifth century), see *Tat und Geschichte* 540, note 73; P. MacKendrick, *CW* 56 (1963) 271; A. Lesky, *Geschichte der griechischen Literatur*[2] (Bern and Munich 1963) 303 and 339, and *Die tragische Dichtung der Hellenen* (Göttingen 1956) 102, note 3.

    [2] For two modern, "non-professional" assessments of the relative merits of Herodotus and Thucydides, see the chapter on Herodotus in R. J. Collingwood's *The Idea of History* (Oxford 1946), and Aubrey de Selincourt's *The World of Herodotus* (London 1962) 22, 36–37, and 373–74.

Herodotus' accuracy in describing the Persian Wars (Hauvette, Grundy), and later the same was done for some of his ethnographic descriptions (Spiegelberg, Sourdille). If these studies remained within the framework of standard nineteenth-century scholarship, the continued discussion of the organization of the work had brought Felix Jacoby, by 1913, to the point where he began to recognize the supreme mastery of Herodotus' organization. Now, though Jacoby himself was interested primarily in the traditional question of the order in which the parts of the *Histories* were actually composed, yet in the course of his analysis he began to see the importance of structure for its own sake: "it is no exaggeration to say that the art of Herodotus in the arrangement of material lies in the manner and the placing of his digressions."[3] Jacoby's study forms the dividing line between the nineteenth-century estimate of Herodotus and that of the twentieth.

In the twenties, however, scholarship at first took a different turn with the discovery of the existence of an archaic style in both prose and poetry. This seemed to its discoverers vastly different from the classical style—a conception that perhaps needs modification today, since it draws too strict a distinction between the archaic and the classical feeling for form. Yet it was this discovery which led Hermann Fränkel to the first definition of Herodotus' style, although he based it upon what Aristotle had observed about early prose style. Simultaneously, the growing understanding of early Greek thought effected a new appreciation of Herodotus' basic ideas; this appreciation is reflected in an important paper by Otto Regenbogen in *Die Antike*. These developments in Germany thus led to the first real appreciation of Herodotus' work: Max Pohlenz' pioneering book of 1937[4]. If Germany thus took the lead in interpreting Herodotus in his own terms, the great edition by Legrand in France, and the recent book by Sir John Myres in England, also show a radical revision of previous judgments on Herodotus.[5]

---

[3] Jacoby, *RE* Suppl. 2.380. For a general survey of scholarship, see Myres, *Herodotus*, Ch. II.

[4] Fränkel, *Stileigenheit*. Regenbogen, *Werk*. Pohlenz, *Herodot*.

[5] Legrand, Budé edition, especially the *Introduction*[2] (1955) and the *Index analytique* (1954). Myres, *Herodotus*. For recent bibliography, see P. MacKendrick, *CW* 47 (1954) 145-52, and *ibid.* 56 (1963) 269-75; G. T. Griffith in M. Platnauer's *Fifty Years of Classical Scholarship* (Oxford 1954) 152 ff.; *EClás* 6 (1961), fasc. 32; W. Krause, *AAlt* 14 (1961) 25-58; Marg, *Herodot* 748 ff. Earlier bibliography: Sieveking, *Herodot*.

II

The change in the estimate of Herodotus is due not only to our greater awareness of the nature of early Greek thought, but also to a strong interest in the non-scientific aspects of history. History, the gift of the early nineteenth century, can again be seen as the most humanistic and least exact of the sciences. As such it is not solely a rational construct based on evidence, but, more than that, a collective memory in which men acquire self-knowledge by the contemplation of the past. History is, as it were, mankind's autobiography, and thus, at any one moment, it reaffirms the relation between past and present in a new way. The historian, in noting and defining these connections, is not a scientist working in isolation, but participates in the "stream of consciousness" of his own generation. The function of the historical imagination consists in the preservation of the important aspects of the past as these are reflected in older traditions, which are formed into a new and living tradition; this is done by selection, emphasis, and combination, on the basis of certain abstract notions which give history its unity. The historian reconstructs the past by using all the aspects of imagination except invention.[6] All history, like poetry, is myth, for history is representation and interpretation in concrete form. Aristotle's famous distinction between history as dealing principally with what happens to occur, and poetry as dealing with what might logically occur, is a most dangerous doctrine, if turned into a fundamental criterion for the definition of history.[7] If history is myth of a special kind (myth restricted to actual events as remembered in tradition), then the historian must be a writer, not in order to beautify history, but in order to understand it. His analysis of events is by no means confined to

[6] The reader might refer, in this connection, to the remarks by Professor F. A. Pottle about the use of imagination (but not of invention) in the composition of Boswell's Journal: see *Boswell's London Journal* 1762-63 (New York 1950) 13-15.

[7] Aristotle, *Poetics* 1451 A 36 ff. This statement should not be understood as an accurate interpretation of this much-debated passage. It is a common prejudice that Aristotle meant to distinguish absolutely between history and poetry; cf. the discussions in A. W. Gomme, *The Greek Attitude to Poetry and History* (Berkeley 1954) 1 ff., 62-63, and 73 ff. Actually he seems rather to have distinguished between a *tendency* of history toward the particular and a *tendency* of poetry toward the universal; see K. von Fritz, "Die Bedeutung des Aristoteles für die Geschichtsschreibung," *Fondation Hardt: Entretiens sur l'antiquité classique* 4 (1956) 85 ff., and, recently, F. W. Walbank, "History and Tragedy," *Historia* 9 (1960) 217 f. (with earlier bibliography). Cf. also T. S. Brown, "Herodotus and his Profession," *AHR* 59 (1953-54) 829 ff.

the question of cause and effect, but also includes the symbolic meaning of actions seen by themselves, as well as judgments concerning these actions based on certain moral or more generally affective standards. The historian cannot do without dispensing praise or blame, for by this means he establishes the significance of the past for the present, and without this significance history loses one of its principal functions. History combines science and art with the educational aim of persuading one's own generation of certain aims in life which are upheld by a particular vision of the past. In this sense, history is always actual.

The combination of educator, scientist, and writer is the chief characteristic of Herodotus, who first discovered history as a method of understanding the world as a whole, and made it the equal of poetry and philosophy. He differs from Thucydides in constructing his account not directly on the basis of evidence, but by combining existing traditions which incorporate such evidence. When he began to collect information, such traditions were still in good part oral. Consequently, what he regarded as the principal way of gaining access to the past was in fact oral traditions, and he was confident that, if evaluated properly, they could be made to mirror past events accurately.[8] His own contribution, in turn, consisted in the combining and arranging of traditions, with the result that his own work became henceforth a living tradition for the present and future. This was possible only by accepting as much as possible of the facts, as well as the bias, in earlier accounts: his work thus presents itself as a summary of past historical thought as well as of facts. This does not mean that Herodotus was uncritical, or that he accepted "all that was told."[9] On the contrary, he has a clear conception of what constitutes the best tradition, and of the *logios anêr*, or knowledgeable man, as the best witness. He also tested traditions by his own experience, set variant accounts against one another, like a judge listening to witnesses,[10] and applied internal criteria of truth by comparison of variants and by his own critical reflection.[11]

---

[8] *Causation* 276.   [9] Ch. I, note 40.

[10] *Causation* 276.

[11] The word used for the comparison of variant accounts is συμβάλλεσθαι (e.g. 2.33.2; 2.112.2; etc. See Powell, *Lexicon* s.v. συμβάλλω, no. 5). It is the basis for forming a judgment (συμβαλόμενος εὑρίσκω, 4.15.1; 7.24.1; 7.184.1; 8.30.1). The word here translated "reflection" is γνώμη; it is formed either by comparison of accounts or sometimes on the basis of general verisimilitude and logical probability (e.g. 2.27:

Traditions were not all of equal value: some could be matched
with fact and others not, a distinction Herodotus expresses by
speaking of the right and false roads "traveled by" tradition,
and of the "*logos* that is" in contrast with the "*logos* that is not." [12]

The work of Herodotus incorporates the memory of the Greeks
about their own history and unifies it by the deeper (because
more comprehensive) understanding of the historian. In particular, his judgments regarding the great Eastern kings, and the
judgment (or myth, as it might properly be called) on the role of
the Greeks in the Persian Wars, were already formed, not without
inconsistencies, in the traditions preceding Herodotus. It should
not be forgotten that the Persian Wars, when viewed from the
Oriental point of view, were not immediately decisive for the fate
of the Persian Empire, as they appear to be in Herodotus' construction, on the basis of Greek tradition, of the myth of the great
struggle between East and West—an interpretation, correct in the
final analysis, that has been accepted not only by scholars, but
by the general consciousness of Western culture. [13] Historical truth
as Herodotus understood it is not simply a matter of factual
accuracy, but includes the overall interpretation of events and
their possible influence on our lives.

Historical knowledge in Herodotus moves on three levels:
events, traditions about events, and the historical work which interprets these traditions. Throughout the *Histories*, Herodotus maintains the fiction that his work is an oral account, even where we
know or surmise it to be based on written sources. [14] He could do so

argument from εἰκός; cf. 2.56.1; 4.31.1; etc.). The whole complex of methods needs
further investigation; cf. *Rev. Crahay* 208. See also A. Lesky, *Gesch. d. griech. Lit.*[2]
(Bern and Munich 1963) 351-52.

[12] We have here two distinct notions: (1) the idea of the road traveled by the *logos*,
for which see O. Becker, *Das Bild des Weges und verwandte Vorstellungen im frühgriechischen
Denken* (*Hermes*, Einzelschriften, Heft 4 [1937]), and B. Snell, "Das Symbol des
Weges," in *Die Entdeckung des Geistes*[3] (Hamburg 1955) 320 ff.; and (2) the idea of the
truth contents of the *logos*, an idea which is expressed by the phrases ὁ ἐὼν λόγος and
ὁ οὐκ ἐὼν λόγος: see e.g. L. Woodbury, *HSCP* 63 (1958) 155-56; W. van Leyden,
Durham Univ. Journal 42 (1949-50) 95 (=Marg, *Herodot* 178).

[13] For the Oriental point of view see A. T. Olmstead, "Persia and the Greek
Frontier Problem," *CP* 34 (1939) 305 ff., and *Hist. Pers.* 151 ff.; F. Schachermeyr,
"Marathon und die persische Politik," *HZ* 172 (1951) 1-35 (but cf. the corrections by
K. Kraft, *Hermes* 92 [1964] 153-58).

[14] E.g. 2.73.3: "they say" (the following about the Phoenix); the story is actually
from Hecataeus, and it includes verbal quotations (Jacoby, *FGrH* I, F 324 b). Herodotus uses λέγειν rather than γράφειν quite consistently both of his sources and of his

because the larger part of his sources was in fact oral, and also because he himself seems to have lectured on historical subjects.[15] The written work as we have it thus has an oral prehistory of some length in Herodotus' own life (and before that, in his oral sources), and it no doubt reproduces Herodotus' style of lecturing,[16] as well as the style of the accounts he used. However, the primary gain that results from the oral fiction is an immediacy through which tradition appears to reflect events directly, and without the intrusion of the historian's own thought.

III

The present investigation is not concerned primarily with the merits of Herodotus as a historian, but attempts to analyze the work as it stands and to define some of its leading ideas. Since his work exhibits a particularly close connection between truth and tradition in the arrangement and unification of divergent stories from the past, its form presents the main clue to its underlying conception of history. The best method of studying Herodotus seems to us a close investigation of narrative structure, and of the stylistic means by which this structure is wrought. On the simplest level, Herodotus' work is a prime example of archaic parataxis, by which short individual items are placed in a row to build up larger compositions. In this manner, individual accounts, or parts thereof, are combined in Herodotus into larger pictures, like the pebbles in a mosaic. The first part of this study is devoted to an investigation of the manner in which such small parts are eventually combined into a large unified whole.

In order to approach this much-discussed problem we must first clear away some misconceptions. For a long time, the study

---

own account. Where he does use γράφειν, there is usually a special reason: either he wants to emphasize exactitude (e.g. 1.95.1; 2.70.1; 2.123.1; etc.), or the notoriety of a person or event (2.123.3; 7.214.3). Differently Powell, *Hist. Herodotus* 31-32.

[15] Jacoby, *RE* Suppl. 2.392 ff., has proved that most of Herodotus' information came to him through his own investigation and was thus oral; cf. now also C. Hignett, *Xerxes' Invasion of Greece* (Oxford 1963) 29 ff. On Herodotus as a public lecturer, see Jacoby, *RE* Suppl. 2.242, and Pohlenz, *Herodot* 208-10. I agree, however, with Powell, *Hist. Herodotus* 34, that Sophocles' imitation of Hdt. 3.119 in *Ant.* 904-20 proves a written version of that story in 442 B.C., but I would hesitate to draw any further conclusions about the composition of the work from this isolated fact. Differently H. Erbse, *RhM*, n.s. 98 (1955) 97-103.

[16] Pohlenz, *Herodot* 208-10. K. J. Dover, *Greek Word Order* (Cambridge 1960) 10-11.

of Herodotean structure has been carried on under the shadow of the genetic problem of how the work came to assume its present form. Insofar as it is interesting to know the intellectual biography of Herodotus, this is in itself an important question, but it has nothing to do with the present investigation. For, apart from the fact that genetic explanations must, by the very nature of the kind of evidence they use, be of the most tentative kind, we would understand the present work no better by knowing that Herodotus had planned earlier to write a work of a different character. Genetic theories operate upon the assumption that traces of such earlier conceptions survive in the final version, and that we can recognize them unequivocally for what they are. This is true, however, only when the final stage is very incompletely finished, and a number of remnants of earlier conceptions are evident which conflict with the final stage and have neither been eliminated nor adjusted. The genetic approach is by necessity largely negative in its judgment of the final version, since it cannot succeed without finding imperfections, and thus is apt to lead us away from a sympathetic understanding of the text. Furthermore, a knowledge of style and structure is a prerequisite rather than a consequence of the study of origins, since all too often the inconsistencies on which such a study is based turn out to be stylistic peculiarities.[16A]

Related to this misconception is the mistaken emphasis often placed by scholars upon the allegedly unfinished state of the work. As Jacoby has summarized the evidence, it is clear that the *Histories* are not a finished book in the modern sense, since they contain several promises by the author which are not fulfilled in the present work.[17] However, such lack of final revision is not necessarily evidence for lack of completion, since the manner of composition of the *Histories* differed substantially from that of a modern book. If the assumption of Herodotus' lecturing activities is correct, the individual parts of the work must have undergone a long process of revision in oral delivery. Under such circumstances, the work did not take shape in a straight line (as it were), but its different layers became inextricably fused. Essentially, the re-

---

[16A] On the genetic question see Jacoby, *RE* Suppl. 2.330 ff., and Powell, *Hist. Herodotus.*

[17] Jacoby, *RE* Suppl. 2.372-79. *Tat und Geschichte* 512, note 25. Cf. E. Meyer, *Forschungen* 1 (Halle/S 1892) 189 f.; How and Wells on 7.213.3.

lation of oral tradition, lecture, and written work resembles the Homeric problem of the relation of short epics to the *Iliad*, except that the process of transformation falls within a single lifetime.

Consequently, the evidence for lack of revision cannot be used to prove lack of completion. Evidence for the latter—definitive in the case of Thucydides—consists for Herodotus largely in the dissatisfaction felt by many scholars with the brevity of the end of the work. This judgment is based on taste rather than logical analysis and cannot be fully supported by proofs. Our notion of an elaborate epilogue basically derives from rhetoric, just as the notion of a climax is dramatic. In Herodotus, the final portion of a story is always open to further attachment, and this is true also of the work as a whole.[18] The end of the work as we have it makes reference to a number of fundamental images and themes, in particular the ideas of the separation and balance between Asia and Europe.[19] While a sequel dealing with the later phases of the conflict with the Persians (perhaps down to the formation of the Delian League in 478 B.C., or even to the peace of Callias in 449 B.C.) could easily be attached to the *Histories*, such a continuation would conflict with the idea of balance by its stress on aggression in the formation of the Athenian empire—a theme perhaps adumbrated, but certainly not developed, in the last chapters of the work. Such a sequel would also devaluate the Greek victories of 480 and 479 B.C., as Xenophon's *Hellenica* destroys the dramatic structure of Thucydides. The break at the end of 479 B.C., as established in Herodotus, was accepted by his successors, in particular by Thucydides himself, and has rightly entered our own historical thinking as self-evident.[20] For this reason and the others mentioned above, I doubt that Herodotus ever thought of extending his work beyond its present limits, but even if he did (such matters can hardly be proved), the assumption of the fragmentary nature of the *Histories* helps little toward a true understanding of the work as we have it. The present study, being devoted to an analysis of what we actually have, excludes any

---

[18] Ch. II, 48–49; Ch. III, notes 188, 189, and 192.   [19] Ch. III, 145–47.

[20] Thucydides in 1.89 ff. begins his account of the fifty-year period following the Persian Wars with the siege and capture of Sestus, which lasted into the winter of 479 B.C. This in turn is the last event mentioned by Herodotus in the work as we have it; see above, note 17, and cf. N. G. L. Hammond, *CR*, n.s. 7 (1957) 100 f., and A. L. Jeffery, *AJP* 83 (1962) 52, note 15 (on page 53). Hammond's divisions differ slightly from ours.

consideration of the reconstruction of a work that was never written.

A third misconception is the importance often attributed to a knowledge of actual historical facts for the study of the organization of a historical work. Since a historian deals with factual truth, and since his aim in reproducing it is (at least in part) to be accurate, the temptation arises to compare his interpretation of events with what we conjecture to have actually occurred and with our view of the importance of the events described by him. Believing ourselves to possess a better knowledge of the period he deals with, we are then apt to judge Herodotus while trying to understand him, and thus fall victim to the tendency to disregard ideas we have reason to think erroneous. Many modern analyses of Herodotean battle descriptions are excellent examples of this sort of misconception, for Herodotus has the reputation of having little understanding of military matters. The fallacy here lies in the assumption that the modern historian has access to a more immediate understanding of history than did Herodotus, an assumption erroneous in principle and particularly dangerous for the period of early Greek history, where other sources are exceedingly scarce. This does not mean that the modern historian does not have the right to criticize Herodotus (for he is in a sense his equal, although never his superior): it does mean that the evaluation of Herodotus as a historical source should not be confused with literary analysis. Thus we have tried, where possible, to avoid discussions involving historical fact, treating the work as an organic unit intelligible by itself. Only in certain cases, where Herodotus' account is incomplete, or elliptic, does outside historical information help to elucidate the text. The analysis of the structure and style of the work may be useful, in turn, to the historian by preventing him from reading modern ideas into the *Histories*, but the two approaches should never be confused.

Thus the task of discovering principles of order in the work is best carried out apart from any other considerations, important as these may be in themselves. I know of no other ancient prose work where the investigation of structure yields so much thematic material. Ideas appearing in the organization are the real aim of this study. Such themes are not identical with Herodotus' opinions as expressed in various direct statements by the historian, although for the most part they do not contradict them. Hence we will not in the first instance discuss what Herodotus thought about religion, political institutions, or even the purposes of his *Histories*, interesting as such statements may be for the history of culture and the understanding of the man. Instead we will try to show how religious, political, and historiographical ideas have shaped the work and are in turn discernible in its form. If I sometimes speak as if I were describing the mind of the author, this is merely a conventional way of referring to themes embedded in the work.[21]

IV

The study of structure in Herodotus should be conducted, as far as possible, on an objective basis. Criteria for such an investigation have long been available in the observations on archaic style described in Chapter II, but they have not been used sufficiently, because outlines of Herodotus have often been made simply as aids to the memory, or have been imposed on the author according to preconceived systems alien to Herodotus. The external organization of the *Histories* differs from later prose by the use made of some peculiar devices, the purpose of which is the delineation of a skeleton structure for the whole work. The reasons for this procedure become plain when one considers the position Herodotus occupies in the development of Greek prose writing. At a later time, rhetoric furnishes both author and audience with formalized schemes of internal organization which, supported as they are by standardized thought and word patterns, do not need to be indicated specifically, since they can be learned and recognized by school doctrine. In poetry, the epic had long possessed a similar system in its formulae and "themes" (using these terms in the sense given them by the school of Parry), which were capable of almost unlimited development, and which made external indications of structure secondary.[22] Drama likewise used underlying patterns, such as certain forms of dialogue, a strict organization by scenes and choruses, and patterns associated

---

[21] Cf. the interesting remarks by H. Fränkel in *Gnomon* 25 (1953) 380 ff., and H. Cherniss, "The Biographical Fashion in Literary Criticism," *CalCP* 12 (1943) 279-92, reprinted in J. P. Sullivan (ed.), *Critical Essays on Roman Literature: Elegy and Lyric* (Cambridge [Mass.] 1962) 15 ff.

[22] On the Homeric formula as a structural device, see C. Whitman, *Homer and the Heroic Tradition* (Cambridge [Mass.] 1958) 115 ff. On the concept of the theme, see A. B. Lord, *The Singer of Tales* (Cambridge [Mass.] 1960) 68 ff.

with the idea of changes of fortune (*peripeteia* and the like), all of
which were familiar to the audience from constant repetition.
When Herodotus constructed the first complex prose work in
Greek literature—a work rivaling the *Iliad* in scope—he had to
invent a system that would be intelligible without the help of a
strongly developed tradition.[23]

For this purpose he used a device of external connection which
is found in early prose and is ultimately derived from the epic,
though it is used in the latter only in a secondary function.[24]
Consisting of repeated introductory phrases or sentences at the
beginnings of sections of the narrative, and of summary ones at
the ends, these elements (which, for want of a better term, we shall
call "framing sentences") provide the work with a relatively clear
external structure. Thus they are able to function as signposts,
marking, so to speak, the stages of the work's progress. On this
foundation, other more complicated patterns could be superimposed without being marked in the same explicit manner:
they derive in part from the motifs found in popular story telling,[25]
early ethnography, Greek wisdom literature, and the moral
patterns of tragedy.[26] Because of the use of framing sentences, these
patterns do not have to support the work to the same extent as
in later authors, but are used with greater variety and freedom.

Previous attempts to analyze the structure of the work have not,
until recently, taken its form entirely seriously. The reason is
partly that Herodotus' ideas of what constitutes a relevant
connection between parts of the narrative (between stories, or the
events themselves) differ widely from ours. It is a mistake, however, to distinguish between real and superficial connections in
Herodotus, and to declare that some are made only for "artistic"
purposes, while others alone are to be taken seriously.[27] Jacoby's
well-known outline suffers from the fact that only historically

[23] Other early prose works are difficult for us to visualize, but the books of Phere-
cydes of Syros and the early philosophers must have been much shorter, and the works
of Hecataeus presumably had a simple organization determined by geography and
genealogy, respectively. The dates of Xanthus and Charon, and of other early Greek
historians, are uncertain; see Ch. I, note 59.

[24] On ring composition in the epic, see Pohlenz, *Herodot* 63; W. A. A. van Otterlo,
*De Ringcompositie als Opbouwprincipe in de epische Gedichten van Homerus. Verhand. d. Kon.
Nederl. Akad. van Wet.*, Afd. Letterkunde, nieuwe Reeks, Deel 51, No. 1 (1948); Ch. II,
54 ff.

[25] Aly, *Volksmärchen*, *passim*; Lang, *Biogr. Patterns*.

[26] Ch. II, 69.   [27] Cf. e.g. the connections of the Arion story, Ch. III, 86.

relevant connections are stressed.[28] Another difficulty has been
the relation of the total contents of a story to the elements stressed
in the connecting phrases. Here Herodotus' method is to preserve
the multiplicity of factors in each account, while stressing one or
another in the outer framing, often not that which most appeals
to modern taste. This has led some scholars to compare his
technique with that of Boccaccio in the *Decamerone*, or with that
employed in the *Arabian Nights*, and to treat the connections as a
mere frame for the development of individual stories.[29] However,
the ultimate aim of Herodotus is never the individual story by
itself, but always the story in relation to others. Because of this
peculiar balance between the individual and the generic, many
scholars have gone to the opposite extreme of imposing an artificial
system of organization on the *Histories*, using perhaps the division
into nine books as a sign of perfect triadic structure, or imposing numerical schemes on the work, under the illusion that harmonious
balance is *ipso facto* meaningful.[30] This last assumption vitiates
(in the opinion of the present writer) the recent treatment of

[28] *RE* Suppl. 2.283-326. The material is there divided into a main line of narrative,
digressions, and digressions within digressions. Cf. also Pagel, *Aitiol. Moment* 41 ff.
A short outline of the work was found among the papers of A. von Gutschmid; see his
Kleine Schriften 4 (1893) 183-87. Further, E. Drerup, *Das Generationsproblem in der
griechischen und griechisch-römischen Kultur* (1933), Appendix "Die klassische Schönheit
der altgriechischen Dichtung" 143-46 (the work divided into 15 logoi) (Studien zur
Geschichte und Kultur des Altertums 18.1); J. Geffken, "Ein Prinzip antiker Erzäh-
lungs- und Darstellungskunst," *Hermes* 62 (1927) 12 ff. B. A. van Groningen, "Over
het ordenend Verband in Herodotus Historiën," *Mélanges Huizinga* (1948) 41-50, is
not available to me.

[29] For the idea of *Rahmenerzählung* in Herodotus, see Aly, *Volksmärchen* 260 ff., and
index, s.v.; E. Howald, "Ionische Geschichtsschreibung," *Hermes* 58 (1923) 128 ff.,
and *Vom Geist antiker Geschichtsschreibung* (Munich 1944) 22 ff.; Schmid-Stählin
1.2.640, note 2; Fränkel, *Stileigenheit* 87.

[30] Most influential has been the theory of R. W. Macan that the work of Herodotus
exhibits perfect triadic structure; see Macan, *IV-VI*, 1.xi ff., and *VII-IX*, 1. 1. xv ff.
Numerical schemes: F. Pfister, "Der Begriff des Schönen und das Ebenmass,"
Würzburger Jahrbücher 1 (1946) 349 (cf. Pfister in *Philol. Wochenschr.* 52 [1932] cols.
1109 ff. [= pp. 165 ff.]). Recently, R. Lattimore has attempted to explain the method
of composition found in Herodotus by the manner of contemporary book-production:
see "The Composition of the *History* of Herodotus," *CP* 53 (1958) 9 ff. However, as E.
Fraenkel has shown (*Aeschylus: Agamemnon* 3.805), postponement of detail is a stylistic
feature of archaic narrative; thus it should not be connected with a mechanical detail
like book-production. Cf. also Egermann, *Geschichtswerk* 239 ff. H. B. Rosén, *Eine
Laut- und Formenlehre der Herodotischen Sprachform* (Heidelberg 1962) 193 ff., attempts
to show that the work was put together by a redactor out of a number of independent
book rolls left by Herodotus: his evidence is the distribution of dialect variants in the
MSS.

the structure of the *Histories* by Sir John Myres,[31] who imposes on Herodotus a general system of symmetrical balances such as he had used earlier for Homer.[32] It is true that in some cases his theory leads to a number of acute observations, but for the most part it is a strait jacket arbitrarily imposed on the text, meant to justify itself by its mere existence. The present analysis of the work is closer to the studies of Pohlenz and Legrand than to that of Myres.[33]

The existence of framing members makes it possible to establish a number of units in the work which, for want of a better term, I have called *logoi*, following therein the practice of Pohlenz, without being entirely satisfied with the word. Herodotus himself does not use *logos* in a formal sense, but rather in the meaning of "story" or "argument," i.e. to indicate contents.[34] For, as we

---

[31] Myres, *Herodotus* 79 ff., and Ch. V. I have made limited use of Myres' observations, but I am in basic disagreement with his methods and the resulting scheme.

[32] Myres distinguishes between two types of composition: frieze and pediment. These terms are metaphors for (1) paratactic composition, for which see Ch. II, 47 ff., and (2) circular composition, for which see *ibid.*, 71–72. Myres does not take into account ring composition, which should not be confused with circular composition; see Ch. II, note 28. Myres' work on Homer: *JHS* 52 (1932) 264 ff.; *BSA* 45 (1950) 252 ff.; *JHS* 72 (1952) 1 ff.; *ibid.* 74 (1954) 122 ff.

[33] Pohlenz, *Herodot, passim.* Pohlenz was the first to publish a book in which Herodotus is studied in the form in which he has come down to us, rather than as a repository of conflicting earlier versions. Legrand, *Introduction* 235 ff. (and throughout the Budé edition), was the first editor to divide the work into units other than the traditional—and somewhat unsatisfactory—divisions according to books.

[34] Cf. *Action* 21, note 11. Herodotus often uses the plural *logoi* to refer to a single unit of narrative (e.g. the Libyan *logoi* 2.16.3, or the Assyrian *logoi*, 1.184), thus showing that he thinks of such a section as a collection of stories. The well-known reference to the Croesus *Logos* as "the first of the *logoi*" (5.36.4) is a reference to the *story* of Croesus rather than to what we would call the "Croesus *Logos*" as a unit of narrative, for his reference is to an appendix to that unit (1.92). In addition to the meaning "story" or "stories," *logos* also means "argument," either concretely (as a section of narrative) or abstractly (as a portion of reasoning). In neither case is the word used for units of narrative in our sense; cf. e.g. 1.140.3 and 7.137.3 ("I return to the former subject"); cf. also 4.82 and 5.62.1; 2.35.1 ("I will lengthen my account of Egypt"). Herodotus conceived of his work as a series of *logoi* (stories and arguments), and not as a single *logos*, as we must do because of our presuppositions concerning the nature of literary works.

I might add that, contrary to many scholars, I believe that the few places where Herodotus speaks of additions to his work are not of any real importance for the understanding of its structure. See the recent discussion of the terms παρενθήκη and προσθήκη by H. Erbse, "Tradition und Form im Werke Herodots," *Gymnasium* 68 (1961) 239-57. Erbse interprets these terms as unnecessary and necessary digressions, respectively; this is correct as far as the use of the words goes, but the "unnecessary digressions" are just as germane to the narrative as are others. Consequently, Erbse's study of digressions is actually a study of certain types of *logoi*.

have seen, it is characteristic of his style that he likes to hide the formal character of his work behind the fiction of informal reporting. In outlining the units of the work we must free ourselves from the notion of subordination, for Herodotus' *logoi* are of every conceivable length; they are in turn composed of other *logoi*, and there is no specific hierarchy of major and minor units. A *logos* is thus basically a series of items, which are themselves smaller *logoi*, held together by certain formal elements signifying in turn a selection (but never the totality) of unifying themes, beside which other elements are left intact. Thus in Herodotus we have a definite distinction between outer and inner structure, the former easy to define, the latter of great diversity. The result is a system of superimposed structures based on different kinds of interconnections. It has seemed best, therefore, in analyzing Herodotus' work, to place primary stress upon those interconnections which can be established as matters of objective fact. The outlines provided in this study are thus not mere memory aids, but are based so far as possible on elements indicated by Herodotus himself. Yet a certain amount of freedom must be permitted here, for Herodotus avoids strict formality, even to the extent of sometimes letting the reader supply the connection for himself. But on the whole, the outlines are intended to have objective validity.

Thus, in Herodotus, literature and history are one and the same, for the form of the work and its insights are mutually dependent. Chapters IV and V, which deal with Herodotus' historical thought, thus describe the consequences which necessarily derive from the study, in the first three chapters, of the structure. Since Herodotus is a classic example of the doctrine that thought appears primarily in organization and structure, the interpretation of his work should always proceed from some aspect of organization to the definition of ideas, and not from the opinions of author or critic. It cannot be denied that this method restricts the limits of interpretation, but it also makes it more certain. Since I have restricted myself to the simpler aspects of structure, it has also been necessary to restrict interpretation to some basic ideas. Fundamentally, Herodotus' conception of history shows it to be an analogue (as well as a part) of nature, or *physis*, as a whole. Civilization is not an accident, nor is it a purely human and conventional creation, as it sometimes appears in sophistic thought, but it exists permanently, like other things in the cosmic order. While individual nations understand only the particulars of their own situations, the historian, in putting together their traditions, acquires a much larger consciousness, not limited to the individual units, but comprehending the true permanent nature of history in its totality. Herodotus' outlook is that of a universal historian, though, as we shall see later, he deals with a particular historical subject; the totality of his work reveals a universality in understanding history.

The last chapter combines the study of structure and of ideas in the analysis of the battles as purely literary compositions, an approach that needs to be pursued further in the study of the ancient historians. In much ancient historiography battle descriptions form the high point of the author's effort to characterize the forces of history. Battle accounts thus have a much wider significance than mere military history, and are particularly apt to show the value of the combined study of form and thought.

Finally the Conclusion considers a number of points insufficiently stressed in the preceding discussions of the work, or omitted, since they are not connected with the study of external structure. These are primarily the well-known ethical and religious ideas of Herodotus and the ethnographic notions of Custom, Equality, and Limit as concepts underlying all history. This brief sketch will place the present investigation in a larger context and will, it is hoped, encourage others to continue it on a broader basis.

Chapter I

THE SUBJECT OF THE *HISTORIES*

I

One major difficulty confronting the modern reader of Herodotus is the lack of an exact title of the work. The word "Histories," although ancient, is not original with the author, and it wrongly arouses the expectation of a collection of disparate stories. Herodotus himself called his work "the setting forth of his research," thereby hinting at his method rather than his subject matter.[1] It is no surprise, therefore, that the book has long had the reputation of being a mere collection of loosely woven tales. In searching for a title, we are in fact looking for unity of subject matter on the simplest level, for an overall plan or pattern, in whatever form.

The remainder of the proem (1.1-5) contains, moreover, comparatively few references to the subject. In this respect, it appears to be old-fashioned (so far as we can judge from the fragments of other early prose proems that survive) and more concerned with the justification of the author's purpose than with the definition of the contents of the work. The proem of the *Histories* may be divided into three principal parts: (1) the famous long introductory sentence giving the author's name and a short description of the character of the work; (2) the accounts of the Persians and Phoenicians as reported by Herodotus, dealing with the mythical origins of the hostility between Greeks and barbarians; and (3) Herodotus' own statements about war guilt and the reign of Croesus as the starting point of his work.[2] In the introductory sentence, once he has opened the work, Herodotus speaks somewhat vaguely of "human events," then of "great

[1] For this phrase, see H. Erbse, "Der erste Satz im Werke Herodots," *Festschrift Bruno Snell* (1956) 209-22. Cf. also W. Schmid, *Phil. Wochenschr.* 52 (1932) 1001 ff.

[2] Ch. III, 80-81 and note 9; proemial topics: Ch. II, 63 ff., and the bibliography cited in Ch. III, note 3. Discussions of prose proems may be found e.g. in M. Pohlenz, *NGG*, Ph.-hist. Kl. (1920) 56 ff., and F. Bizer, *Untersuchungen zur Archäologie des Thukydides* (Diss. Tübingen 1937) 1 ff.

and marvelous deeds performed by Greeks and barbarians," [3]
and finally he states that Greeks and barbarians "came to war
with one another." [4] Thereby the definition of the subject is
gradually restricted to a quarrel (or to quarrels) between Greeks
and barbarians, and this idea is further defined in the Persian
account (1.1-4): originally a series of private disagreements
(*diaphorai*) [5] over rapings of women, East-West actions began to
take the form of real warfare (*polemos*) at the time of the Trojan
War. The result was a permanent state of hostility (*echthrê*)
between the two parties, who are then identified as Europe and
Asia. This hostility found expression in repeated acts of retaliation, and the reader (today as in antiquity) feels that the Persian
Wars will be another step in this series. Yet Herodotus mentions
the Persian Wars (the high point of his work) nowhere directly in
the proem, and thus the emphasis remains upon the idea of a
permanent state of hostility as the underlying cause for certain
future actions which are not yet enumerated. [6]

In the final section of the proem (1.5.3-4), Herodotus gives us
the beginning of the series of "unjust acts" in the historical period,
namely the attacks by Croesus of Lydia upon the Greeks, and he
then announces that he will proceed with his narrative. Again,
in what direction he will go, he does not say, but we expect further
aggression: here again the Persian Wars are implied without
being mentioned. Thus the proem of the work foreshadows a
specific subject matter without naming it. In this respect Herod-

---

[3] See *Ergon* 263 ff.

[4] The reader, coming upon the word ἐπολέμησαν in the proem, is naturally
inclined to translate "they fought" and finds here a reference to the Persian Wars.
However, the aorist may be ingressive, "they came to fight" (this is not uncommon
in Herodotus), and may refer to all wars between Greeks and barbarians. That this
interpretation is the correct one is shown by the term διαφορή ("quarrel") in the
following sentence, which takes up ἐπολέμησαν, and further by 1.4.4 (the Persians
always considered the Greeks their enemies), 1.5.1 (the beginning of the hostility),
and 1.5.3 (he began with unjust deeds, in the plural). The most precise reference to
wars between Greeks and Persians after the introductory sentence is 1.4.1: (the Greeks)
προτέρους γὰρ ἄρξαι στρατεύεσθαι ἐς τὴν Ἀσίην ἢ σφέας ἐς τὴν Εὐρώπην, but that
would include such campaigns as Darius' Scythian war. Thus the proem defines a
state of hostility rather than naming the Persian Wars directly.

[5] Cf. Pohlenz, *Herodot* 10. Despite the phrase πόλεμον διαφέρειν in 1.25.1 and 74.2,
διαφορή, διαφέρειν, and διάφορος almost always refer to private grievances causing
a quarrel, i.e. to states of mind. See Powell, *Lexicon* s. vv.

[6] Characteristically, Herodotus, while rejecting the bias of the Persian account,
accepts its underlying principles, and so the story comes to contain several themes
fundamental to the whole work.

otus differs substantially from Homer, who in the proems of both the *Iliad* and the *Odyssey* announces at least the central character and the earlier portions of the poem, although he does not give the end: the epic poet need not justify his work as does the prose writer, since its "truth" is guaranteed by the Muse, i.e. tradition, and hence he is free to be more specific. In Herodotus, we realize only that the work is not designed as a universal history, but as an account of specific interactions between Greeks and Asiatics. However, the reader must identify these actions for himself, as well as conjecture where the work will come to an end.

There is a further difficulty: if we apply the idea of a hostility between East and West to the whole work (as Pohlenz has attempted to do), we find that there are a good many events that do not fit the formula. Among such events are certain Eastern wars in which the Greeks do not participate at all; further, some Eastern attacks on non-Greek Europeans, e.g. the Scythians; and many shorter stories. The conflict between East and West mentioned in the proem cannot, therefore, be considered as the real subject of the *Histories*, as Pohlenz thought. At the same time, it is equally impossible to define the subject as a history of the East, since the work ends abruptly with the Persian Wars and omits a number of preceding Eastern events.[7] One of Pohlenz' critics has suggested, as the subject of the work, "The Rise and Fall of Asiatic Power"; but this fails to account for the large amount of Greek material and anyhow is not even mentioned in the proem. Unless we wish to follow those who would deny altogether any real consistency of subject matter, we are faced with a choice between "East-West conflict" and "account of Asiatic power," and yet neither of these seems to include the whole of the extant work.[8]

In this dilemma, it may be of advantage to abandon the proem for a moment and to look at the whole work as Herodotus has constructed it, namely as a series of historical accounts following one another in a single sequence. These accounts, or *logoi*, are in large measure identifiable by recurring introductory and summary statements, and sometimes by anecdotes, notes, or other material

---

[7] Below, 42.

[8] Previous opinions on the subject of the work vary considerably: see Egermann, *Geschichtswerk*; Jacoby, *RE* Suppl. 2.347 ff.; Pohlenz, *Herodot* 1 ff.; Legrand, *Introduction* 227-35; Myres, *Herodotus* 60 ff. Cf. Sieveking, *Herodot* 111; M. B. Sakellariou, "Motive und Zielsetzung des Herodoteischen Geschichtswerkes," *Prakt. Acad. of Athens* 15 (1940) 131-39.

placed in the breaks between.[9] Thus we have objective means for distinguishing the parts of the work and for discovering the overall organization of the *Histories*, if such exists. The plan of the work may in turn elucidate the problem of its subject.

The sequence of *logoi* and their connections show that the work consists principally of a series of military actions beginning, by the traditional dating, around 560 B.C. with Croesus, and continuing, with some well-marked interruptions, to the battle of Salamis in 480 B.C. and beyond, to the end of the Persian Wars in 479. With few exceptions,[10] the connection between the *logoi* before Salamis is through the Oriental, rather than the Greek, line of action. Herodotus thus follows, in the main, Eastern initiative, although this does not necessarily imply that he is writing a history of the East, for his Eastern account is not always complete, and its beginning and end are arbitrary if seen merely from an Eastern point of view.

The work begins with Croesus at the height of his power (1.6.1). Two statements are made about him: (1) he ruled the nations west of the Halys river, and (2) he was the first to conquer the Greeks of Asia Minor.[11] These statements are related to the two themes which we considered before: the Power of the East, and the East-West Conflict. It is important to realize that in the account of Croesus (for the moment I omit the proem) the East-West theme is mentioned in the second place only, i.e. it has the inner position both at the beginning and at the end of the Croesus *Logos*.[12] Thus the idea of the growth of Asiatic power is clearly more important than that of the Eastern contacts with the Greeks, so far as the connection of this *logos* with the subsequent narrative is concerned. The same is true internally: Herodotus tells us much of the accession of Gyges as the first king of the Mermnadae; the climax of the Croesus *Logos* is Croesus' ill-fated attack on Cyrus, whereby the power of Lydia was added to that of Persia.[13] By a

---

[9] Ch. II, 61.

[10] Below, 40.

[11] See, more fully, *Causation* 254 ff.

[12] That is to say, the motif of Eastern power and that of the East-West conflict frame the Croesus *Logos* at the beginning and end in the order AB . . . BA. Mention of the Greeks recurs only once at the end of the Croesus *Logos* (1.92.1), while elsewhere the Greek motif is dropped, and only the outer connection with Cyrus' campaigns is established (1.94.7 and 1.130.1 = 141.1). See also note 83.

[13] The main sections of the Croesus *Logos* all deal with Eastern history, if we take the Solon story as a warning of Croesus' downfall.

series of cross references, Herodotus then connects Croesus' defeat by Cyrus with the latter's further conquests, which lead to complete Persian control of Asia.[14] Here Herodotus' thought must run something like this: Lydia had unified Western Asia Minor; through Croesus' defeat this part of Asia became a part of Persia, which thus acquired total control.

The origin of Persia, as well as the previous history of the Medes and the accession of Cyrus, are told by Herodotus in a section clearly marked as an interruption of the direct line which connects Croesus' defeat to the subsequent campaigns of Cyrus (1.95.1). At the end of his account of Cyrus' accession, Herodotus tells us that he is returning to "the previous account" (1.130.3 and 1.140.3, interrupted by the section on the customs of the Persians). This "previous account" is the overthrow of Croesus by Cyrus.

After the story of Cyrus' conquest of Lydia, the work presents a straight line of Persian action. Cyrus settles the affairs of Lydia and then proceeds eastward to complete the conquest of Asia (1.153.3-4). Meanwhile, the campaign against the Ionians is conducted by Cyrus' generals Mazares and Harpagus (1.156 ff.). At the end of this account, we return to Cyrus, who is subduing "Upper Asia" (1.177). Then follow the two campaigns against the Assyrians (i.e. the Babylonians) and the Massagetae; in the latter Cyrus loses his life.

Cambyses, the son and legitimate successor of Cyrus, at once attacks the Egyptians, whom his father had planned to conquer (cf. 1.153.4).[15] After the account of Cambyses' victory at the Pelusian branch of the Nile, we follow that of his stay in Egypt, first in Memphis and then in Sais. He plans campaigns against the Carthaginians, the Ammonians, and the long-lived Ethiopians, but he fails to conquer any of them. From Ethiopia he returns to Thebes, and then to Memphis, where he becomes insane. The account of Cambyses' madness forms a coda to the story of his campaigns, and is thus the end of the Cambyses *logoi* (2.1-3.38).

At this point there occurs a minor break in the work, for Herodotus tells about a Spartan war against Polycrates of Samos before he turns to the Revolt of the Magi and the accession of Darius to the throne of Persia (3.39-60). The intercalation of this

[14] Above, note 12, and Ch. III, 89.

[15] In this survey of structure, I omit the ethnographic *logoi* (including the Egyptian). On their position, see below, 34.

logos guarantees the correctness of making a major division at this point, before the death of Cambyses. That story, in turn, introduces the Revolt of the Median Magi, which is closely tied to the Accession of Darius (3.61-87). Here again, Herodotus' main concern is with the power situation in Asia, which is first weakened by the revolt and then re-established by Darius. Now Darius is the king who represents the high point of Persian might; Herodotus describes that power in the account of Darius' marriages, his division of the empire into satrapies, and the revenues he derives from them. Action is here suspended; before returning to the main story, Herodotus adds an account of the Ends of the World,[16] and in a series of five anecdotes he skillfully establishes a link between the accession stories and those of Darius' subsequent campaigns.[17]

The Conquest of Samos by the Persians under Darius initiates a long sequence of Persian campaigns ending with Marathon and intimately connected with Xerxes' campaigns against Greece. Therefore Herodotus calls Samos the first of all Greek and barbarian cities conquered by Darius (3.139.1).[18] There follow the Babylonian and Scythian campaigns, and it is with the latter that the narrative assumes greater compactness. Not only is the Scythian campaign treated in greater detail than the preceding, but at its conclusion Herodotus establishes a number of precise connections with the Ionian Revolt, which in turn is the beginning of interactions between East and West, and thus leads to the Persian Wars. These connections consist first of the accounts of the European campaigns of Megabazus and Otanes, where the emphasis lies upon the Hellespont—the boundary of Asia and Europe later crossed by Xerxes. They also comprise the story of Histiaeus of Miletus, the transfer of the Paeonians to Asia, and the movement of Darius himself to his capital, Susa, from which he is to direct all subsequent campaigns against the Greeks. This connection is so strong that the contemporary Libyan campaign is treated as an aside.[19] It is often assumed that the Graeco-Persian narrative starts with the Ionian Revolt, but the links referred to prove that the earlier Scythian campaign is the real beginning of this series of events. The reason, as will be seen later, is the parallel between

[16] For the section on the "Ends of the World," see Ch. III, 102-103, and IV, 72.
[17] Ch. III, 103-104; *Samian Stories* 314 f.
[18] For the interpretation of this sentence, see Pohlenz, *Herodot* 77, note 3.
[19] Ch. III, 111; *Causation* 269-70; *Tat und Geschichte* 508, note 18.

Scythians and Greeks as defenders of the freedom of Europe against Asiatic expansion.[20]

The Ionian Revolt ends with Persian naval action near the Hellespont (6.33 and 42). The next action of Darius' generals begins with Mardonius' crossing of the Hellespont to attack the mainland Greeks and punish the Athenians and Eretrians for their participation in the Ionian Revolt (6.43 ff.). This expedition fares badly at Mt. Athos and returns to Asia without accomplishing its mission. Darius next orders the Thasians to take down their walls, and he sends heralds to all the Greeks asking for earth and water as tokens of submission. Simultaneously, he orders new preparations for an attack on Greece; these result in the campaign against Athens and Eretria, which fails at Marathon.[21]

There is some difference of opinion among scholars concerning the exact place at which to make the break between the campaigns of Darius and the later campaigns of Xerxes.[22] It seems to me that the most natural division occurs in the first chapter of Book 7, where we return to an earlier point of the narrative and see Darius receive a message about the defeat at Marathon.[23] He is now anxious to campaign in person against the Greeks, and upon hearing of the outbreak of a revolt in Egypt, he wishes to attack both countries, but death prevents the execution of these plans (7.4). Thus both campaigns fall to Xerxes as his heir. The death of Darius does not constitute a break in the narrative, and the Persian Wars of 480 B.C. are seen by Herodotus as the direct result of Darius' last plans.

Xerxes' campaign against Greece (his Egyptian campaign is not described in detail by Herodotus) is a closely-knit narrative in which, after describing the decision and plans of Xerxes, Herodotus follows exactly the movements of the army and navy, beginning in Asia Minor and continuing across the Hellespont into Greece, until we find the army on the road to Athens and the navy anchored in her harbor.[24] It is with the

---

[20] Ch. III, 106 ff.

[21] Hdt. 6.46 ff. (Thasos), 48.1 ff. (heralds), 48.2 (first preparations for Marathon), 94 ff. (Marathon).

[22] Jacoby, *RE* Suppl. 2.311 and 314, divides after 7.4 (death of Darius), but the majority divide at 7.1: see How and Wells 2.124; Macan, *VII-IX* 1.1.xix ff.; Pohlenz, *Herodot* 120; Myres, *Herodotus* 105 ff.=217 (cf. 126); Legrand, Budé.

[23] The break consists primarily in the group of stories at the end of Book 6, especially Chs. 125-31 and 137-40. Cf. Ch. III, 125, and note 142.

[24] Hdt. 8.34 (army) and 66.1 (navy).

antecedents of the battle of Salamis that the structure of the work changes (8.42 ff.). From here on, with some interruptions during the campaign of Mardonius in 479 B.C., the narrative follows the actions of the Greeks, who will be the victors in the war.[25]

Thus the major part of Herodotus' work presents a connected series of Persian actions beginning with Cyrus' campaigns after the overthrow of Croesus (1.141 ff.) and ending just before Salamis. This chain is clearly marked throughout by introductory and summary statements which it has not been convenient to quote in detail.[26] The great majority of these *logoi* begin with Persian action, if we except smaller *logoi* which are placed in the breaks between major units.[27] Three major *logoi*, however, also differ from the norm by beginning with Greek action, thus foreshadowing the about-face of the narrative at Salamis. These are the first Persian conquest of Ionia (1.141 ff.), the Spartan campaign against Polycrates of Samos (3.39-60), and the Ionian Revolt (5.28 ff.). With these exceptions, Persian action determines the course of the narrative in the *Histories*.

This arrangement is disturbed, however, at the beginning and the end. The campaign of Croesus against Cyrus should properly have formed a part of the campaigns of Cyrus, but taking into consideration no doubt the fact that Croesus was here the aggressor, Herodotus has placed the history of Lydia at the beginning of his work.[28] At the end he has cut off the line of Persian action

[25] The Greek line of action after Salamis consists primarily of the advance of the Greek navy: 8.108 ff. (siege of Andros), 8.131 f. (movement to Delos), 9.90 ff. (movement to Samos and Mycale), 9.114 ff. (movement to Hellespont and capture of Sestus), 9.121 (return to mainland Greece). In addition, the campaign of Mardonius shows that the Greeks have the initiative to an extent; see Ch. VI, 289. The return of Xerxes and the stories concerned with Artabazus (Ch. VI, 285, 297) are secondary. See further, Ch. III, 140-41.

[26] E.g. Hdt. 1.177 (Cyrus conquers upper Asia while his generals subdue Ionia); 2.1 and 3.1 (Cambyses against Egypt); 3.61.1 (Revolt of Magi synchronized with Cambyses' stay in Egypt); 3.139.1 (Darius' first campaign directed against Samos); 4.1 (Scythian campaign chronologically related to Babylonian); 3.143.1 (Darius, on return from Scythia, begins European campaign); 5.28 (Relation of Ionian Revolt to European campaign); 6.43.1 (Mt. Athos campaign); 6.46.1 (Thasians); 6.48.1 (heralds sent to Greece); 6.94 (Marathon). 7.1 establishes the connection between Darius' and Xerxes' campaigns: above, notes 22 and 23.

[27] E.g. certain ethnographic sections at the end of the campaigns of Cyrus against the Babylonians and Massagetae (1.192-200 and 1.215-16), or the first Miltiades *Logos* (6.34-41).

[28] G. DeSanctis, *RFIC* 54 (1926) 289 ff., and 64 (1936) 1 ff., first proposed the well-known theory that this "displacement" indicated a shift in plan, but we are here concerned only with the work in its final form.

by the victories of the Greeks. We may say then, provisionally, that the beginning and end of the work are determined by considerations other than the rise and fall of the East. We shall see later what these considerations are.

II

Apart from the beginning and end of the work, it is clear that the main sequence of *logoi* is not primarily an account of East-West conflicts, but a description of the activities of Eastern powers, among which their wars with the Greeks are only a part. Already the Lydian and Median kings exhibited what, to Herodotus, is the essentially Asiatic characteristic of basically unmotivated expansionism.[29] By overthrowing both nations, the Persians established a unified Asiatic empire which combined the regions east and west of the Halys river.[30] Cyrus and Darius, the two greatest Persian kings, attempted, with varying degrees of success, to continue this expansion, and Cambyses and Xerxes took their plans of empire directly from their fathers.[31] For much of the *Histories* the unity of the narrative is based on unity of action driven forward by a single basic motivation.

This view runs counter to the commonly expressed argument that at least a portion of the work is a history of Persia. Jacoby implies that the elements of such a history would consist of chronicles of kings and their deeds.[32] More recently, J. E. Powell has outlined his proposed original form of Herodotus' Persian History: it too forms a straightforward chronicle beginning with the Assyrians (1.95.2) and continuing with Median and Persian history, with the Lydian history following upon Cyrus' accession. Powell thinks that this history originally extended as far as the Libyan Campaign (4.205) and was actually published separately. Later Herodotus conceived the plan of extending the

[29] *Causation* 253 ff.

[30] Throughout the histories of Croesus and Cyrus, Herodotus emphasizes first the division, and then the unification of Asia. See Pohlenz, *Herodot* 21 ff.; *Causation* 258-59, and note 31.

[31] Cyrus, who "came to rule over all of Asia" (1.130.3), finds his limit, before he can conquer Egypt, in the campaign against the Massagetae. Darius, edged on by his wife at the beginning of his rule (3.134), finds his limit in premature death before the conquest of Egypt and Greece (7.4). Cambyses conquers Egypt, and Xerxes reconquers it, according to the wishes of their fathers. Xerxes' second task—the conquest of Greece—ends in failure.

[32] Jacoby, *RE* Suppl. 2.348 ff.

work into the fifth century and began to rewrite it, but eventually
he used both versions for the antecedents of his History of the
Persian Wars.[33] Jacoby and Powell differ only in certain details:
Jacoby's Persian History extends through Book 6, while Powell's
first draft stops in Book 4. These theories are based on the observation that Herodotus did in fact conceive of Eastern history in
the (no doubt traditional) pattern of kings' chronicles, as is
apparent from the formulaic language he uses for royal succes-
sions.[34] They neglect, however, the considerable freedom with
which Herodotus handles chronicle data.

The history of the Egyptian kings may serve as an example
(2.99-182). Its first section (2.99-146) begins with the mention of a
list of 331 kings which Herodotus claims to have received from
the Egyptian priests. This list is not reproduced in the work,
however, and Herodotus confines himself to the first and the last
kings (Min and Moeris), and to one other person (Queen Nitocris),
whose exact place in the series is not given.[35] This selection is
determined not only by the paucity of sources available, but also
by Herodotus' desire to mark the beginning and end of the series,
as well as by characteristic Herodotean ideas of historical relevance: Nitocris had built great buildings, her cruel vengeance on
the murderers of her brother was to be counted as a great deed,
and the paradox of a woman ruling over men paralleled the story
of her namesake, the queen of Babylon.[36] The first list is followed,
without a break, by another of ten kings from Sesostris to Setho,
which is given in complete and consecutive form, except that the
lengths of the kings' reigns are mentioned only where the numbers
have a special symbolic value; these kings were either exceptionally great or exceptionally wicked.[37] By contrast, the history of the

[33] Powell, *Hist. Herodotus* 24, 60, and 63 ff. Powell is much influenced by Jacoby
(above, note 32) and DeSanctis (above, note 28).

[34] The full formula is: After such and such an event, king X died, having ruled n
years, and king Y acquired the rule; see e.g. 1.25.1 and 26.1; 1.214.3 and 2.1.1;
3.10.2; 7.4. Since the dating of other fifth-century historians is uncertain, we do not
know in what form Herodotus knew this chronicle pattern; see below, note 59. But
see Jacoby, *Abhandlungen z. griech. Geschichtsschr.* (Leiden 1956) 198-200.

[35] Whether or not Herodotus actually had such a complete list, he maintains that
he did, and this means at least that he assumed the priests could have procured it
for him.

[36] Hdt. 2.100.

[37] Cheops ruled for 50 years, his brother Chephren for 56, and these 106 years
together brought great evil to Egypt (2.128). While the four predecessors of Cheops
had been a boon for Egypt, the following three kings ruined her (2.124.1 and ff.), for

later Saite dynasty (2.147-82) is complete in all respects: Herodotus' sources (being, as he gives us to understand, partly Greek) were here more accurate, and he reproduces them more exactly, in the manner of a chronicle. Herodotus appears to have adapted his material to a theory about the history of Egypt, according to which it fell into four periods: (1) a legendary period of 331 kings who were of little importance, (2) the great and prosperous rules of Sesostris, Pheron, Proteus, and Rhampsinitus, (3) a period of decline under the remainder of the ten kings (the Pyramid Builders), and (4) the Saite revival.

The king lists of Lydia and Media are treated even more summarily by Herodotus. The Lydian emphasizes mainly the campaigns against Greeks. The war of Alyattes with the Medes is transferred to a different part of the narrative, and there are a number of other irregularities, mostly affecting purely Oriental events.[38] The Median history stresses the overall expansionist

---

the gods had decreed altogether 150 years of misfortune for Egypt (2.133.3). However, the third of the bad kings, Mycerinus (successor of Chephren and son of Cheops), upset the gods' calculations by bringing Egypt relief from her troubles before the appointed time. For this he was punished by having his reign shortened (2.133). Since Herodotus does not give the total length, it is not clear how long altogether the three bad kings ruled, except that it was less than 150 years, and that Mycerinus' reign lasted $x+7$ years, this being considerably less than 44 years, since Mycerinus complained that he was to die so young (2.133.2). I should add that I cannot accept the transposition (by B. Apostolides and Sir Flinders Petrie) of 2.124, line 25 (Hude)— 2.136 to stand between 2.99 and 2.100, since that destroys the contrast between εὐνομία and κακότης in 2.124 (beginning), a problem not solved by the recent defense of the transposition by H. T. Wallinga, *Mnemosyne*, ser. 4, 12 (1959) 204-23. Cf. also von Fritz, *TAPA* 67 (1936) 331, note 15. Clearly we are dealing here with a whole web of symbolic numbers (50; $56 = 50 + 2 \times 3$; $4 + 3 = 7$; 3×50; $x + 7$). The passage is not properly treated by J. W. S. Blom, *De typische Getallen bij Homeros en Herodotus* (Nijmegen 1936). W. H. Roscher, *Die Zahl 50 in Mythus, Kultus*, etc., *ASAW* 33, No. 5 (Leipzig 1917), is not available to me.

Evils are connected with numbers in the story of the Ethiopian Sabacos, whose rule in Egypt lasted 50 years, again a divinely ordained time (2.139.1-3). By contrast, the total given for the 341 Egyptian kings is an arbitrary calculation by Herodotus himself on the basis of his belief that three rules would last 100 years (2.142.2); differently F. W. Mitchel, *Phoenix* 10 (1956) 62-63.

[38] War of Alyattes with Cyaxares: 1.16.2 = 74 = 103.2. Other irregularities: the notorious phrase καὶ οὗτος in 1.14.4 compares Gyges with his successors, not his predecessors; cf. Stein *ad loc.* and Pohlenz, *Herodot* 10, note 1. Further, Sadyattes' reign is treated partly under his son's (1.18.2). The Milesian war of Alyattes is told after the mention of his other campaigns (which could not have preceded it) to achieve a climax at the end of his life (1.16.2 ff.; see below, note 81). Likewise, the separation of Croesus' Greek campaigns from those against native populations (1.26-27.1, and 1.28) is not necessarily chronological.

policy of the kings rather than their individual reigns.[39] In each case the history is treated in a manner suitable to the particular place it occupies in the work as we now read it. Furthermore, both the Egyptian and Median chronicles are cut at the end to connect them with the subsequent narratives: mention of the death of Amasis is shifted to Cambyses' attack on Egypt (3.10.2), and the reign of Astyages is not given in detail except for his relations with Cyrus. We should then be careful to avoid over-emphasizing the significance of the elements of chronicle form. In the Persian history, the death of Cyrus marks the end of a *logos*, since he died in action, namely in the campaign against the Massagetae (1.214.3). Cambyses' death, on the other hand, is told in connection with the Revolt of the Magi (3.66.2), and the death of Darius is a part of the section which introduces the campaigns of Xerxes (7.4). This alone suggests that the Persian chronicle is for Herodotus merely a received traditional pattern, and not the main basis of his work.

Furthermore, it can be shown that Herodotus does not always give a complete and evenly balanced account of all the events in a king's reign which are known to him. In certain instances, he himself tells us that he has been selective. Elsewhere, he casually mentions important elements of a king's history which he has not seen fit to include in their proper place. Contrary to a commonly held view, Herodotus did not uncritically include every piece of information that had come to his attention.[40] On close analysis, one is struck by his selectivity more than by his inclusiveness. This selectivity furnishes several clues to the unity of the subject of the work.

In the Croesus story, two items that would have been important in a Lydian history are neglected by Herodotus: one is Croesus'

[39] Pohlenz, *Herodot* 23 f.

[40] It is a common, but quite erroneous, assumption that Herodotus is all-inclusive, a feeling expressed in Rawlinson's mistranslation of the famous phrase ἐγὼ δὲ ὀφείλω λέγειν τὰ λεγόμενα, etc. (7.152.3): "my duty is to report all that is said . . .," where "all" is added gratuitously. Herodotus means that he must tell a story (once he tells it at all) as it is told, regardless of whether he believes it. Jacoby, *RE* suppl. 2.350, line 67, assumes that Herodotus tells all he knows about Greek history, which is manifestly not the case. Even Pohlenz, *Herodot* 43 ff., assumes that the work contains more investigation (*historiê*) than the *logos* requires. In making these judgments, we are guided by modern notions of relevance, not by Herodotus' own. Cf. also Introduction, note 34 (on "digressions"). G. Gottlieb, *Das Verhältnis der ausserherodoteischen Überlieferung zu Herodot* (Bonn 1963) 130 ff., states that Herodotus is very selective before the Persian Wars, and for the latter period somewhat selective also.

struggle to gain possession of the throne, the other, the series of his early conquests in Asia Minor. In an appendix to the Croesus *Logos* (1.92.2-4), Herodotus tells of certain dedicatory offerings, made by Croesus soon after his accession, which must be distinguished from the dedications made later in connection with his great war against Cyrus. These earlier dedications, Herodotus thought, derived from the patrimony of a man who had tried to help a half-brother of Croesus in seeking the throne.[41] Nothing of all this is mentioned in the description of Croesus' accession earlier in the *Histories* (1.26.1 ff.), since there the emphasis is on Croesus' great power from the beginning of his reign. This evaluation is actually a Herodotean, or at least a Greek, invention, for it has been shown that Croesus' father Alyattes was the more powerful king, and Gyges, the founder of the dynasty, was probably also a greater conqueror than he appears in Herodotus' account.[42] In view of the Herodotean conception of Croesus, it is all the more remarkable that his non-Greek conquests in Asia Minor are condensed, at the cost of some inconsistency, into a single sentence, which connects his Greek campaigns with Solon's visit to Sardis (1.28-29).[43] Herodotus stresses primarily the result

[41] In 1.92, Herodotus lists all the dedications made by Croesus, except those at Delphi and the sanctuary of Amphiaraus just before the war with Cyrus (these had been mentioned earlier). He then declares that these other dedications were made from the patrimony of a supporter (unnamed) of Croesus' half-brother Pantaleon, i.e. they were made right after Croesus' accession (1.92.4). Herodotus is here completing a pattern stressed for all the Lydian kings, according to which the accounts of their reigns consist of campaigns and dedications, since both are great accomplishments (*erga*), cf. e.g. 1.14 (Gyges). Nevertheless, the appendix gives us *de facto* a piece of Croesus' earliest history, and one which would have conflicted with the description of Croesus' great power at the beginning of the work (1.6 ff.). The idea that these dedications were early is doubtless derived from the Pantaleon story. Nicolaus of Damascus has, perhaps from Xanthus, a different version of the same story; he names the supporter Sadyattes and gives a private motivation for Croesus' hatred (fr. 65; Jacoby *FGrH* II, A 360-61 and II, C 250-51). See, in general, Weissbach, *RE* Suppl. 5, s.v. Kroisos.

[42] For Alyattes see E. Meyer, *Geschichte des Altertums*[2], ed. H. E. Stier, 3 (1937) 166 and note 1. Cf. G. Radet, *La Lydie et le monde grec au temps des Mermnades* (Paris 1893) 193 ff. For Gyges, see Radet, *op. cit.*, Ch. V; K. J. Beloch, *Griechische Geschichte*[2] 1.1 (1912) 343-46; D. G. Hogarth in *CAH* 3 (1929) 501-24; Lehmann-Haupt, *RE*, s.v. Gyges, 1957 ff.

[43] I believe that the text of 1.28 is sound, except that we should read προσεκτημένου instead of προσεπικτωμένου. (Krüger had already suggested προσεπεκτημένου.) The account is so condensed here that the impression is created that Croesus was the first to reach the Halys river; yet Herodotus knew that Alyattes had fought the Medes, and thus must have been their neighbor (cf. Stein on 1.29, line 2); contrast also 7.30 with 1.74 (but note that Herodotus does not speak of the Halys as boundary in the time of

of these conquests, namely that Croesus had subdued nearly all nations west of the Halys river.

In the *logos* dealing with Cyrus, Herodotus himself tells us that he is using only part of the available material. The story of Cyrus' birth is only one out of four versions known to him (1.95.1), and for the account of Cyrus' death a similar statement is made (1.214.5).[44] As we have seen, the birth and accession of Cyrus are told in a *logos* separate from the *logoi* of Cyrus' campaigns, a treatment which has caused some obscurities in the narrative, especially at the beginning and end of the accession *logos*, where the locale of the action is not always clear.[45] This isolates the *logos* of Cyrus' origin from his campaign *logoi*, as well as from the earlier war of Croesus, in both of which the locale (Sardis) is clearly named.[46] The campaigns of Cyrus, in turn, show evident traces of condensation. They fall into two sections: the first deals with the Ionian campaign, in which we get only a glimpse of Cyrus at Ecbatana, without any details of his Eastern campaigns (1.153.4). The second part is introduced by the statement that most of the nations conquered will be omitted, except for what is most worthy of account (1.177.1). The two campaigns which qualify from this point of view are the Babylonian and Massagetan. Babylon is evidently of great interest to Herodotus, for he tells later on the story of its second conquest by Darius and

---

Alyattes). These apparent inconsistencies could be adjusted, but Herodotus does not face the problem. For a suggested adjustment, see Weissbach, *RE* Suppl. 5.459. Similarly, the apparent conflict between the statement that Croesus was the first to subdue the Greeks and the stories of earlier Mermnad wars against Greek cities has caused much perplexity (see, however, Pohlenz, *Herodot* 10-11: the difference is one between raids and real conquest). Like the brevity with which Herodotus tells of Croesus' foreign alliances other than the Spartan (1.77.1-3 and 82.1), these omissions betray Herodotus' purposes: first his intention to depict Croesus as the greatest of the Mermnad line, and secondly his emphasis on Eastern relations with the Greeks. Cf. also above, note 38.

[44] For the Greek versions of Cyrus' birth and death, see Weissbach, *RE* Suppl. 4, s.v. Kyros No. 6, 1129 ff.

[45] The action takes place throughout near Ecbatana, which is, however, named only once (1.110.2). The home of Cyrus is simply called "Persia" (1.108.2; 123.3; 123.4; 126.1): on this term see below, note 51. At the end, the capture of Ecbatana is only vaguely hinted at (1.128.2), although this is stressed in the cuneiform tradition: see Olmstead, *Hist. Pers.* 37. In the Croesus *Logos*, it is not stated where Cyrus came from when he attacked Croesus (1.76.2).

[46] The Croesus *Logos* ends with Cyrus in Sardis, and the campaign *logoi* begin in the same locale (1.141.1), whence we follow Cyrus' travels into "Upper Asia" (1.153.3, etc.).

promises a fuller treatment of its history (in the so-called Assyrian *logoi*, which were probably never written). The reason for this fullness becomes clear when we read of the importance of Babylon for the resources of the Persian empire.[47] The city represents symbolically the center of power in Asia, and its conquest by Cyrus stands for Persian conquest of all Asia. Similarly, the campaign against the Massagetae has a symbolic importance, since it illustrates the downfall of a ruler: on this campaign, Cyrus came to the limit of his aggressive military plans, and lost his life in defeat.[48] Cyrus' campaigns are thus treated on three levels: the majority of his Eastern campaigns are barely mentioned, the Babylonian and Massagetan campaigns are stressed because of their symbolic importance, and only the Greek campaign is given in full detail.

The story of Cambyses shows only two inconsistencies due to the adaptation of received tradition. One is the curious remark in the description of Darius' empire (3.88.1) that the people of Asia had been conquered for Darius by Cyrus, "and then again by Cambyses." Since Herodotus, as is probable, did not consider Egypt as part of Asia, we should not refer this statement to Cambyses' Egyptian campaign, but to troubles which arose after his accession and which Herodotus does not mention elsewhere, since he wished to present Cambyses as the legitimate successor of Cyrus.[49] The second inconsistency is the mention of Cambyses' conquest of the "Ethiopians living near the border of Egypt" (3.97.2), a conquest not referred to in the account of Cambyses' Ethiopian campaign, since even this minor success would have destroyed the picture of utter failure which was Herodotus' aim.

The account of Darius is the fullest of the Persian *logoi*, for he symbolizes for Herodotus the height of Persian power. Yet even

---

[47] Hdt. 1.192. For the notorious promise of Assyrian *logoi*, which are not found in the extant work, see e.g. Schmid-Stählin 1.2.561, note 3. Myres, *Herodotus* 94-95, follows Powell, *Hist. Herodotus* 18-20 and 35, in assuming that this section was actually written, but has been lost. This is based on an uncertain reading in Aristotle (Powell, *op. cit.* 35).

[48] The campaign against the Massagetae has the same function in the work as Cambyses' Ethiopian campaign and Darius' Scythian expedition. These three are the main failures of Oriental expansionism before the attack on the Greeks.

[49] On the geographic position of Egypt, see *Causation* 260, note 38. In the Hippocratic treatise *On Airs, Waters, Places*, Ch. 12, Egypt is listed on a par with the three continents, and coupled with Libya; cf. also van Groningen, *Comp. litt.* 252, note 2. I follow Stein in the interpretation of 3.88.1, but cf. e.g. How and Wells, and (apparently) Powell, *Lexicon*, s.v. αὖτις.

here the story is not quite complete. Herodotus knew the entire ancestry of Darius back to Achaemenes (7.11), but in the early parts of the work Darius appears merely as the son of the noble Hystaspes and is not of royal blood.[50] Another puzzling aspect of the story about young Darius is the abruptness of his arrival in Susa "from the Persians" to plot the overthrow of the Magi (3.70.3). Elsewhere, Herodotus tells us that, at the time of Cyrus' death among the Massagetae, Darius (then only twenty years old) was living in Persia (1.209.2), but that he later accompanied Cambyses to Egypt as a spearbearer (3.139.2) and married a daughter of Gobryas (7.2.2), the man who later became one of the seven conspirators against the Magus. None of these facts is alluded to in the account of the overthrow of the Magi. We are not told how Darius had returned from Egypt to his home "in Persia,"[51] nor how he happened to suspect that the Magus and his brother were ruling. Herodotus has simply excluded, at the beginning of the *logos* on the overthrow of the Magi, such information concerning the young Darius as would have conflicted with the picture of a usurper appearing suddenly on the scene to take over the control of Asia and resurrect the Persian empire.[52] His main concern is the re-establishment of power in Persia.

This interpretation is confirmed by Herodotus' account of the beginning of Darius' reign. Here also, the historian knew a fuller story of troubles and revolts against the new king, but when Darius comes to the throne, we are told merely, "all was full of his power" (3.88.3). We cannot ascertain, of course, whether Herodotus knew the list of campaigns mentioned by Darius himself in the Behistun inscription,[53] but in another place he hints at the ferment existing at that time (3.127.1), and he gives us to understand that Darius had made extensive preparations against

[50] On the genealogy of Xerxes in 7.11, see Ch. IV, note 63.

[51] Herodotus uses the words "Persians" and "Persia" in three geographical meanings: (1) the homeland of the Persian tribes listed in 1.125.3-4. This is the residence of Cyrus' parents (1.108.2; 120.6; 123.3-4), and the province of Hystaspes (1.209.2 and 3.70.3, etc.). It is described as distant from both Ecbatana (1.121 and 123.4) and Susa (3.70.3; 97.1, cf. 91.4 and 5.49.7). Cf. also 4.39.1. This region (Parsamash) is Darius' home at the time of the overthrow of the Magus. (2) the heartland of the Persian empire, including Susa, as in Aeschylus' *Persians* (3.1.1, cf. 30.3; 8.98.1, cf. 99.1). (3) the Persian Empire as a whole (7.8c.1; 53.2, both in speeches).

[52] Ch. IV, 170-71.

[53] F. H. Weissbach, *Die Keilinschriften der Achämeniden* (Leipzig 1911) 8 ff., especially para. 16-52.

the Magi before the conspiracy of the Seven.[54] Elsewhere, he alludes to a revolt of the Medes, which we know to have occurred at this time (although Herodotus does not date it), and he knows that Darius was at one time in Egypt, an event perhaps to be connected with the same series of early revolts.[55] We are not in a position to know, of course, whether Herodotus was aware of the exact chronology of these events, but it is tempting to connect his scattered references with the troubles of Darius' early reign. In a similar off-hand manner, Herodotus twice alludes to Darius' Indian campaign, but does not include it among the campaigns he describes in full.[56]

The picture of Darius, although very detailed, is nevertheless stylized to a certain degree. A complete account is given of his accession, but very little is said about his origins or about his early reign. The Far Eastern campaigns (India) are not described. Stress is laid on campaigns in the West (the region of the Hellespont, Libya, Samos, Ionia, Greece) and on campaigns of symbolic significance (Babylon and Scythia). Thereby Herodotus has taken from Darius some of his greatest successes and emphasized instead his limitations.[57] This selectivity is even more pronounced in the case of Xerxes, whose Greek campaign is alone treated in full, whereas the Egyptian is mentioned in two short sentences (7.7).

[54] I believe 3.126.1-2 should be understood in this sense, although the passage is difficult. Oroetas, who had killed Polycrates while Cambyses was still living, was punished "not much later" by Darius for other misdeeds, which occurred, according to the received text, "after the death of Cambyses and the rule of the Magi," but before Darius' accession (3.127.1). If the text is sound, this can refer only to the time when the rule of the Magi came to an end, i.e. during the conspiracy of the Seven. At that time Oroetas killed a messenger of Darius: the message sent can only have been an appeal to come to Susa to participate in the conspiracy, since Darius was then still a private individual. I believe that this is meant by Darius when he says: "and he (Oroetas) kills those that summon him and are sent by me" (3.127.3). Thus the story of the messenger should be placed before Darius' accession, although it has usually been understood in the sense that Darius, after his accession, was recalling Oroetas. See e.g. Powell, *Hist. Herodotus* 50; How and Wells *ad loc.*

[55] Median revolt: 1.130.2. Darius in Egypt: 2.110.2-3. The Behistun inscription shows that the Median revolt was a part of the general upheaval after Darius' accession; see Weissbach, *op. cit.* (above, note 53), para. 24. Olmstead, *Hist. Pers.* 142, dates the Egyptian campaign in 518 B.C., and others date it early also, on the basis of the mention of an Egyptian revolt early in Darius' reign (Behistun inscription, para. 21); see H. Swoboda in *RE*, s.v. Dareios No. 1, 2189, and G. B. Gray in *CAH* 4.181.

[56] Hdt. 4.44.1-3 and 7.9.2. The Indian campaign also seems to have taken place early in Darius' reign; see Olmstead, *Hist. Pers.* 144-45; Gray in *CAH* 4.183.

[57] Ch. IV, 173.

Thus Herodotus' use of material (besides giving an inkling of the nature of his sources) shows certain guiding ideas. His history of the Eastern kings is organized as an Eastern narrative rather than as an account of the reciprocal quarrels between East and West, yet it is not a history of the East. The emphasis is on the portraits of the Eastern kings as elements in the story of the growth of Asiatic power. Nevertheless, Eastern development is not delineated for its own sake; we note that certain conquests are not described in detail, so that only the resulting increase in empire is stressed, and that a selection of other conquests is made principally for their symbolic significance. What is developed with great clarity concerns the history of the campaigns of the Eastern monarchs in the West, whether directed against Greeks or against barbarian peoples in Europe and Africa. Despite the pattern of the Oriental chronicle, Herodotus has not written a history of Persia.

III

How does the Greek element fit into this unevenly balanced history of the East? From the structural point of view, it must be emphasized that prior to the account of Salamis, except for the three *logoi* mentioned earlier, the Greek material (regardless of its real importance in the work) is throughout formally subordinated to the Eastern sequence by being attached to Eastern accounts in sections. In this respect, the Greek stories are treated in a manner resembling (in a general way) the ethnographic material. It has been observed that ethnographic *logoi* are nearly always attached to the Eastern accounts at the point where the nation in question is conquered, or attacked, by the East; and further, that the history of such nations always ends at the time of conquest, i.e. where they cease to have an autonomous existence.[58] Herodotus here undoubtedly follows or adapts previously established patterns of ethnography. It is less clear that similar patterns already existed for purely historical accounts.[59] At any

---

[58] Jacoby, *Entwicklung* 93 ff.; Regenbogen, *Werk* 67 f. (=Marg, *Herodot* 69 f.).

[59] The solution to this difficult problem depends in part on the dates that should be assigned to the earliest Greek historians who dealt with the East, in particular Charon of Lampsacus and Xanthus the Lydian, who are the best known. See Schmid-Stählin 1.1.683 ff. L. Pearson, *Early Ionian Historians* (Oxford 1939) 2 ff., 116 (Xanthus), 139-40 (Charon), supports the early dating, and Jacoby, *FGrH* III, C, Vol. 2 (Leiden

rate, Herodotus has extended the principle used for barbarian ethnographic material to the more properly historical material dealing with the Greeks. Before Salamis, the principal Greek *logoi* are attached to the Eastern narrative at points of contact between the East and the Greek states. It follows that Herodotus nowhere presents us with a continuous Greek history, but that his method shows here an even greater selectivity than in the Eastern accounts.[60]

The first separate Greek *logos* in the work (although not the first mention of the Greeks) is the story of Arion and the Dolphin (1.23-24). As Myres has pointed out, the story involves two separate motifs: (1) the greatness of the Corinthian tyrant Periander and (2) the miraculous rescue of Arion.[61] By placing the second motif in the center of the story, and the first at the beginning and the end, Herodotus was able to connect it formally with the East, for Periander had helped Thrasybulus of Miletus in his war against Alyattes king of Lydia. This connection has often been criticized as superficial,[62] but the principle is the same as that used for the next Greek *logos*, the history of Athens and Sparta down to the time of Croesus (1.56.2-68).

Jacoby and Pohlenz have suggested convincingly that, in attaching this *logos* to the story of Croesus' search for Greek allies, Herodotus follows the pattern of the later account, which concerns a similar quest by Aristagoras of Miletus at the beginning of the Ionian Revolt (5.39-96). This quest was in fact better known to Herodotus, and it has a much better claim to historicity.[63] Aristagoras first went to Sparta, and having been refused there,

1958) 750 (Xanthus), and III, A (1943) 1-2 and 17-18 (Charon), the late. In *Entwicklung* 89-90, Jacoby thinks, nevertheless, that the historical sections in ethnographic *logoi* derive from earlier historical literature on Persians and Lydians (a literature which itself derived from ethnography); but he admits that historical notices occurred already in purely ethnographic works. (So also E. Norden, *Die Germanische Urgeschichte in Tacitus' Germania* [1922] 25.) However, historical works earlier than Herodotus are very shadowy; hence the origins of the Herodotean combination of history with ethnography are uncertain.

[60] Differently Jacoby, see above, note 40; cf. also below, note 67.

[61] Myres, *Herodotus* 83-84. Cf. also H. Erbse, *Gymnasium* 68 (1961) 250, and C. M. Bowra, *MH* 20 (1963) 121-34.

[62] E.g. Schmid-Stählin 1.2.604 f.

[63] Jacoby, *RE* Suppl. 2.382-83; Pohlenz, *Herodot* 41, also 34 and 36. Jacoby's aim is to show that the Athenian and Spartan history originally formed an independent lecture. Pohlenz is concerned with the work as it stands, but if I understand him correctly, he also thinks of the history of Athens and Sparta as a unit.

concluded an alliance in Athens. The order of the inquiries is here
the reverse of that followed by Croesus, since the latter concluded
an alliance with Sparta, and the Greek city concluding the alliance
is of course placed second. In both instances Herodotus has added
certain specific accounts to explain the power (or lack of power) of
Athens and Sparta in these two periods. Jacoby and Pohlenz,
however, went one step further and claimed that the four resulting sections, together with their short introduction, are really
a unified history of Athens and Sparta respectively, each artifici-
ally rent asunder. The whole complex would have the following
form:

1. Introduction: origins of Dorian Sparta and Pelasgian Athens
   (1.56.2-58).
2. Athens under Peisistratus (1.59-64).
3. Sparta's early history down to the war with Tegea (1.65-68).
4. Sparta's trouble with her royal house (5.39-48).
5. Athens, from the end of tyranny to the time of the Ionian
   Revolt (5.55-96).

This scheme is based in part on the correct observation that
the second Spartan section begins with a direct reference to the
end of the first.[64] This backward reference, however, is occasioned
by the fact that the Athenian and Spartan *logoi* follow each other
in the order ABBA, with the Spartan *logoi* occupying the inner
positions. Between the two Athenian sections there is no such
continuity.[65] There is, to be sure, a contrast between Athens
held down by tyranny and Athens strengthened by the establishment of democracy, with the murder of Hipparchus at the
beginning of the second Athenian *logos* (5.55) forming a connecting
link between these two pictures. At the same time, between the
two accounts there exists a gap, which comprises the later rule
and death of Peisistratus and most of the rule of his sons. Thus the
two Athenian *logoi* do not present a continuous history of Athens.
The same is actually true of the two Spartan *logoi*, for a third *logos*
on Sparta, describing hostilities with Argos over Thyrea, inter-
venes between them and is not in any way tied in (1.82.1-83).
This last *logos* tells only that part of the strife over Thyrea which is
contemporary with Croesus, although friction over the territory

[64] Hdt. 5.39.1, cf. 1.67.1. Pohlenz, *Herodot* 34.
[65] Differently Pohlenz, *Herodot* 36.

was of much longer duration: thus it is simply another Greek *logos* attached to Eastern history.[66] Therefore, despite the general introduction to the first Athenian and Spartan *logoi*, which forms a kind of prehistory of Greece, Herodotus has selected his material to fit the immediate surroundings of his several *logoi*. How much he has omitted can be seen from Myres' list of Athenian and Spartan events mentioned in other parts of the work.[67]

No other Greek *logoi* occur until the end of Cambyses' campaigns in Book 3. There the Spartan war against Polycrates of Samos (which follows the story of Cambyses' madness) is connected with the account of Cambyses by an initial synchronism to the effect that the war took place "while Cambyses was fighting against Egypt," i.e. at a time already passed in the narrative.[68] Hence this *logos* is told in retrospect, as an afterthought to the Cambyses *logoi*. The story of the death of Polycrates, on the other hand, is shifted forward in the narrative (it actually occurred "approximately at the time of Cambyses' illness," 3.120.1) and attached to the story of the fate of his murderer, the Persian Oroetas, who was killed by command of Darius after the latter's accession (3.126-28). In the same way, the story of the Greek doctor Democedes is treated as a Persian story, depending as it

[66] We learn from Thucydides 5.41 that Thyrea and all Cynuria were a constant source of friction well into the Peloponnesian War, but the story in Herodotus is of the time of Croesus. Sparta occupied Thyreatis shortly before the battle of the 300 (so G. Busolt, *Griechische Geschichte*[2] 1 [Gotha 1893] 595, note 3), i.e. during the reign of Croesus. Argos assisted her territory, and this led at once to two battles: (1) the battle of the 300, in which both sides claimed victory; it was famous in antiquity, and is the only battle cited in Thuc. 5.41. (2) a mass battle, in which Sparta was victorious (cf. Plutarch, *Apophth. Lac.* 231E). After this the Argives cut their hair and forbade their women to wear gold until they had regained Thyreatis. Thus, when Croesus' messengers arrived, the Spartans must have expected a renewed attack; despite this, they made ready to assist their Lydian friend, but were too late, since Sardis was captured unexpectedly early (Herodotus does not imply that the war with Argos delayed the Spartans). The second battle was decisive: at the time of Cleomenes' Argive expedition Thyrea was held by Sparta (6.76.2; Stein's comment on 1.82, line 5 is in error), and Thucydides also implies no further battles (5.41, cf. 4.56 and 5.14). Hence 1.82-83 may be considered a continuation of Spartan activities in the Peloponnesus, mentioned in the first Spartan *logos* (cf. 1.68.6), but Herodotus does not stress this connection. What is important to him is the contrast in the fortunes of Sparta and Croesus' *symphorê*, which is paralleled by the changes of custom (as the result of changes of fortune) in Sparta and Argos. For historical detail see Pieske, *RE*, s.v. Kynuria, 44-45; Wade-Gery, *CAH* 3.569; and A. Brelich, *Guerre, agoni e culti nella Grecia archaica* (1961) 22 ff. Cf. also Ch. II, note 26.

[67] Myres, *Herodotus* 177 ff.

[68] Hdt. 3.39.1. For further synchronisms with Cambyses' activities, see Ch. III, 98-99.

does on the illnesses of Darius and Atossa (3.129.1 and 3.133.1);
the central episode of the *logos* is the bedchamber scene, in which
Darius and Atossa discuss the conquest of both Greece and
Scythia.[69]

From the Ionian Revolt on, the narrative concerns primarily
the interaction of Greeks and Persians, but there are still several
independent Greek *logoi*. We have already seen how the accounts
of Sparta and Athens are attached to the visits of Aristagoras at
the beginning of the Ionian Revolt. Later on, the story of Miltiades
is divided into a number of sections, some of which are in the
form of separate *logoi*. The first of these shows Miltiades fleeing
the Chersonese and pursued by the Phoenician navy after the
Ionian Revolt (6.34.1-41.4). Following the account of the battle of
Marathon, there is the *logos* of Miltiades' attempted conquest of
Paros, his injury and his death, a story to which is added his earlier
conquest of Lemnos for the benefit of Athens, in fulfilment of an
oracle (6.132-36; 137-40). The attack on Paros belongs with the
aftereffects of Marathon and thus differs somewhat from the *logoi*
here discussed, for it resembles rather the independent narrative
after Salamis (in particular, Themistocles' punitive campaign
against Andros).[70] The capture of Lemnos in turn is an explanation added to the Parian adventure (the capture had been mentioned, in fact, during the last trial of Miltiades), but it does have
an indirect connection with the Persian narrative in the reference
to the Hellespont at the end.[71] These last two *logoi* thus have a
more remote connection with Persian action, through their
dependence on Marathon and its consequences.

More closely connected with Persian history is the long account
of Greek affairs which follows the embassies sent by Darius to the
Greek states with the demand of earth and water (6.49-94.1).
This *logos* contains a good deal of Spartan royal history, among it
especially the last part of Cleomenes' reign, but from the structural
point of view it should be called an Aeginetan *logos*, since it begins
and ends with the story of the hostages exacted from Aegina and
deposited in Athens. The reason for the collection of hostages was
the fact that the Aeginetans, like other Greek islanders, had given
earth and water to Darius (6.49.1). Thus the organization of this

[69] Hdt. 3.134. *Causation* 261 and 271, note 60.
[70] Ch. III, 140.
[71] *Action* 25.

logos depends entirely on the point of contact between Darius and the Aeginetans.[72]

The famous digression on the Alcmaeonids, which follows the account of Marathon and precedes the story of Miltiades on Paros (6.121-31), likewise owes its place to a connection with the Persians, for Herodotus begins it by defending them against the charge of flashing a shield-signal to the enemy during the invasion of Attica (6.121.1). Oriental connections are still basic for the last of the great Greek *logoi*, the preparations of the Greeks against Xerxes' invasion (7.132-78). This account is usually analyzed as action parallel with the preparations and march of Xerxes,[73] but it is in fact subordinated to the Eastern narrative in two ways. First, it is attached to Xerxes' stay in Pieria after his arrival in Greece (7.131 and again 177),[74] and specifically to the statement that Xerxes' invasion, while nominally directed against Athens, really concerned all of Greece (7.138.1). Secondly, its internal structure is entirely dependent on the stages of Xerxes' march as given in the narrative.[75] It is the last *logos* in the work to be so treated.

These details concerning the independent Greek *logoi* have been necessary in order to show their attachment to the Eastern narrative in the manner of ethnographic *logoi* for non-Greeks. These are, of course, by no means the only places where Greek material is found in the work. Much of it occurs in the campaigns of the Lydian and Persian kings (especially the campaigns of Croesus and his ancestors, the several Ionian campaigns, the conquest of Samos, the campaign against Cyrene in Libya, and the Persian Wars in the widest sense), but not the least part is found worked into the remainder of the Eastern narrative wherever possible. Throughout the *Histories*, as Pohlenz has shown, Herodotus emphasizes all possible Greek connections with the East.[76] We must distinguish, therefore, between internal emphasis on Greek material and outer connections between the principal *logoi*, connections which are mainly based on the Eastern narrative. In outlining, as we have done, the overall organization, we cannot do full justice to the Greek subjects treated in the

[72] See Ch. III, 121-22.
[73] Cf. generally Pohlenz, *Herodot* 42 and 89, and Ch. III, 133-37.
[74] For details, see Ch. III, 133.
[75] Ch. III, 136.
[76] Pohlenz, *Herodot* 9 ff.

work, but we may discover its general plan. We note, then, that from the beginning to the battle of Salamis the external structure of the work is almost entirely based on the Eastern accounts, to which the Greek material is subordinated.

IV

The work of Herodotus is arranged as a chain of *logoi*, with the individual items strung along in a single row and usually framed by introductory and concluding sentences. This series is arranged according to the simple principle of action and counteraction. Whenever the East has the initiative (and that is true for most of the work), the narrative follows the Eastern line of development, and only where the Greeks themselves initiate action does a change in structure occur. Herodotus' history is primarily a history of action.[77] As mentioned above, the Greeks show such initiative three times (in the Persian conquest of Ionia, the Spartan war against Polycrates, and the Ionian Revolt), until with Salamis the narrative as a whole changes to the affairs of the victors. The battle description, with its symmetrical arrangement of action and counteraction around a central point, quite naturally lends itself to a shift of emphasis from one contestant to the other.[78]

The central stories in the Eastern series are those of the accession and campaigns of four Persian kings who form two pairs of father and son: Cyrus and Cambyses, and Darius and Xerxes. The accession-stories of Cyrus and Darius are important to Herodotus as the crucial links in the development of power in Asia. The campaigns of the four kings are treated with a definite Western bias, so that their Asiatic wars are described only in part. This portion of the *Histories* (from Cyrus' Ionian conquest to Darius' Greek campaigns) shows a straightforward development and close inner unity.

At the beginning and end of the chain, the situation is not so simple. The direct line from the predecessors of the Persians (the Assyrians and Medes) to the campaigns of Cyrus, the founder of the Persian empire, has been disturbed by placing the defeat of Lydia first in the work, a procedure which necessitated putting the history of Assyria and Media into a "digression." We are not here concerned with the question of when Herodotus

[77] *Action* 16 ff.
[78] Ch. VI, 238-39.

did this, but only why it was done.[79] We have previously
noted the double framing of the Croesus *Logos* with statements
regarding Croesus' empire over Western Asia and his attacks on
the Greeks. We may now say that, in the first place, the transposition of the Croesus *Logos* helps to underline the theme of the
unification and growth of Asiatic power; Herodotus stresses the
unification of the Western part and its absorption into the Eastern,
before giving an explanation of the earlier conquest of the Eastern
portion by the Persians.

It is clear, however, that this idea could have been expressed
equally well by telling the story in its proper chronological order:
Assyria—Media—Founding of Persia—Overthrow of Lydia. We
must therefore use the second framing statement (the attack on
the Greeks) in explaining the shift of the Croesus *Logos* to the
beginning of the work. Herodotus begins with the part of Asia
situated nearest the West, because the Western expansion of
Persia is his main concern from the start. Among the Western
campaigns, those directed against Greece are in turn the most
important to him. Since Herodotus considered the Greeks the
"forefighters" (as he would have called them) in the battle of all
Europe against all Asia,[80] he employs the Greek narrative as
the focus of his general Western emphasis. Consequently, we
find in the Croesus *Logos* a cluster of Greek *logoi* and other Greek
references, such as the attacks on Greek cities in Asia Minor by
each of the Lydian kings, even where they were mere raids (*harpagai*). The first major war of the work is the siege of Miletus by
Alyattes,[81] to which the story of Arion and the Dolphin is an

---

[79] See above, note 28.

[80] On the contrast between Asia and Europe, see briefly *Causation* 263, note 42. H.
Berve, "Der Europabegriff der Antike," in *Gestaltende Kräfte der Antike* (1949) 170-87.
Pohlenz, *Herodot* 21 ff. and 205 ff. C. van Paassen, *The Classical Tradition of Geography*
(Groningen 1957), Ch. 3, *passim*, esp. 96, and note 36. Cf. also Oliver, *Demokratia*
118-20, and Plate 1. D. Hay, *Europe: The Emergence of an Idea* (Edinburgh 1957). A. J.
Toynbee, *A Study of History*, Vol. 8 (1954) 708-29. G. Pugliese Caratelli, *PP* 40 (1955)
5-19. *Times Lit. Suppl.* (January 17, 1958) 34.

[81] Hdt. 1.16.2-22.4, and 25.1. The war is told slightly out of context: (1) it originated with Sadyattes, the predecessor of Alyattes, but it is not mentioned under his
rule (1.16.1). (2) it was Alyattes' first war (since he inherited it from his father), but it
is told at the end of his reign, after the mention of his wars with Cyaxares and the Cimmerians and his raids against Smyrna and Clazomenae (1.16.2). Herodotus calls the
war with Miletus "most worthy of mention" (1.16.2); however, he tells it not out of
curiosity, but because it was the first real conflict between Greeks and the East known

addition. Arion, Periander, Solon, and Bias or Pittacus (depending on the version we follow) form a series of Greek personalities who contrast with Croesus the Oriental ruler, and the latter's relations with Delphi initiate an important religious theme in the work.

Another and much larger cluster of Greek *logoi* develops naturally in the second half of the work, beginning with the Ionian Revolt and ending with the capture of Sestus in 479 B.C. These references may be divided into two phases: before Salamis the Greek material is still largely subordinated to Persian actions, while afterwards it is really independent. Looking at the work as a whole, we may say that the Greek material has the function of establishing the two cuts which begin and end the chain of Eastern action. The work begins with Croesus and ends with the expulsion of the Persians from Europe.

The structure of the *Histories* is very simple. The work is a chain of *logoi* with special emphasis at the beginning and a similar, if greater, emphasis at the end. Such a chain of stories is itself a typically Herodotean *logos*, as we shall see in the next chapter. The formal arrangement of the work is characteristic of early Greek prose. The problem now is to determine whether a unified conception of the subject underlies this plan.

The *Histories* begin and end with Greek relations with the East: first enslaved by Croesus, Greeks finally defeat the Persians on Greek soil. Between these two extremes, however, the subject of the work is the growth of the unified power of Asia under the Persians—a theme very much larger than East-West relations (although it includes them). The Greek material, by establishing the outer limits of the Eastern *logoi*, helps to define a special period of Eastern history, namely that in which the Eastern empires attacked the West. In this manner the Greek stories contribute to the definition of the subject of the Persian *logoi* themselves: the *Histories* deal not with Persian history per se, but with the unification of Asia, the attempted extension of empire beyond the borders of the continent, and the failure of this attempt. This period began at the time of Croesus and was checked when the Persians were driven out of Europe by the Greeks. Unlike a modern historian, who would show the gradual development of

to him that could find its place at the beginning of the work. Subsidiary themes of the *logos* are Alyattes' religious crimes, the Delphic motif, and the cooperation of Greek states in the time of the tyrants.

power politics, Herodotus assumes that the basic motivation—
expansionism—was a permanent feature of Eastern monarchy.
This desire for aggrandizement first became apparent during the
conquest of Western Asia by the Lydians (a conquest which
necessarily included the Greeks of Asia Minor), as well as in the
subjugation of the Eastern part by the Medes. Expansion continued further through the conquests of Cyrus both in the East
and in the West, and advanced still another step in Cambyses'
conquest of Egypt and his attempted attack on the African
Ethiopians. Under Darius, expansionism became the attempt to
conquer all continents: Europe, in his attacks against the Scythians
and the Greeks; and Libya, through a war conducted by one of
Darius' satraps. This policy was checked forever by the valor of
the Greeks who opposed Xerxes.

The work begins and ends at points that are not at all arbitrary.
The end is particularly appropriate, for it comes when the
Persian has left Europe and the continents are separate, as they
had been originally. It is hard to believe, therefore, that Herodotus' work has been left incomplete.[82] The symbolic conclusion
of the *Histories* is the dedication of the broken Hellespontine cables,
with which Xerxes had once connected Asia and Europe.

The proem likewise must be understood from the basic thematic structure of the work. It is closely connected with the
Croesus *Logos* and in particular develops (as Pohlenz has rightly
observed) the idea of the East-West conflict between Greeks and
barbarians. The proem stresses the second framing element of
the Croesus *Logos* more than it does the first.[83] This is natural,
since its aim is to establish the figure of Croesus firmly at the
beginning of the work, but we must not take ·the East-West
conflict as a complete description of the subject. Dealing primarily
with purpose and method, the proem defines the contents of the
work merely by establishing the beginning of the series of actions
that make up the *Histories*. So far as the subject of the work is
concerned, the proem stresses mainly a basic theme, namely the
permanent hostility between Greeks and Persians, or between Asia

[82] Above, Introduction, 8-10.

[83] The relation of the proem to the work may be schematized as follows (A stands
for the motif of the growth of Asiatic power, B for the East-West conflict):

B, Proem.   A B, Croesus *Logos* . . . B A.   A, Origins of Persia . . . A, etc.

and Europe (1.4.4). At the same time, the proem calls attention to Persia's hybris in seeking world dominion by stating that the Persians themselves considered Asia to be theirs, but Europe to be separate. The unity of the work consists partly in the emphasis on the disregard shown by the Persian kings, in their Western attacks, of this native doctrine, which is recalled at the end of the *Histories*.[84]

A characteristic feature of early Greek literature is its refusal to conceive of unity in the abstract; instead, it perceives it in the concrete development of a series. Hence the unity of the work must be established by looking at the whole chain of *logoi*, rather than by the analysis of the proem. This unity is nevertheless real. It consists of the history of Persian power and aggressiveness in a well-defined period in which aggression affected the Greeks. It does not consist of Persian history per se, or of the East-West conflict alone. The latter is a subsidiary theme, no matter how decisively it may influence the presentation of the main subject.

The *Histories* derive their subject from the particular view which the Greeks had of the importance of their fight against Persia, and is therefore similar to the views found in the *Persians* of Aeschylus. The two works have in common their Oriental structure, by which the unity of viewpoint is manifested in the description of the effect of the Persian Wars upon the Persians themselves rather than the effect upon the Greeks. Aeschylus and Herodotus treat the same subject, which is "*Persai*"—the nation that came to destroy "us" and instead destroyed themselves by frustrating their own aspirations.[85] In filling in the antecedents of this struggle (a problem which Aeschylus did not have to face to the same extent), Herodotus simply assumed that the character of Persia, and of the East in general, had always been what it was known to be during the Persian Wars. Therefore he wrote the history of those Persians (and their predecessors) whose expansionist drive had always been a danger to "our" existence. Herodotus' history is thus in the first instance patriotic history,

---

[84] Hdt. 1.4.4=9.116.3.

[85] On the relations between Herodotus' work and Aeschylus' *Persians* see Hauvette, *Hérodote* 125, note 2, and Pohlenz, *Herodot* 116, note 3. The etymology of "Persians" from πέρθω (to destroy), by which the Persians are seen as destroyers and self-destroyers, is fundamental to the play (e.g. line 65), but it is found in Herodotus only in the text of two oracles, 7.220.4 and 8.77.1. Nevertheless, the self-destructive tendencies of Persia are also stressed by the historian, although in different ways, e.g. in the final story about Xerxes' loves in Book 9, on which see now the paper by E. Wolff cited below, Ch. IV, note 96.

but he gave his theme a wider significance by describing the Greeks as the exponents of a particular way of life and as representatives of a whole continent on which this way of life was able to flourish. He also showed by what laws in the world of history absolutism was bound to fail. The treatment of Eastern history and of the wars of Asia with Greece is thus developed intuitively from a general conception of what the Greek struggle for freedom really meant for the history of the world. It is difficult to formulate such a conception with precision, and perhaps for this reason Herodotus' work has never had a precise title.

Chapter II

STYLE AND STRUCTURE

I

Since 1924, when Hermann Fränkel's fundamental paper, "A Stylistic Peculiarity of Early Greek Literature," laid the foundation for the study of the style of early Greek poetry and prose, there have been repeated attempts to cite Herodotus as an example of that style. Fränkel himself used Herodotus with much insight, but stopped short of admitting the unity of the work, since in the view then prevalent the *Histories* were a compound of heterogeneous parts composed at different times—a view which had been only recently upheld by Felix Jacoby (1913).[1] Furthermore, the stylistic analysis of early Greek literature, by following Aristotle's observation of a contrast between a paratactic, or "strung-along," and a periodic, or "knit-together" style,[2] was carried on under the shadow of a superior classical model, the periodic style of fourth-century oratory. This method emphasized unduly (and the same bias is still found in more recent studies) the negative aspects of the "archaic" as contrasted with the "classical" style: a book on early Greek composition published a few years ago still contains the statement that archaic works show only restricted organic unity.[3] This classicistic prejudice (if I may call it that) has tempted some scholars who have continued the studies of Fränkel (among them especially the Dutch scholars van Otterlo and van Groningen) to construct stylistic systems that look suspiciously like attempts to replace classical by an earlier archaic rhetoric. However, ancient rhetoric is a matter of giving practical advice (in the form of rules) to contemporary writers, and in the early period such rules did not exist. Stylistic analysis of early Greek literary works aims at the discovery of patterns observable in actual practice, which do not have the authority of school maxims and are not systematized. Despite the interest in early

---

[1] Fränkel, *Stileigenheit*. Jacoby, *RE* Suppl. 2.281 ff.   [2] Arist. *Rhet.* 3.1409 A 24.
[3] Van Groningen, *Comp. litt.* 8 ff. and 337. Cf. G. M. Kirkwood in *Gnomon* 32 (1960) 414-21.

Greek poetry and prose, a full investigation of Herodotus' style has not been made, although his work has been a fertile source of examples to illustrate the style of other authors.[4] The present chapter likewise makes no attempt at such an analysis, but tries to present a few guiding ideas that may be useful for the understanding of the organization of the work. In doing so, it relies heavily on the studies of earlier writers.

It is a basic feature of early prose that the principles underlying large units of composition are equally applicable to smaller entities down to a short phrase, a sentence, a brief remark, or a story.[5] In the preceding chapter, we have used one ubiquitous feature of this sort, the paratactic chain of items, in that case the individual *logoi* of the whole work. Eduard Norden has called such items, in their simplest form, "*kai*-members."[6] Herodotus inherited this style from Hecataeus and other predecessors, among whom it flourished by virtue of its appropriateness for lists of geographical names and for the description of animals and human customs.[7] In fact, some of the Herodotean passages of this

---

[4] Aly, *Formprobleme, passim.* Van Groningen, *Paratact. Comp.* 11 ff., and *Comp. litt., passim.* J. Haberle, *Untersuchungen über den ionischen Prosastil* (Diss. Munich 1938). K. Marót, "Herodots Prosastil," *Egyetemes Philologiai Közöni* (Budapest 1943) 1-25, is not known to me. J. Notopoulos, "Parataxis in Homer: A New Approach to Homeric Literary Criticism," *TAPA* 80 (1949) 2-5; cf. also Notopoulos in *TAPA* 82 (1951) 81 ff. Van Otterlo, *Ringkomposition*, esp. 164, notes 1-2, and *passim.* Van Otterlo (see above, Introduction, note 24), and H. Mette in *Gnomon* 23 (1951) 223. G. Pöhlmann, *De arte qua fabellae Herodoteae narratae sint* (Diss. Göttingen 1912). T. B. L. Webster, *Language and Thought in Early Greece*, Memoirs and Proceed. *Manchester Lit. and Phil. Soc.* 94 (1952-53) 17-38, bears only indirectly on Herodotus. More generally on Herodotus' style: Fränkel, *Stileigenheit*, section reprinted in Marg, *Herodot* 726 ff. Pohlenz, *Herodot* 207 ff. (=Marg, *Herodot* 737 ff.). J. D. Denniston, *Greek Prose Style* (Oxford 1952) 5 ff. Cf. also J. A. K. Thomson, *The Art of the Logos* (London 1935), *passim.* W. J. Verdenius, "L'Association des idées comme principe de composition dans Homère, Hésiode, Théognis," *REG* 73 (1960) 345-61.

[5] Van Groningen, *Comp. litt.* 91, note 1.

[6] E. Norden, *Agnostos Theos* (Leipzig 1913), Appendix VII: "*Lexis eiromenê.*" On the *kai*-style in Attic and later Greek literature (a broader view than is presented here) see S. Trenkner, *Le Style* kai *dans le récit attique oral* (Assen 1960), known to me only from reviews in *CR*, n.s. 11 (1961) 290 (Hudson-Williams) and *Mnemosyne*, ser. 4, 14 (1961) 242-47 (Bolkestein). I am not familar with Trenkner, "*Lexis eiromenê* Herodots," *Charisteria . . . G. Przychocki* (Warsaw 1934) 295-311.

[7] On the style of Hecataeus and its relation to that of Herodotus, see Jacoby, *RE* s.v. Hekataios, 2748-50; Fränkel, *Stileigenheit* 62 ff.; L. Pearson, *Early Ionian Historians* (Oxford 1939) 29 ff. For the relation of style and subject matter, see also Aly, *Formprobleme* 44 ff. Aly criticizes Fränkel's distinction between the style of Hecataeus and that of Herodotus, and claims (with some exaggeration) that style goes with subject matter, not with the individual author.

kind are quotations from Hecataeus. On a large scale, the principle is used by Herodotus in his great lists: the Persian satrapy list of Book 3, the Persian army and navy lists in Book 7, and the various rosters of Greek forces. Other applications of the same principle are the march sections of some campaign *logoi*, especially Darius' march into Scythia and Xerxes' march into Greece.[8] More significant, because more pervasive, are the chains of *logoi* in the accounts of the Eastern kings, especially the sequences of their military exploits.

The paratactic style is not, as is sometimes thought, a continuous style; on the contrary, its effect is discontinuity. The basic effect of parataxis is the safeguarding of the autonomy of the individual members in the chain. The description of Thermopylae contains the following group of statements:

> There are in this entrance warm springs, which the natives call cauldrons ‖ and an altar of Heracles is built above them. ‖ A wall had been built across the entrance ‖ and of old there was a gate in it. (7.176.3)

It cannot be denied that in this description the single items, which are of great importance for the account of the battle, stand out very clearly. The discontinuous character of parataxis can be seen further in the insertion of short items into the breaks between the *kai*-members of the original chain; this is especially common in the description of Xerxes' march, where notes of various sorts are added to almost every stage of the march.[9] Thus the paratactic chain, through the simple expedient of filling the pauses between its members with independent stories or other items of information, is capable of unlimited development, which can create considerable complexity, although it can hardly build dramatic tension. One feels in these descriptions a relaxation of pressure toward the end of the narrative, and, because of constant interruptions of uneven length, a certain "jerkiness" in the progression.

At the same time, early prose develops a number of devices, some of them borrowed from poetry, in order to connect the independent items of the chain. These devices take the place of the subordination which is found in the later periodic style. We find here a number of separate elements which initiate the several

[8] Hdt. 4.83 ff. and 7.26 ff.
[9] Ch. III, 130-33.

units of the chain, among them (besides simple connective particles) repeated nouns and adjectives, participial phrases summarizing certain aspects of the preceding narrative, and even separate phrases related both to the end of the last item and to the beginning of the next.[10] Such features are found well developed in Hecataeus, and in Herodotus, as Fränkel has well said, they are developed to such a degree that at times they tend to become almost independent units in themselves.[11] Whereas Hecataeus connects where he must, Herodotus connects where he can, and his style is an ornate form of early prose.

Eduard Norden derived the style of early literature from two types of relationships: parataxis and antithesis, or *kai*-members and *de*-members.[12] However, antithesis is not, in Herodotus, or for that matter in early prose generally, on a par with parataxis. The disjointed paratactic style leads naturally to the addition of members that stand in opposition to the main sequence in a list or an argument, and it is this subsidiary use of antithesis that is characteristic of Herodotus. True antithesis is avoided even where we would expect it. This is deliberate, for Herodotus knows the antithetic style; he uses it in conversations and, especially, in formal speeches found primarily in the later books.[13]

In ordinary narrative, antithesis is principally an aspect of polarity, by which both elements of an antithesis are thought to coexist.[14] Thus we find antithesis commonly used for statements which are really complementary. On a very simple level we have:

> Croesus, on the one hand, was a Lydian by birth, on the other hand, he was the son of Alyattes. (1.6.1)

At the same time, antithesis is avoided where we might expect to find it:

> The ends of the world possess the most beautiful things, just as Greece possesses seasons most beautifully mixed. (3.106.1)

[10] Fränkel, *Stileigenheit* 63 f. Van Groningen, *Comp. litt.* 36 ff., etc. Pohlenz, *Herodot* 209 f.

[11] Fränkel, *Stileigenheit* 65.

[12] E. Norden, *Agnostos Theos* (Leipzig 1913), Appendix VII.

[13] Schmid-Stählin 1.2.574, note 2, lists 57 cases of antithesis in Herodotus. Of these, 30 occur in speeches. Actually, only 29 out of the 57 examples are in true antithesis, and of these 19 are in direct discourse. The only frequent expression is "word and deed," which is not, of course, a true antithesis.

[14] On polarity, see H. Fränkel, *Dichtung und Philosophie*, index 603-05. E.g. Hdt. 3.127.1: Darius knew that the Persian Oroetas had great power, τὸν χίλιοι μὲν Περσέων ἐδορυφόρεον, εἶχε δὲ νομὸν τόν τε Φρύγιον καὶ Λύδιον καὶ Ἰωνικόν.

The underlying idea here is that of a contrast between the ends of the world, where we find the most beautiful things, and the center of the world (namely Greece) where we do not find such extremes. This is expressed, not as an antithesis, but as a comparison between two states that are equally "beautiful," namely a state of extremes and a state of mixture or balance.[15] This implies that both the ends and the center of the world are parts of the same world order and that they are both equally desirable. The element of complementary balance outweighs that of antithesis.[16]

True antithesis, then, is used in the narrative only in a very restricted sense: additions to the chain of *logoi* (which are really complementary), some argumentative passages, comparisons of customs of foreign peoples, and at times special expressions used for dramatic effect.[17] This last use, of oxymoron, is perhaps due to the influence of tragedy:

> (The Persians) showed clearly to everybody, and not least to the King, that they consisted of many people, but few men. (7.210.2)

Or again:

> (The Persians) chose to rule while living in an unpleasant country, rather than to be slaves while sowing on the plains. (9.122.4)[18]

The second example is the last sentence of Herodotus' work.

The relative lack of antithesis is surprising in an author in whose thought opposites play an important part. Antithetical relations are thus commonly expressed in non-antithetical ways by Herodotus. This "inner antithesis," as I would like to call it, pervades the work in the explicit and implicit comparisons of nations, especially of Greeks and Persians and, in Greece, of Athenians and Spartans. It is even more important in the contrasting pictures of monarchs, and in changes of fortune of

---

[15] The Hippocratic essay *On Airs, Waters, Places*, Chs. 12 and 16, stresses the difference rather than the comparison.

[16] On the section on The Ends of the World, see further Chs. III, 102-103, and IV, 172.

[17] Additions to *logoi*: e.g. 1.140 (added note to *logos* on Persian customs, concerning burial). Argument: e.g. 1.5.3 (Herodotus' opinion contrasted with that of Persians and Phoenicians). Comparison of customs: e.g. 1.56.2 (Pelasgians and Dorians) and 2.35.2 ff. (Egyptians and the rest of mankind).

[18] On oxymoron in Herodotus, see Schmid-Stählin 1.2.653, note 3.

individuals and nations, as well as in pictures of contradictory behavior of one and the same person, especially in the figure of Xerxes and of the Persians during the invasion of 480 B.C. None of these themes finds an adequate representation in antithetical structure. They are described rather in the juxtaposition of autonomous members of a chain, often with the implication that they should be compared with each other by the reader.

II

In what manner was Herodotus able to build a large unified work out of a mosaic of small elements—his inheritance from the archaic type of composition we have described? The connecting links between individual units seem to reach out only so far as the immediately preceding and following narrative, and this is hardly enough to establish a substantial connection between major units of narrative. However, the paratactic style allows for great variety in the size and composition of its members, and by this means complexity is introduced as an aid to unification. We may speak of *irregular emphasis*. It is true that early narrative pays little attention to the individual length of different items, as is particularly apparent in the king-lists, where long and short descriptions follow one another, by necessity, in an irregular order. Yet, by virtue of this very irregularity, a complex action, when told as a series of individual items, will show emphasis at different points, among which the beginning and end tend to stand out. We have seen this principle operate in the list of the earliest Egyptian kings.[19] Herodotus (it would seem) derived it from earlier ethnographic and historical writing rather than directly from Homer, its ultimate source. In his own ethnographic sections, and in some of the smaller historical units, the beginning is the place of principal emphasis.[20] The ethnographic sections added to the first capture of Babylon may serve as an example (1.178 ff.). The first of these begins with an introductory statement that among the cities of Assyria Babylon is the most illustrious and has been the capital since the destruction of Nineveh (1.178.1). The subsequent description of the city is followed by a historical section introduced by a parallel statement (among the rulers of Babylon two queens

[19] Ch. I, 26-27.
[20] Cf. also van Groningen, *Comp. litt.* 53.

are outstanding, 1.184).[21] Later on, the section on customs is introduced by a third statement stressing Herodotus' selectivity (1.192.1: on the resources of Babylon), followed by still other introductory statements (1.193.1; 194.1; 195.1; 196.1).

It appears, however, that in the historical narrative Herodotus tends to emphasize the end of a unit more than its beginning. Roughly speaking, the following types of final statement are found:

(1) The emphatic presentation of the last stage of an action, as in the justly famous sentence that serves as the conclusion of the Atys story:[22]

> Adrastus, the son of Gordias, the son of Midas—he who had become the murderer of his brother, and the murderer of him who had cleansed him—when the tomb had been deserted by the people, slew himself over it in the knowledge that of all humans he knew he was the most unfortunate. (1.45.3)

(2) A summary of the action, or of an aspect of it:[23]

> Thus the Mermnadae acquired the rule (of Lydia), having taken it from the Heracleidae. (1.14.1, after the Gyges story)

(3) A statement by the author about the significance of the past story:

> With regard to the death of Cyrus, the account above is the most certain out of many that are told. (1.214.5)

and

> Everything was done by the divine (in the storms at Artemisium) that the Persian forces should be equal with the Greek and not be too much larger. (8.13)

(4) A tag showing that the action is completed:[24]

> This is what the Persians say happened. (1.5.1)

---

[21] Another parallel to these passages occurs internally, 1.185.1.

[22] It is true that the sentence continues into 1.46.1: Fränkel, *Stileigenheit* 84. Other examples: 1.119.7 (last sentence of the murder of Harpagus' son); 3.43.2; 3.75.3; 3.125.4. It is from sentences such as these that Regenbogen has denied *lexis eiromenê* in Herodotus (*Werk* 65-66 [=Marg, *Herodot* 66-67]). For a more judicious view, see J. D. Denniston, *Greek Prose Style* (Oxford 1952) 5-8.

[23] Sometimes found coupled with type (1): e.g. 3.75.3. Type (2) is perhaps the most common of all.

[24] Often employed mechanically to show that a story is finished: e.g. 4.82 (τοῦτο μέν νυν τοιοῦτόν ἐστι), or 2.135.6 (I have finished with Rhodopis).

The style of these remarks varies from case to case, but they have in common the idea of giving a *summary*, however incomplete. It must be admitted that some accounts do not have such a concluding section, and that even where we do find one, it often refers to only a part (usually the last part) of the preceding chain. Nevertheless, these statements are important in turning the work from an amorphous mass into an organized whole.

Emphatic statements of the kind described above lend themselves to *repetition*. Repetition, it is true, sometimes occurs within the narrative in an irregular manner,[25] but usually it has a tendency to mark a rest or stop. In historical narrative, it is particularly important in the form of *anticipation* at the beginning of a chain.[26] Hence, at the beginning of a *logos*, introductory statements may correspond to the types of summary statements at the end.[27] However, the summary of the first stage of the action is less common in the historical sections, and is sometimes less strongly worded, than the summary at the end; instead we find often a *brief* announcement or anticipation of the conclusion. Several variations of this short form of introduction also occur: a brief statement may deal with the intention of the main actor of the story, or his basic motivation; or Herodotus, speaking for himself, may declare an opinion about the sequel of the narrative, or his own purpose in telling the story. This last type, which is of course not found at the end of a *logos*, has a connection with the standard topics of proems and will be discussed later. Caution is again needed in analyzing these statements, since frequently they are even less mandatory or complete than statements at the end. The beginning of a *logos* is often more vague than its end: this has caused some confusion in the interpretation of the work, since the modern reader expects rather the reverse. We will understand the beginning of a *logos* better if we think of it as a place in which a part of the coming story is anticipated, rather than as a clear announcement of what is to come.

[25] Van Groningen, *Comp. litt.* 91 ff. See also below, notes 26, 38, and 39.

[26] Anticipation can also be used internally: see van Groningen, *Comp. litt.* 93, who connects it with epic foreshadowing.

[27] Introductory statements may be classified in a manner similar to concluding statements: (1) The emphatic presentation of the first stage of the action, but usually weaker than the emphatic presentation of the end of an action. This type is more common for description than for action proper. (2) The brief announcement of the action, a form preferred to (1). (3) Anticipation of the conclusion. (4) A general statement about the significance of what follows. (5) A tag.

The combination of final and anticipatory statements has received much attention under the name of *ring composition*,[28] a construction that results from a close (but not necessarily exact) correspondence between anticipatory and summary statements. For an example, we may return to the account of the ends of the world in Hdt. 3.106.1-116.3. I recall the beginning:

> The ends of the world possess the most beautiful things, just as Greece possesses seasons most beautifully mixed. (3.106.1)

This sentence introduces an account of the riches of the four corners of the earth, in which the South is treated more fully, while East, West, and North are treated much more briefly. In the account of the South, the main stories concern the difficulties encountered by the Arabians in collecting spices and incense; this leads at one point to a disquisition on divine providence. However, the closing sentence is written as if a complete account had preceded dealing equally with the four ends of the world:

> The ends of the world, which enclose the rest and hold it within, appear to possess what seems to us the most beautiful and the rarest. (3.116.3)[29]

The two summary statements thus do not exactly summarize the contents of the *logos*, since they do not include the important idea of the difficulty of acquiring precious goods. They also do not exactly correspond to each other, since the second sentence no longer expresses the idea of a comparison of the ends of the world with the center, but instead adds the concept of the rarity of "beautiful things." The lack of exact correspondence is due first of all to a general principle of *variation*, which enables Herodotus to present his own ideas more easily under the guise of inferences

[28] History of the term and bibliography in van Otterlo, *Ringkomposition* 131-33. See further K. Jost, *Das Beispiel und Vorbild der Vorfahren bei den attischen Rednern und Geschichtschreibern* (1936) 45, note 1; W. Schadewaldt, *Iliasstudien*, ASGW 43, No. 6 (1938) 84 (Homer); van Otterlo (above, Introduction, note 24), reviewed by Mette, *Gnomon* 23 (1951) 223; J. A. Notopoulos, *TAPA* 82 (1951) 81 ff.; R. Katičič, "Die Ringkomposition im ersten Buche des Thukydides," *WS* 70 (1957) 179-96; van Groningen, *Comp. litt.* 52 f. Fränkel, *Dichtung und Philosophie*, index, 594 (Schleifengang); A. Lesky, *Die Tragische Dichtung der Hellenen* (Göttingen 1956) 92. Ring composition should not be confused with circular, or (as Myres, *Herodotus* 81 ff., calls it) "pedimental" composition, which is more regular and not based on verbal repetition. Cf. Introduction, note 32. The two terms are confused in C. Whitman, *Homer and the Heroic Tradition* (Cambridge [Mass.] 1958) 252-54.

[29] For the structure of the *logos*, see Ch. III, 102, and note 75.

arising naturally out of the material itself. Secondly, it is due to a close connection of the second sentence with the part of the story that immediately precedes, in which the rarity of fine things and the idea of the ends of the *whole* world are stressed. Since Greece does not play a part in the *logos*, the second statement is more accurate than the first.

There are many examples to show that in so-called ring composition the correspondence between initial and final statements is not exact, but purposely varied. Exact verbal repetition is more germane to the style of the epic, where ring composition was first developed.[30] It is consciously avoided by Herodotus, who at times even shuns the repetition of the main feature of a story in favor of some detail. Hence the term ring composition (which implies the idea of perfection) is misleading when used for the approximate correspondence of the margins of narrative without reference to the center of that narrative. However, I know of no better term.[31]

In a good many cases, the statements at the beginning and the end, while referring to the same events, do not use the same phrasing, so that they are somewhat hard to recognize. Thus the *logos* of the Origins of the Persians and of Cyrus, mentioned in Chapter I,[32] begins with the well-known statement:

> At this point my argument inquires who this Cyrus was who destroyed the empire of Croesus, and in what manner the Persians came to rule over Asia. (1.95.1)

At the end of the story the two main ideas found in this sentence (Cyrus' origins and Persia's rule over Asia) can be discovered in the following series of remarks:

> At that time the Persians and Cyrus revolted against the Medes under Astyages, and ruled from then on over Asia. Cyrus kept Astyages with him until he died, without harming him any further. Cyrus, being thus born and reared, came to the throne and later on conquered Croesus, who had begun the injustice, as I have said before. Having subdued him he thus came to rule over all of Asia. (1.130.2-3)

[30] See the examples listed in van Otterlo, *Ringkomposition* 149 ff. (recapitulation in the form of ring composition), and in Pohlenz, *Herodot* 63.

[31] Cf. however the German term "Schleifengang." See also the criticism by van Groningen, *Comp. litt.* 52 f.

[32] Ch. I, 21.

Here the first and third of the sentences cited summarize the preceding narrative, the first referring to the revolt of Cyrus against the Medes (i.e. the immediately preceding narrative), the third both to the miraculous origin of Cyrus (i.e. the first part of the preceding narrative) and to the Croesus *Logos*, which it attempts to tie in here. Because of this last aside, the statement of the introductory sentence in 1.95, "in what manner the Persians came to rule over Asia," is repeated twice in 1.130, the second time with increased emphasis ("all of Asia"), since the unification of Eastern and Western Asia was achieved through the victory over Croesus.[33]

This type of summary statement brings us to another, in which the statements at the beginning and end refer to quite different aspects of the narrative. The story of the death of Polycrates, the tyrant of Samos, is introduced as follows:

> At about the time of Cambyses' illness the following happened. Oroetas, a Persian, had been established at Sardis by Cambyses. This man desired an unholy deed . . . (3.120.1)

After the murder of Polycrates by Oroetas, we read:

> Polycrates' great luck thus came to such an end, as Amasis the king of Egypt had foretold, but not much later vengeance for Polycrates overtook Oroetas also. (3.125.4-126.1)

Here the final sentence falls into two parts, the first of which summarizes the preceding *logos*, while the second announces the following narrative. The summary concerns specifically the end of the Polycrates story, but it also refers to the much earlier account of the friendship of Polycrates and Amasis (3.40).[34] Thus the reader must deduce the unity of the different accounts from the story itself.

As a variety of this type, we may note those stories where only the beginning of the following action is announced, whereas subsequent actions are appended without any further announcement. This is especially common in the latter parts of the

---

[33] The phrase "all of Asia" has been used to show inconsistency in Herodotus' final draft: see Powell, *Hist. Herodotus* 11. There is no inconsistency, however, if we consider the aorist to be ingressive (cf. *Causation* 259, note 31).

[34] See *Samian Stories* 318. The sentence which mentions Amasis' prediction should not be bracketed. An excellent example of the same technique is the Democedes story (3.129-38), where the different sections are framed by summary sentences, each of which refers to a different event, and yet the overall structure is quite clear.

Histories, and it has given rise to the theory that Herodotus wrote those parts later, when he had finally developed a sense for true historical narrative. The truth is, however, that the accounts of the Persian Wars do not require such elaborate punctuation. Wherever the material of later books becomes more digressive, we find again the method of summary statements. Herodotus' style thus adapts itself to the subject matter.[35]

Van Otterlo distinguishes two types of ring composition, one in which the sentences that frame a *logos* refer to the narrative which they contain, and the other in which the framing sentences take up the broken thread of a narrative interrupted by a digression on matters unrelated to it.[36] The second type (the anaphora of an interrupted idea, or narrative) can be exemplified by the repeated statements that Cyrus defeated Croesus, one example of which we have just cited. These statements, repeated thrice over, are designed to connect the story of Cyrus' origins with his first and later campaigns.[37] In its first occurrence the statement summarizes the preceding account; through further repetition it comes to be anaphoric. In general, anaphoric statements are simply repetitions of regular framing sentences of the first type. If we describe the regular type as follows:

$$a \text{ -I- } a\_b \text{ -II- } b\_c \text{ -III- } c, \text{ etc.,}$$

where I, II, III stand for different *logoi*, and a, b, c, for framing sentences, then the so-called anaphoric type may be analyzed as follows:

$$a \text{ -I- } a\_b \text{ -II- } b\_a \text{ -III- } a, \text{ etc.}$$

Hence the distinction between the two types is unnecessary. Anaphoric ring composition is merely an example of repetition carried out more than once. Such continuous repetition, termed "refrain composition" by van Otterlo, enables Herodotus to carry certain key themes or ideas through a large part of the work,

[35] A great difference in style between the first and the second parts of the work is assumed by Aly, *Volksmärchen* 297 ff.; cf. also Aly, *Formprobleme* 63, and Jacoby, *RE* Suppl. 2.353. But statistical attempts to define the difference have led to no certain results: Schmid-Stählin 1.2.594, note 8 (atticisms), and van Otterlo, *Ringkomposition* 153 ff. Cf. also Jacoby, *RE* Suppl. 2.489, lines 30 ff.
    Note the use of framing sentences in the battle descriptions of Salamis, Plataea, and Mycale, Ch. VI, 270, and notes 155 and 177.

[36] Van Otterlo, *Ringkomposition* 137. This terminology is also criticized by van Groningen, *Comp. litt.* 52-53. The terms are *inklusorisch* and *anaphorisch*.

[37] Hdt. 1.92.1; 1.94.7; 1.130.3; 1.141.1.

and has been fundamental to Pohlenz' study of the *Histories*. Since we derive ring composition in its simple form also from repetition, we do not need an elaborate terminology for multiple repetition.[38]

More important than anaphoric connections are the combinations a_b, b_c, etc., shown in the first of the diagrams above, for it is here that different *logoi* are joined together by means of the well-known *men-de* sentences so common in Herodotus.[39] Sometimes the connection is purely mechanical:

> The Delphians, on the one hand (*men dê*), in accordance with the oracle, pray to the winds to this day, but (*de*) the naval armament of Xerxes started from Therma ... (7.179)

The first part of this sentence closes the story of the oracle which the Delphians received concerning the winds, a story which in turn closes the great account of the Greek preparations against the Persians. In its second part, the sentence initiates the account of the movement of Xerxes' fleet into Greece. Often, however, *men-de* sentences are not used so mechanically, but help greatly in the understanding of Herodotus' main ideas. It is not too much to say that this type of connection furnishes the basic structure of the work; many examples will be cited in the next chapter.

[38] Van Otterlo, *Ringkomposition* 162, has named this type of ring composition *Ritornellkomposition*; cf. also his paper in *Mnemosyne*, ser. 3, 12 (1945) 192-207. Similar are some of the repeated themes stressed by Pohlenz, *Herodot* 9 ff. ("Das Leitmotif"). The idea of *Rahmenerzählung* also owes something to this phenomenon (cf. Introduction, note 29). Repeated framing sentences of this type may be either simply factual portions of a *logos* (e.g. in the Spartan War against Polycrates, Ch. III, 98-99, or in the antecedents of Salamis, Ch. VI, 270), or they may stress certain themes of importance for the work as a whole (e.g. below, note 59). Similar repetitions also occur internally within *logoi*, and sometimes at great intervals; thus some metaphysical statements recur in the Solon-Croesus story, the Polycrates-Amasis story, and the Xerxes adviser scenes; cf. *Samian Stories* 318-19. Internal repetition may be confined to a single *logos*: cf. e.g. the repeated references to the conquests of Upper Asia by the Medes, 1.102.2; 103.2; 104.2; 105.1; the wording varies throughout. Internal repetition does not, however, establish units of narrative, and is therefore little stressed in this study. Yet it must be admitted that the distinction is sometimes rather arbitrary.

[39] Fränkel, *Stileigenheit* 83. Van Otterlo, *Ringkomposition* 171 ff. The first part commonly uses the particles μέν, μὲν δή, or μέν νυν. This type of sentence also occurs internally, e.g. in the story of the rape of Io (1.1.4): "On the one hand (μὲν δή) the majority of the women escaped, but (δέ) Io and others were seized," where the μέν-clause disposes of a part of the story before Herodotus turns to the main event. Some connecting sentences have only the second, or δέ-portion, e.g 5.82.1 (the beginning of the story of the old hostility between Athens and Aegina, taking up the idea expressed in 5.81.2); cf. also 1.34.1 (beginning of the Atys story) and 8.65.1 (beginning of the Dicaeus and Demaratus story).

III

It is by a simple system of external repetition between semi-autonomous parts of his narrative (and to a lesser extent by some internal repetition as well) that Herodotus has created a large unified work. Throughout this work descriptions of single events reach out to find connections with other events, especially at the beginning and end of a story. Thus Herodotus' style everywhere exhibits the single chain rather than complex interweaving. Subsidiary action tends to be attached to the primary chain at a single point, or at least at one of a restricted number of points. The most precise attachment in Herodotus is the synchronism. Even where a synchronism is made with an extended series of events, it is often treated as a synchronism with a single point in time.[40] In the same manner, ethnographic *logoi* are attached to the single moment, as it were, of conquest, and Greek *logoi*, to precise points of contact between East and West.[41] Some accounts, it is true, contain a series of synchronisms with the main action, but such *logoi* can usually be analyzed as separate sections, each depending on its own synchronism. Conspicuous examples of this more complex method are the Spartan War against Polycrates of Samos and the Greek Preparations *Logos* in Book 7.[42]

Thus, on the whole, the term "parallel action" should not be applied to the work of Herodotus.[43] Elaborate parallel

[40] Synchronisms are discussed in detail by F. W. Mitchel, *An Investigation of the Chronological Systems used by Herodotus* (unpublished Yale Diss. 1954); cf. also Mitchel in *Phoenix* 10 (1956) 48-69, and H. Strasburger, "Herodots Zeitrechnung," in Marg, *Herodot* 677-725, a revised version that supersedes the paper in *Historia* 5 (1956) 129-61.

[41] Ch. I, 34-35.

[42] Ch. III, 98-99 and 136-37.

[43] Herodotus uses "meanwhile" (ἐν ᾧ) mainly to connect a single action with a preceding state of affairs. Powell, *Lexicon* s.v. ὅς B III 4, lists 17 examples of this expression, of which only three introduce *logoi*: 3.74.1 (while the seven conspirators deliberate, Prexaspes hurls himself from a tower); 5.108.1 (Introduction to Cypriote Campaign in Ionian Revolt); 7.26.1 (Beginning of Xerxes' March). For these three *logoi*, see Ch. III, 110, 115, and 129. Other places where I have noted parallel action are: a part of the Scythian Campaign (Ch. III, 110), a portion of the account of Plataea (9.54 f.), and the beginning of the Babylonian Revolt (3.150, cf. Jacoby, *RE* Suppl. 2.306). On the whole, both Jacoby and Pohlenz make too much of parallel action in Herodotus. Parallel accounts in Homer: W. Schadewaldt, *Iliasstudien* (above, note 28) 93, 97 f., etc. Basic is T. Zieliński, *Philologus*, Suppl. 8, 407 ff. Cf. D. L. Page, *The Homeric Odyssey* (Oxford 1955) 64 f. and 77, note 11. See also S. E. Bassett, *The Poetry of Homer* (Berkeley 1938) 34 ff. I would urge, against Bassett and Page, that it is erroneous to consider only the question of time-sequence in

compositions such as are found in Homer are basically alien to him. Seeming exceptions can usually be explained differently. In the middle of the account of the Ionian Revolt, Herodotus turns from the description of certain actions of Darius to a new *logos* of the campaign in Cyprus, which took place during the Ionian Revolt and was related to it. The introductory statement is as follows:

> While (*en hôi de*) the news about Sardis had come to the King, and Darius had shot his arrow and had spoken to Histiaeus, and Histiaeus, having been released by Darius, was traveling to the coast, in this whole period there happened the following. (5.108.1)

Here we seem to have two stretches of time correlated, but actually the time intervals are not measured at all, and the first part of the sentence simply summarizes one by one the preceding three stories of Herodotus' own narrative (5.105-107). At the end of the Cypriote Campaign there is no further reference to the events summarized in the introductory sentence, and thus that sentence looks forward perhaps only to the beginning of the Cypriote Revolt. Likewise, in Book 3, the death of Prexaspes is attached to the actions of the seven conspirators against the Magi with the following words:

> While these (the Seven) were thus deliberating, there happened by coincidence the following . . . (3.74.1)

The story which follows immediately upon this concerns Prexaspes and his relations with the Magi, and it ends with his death. Now obviously the death alone, and not the whole narrative, is contemporaneous with the conspirators' deliberations.[44] In several instances where we expect parallel action, it does not occur, such as for the synchronism between Croesus' and Cyrus' reigns, or the parallelism between the battles of Salamis and Himera, or that between Plataea and Mycale. In all these cases, the connection is made at a single point.[45] On the whole, the *Histories* are based

---

parallel accounts; Homer seems to me to work throughout with very elaborate analogical compositions (e.g. suitors and Telemachus scenes in the *Odyssey*.). This Herodotus does not do.

[44] Cf. 3.76.2, where the conspirators hear of Prexaspes' death "on the road." This constitutes an additional synchronism, a procedure basically related to proems of the second type discussed below, 65 ff.

[45] The parallelism of the battles cited above is noted by Herodotus only in one passage in each case; see Hdt. 7.166.1, and Ch. VI, 257. (The synchronism in 9.90.1 merely anticipates 9.100-101).

on the single chain of events, with single attachments of smaller accounts, rather than on elaborate synchronous structures.

The irregular sequence of emphatic and less emphatic statements produces a narrative that may be called *rhythmic*. There is no clear-cut subordination; instead repetition, anticipation, and summary create units of unequal length. These in turn form a chain, with certain interruptions attached at definite points. It is well not to apply to these latter the term digression, since it is frequently impossible to say whether the digression is more or less important than the main narrative.[46] From the purely formal point of view, we can make a distinction between smaller and larger units, and sometimes we find the smaller units inserted within the framework of larger ones. The general principle of composition here is that *the place between logoi forms a pause*. Thus a possible place for short remarks, or even short stories, is between the two parts of a connecting sentence of the *men-de* type. Such a sentence occurs between Darius' questioning of Greeks and Indians about their burial customs and the Spartan war against Polycrates:

> Such, then (*men nyn*), are these customs, ∥ and Pindar appears to me to have been right in saying that Law is king of all, ∥ but (*de*) while Cambyses had been fighting against Egypt, the Lacedaemonians had also waged a war against Samos and Polycrates . . . (3.38.4-39.1)

The remark about Pindar is a note placed between the two parts of a single connecting sentence.[47] The same phenomenon occurs on a larger scale in the monster sentence which connects the early achievements of Croesus with the visit of Solon to Sardis: there a statement about Croesus' conquests of barbarians, with a list of subject peoples, is placed in the middle of the connecting statement.[48] The same principle is finally used to place whole *logoi* between the main sections of the narrative. In this manner, the

[46] See the comments on the study by Erbse cited above, Introduction, note 34. Erbse distinguishes among others three principal types of digression: (1) those furnishing geographical background, (2) those introducing a new character, and (3) metaphysical explanations.

[47] Similarly 2.31 (the continuation is made with ἀλλά); 3.105.2 (last sentence); 4.63; 7.131. In 3.138.4 the final statement about the significance of the preceding *logos* is placed in the middle of a connecting sentence.

[48] Ch. I, note 43.

accounts of Croesus' dedications and the marvels of Lydia are placed between the Croesus *Logos* and the *logos* on the origins of Persia, and the *logos* on Persian customs is interpolated between the origins of Persia and the accounts of Cyrus' campaigns.[49] It follows that such small notes or *logoi* are useful in determining the main groups of *logoi* in the work, and that in determining a break between major *logoi* we must make it where Herodotus shows us a pause, whether or not this corresponds to our own notions of the unity of subject matter.

The notion of a pause is also useful in studying the beginnings and ends of units not otherwise clearly marked by anticipatory or concluding statements. Both the Egyptian and Scythian ethnographic *logoi* lack such statements (although there is in each case anaphora of the surrounding narrative), and instead they each begin with an anecdote. The Egyptian account begins with the story of the linguistic experiment of King Psammetichus, through which he discovered that the Egyptians were not the earliest of mankind, and the Scythian begins with the story of the war between the Scythians and their slaves, in which the theme of freedom and slavery is prefigured. Similar anecdotes also occur at the end of some *logoi*, such as the story, already mentioned, of the Delphic oracle concerning the winds, a story which comes at the end of the *logos* on Greek preparations. In certain *logoi*, Herodotus enters slowly upon his subject and shows a certain reluctance, as it were, to leave it. A significant development of this stylistic peculiarity is the fact that Herodotus sometimes puts personal remarks and accounts of great theoretical importance between *logoi* dealing with concrete events, so that the former take on the shape of "digressions."[50]

[49] Hdt. 1.92-94 and 1.131-40. In both cases the framing sentence is repeated after the *logos*.

[50] Cf. above, note 46. Similar introductory anecdotes occur e.g. in the European Campaign *Logos* (Ch. III, 110) and in the account of Plataea (Ch. VI, note 170). Anecdotes at the end of a *logos*: see the Libyan Ethnographic *Logos* (Ch. III, 113), the Scythian (Ch. III, 107), Darius' inquiry into burial customs at the end of the Cambyses *logoi* (3.38). "Digressions" of theoretical importance: 2.51-53, on Greek and Pelasgian religion, part of a series of *logoi* on Egyptian and Greek religion, divination and festivals, and placed between the sections on Egyptian sacrifices and sacred animals (Ch. III, 96); 3.108-109, on divine providence in the animal kingdom, placed at the end of the story of the collection of incense by the Arabians (Ch. III, 102); 4.36.2-45.5, discussion of the geography of the world, placed after the story of the Hyperboreans, which closes the geographical part of the Scythian Ethnographic *Logos*.

IV

The proem is one further device by which emphasis can be placed at certain specific points in the chain of *logoi*. As such it always has a strong connection with the narrative immediately following, so that it is never a complete survey of what is to come, but merely initiates in some way a sequence, the end of which is usually not indicated. The proem is simply a more elaborate form of the initial statement by anticipation. This is true, as we have seen, of the proem at the beginning of the work, which initiates the work without foretelling its future course.[51] At the same time, the external proem (i.e. the proem at the beginning of a work) makes use of a number of standard topics, such as the name of the author (and later on, but not in Herodotus, a title), the author's justification for making his work public, his purposes and methods, and an indication of the importance of the work, or of its subject. This last topic is not fully treated by Herodotus in the external proem of the work.

Internal proems may be defined as statements within the work which introduce not merely a single *logos*, but more generally a larger section of material, or as statements calling attention to the importance of a *logos* in more general terms than do simple anticipatory statements. Such proems are not very common in Herodotus, and so far as I can see there is not always a necessary correlation between their occurrence and the importance of the following narrative. Hence internal proems are only a secondary device in the structure of the work as a whole.

Internal proems fall into two classes: the first uses the topics of the external proem (it speaks of the author's qualifications or praises the topic that follows), while the second uses the topics common for introductory statements in a fuller, or more complicated, form. These two types do not appear to be combined in Herodotus. The first appears in the well-known comparison of Xerxes' invasion with four previous campaigns between Europe and Asia (at the beginning of Book 7), which is sometimes called the second proem of the work.[52] Despite the fact that this proem is introduced by *gar* as an explanation, its topics are those of external proems: the comparison (*synkrisis*) of the coming campaign with earlier ones, and the *auxêsis* of the campaign by listing

---

[51] Ch. I, 18.   [52] Hdt. 7.20-21. See Ch. III, 129.

the size of the armament; thus Herodotus adapts the standard
topic of the praise of subject to the immediate surroundings,
while introducing the section on preparations.

Other conspicuous examples of the use of topics properly
belonging to the external proem occur in the ethnographic *logoi*.
In the Egyptian ethnographic account such proemial statements
furnish the basic internal structure of the *logos*. We have seen
earlier that this *logos* starts without an introductory sentence;
instead it is introduced by the story of Psammetichus' linguistic
experiment, which deals with the idea of the antiquity of the
Egyptians. To this story are added some remarks on sources:
Herodotus heard this and other stories from the priests in Memphis,
Thebes and Heliupolis, and thus his account is based on the best
native informants (2.2-3). All this is introductory to the description of the country of Egypt (the *chôrê*), which is the first standard
topic of ethnographic *logoi*. At the beginning of the next section,
the description of customs (*nomoi*), we read:

> I am about to lengthen the *logos* about Egypt because (this
> country) contains the most marvels and has works beyond
> description as compared with other countries; therefore, more
> will be said about it. (2.35.1)

This introduction cannot be taken at face value, because a *nomoi*-
section is mandatory in ethnography. The statement is an internal
proem using the topic of praise of subject matter. There follow
two sections on Egyptian history.[53] The first is introduced as
follows:

> Up to this point my account has been based on my own
> observation, opinion, and investigation, but from now on I
> shall tell the stories given by the Egyptians as I have heard
> them; a bit of personal observation will be included. (2.99.1)

Again, the statement does not mention the subject matter that
follows, but uses the topic of the reliability of sources: history is
not based on direct observation, but on oral accounts.

A similar proemial statement introduces the more recent
history of Egypt:

> The (above) is what the Egyptians themselves say, but what
> both the rest of mankind and the Egyptians agree in declaring

[53] On these sections, see Ch. III, 97 and 99.

to have happened in this country, that I shall now relate; a bit of personal observation will be included. (2.147.1)

Herodotus has divided the history of Egypt into two periods: that before the arrival of the Greeks in Egypt in the seventh century is based on Egyptian accounts alone, while the period after the Greeks had come to know Egypt (the history of the Saite dynasty) was better known, since Egyptian accounts could now be checked against Greek accounts (the phrase "the rest of mankind" in the quotation above refers primarily to the Greeks). Consequently, he has used the topic of the reliability of sources for proemial introductions to both sections, each written with the other in mind, especially as regards the mention of his own personal observation (i.e. the use of monuments in each section to substantiate Egyptian history).[54] We notice, then, that the passage at the beginning of the Egyptian *Logos*, which also deals with sources, is proemial as well, although, somewhat in the manner of the so-called second proem in Book 7, it is in form merely an addition to the preceding narrative.

Other ethnographic *logoi* lack the completeness of this scheme, but we may cite two isolated instances from the Scythian Ethnographic *Logos*:

> But I laugh when I see those who have written surveys of the earth in great number, without giving sensible explanations. (4.36.2)

This introduces a section on Herodotus' ideas about the map of the world. A little further on, a similar statement occurs:

> I marvel at those who have defined and separated Libya, Asia, and Europe. (4.42.1)

Both proemial statements recall the proem of Hecataeus' *Genealogies*.[55]

The second class of proems owes its character to a combination of framing sentences, for it is possible for certain statements and their repeated counterparts to overlap in such a way that several

---

[54] On the topics used in proems, see below, Ch. III, note 3, and for the schemes used in ethnographic *logoi*, see this Chapter, note 60. A similar phrase on sources occurs e.g. in 4.150.1, and a similar phrase on purpose in 1.177; 3.60.1 and 4.

[55] Jacoby, *FGrH* I, 318-19 (1 F 1). Hdt. 4.42.1 introduces a separate section. A further example of a proem of the first type is 4.46.

come together at one point. This may be represented in the
following diagram:

$$\overline{a \text{ -I- } \ldots, \; \overline{b \text{ -II- } \ldots, \; \overline{c \text{ -III- } \ldots, \quad c+b+a.}}}$$

Or, if the combined statements are anticipatory rather than
summary:

$$\overline{a+b+c \quad \overline{c \text{ -I- } \ldots, \; \overline{b \text{ -II- } \ldots, \; a \text{ -III- } \ldots}}}$$

We have already seen an example of the first alternative in the
introduction to the Cypriote Revolt.[56] The first and second
alternatives both appear in what I would like to call the proem to
the *logos* on Marathon:

> The Athenians had joined in war with the Aeginetans, and the
> Persian was carrying out his own plans, for the servant was
> reminding him constantly of the Athenians, the Peisistratids
> were urging him on and accusing the Athenians, and at the
> same time Darius himself desired to use this pretext for the
> conquest of those in Greece who would not give him earth and
> water. Mardonius, who had done poorly on his (previous)
> expedition, he dismissed from the command, and appointing
> other generals he sent them against Eretria and Athens, namely
> Datis, a Mede by birth, and Artaphernes son of Artaphernes,
> his own nephew. In sending them he told them to enslave
> Athens and Eretria and to bring the slaves before him. (6.94)

In this elaborate statement, the first sentence summarizes: the
slave's reminder refers to a chapter in the Ionian Revolt (5.105),
the Peisistratid entreaties recall the end of the second Athenian
logos (5.96.1), and the demand for earth and water harks back
to the beginning of the Aeginetan *Logos* (6.48.2). The whole is
introduced by a statement summarizing the end of the Aeginetan
Logos, i.e. the chapter immediately preceding (6.93). Except for
this last, all summary statements are combined in a causal scheme
according to which vengeance and provocation are minor causes
when compared with expansionist desire.[57] The second portion
of the chapter looks forward and closes with an anticipatory
statement which is fulfilled for the Eretrians at the end of the

---

[56] Above, 60. A similar summary, Hdt. 3.140.1.
[57] *Causation* 272-73.

campaign (6.119). This type of proem, then, is no more than a combination of features found elsewhere in individual framing sentences.

V

If in the preceding pages we have paid a perhaps inordinate amount of attention to the mechanical connection between *logoi*, this is because these connections are most easily classified and therefore have been studied more fully than other aspects of structure in Herodotus.[58] In turning now to individual *logoi*, we shall find that their internal structure likewise falls into patterns, which are, however, less easily identified. This is true despite the fact that internal unity is in large measure based on the same principles as external unity. A *logos* may be a chain of events or a more balanced or dramatic composition, but its basis will always be parataxis modified by irregular emphasis, especially at the beginning and end. An essential feature of Herodotean style is the fact that the elements of external connection are also found in internal construction. Thus we have irregular emphasis through repetition, anticipation, and summary, occurring within *logoi* and leading to a system of cross references and verbal echoes between different units of composition as well as within a single *logos*. Some of these connections will be pointed out in the next chapter.[59]

It may be useful to distinguish certain types of *logoi* on the basis of form and subject matter. There can be little question that definite arrangements of subject matter had already become associated with geography and ethnography before Herodotus, but it is less certain that historical sections were a regular part of such *logoi*.[60] However that may be, Herodotus gives his own complete scheme only in the Egyptian Ethnographic *Logos* in

[58] Not all *logoi* employ ring composition for outer connection: e.g. the Gyges story (1.8.1-12.2) uses repetition of participial phrases at the beginning, cf. Fränkel, *Stileigenheit* 65 f.; similarly, the Pigres story, 5.12.1 ff.

[59] Direct cross references: Schmid-Stählin 1.2.592, note 8; Powell, *Hist. Herodotus* 89-90. Verbal echoes: Pohlenz, *Herodot* 9-21 and 209; above, note 38. "Ritornellkomposition" is related to this.

[60] For ethnographic patterns see Trüdinger, *Studien* 15 ff., esp. 21; Jacoby, *Entwicklung* 88 ff.; E. Norden, *Die Germanische Urgeschichte in Tacitus' Germania* (Leipzig 1922) 46 ff.; Pohlenz, *Herodot* 71 ff.; E. Wolff, *Hermes* 69 (1934) 136 ff. For the question of the relation between historical and ethnographic *logoi*, see above, Ch. I, note 59.

Book 2; it consists of Origins, Description of Country, Customs, and History, and the Customs section is divided into Religious Customs and Secular Customs, in that order. In the section on customs Herodotus relies heavily on the archaic joining of the parts of narrative by intermediate links, a fact which tends to confirm the traditional character of this kind of *logos*.[61] His other ethnographic *logoi* vary this scheme, with some (such as the Libyan) preserving the traditional form to a considerable extent, while others (in particular the Scythian) modify it to conform to the particular historical situation with which they are connected.[62] Certain other short *logoi*, such as place descriptions, notes on natural history, and scientific arguments, likewise give the impression of being heavily indebted to a pre-existing tradition.[63]

Among the historical *logoi*, we have already noted the chronicle of kings, which is used for long stretches of the narrative, but always in modified form. The most outstanding feature of the chronicle of kings is the series of campaigns. For their description Herodotus has a fixed order of topics, varied of course according to circumstances, but ideally present in all *logoi*. The complete scheme is as follows:

1. Plan of aggressor.
2. His preparations.
3. Section on causation (*aitiê*-section).
4. March of aggressor to place of action.
5. Preparations of defender.
6. March of defender to place of action.
7. Battle.
8. Epilogue: consequences of battle (retreat and pursuit; stories about victors in valor; further pursuit of enemy).

It should be noted, however, that a considerable amount of variation is possible within this scheme. The causation section always deals with the immediate grievances (*aitiai*), rather than

---

[61] For the outline of the Egyptian Ethnographic *Logos*, see Ch. III, 96-97.

[62] See the comparative tables in Aly, *Formprobleme* 48; Myres, *Herodotus* 73; Pohlenz, *Herodot* 79 ff.

[63] Place descriptions: especially the short ones are no doubt in a form that is traditional, e.g. those in Xerxes' march (7.30, etc.). Natural history: the phoenix story is from Hecataeus (Jacoby, *FGrH* I, 1 F 324); cf. also the winged snakes (3.107-109); the fox ants (3.102) and camel (3.103), etc. Scientific argument: sources and floods of the Nile in Book 2; shape of the continents (4.42.1), etc.

with underlying causes.[64] The crucial stage is the battle section, which is essentially a circular composition around some central point, not necessarily the military decision, but sometimes another element. The full form is as follows:

1. Movement of aggressor into position.
2. Movement of defender into position.
3. Council of defender.
4. (Less commonly) a council for the attacker.
5. Description of action.
6. Epilogue, i.e. No. 8 above.

The last chapter will show examples of the variety of composition possible under this scheme, especially in the great battles against the Persians in 480 and 479.[65] It is characteristic of Herodotus that the sections preceding and following the action are always more important that the battle itself.

More difficult (and perhaps less fruitful for our purposes) is the analysis of the minor types of *logoi* in the work,[66] but there are at least two types of highly organized *logoi*, not dependent on subject matter and thus recurring in various situations. One is the *dramatic logos* and the other the *circular logos*. Of these, the former clearly bears a relation to Attic tragedy.[67] Its elements are the same as those found in other, non-dramatic *logoi*, but they are arranged in such fashion as to produce a definite tragic development. In this group are found the most famous of Herodotus' compositions,

[64] *Causation* 243 ff. On causation in Herodotus, see now also R. Sealey, *CQ*, n.s. 7 (1957) 1-12, and A. E. Wardman, *AJP* 82 (1961) 133-50.

[65] See Ch. VI, *passim*.

[66] For patterns of advice, see below, 74. On wisdom literature connected with the Seven Sages (an important model for Herodotus), see Barkowski in *RE*, s.v. Sieben Weise; M. P. Nilsson, *Gesch. d. griech. Rel.*[2] 1 (Munich 1955) 650 f.; and B. Snell, *Leben und Meinungen der Sieben Weisen*[3] (Munich 1952). Generally, Aly, *Volksmärchen* 15 ff. and 236 ff. Literary patterns of oracles: Crahay, *Litt. orac.* 46-57. Conversations: R. Hirzel, *Der Dialog*, 1 (1895) 2-42. Speeches: E. Schulz, *Die Reden im Herodot* (Diss. Göttingen 1933); A. Deffner, *Die Rede bei Herodot und ihre Weiterbildung bei Thukydides* (Diss. Munich 1933). On the parables in the speeches of Socles and Leotychidas, see Ch. V, 194 and 213.

[67] For Herodotus and tragedy, see H. Fohl, *Tragische Kunst bei Herodot* (Diss. Rostock 1913); B. Snell, *Aischylos und das Handeln im Drama, Philologus*, Suppl. 20, No. 1 (1928) 72 f.; Myres, *Herodotus* 27 and 137-38; F. W. Walbank, "History and Tragedy," *Historia* 9 (1960) 221 ff. Unknown to me: J. Casseur, *Hérodote et les tragiques du Vᵉ siècle* (Thèse Brussels), cf. *RBP* 20 (1942) 535. Recently, D. L. Page, "An Early Tragedy on the Fall of Croesus?" *PCPS* 188 (1962) 47 ff. On the relation of Herodotus to the Gyges tragedy, a fragment of which is known from a papyrus, see e.g. A. Lesky, *Hermes* 81 (1953) 1 ff.

such as the Gyges story, the Atys story, the birth of Cyrus, the Periander and Lycophron story, and the death of Polycrates. On a larger scale, the whole Croesus *Logos* shows dramatic structure.[68] In the Atys story, which is one of the most elaborate, the main sections are set off by short summary phrases, so that the analysis has an objective basis.[69] The resultant structure is as follows:

    I. Introduction:
        a. Connecting sentence: punishment overtakes Croesus for hybris in front of Solon.
        b. Warning dream: son will be killed.
        c. Croesus attempts to foil the dream by protecting his son.
    II. Adrastus:
        a. His arrival and cleansing by Croesus.
        b. Conversation of Croesus and Adrastus (in 3 parts).
    III. The boar:
        a. He ravages the country.
        b. Embassy to Croesus: request to get Atys to help; negative reply.
    IV. Conversation of Atys and his father:
        a. Atys asks for permission to go.
        b. Croesus explains his dream.
        c. Atys interprets the dream differently.
        d. Croesus is persuaded.
    V. Adrastus:
        a. Croesus asks him to accompany Atys.
        b. Adrastus is unwilling, but he is finally convinced by Croesus.
    VI. The Hunt:
        a. Hunt and accident: Adrastus kills Atys.
        b. Croesus hears it, accuses Zeus.

[68] Myres, *Herodotus* 137. Structure of Polycrates stories: *Samian Stories* 312 ff. Cf. also *Tat und Geschichte* 535, note 66.

[69] Summary phrases establish the six main sections, but not the subsections. Thus at the beginning of Section II we have a gen. absolute about Atys' wedding (1.35.1, beg.); Section III begins with a reference to Adrastus' stay in Sardis (1.36.1, beg., with μὲν δή); Section IV, again, starts with a gen. absolute concerning the Mysian requests (1.37.1, second line); Section V has a simple participle (1.41.1, beg.); Section VI, a temporal clause; the last two examples refer to the preceding conversations. Such subdivision is a sign of elaboration and is not used in all *logoi*. It is absent e.g. in the Arion story (1.23-24) and the story of the ring of Polycrates (3.40-43).

    c. Arrival of corpse and Adrastus.
    d. Croesus sees and forgives Adrastus.
    e. Suicide of Adrastus.

The structure of the story is based largely on a rigid distinction between speeches and action. The action is reduced to a minimum. The central structural problem of the story is the fact that there are two victims of misfortune (Atys and Adrastus) and two deaths. This is solved by arranging the speeches so as to make the two Adrastus episodes connecting links between the Croesus-Atys scenes. Hence the conversation between father and son is central, for in it Croesus is persuaded to an action which brings about his son's death. The conversation consists of two pairs of speeches, and the two speeches of Atys are parallel in structure, each consisting of an address to the father, the main argument in the form of rhetorical questions, and a request.[70] Thus the core of the whole story is Croesus' decision to let his son go on the hunt. Croesus is the tragic hero of the story, for it is he who tries to outwit the oracle, yet accepts the murderer Adrastus in his house; it is he who is persuaded by his son to let him go on the hunt, where Adrastus slays him. At the end Croesus recognizes the truth: he accuses the gods and forgives Adrastus (who nevertheless slays himself). In this scheme Adrastus is the connecting link and not a major figure.[71] We have here a sequence which is truly organic in the sense of tragedy, i.e. each part derives its meaning only from the exact place it occupies.

    Recently Myres has laid great emphasis upon *circular compositions* (under the name "pedimental compositions"), which he takes to be the main structural feature of the work of Herodotus

---

[70] *First speech.*

Father, formerly I was proud to go to war and hunt, but now you lock me up.

To whom can I show myself? What man will I seem to citizens, what man to my wife? What man will she think to have for a husband?

Let me go on the hunt, or convince me that it is better otherwise.

Second speech.

Father, I understand that you are worried, but you misinterpret the dream.

You say I shall die from an iron spear? What hands has a boar? What iron spear?

Since the battle is not against me, let me go.

The organization of the speeches calls to mind Corax' tripartite division of speeches into proemium—agon—epilogue (O. Navarre, *Essai sur la rhétorique grecque avant Aristote* [Paris 1900] 15 f.).

[71] Differently Hellmann, *Kroisos-Logos* 58 ff. Cf. Ch. IV, 157.

as a whole.[72] We have seen that this is erroneous. Circular compositions (one wishes the term "ring composition" were available for them) occur only on a relatively restricted scale, because they presuppose an exact correspondence between a small number of sections of a *logos* in such a way that the main action occurs in the center of the *logos*, and the preceding and following sections correspond to each other in inverse sequence. I have tried to show elsewhere that the story of the ring of Polycrates bears such a circular arrangement.[73] Another story of this type is that of Arion and the Dolphin, rightly analyzed by Myres as circular.[74] At the center of such stories there is always a particularly vivid scene (the fisherman bringing back the fish with the ring in it; Arion flinging himself into the sea). These are often stories in which the resulting fortune or misfortune is not primarily the consequence of the hero's decision. A fine example, on a somewhat larger scale, are the sea skirmishes before Artemisium:

1. Three Greek ships attacked by ten Persian, and worsted. The Greeks withdraw from Artemisium to Chalcis. The Persians advance to Cape Sepias.
2. The numbers of the Persian navy and army up to this point.
3. The storm off Magnesia reduces that number. (Stories of Boreas and of Ameinocles.) Prayers of Magi assuage the storm.
4. Greeks sacrifice to Poseidon and return to Artemisium. The Greeks worst fifteen Persian ships.

   (7.179-95)

The central complex here is the story of the storm which caused a reversal of fortune, a theme reinforced by the preceding account of the size of Persian armament. The two stories of sea skirmishes underline this reversal: again it is due to an outside agency rather than to human decision.[75]

VI

The last examples of the preceding section have been based on certain patterns of narrative which are not strictly formal in the sense of verbal repetition. In addition to such narrative patterns,

[72] Myres, *Herodotus* 79 ff. Introduction, note 32.   [73] *Samian Stories* 317.
[74] Ch. I, 35 and note 61.
[75] Ch. VI, 264. The figures for the land army, which are irrelevant to the story, are added because the computation completes the army and navy lists given for the Persians in 7.61 ff.

a number of thought patterns recur throughout the work; they are of great importance in reinforcing the continuity that exists between the separate *logoi*.

One elementary thought pattern concerns the Herodotean analysis of human events into *thought and action*. H. Bischoff, in a valuable dissertation, has noted the proclivity of Herodotus (ultimately derived from Homer) for separating a previous stage of counsel from the action proper, even where this is not necessary:

> As soon as Croesus had withdrawn after the battle of Pteria . . ., Cyrus took counsel and found it to be his business to go to Sardis as soon as possible . . . And as he had decided, so he acted with speed. (1.79.1)

The full pattern of this type consists of counsel, decision, and action, but shorter forms (counsel and action, or simply word and action) are also found.[76] With this intellectualization of the action (if I may call it that) we may contrast a formula where action is based on passion:

> When the army had been counted and arranged in order, Xerxes desired to pass it in review in person. Afterwards he did this . . . (7.100.1)

In some instances the desire is felt to be so important that it replaces the account of the action itself.[77] The intellectual, rather than the emotional, formula is the fountainhead of the numerous counsel scenes in Herodotus, for a man must either take counsel with himself or receive it from others:

> Be it that someone else suggested it to him when he was in a quandary, or that he himself learned what had to be done, Cyrus acted as follows . . . (1.191.1)

In Herodotus, to be one's own counselor, or to receive advice, are

---

[76] The remarks above and the section following are based largely upon Bischoff, *Warner*. See also R. Lattimore, "The Wise Adviser in Herodotus," *CP* 34 (1939) 24-35. Further, C. M. Bowra, *Early Greek Elegists* (Cambridge [Mass.] 1938) 79-80, and *Sophoclean Tragedy* (Oxford 1944) 106; *Tat und Geschichte* 529-34; H. D. Kemper, *Rat und Tat. Studien zur Darstellung eines antithetischen Begriffspaares in der klassischen Periode der griechischen Literatur* (Diss. Bonn 1957, published by the author in 1960) 47-48. Examples are: (1) word and action, 3.134.6; (2) counsel and action, 2.30.3; cf. 3.119.4; 4.102.1; (3) counsel, decision, and action, 3.17.2 and 25.1 ff.; 3.153.1-154.1. A common formula is βουλευομένοισι ἔδοξε; see Powell, *Lexicon*, s.v. δοκέω 3 c.

[77] The full formula is used e.g. in 2.135.3-4; 7.128.2; but the short formula is actually more common: 1.24.1; 1.201=204.1; 3.120.1=120.4; 3.127.1, etc.

equivalent situations.[78] This intellectual element is so important in Herodotus that council scenes sometimes overshadow the account of the action itself, e.g. in the accounts of the great battles in the Persian Wars.

Between thought and action a pause occurs, which may be filled (strange as that may seem to us) by other material. Thus Cyrus' campaign against the Massagetae is introduced as follows:

> When Cyrus had conquered (the Assyrians) as well, he desired to bring the Massagetae under his yoke. (1.201)

This is followed by some ethnographic material, after which the idea of a desire to attack is repeated (1.204.1). Then follows a short *aitiê*-statement, plus an account of Cyrus' attempt to gain his objective peaceably. This is finally followed by the action itself (1.205.2). Similarly, the narrative may be broken between the stages of the action itself, a fact especially noticeable in campaign *logoi*. Thus we often find material added in the pauses between the stages: plan—preparations—march—battle—retreat, but the preferred place for such interruptions is between the planning stage and the other phases of a campaign. This corresponds to the dichotomy of thought and action.[79]

Advice and warning thus occur in certain specified positions in the narrative. The occasion is usually the seeking of advice by the ruler, but sometimes the adviser appears unexpectedly, prior to the action. The form in which advice is given varies from a pithy saying to a short speech, a conversation, or an elaborate oration. There is a definite *pattern of advice*, which in its full form consists of three main parts: gnomic sayings embodying a view of the world, a general warning often of a negative kind ("don't act rashly," or the like), and specific advice dealing with a practical problem and usually embodying a positive plan. The effect of the advice given depends on whether or not it is accepted: usually, but not always, general advice is rejected, and thus it becomes a

---

[78] Bischoff, *Warner* 8-11 and 26 ff. This contrasts with the well-known lines in Hesiod, *Erga* 293-97, where to be counseled by another is inferior to taking counsel with oneself. In Herodotus, counselors sometimes address their audience as if the latter were taking counsel with themselves; so Artabanus, 7.10d.2, and Themistocles, 8.60c.1 (cf. also 7.157.3). Cf. also the advice of Mnesiphilus and of Aristeides to Themistocles, Ch. V, 224 and Ch. VI, 277.

[79] Pause between planning and action, e.g. 3.17 ff. (Cambyses' Ethiopian campaign). Pauses between stages of action, especially the march of Xerxes, Ch. III, 132. Adviser scenes are often placed in these pauses, e.g. 1.27.1-2 and 1.71.2.

warning which has a dramatic effect within the course of the narrative. In this case, the wise adviser appears as the warner who shows up the folly of the ruler. Specific advice, on the other hand, is usually accepted, so that the adviser then appears as the wise counselor. The full form of advice is present only in a single case, the advice given by Artabanus to Xerxes at the Hellespont.[80] There Artabanus begins by describing the troubles of life (general *gnômê*), then warns Xerxes of the dangers of land and sea (general advice, here rejected), and finally advises him to leave the Ionians behind (practical advice, here also rejected). The same pattern is presupposed in the advice given by Croesus to Cyrus before the latter enters the country of the Massagetae, a scene which is often misunderstood. There the question is specifically whether or not to cross the river Araxes to give battle to the queen of the Massagetae. Croesus begins by describing the wheel of fortune in all human affairs (general *gnômê*), thereby implying that he cannot give advice on whether Cyrus will be victorious (i.e. he refuses to pronounce upon the question of general advice), and finally advises crossing the river, since this will save the empire even if Cyrus should be defeated (specific advice, which is accepted).[81] Elsewhere, there are various combinations of one or more of the three elements of the pattern of advice.[82]

These examples may suffice to show the importance of thought patterns for the analysis of the work. Similar patterns may be found for omens and predictions, and in other cases where the outcome of action is prefigured in the narrative. In order to understand these cases, it is necessary to be aware of what I have called the full form in each instance, for the narrative of Herodotus is often elliptic, and a short story or phrase may be unintelligible without reference to the complete pattern.

One further pattern must be discussed in detail, since it furnishes a basic clue to the structure of the work in at least three

[80] Hdt. 7.46-51. *Action* 41-44.

[81] Hdt. 1.207. It is not true (as is claimed e.g by How and Wells *ad loc.*, perhaps following Cambyses, 3.36.3) that Croesus is responsible for Cyrus' defeat, or has lost his wisdom. The correct interpretation is given by Hellmann, *Kroisos-Logos* 83, note 1. Cf. also Bischoff, *Warner* 43-44.

[82] Based on the lists in Lattimore, *CP* 34 (above, note 76), the evidence for the different types is as follows: (1) warning, advice, and *gnômê*: 7.46-51. (2) warning and advice: 7.10; 5.36; 8.68; 9.2; 9.41. (3) advice and *gnômê*: 1.207; 3.40. (4) warning and *gnômê*: frequent, e.g. 9.122; 6.11; 6.109.

crucial sections. This is the pattern of the rise and fall of rulers, which is basic for the *logoi* dealing with Croesus, Cyrus, and Darius. This pattern in turn is based on the idea of a reversal of fortune, which is so basic to Herodotus' philosophy of history that he sometimes seems to report on the complete life story of an individual merely to give emphasis to a change of fortune:

> Ameinocles the son of Cretines, a Magnesian who farmed near Cape Sepias, found the shipwreck (of the Persians) much to his advantage. He collected many gold and silver cups later cast ashore, and finding hoards of Persian treasure he acquired untold wealth. However, although he became very rich by his finds, he was not otherwise lucky; for he too was hit by an ugly and grievous misfortune, the death of his son. (7.190) [83]

The last statement is added not so much for the purpose of drawing a moral lesson as to show a difference in fortune. In other cases the statement is so short that it may be misunderstood unless one has the whole pattern in mind.

Reversal of fortune is the climax of the elaborate *pattern of the rise and fall of a ruler*. The full pattern may be outlined as follows:

1. Origin of the ruler (how he was born, or how he came to power).
2. Early reign until full power is achieved. (This is usually brief, and there is a sudden rise to high fortune.)
3. Further reign, told at length, and leading to destruction, or at least to a decline.

---

[83] On this story cf. also Ch. V, 189. "He too:" presumably like the Persians; the story draws a parallel between the fate of the Persians and that of a Greek. However, two points in the story are obscure: (1) did the death of Ameinocles' son precede or follow the acquisition of the treasures? The second seems more likely; thus the fate of Ameinocles would parallel directly that of the Persians. (2) Did Ameinocles kill his son, or did he lose him by a natural death? The fact that Dionys. Halic., *Arch.* 3.21.1, and Plut., *Mor.* 864, interpret the story in the former sense does not prove its correctness, and the matter remains a puzzle. See Macan on 7.190, line 10. συμφορή is used by Herodotus both for accidents and for crimes (involuntary, 1.35.1, etc., but is not 3.52.4 voluntary?); see Powell, *Lexicon* s.v. Fränkel, *Stileigenheit* 67, note 3, is surely wrong in connecting the expression "an ugly misfortune" (ἄχαρις συμφορή) with aristocratic feelings alien to Herodotus, for the latter uses it in an almost formulaic way both for accidents and for crimes; see Powell, *Lexicon* s.v. ἄχαρις. The opposite to ἄχαρις is εὐχάριστος as used by Solon before Croesus: . . . καὶ ἔπειτα τελευτήσῃ εὐχαρίστως τὸν βίον (1.32.9). This is a widespread terminology, which looks at events

Throughout the work, Herodotus emphasizes the origin of a king or a dynasty; the story of Candaules' wife is important for the accession story of Gyges, the founder of the Mermnad dynasty in Lydia (1.8-13). Deioces, the judge of the Medes who made himself into the absolute ruler of his people, initiates the Median dynasty (1.96-101). In the same way, the origins of Cyrus and (in a more restricted form) the accession of Darius are fundamental both for the Persian dynasty and for the fate of the individual rulers concerned. The same stress on origins is present in the accounts of some of the Egyptian kings, and on the Greek side in the stories of the Greek tyrants and the Cyrenean and Spartan kings.[84]

The second element in the pattern is usually more briefly treated, since what interests Herodotus in his accounts of tyrants and foreign kings is the descent from power rather than the ascent thereto. Therefore, a warning is often added at the height of fortune: Gyges was warned by the Delphic oracle after his accession; Croesus was warned by Solon and also by the death of his son Atys; Cyrus is more obscurely warned by Astyages after the latter's defeat; Darius receives no warning because he is not destroyed, but the section on the Ends of the World following directly upon the account of Darius' great prosperity has a similar function for the reader. The warnings received by Xerxes are numerous. The connection between high fortune and warning is best shown in the case of Polycrates, whose constant good luck is the occasion of the warnings of Amasis, king of Egypt.[85]

The last section of the pattern of rise and fall usually consists of the later reign of the king or tyrant (so far as Herodotus tells it).

---

not directly from the moral point of view, but considers first whether they give a human being (either the sufferer or, vicariously, a bystander) pleasure or pain.

Cf. further the story of Pytheas of Aegina, Ch. V, 190; Sandoces, 7.194.3; the Thebans at Thermopylae, 7.233.2; Sophanes, 9.75; Hegesistratus, 9.37.4. It is not accidental that such stories abound in the narrative of the battles of the Persian Wars.

[84] Egypt: Min (2.99.2 ff.), Cheops (2.124 ff.), Psammetichus and the twelve kings (2.147.2 ff.), Apries and Amasis (2.161.3 ff.). On the Greek side: the rise of Polycrates (3.39), of Peisistratus (1.59.1-3), of the Cypselids (5.92b ff.), the Battiads (4.150 ff.), and the Spartan kings (6.51 ff., etc.). See also Ch. V, 191-98.

[85] Gyges, 1.13.2; Croesus, 1.30 ff. and 34 ff.; Cyrus, 1.128.1; Darius, 3.106 ff. (Ends of the World); Xerxes, 7.10; 37.2, etc. Polycrates: 3.40 ff. The Atys story (1.34 ff.) may be considered a warning in deed, and thus similar to the story of the ring of Polycrates, 3.40.2 ff., cf. 3.124.1. The section on the Ends of the World differs, to be sure, from the other stories, since it foreshadows the end of Darius for the reader, but not for the main character himself. See further, Ch. IV, 172.

The campaign *logoi* of a particular king thus partake of both the elements of height of fortune and of decline or destruction, but there is always a particular emphasis on reversal of fortune in the accounts of campaign failures, which are usually heavily stressed.

The whole pattern is found in the accounts of the great rulers (as well as in several shorter *logoi*), and its recurrence establishes a basic similarity for the royal histories, which culminate in the story of Xerxes. The history of the Mermnadae is related to Croesus as the history of the Medes is related to Cyrus, and the history of the Persian kings to Xerxes (Origins). The wealth of Croesus corresponds to Cyrus' conquest of Babylon, Cambyses' conquest of Egypt, Darius' wealth as described in the satrapy list, and Xerxes' war preparations (High Fortune). The further wars of the kings are largely examples of their failures (Decline). The cumulative weight of these examples of one recurrent pattern forces the reader to accept the Herodotean interpretation of Xerxes' ill success in the Persian Wars as a decisive defeat.[86]

The ideal pattern of rise and fall at times conflicts with the actual situation (both Cyrus and Darius fought for some time to gain mastery over Asia). It is nevertheless a historical pattern and not a purely moral one. Both the sections on origins and those dealing with campaigns are detailed historical accounts explaining the fortunes of great nations and not merely of individuals. The variety of *logoi* used in this pattern shows that it is no more than a general scheme into which historical material is molded, and by which that material is explained in its interrelations.

The historical narrative of Herodotus is arranged primarily in two groups of compositions: Origins and Campaigns. The ethnographic *logoi*, despite their great length, are clearly subordinated to these main groups. The accounts of great fortune are more briefly treated, except for the two Babylonian conquests, which are symbolic of mastery over Asia, and the account of the Power of Darius, whose reign stands at the ideal center of the work. This simplicity of arrangement in two groups of narrative is the foundation of the unity of structure.

[86] Ch. IV, 176.

Chapter III

THE UNITS OF THE WORK

I

We have described the work of Herodotus as a single *logos* with special emphasis at the beginning and end, a *logos* consisting in turn of a sequence of smaller *logoi*. These are arranged in a single row from which are suspended, as it were, separate ethnographic and Greek historical *logoi* at irregular intervals. In the present chapter, we shall consider the internal structure and the interconnections of these individual *logoi*, so far as they can be established by the criteria discussed previously. Here we will find that Herodotus emphasizes certain events (which are embedded in stories he found in the tradition) by referring to them repeatedly in certain places of his narrative, especially at the beginning and end of a *logos*, with the effect that these items become fixed elements in the development of the work and can be referred to as literary "motifs" which tie the work together. This term does not imply, of course, that we doubt their factual nature, or that we treat the *Histories* as fiction. Outlines of the work such as that given in the present chapter have been made before, but previous attempts are perhaps somewhat inadequate because of a lack of confidence felt by their authors in Herodotus' ability to organize.[1] I disregard the traditional non-Herodotean division of the work into books and chapters, although I doubt that the present division (or any division based on *logoi*) is usable in making an edition.[2]

[1] See Introduction, notes 27-33.

[2] The ancient (but not Herodotean) division into nine books breaks apart the *logos* of the Ionian Revolt (Books 5 and 6), and the antecedents before Plataea (Books 8 and 9); see below, 115 f. and 142. In the latter case, however, there results an interesting parallelism between the end of Book 8 and the beginning of Book 9, such as exists between Books 6 and 7 of Thucydides also: cf. J. de Romilly, *Histoire et raison chez Thucydide* (Paris 1956) 73, and note 1. A division into six books would perhaps be more rational (1.1-216; 2.1-3.60; 3.61-4.205; 5.1-6.140; 7.1-8.39; 8.40-9.122), but only a division into *logoi*, such as that of Legrand, would be in the spirit of the work. Chapter-divisions pose a similar problem, since they are masked by the ubiquitous *men-de* clauses. Hence Stein begins chapters with the *men-* portions, Hude with the *de-* members. The former seems preferable.

1. *The Proem* (1.1-5)

The Proem begins with the author's name and the brief
statement that he is making his research public (*Hêrodotou
Halikarnêsseos historiês apodexis hêde*), by which Herodotus asks the
reader to accept the work not so much because of the importance
of its subject matter, but for his skill in assembling his material.
The "title" of the work thus resembles the internal proemia of the
ethnographic *logos* on Egypt discussed in the last chapter.[3] As I have
mentioned elsewhere, the proem in its entirety is defined as a separate entity both by the asyndeton of 1.6.1 (which contains the beginning of the Croesus story) and by its internal structure, as follows:

> 1a. Heading and statement of purposes and methods.
> 2. Persian account of who is to blame for the quarrels between
>   Greeks and barbarians.
> > Phoenician variant.
> 1b. Herodotus' own opinion with respect to who is to blame,
>   and further statements on his method.[4]

The points made in the first and last sections, where Herodotus
speaks on his own behalf, are four:

> A. Concerning his purpose:
> > a. The preservation of the record.
> > b. The evaluation of the record (its praise).
> B. Concerning his method:
> > a. Fixing the responsibility for the wars between Greeks
> >   and barbarians (*aitiê*).
> > b. Impartiality and a certain comprehensive objectivity in
> >   relating events, because all humanity is liable to the
> >   cycle of fortune.[5]

The proem is thus devoted primarily to a justification of the
work, in conformance with the nature of early prose proems,

---

[3] Ch. II, 64. For a bibliography of the proem, see *Causation* 247, note 11, and
Ergon 264, note 6. Cf. also van Groningen, *Comp. litt.* 62 ff., 74, and 224 ff.; W. Kroll,
"Theognisstudien," *Philologus*, Suppl. 29, No. 1 (1936) 72-73.

[4] Ch. I, 17-19. *Causation* 248.

[5] In *Causation* I discussed only B, not A. The preservation of the record (ὡς μήτε τὰ
γενόμενα ἐξ ἀνθρώπων τῷ χρόνῳ ἐξίτηλα γένηται) and the praise of great achievements
(μήτε ἔργα μεγάλα τε καὶ θωμαστά ... ἀκλεᾶ γένηται) are found in the introductory
sentence; for the meaning of *erga*, see *Ergon*. Section Ba also originates in the introductory sentence (τά τε ἄλλα καὶ δι᾽ ἣν αἰτίην ἐπολέμησαν ἀλλήλοισι), and is continued,
after the Persian and Phoenician *logoi*, in 1.5.3-4. The Persian *logos* thus does not affect
the sequence of thought.

since the prose writer differs from the epic poet in being unable to rely upon the Muses, i.e. tradition, in establishing his authority. Hence early prose proems stress the author's individuality and his manner of acquiring knowledge, as well as his purpose in making it public.[6]

The Persian account (with its Phoenician variant) is added to the third point of Herodotus' own account, attaching itself to the question of responsibility. Much has been written in conjecture of the true source of the story of mutual wrongs committed by Greeks and barbarians in the mythological period.[7] For while Herodotus attributes the story to the Persians, it is clearly a Greek rationalization of Greek mythology. But whatever the actual source, there is no doubt why Herodotus calls it a Persian account. Responsibility (aitiê) involves recriminations between two guilty parties, and Herodotus, where possible, follows the principle of questioning both parties to a dispute. In this case he contrasts his own opinion with that of the Persians, since the Persians will appear, in the course of the work, as the party primarily responsible for the Persian Wars and their antecedents.[8]

The treatment of the subject matter of the work in the proem has been discussed in Chapter I.[9]

2. The Croesus Logos (1.6-94)

The outer connections of this logos are made through the repetition of the two motifs of the unification of Western Asia and Croesus' attacks upon the Greeks, which frame the logos at the beginning and the end, but are also used internally to set off several sections of the logos.[10] In the process, both motifs undergo some change.

The idea of the unification of Western Asia appears first as the initial statement that Croesus was "ruler over the nations this side

[6] On these topics, see above, note 3.

[7] Wells, Studies, Ch. 5. Pohlenz, Herodot 6, note 1. Schmid-Stählin 1.2.627, note 5. Daniels, Rel.-hist. Studie 111 ff.

[8] Cf. the two versions of the expulsion of the Pelasgians by the Athenians, one from Hecataeus (who said it was done unjustly), the other from the Athenians (who said it was done justly); Hdt. 6.137 ff. Similarly, 1.70.2-3 (Spartans and Samians) and 5.44 (Sybarites and Crotoniates).

[9] The proem may be discussed from three points of view: (1) use of standard topics of prose proems; (2) development of subject matter, see Ch. I,17-19; (3) themes developed internally, especially in the Persian logos, cf. below, 146.

[10] Ch. I, 20, and Ch. II, note 37.

of the Halys river"(1.6.1), and this is repeated at the end of the
first section of the Croesus *Logos* (the History of the Mermnadae)
in the form "when nearly all those who lived this side of the
Halys river had been subdued"(1.28). Then the motif as such
disappears, but it undoubtedly furnishes one motivation for
Croesus' campaign against Cyrus, according to which Croesus was
anxious to acquire Persia in addition to his own empire (1.73.1
and very briefly 75.2).[11] The Halys river is mentioned prominently
at the beginning of Croesus' campaign (1.75.3). Another motif, also
related to the motifs of the Western empire and the contemplated
acquisition of Persia, appears at the end of the *logos*, where the
phrases "the affairs of Croesus' empire"(1.92.1), and "the
Lydians were enslaved by the Persians"(1.94.7), are closely associated with the story of Croesus' downfall; between them come
the short *logoi* on Croesus' dedications and the marvels of Lydia.[12]
Thus these sentences apply only to certain parts of the narrative:
the first group to the conquests of Croesus, the second to his
campaign against Cyrus, and the last to his defeat. Croesus, at first,
is satisfied with Western Asia, then he attempts to conquer the
portion held by the Persians, and finally he loses everything.
     The motif of Croesus' attacks on the Greeks also furnishes
framing sentences of various kinds. At the beginning, Herodotus
states that Croesus was "the first of the barbarians, to our
knowledge, who subdued some of the Greeks and made others
his friends."[13] This statement announces both Croesus' Ionian
conquests and his alliance with Sparta (1.6.2). Its first portion
recurs, and is developed, at the end of the History of the Mermnadae: "Croesus . . . who attacked the Ephesians first among the
Greeks" (1.26.1 and ff.). The second part does not recur except as
the *story* of Croesus' alliance. At the end of the Croesus *Logos*, the
first part of the statement is repeated in the reference (linked to the
Western empire motif) to "the first conquest of Ionia," a statement which looks forward to the other conquests of Ionia[14] by the

---

[11] More exactly, Hdt. 1.73.1 mentions only Croesus' desire to add Cappadocia to
his empire, but 1.71.1 and 75.2 show that the conquest of Persia was part of his plan.
[12] The same idea is taken up again in 1.130.3.
[13] Pohlenz, *Herodot* 10-11, has shown that there is no inconsistency between this
statement and the attacks by Croesus' predecessors, since they resulted in raiding, not
in real conquest.
[14] Second conquest: 1.169.2; third: 6.32 (there the three conquests are added up).
Cf. the two Ionian revolts: 9.104. Pohlenz, *Herodot* 18, etc.

Persians (1.92.1). Thus this statement is also freely varied, and it occurs only in some sections of the *logos*.

It is therefore impossible to establish the inner structure of the Croesus *Logos* entirely by following the two motifs which furnish its outer connections. In its entirety, the *logos* consists of the following main sections:

(a) *The History of the Mermnadae from Gyges to Croesus' Accession*, including Croesus' early conquests, is framed by the two motifs described above (1.6-29.1). This section comprises origins, accession, and rise to fortune by conquest, thus illustrating the first two elements in the pattern of the fate of the ruler.

(b) *Solon's Visit* and the *Tragedy of Atys* (1.29-45) are two stories treated entirely apart from the other sections, and without framing sentences. They are closely connected with each other by the statement that the death of Atys was, in Herodotus' opinion, due to divine anger at Croesus' pride in considering himself, before Solon, the happiest of mortals (1.34.1). The Solon story is attached to the sentence listing Croesus' conquests with an emphatic "and" (*kai dê kai*, 1.29.1), and it has only the briefest closing phrase (1.34.1). The Atys story in turn is closed by a sentence describing the effect on Croesus of his son's death: for two years he sat in mourning (1.46.1). These two stories are not autonomous sections of the main narrative. They function as warnings, one in word, the other in deed, of what is to befall Croesus later on.[15] They are thus placed between the section on origins and the following sections on the war with Cyrus, i.e. in a pause.

The main sections concerning the war with Cyrus are introduced by initial statements on Croesus' motivations and have been discussed elsewhere.[16]

(c) *Planning and Preparations Section* (1.46-70), in which Croesus first tests and then consults the Greek oracles and, on the advice of Delphi, concludes an alliance with the Spartans as the most powerful Greek state. This is introduced by a statement stressing Croesus' fear of the growing power of the new Persian state

---

[15] Solon's advice to Croesus is not in form a warning, but after Croesus' downfall turns out to have been just that (see 1.86.5: ὥς τε αὐτῷ πάντα ἀποβεβήκοι τῇ περ ἐκεῖνος εἶπε). In the Polycrates story, we have a similar indirect warning in the letter of Amasis (3.40.2-4, cf. 3.125.4 and *Samian Stories* 318), and a warning in deed in the story of the fish.

[16] *Causation* 255 ff.

(1.46.1), an idea briefly repeated at the end (1.71.1). The preparations for this campaign consist entirely of alliances (1.56.2 and 69), and real military preparations are not mentioned.

(d) *Advice of Sandanis* (1.71.2-4): a warning, not heeded, against the campaign. This section is introduced by the announcement of the campaign (1.71.1), an announcement which is coupled with a reference backward to the false oracle received by Croesus, and with the repetition of Croesus' desire to destroy Persia's power. The advice is followed (1.72) by two notes, placed in the pause, about the Cappadocians (who are Croesus' immediate objective), and the course of the Halys river (which Croesus must cross in order to reach the Cappadocians).

(e) *The Aitiê-section* (1.73-75.1) begins, as seems fitting, with a complex statement on motivations, the last of which concerns Croesus' desire to take vengeance on Cyrus for having conquered Croesus' brother-in-law Astyages, king of the Medes. What follows, however, is not the story of that conquest (which is postponed to the Accession *Logos* of Cyrus, 1.107 ff.), but the story of how Croesus had become Astyages' brother-in-law. This story draws a contrast between the peaceful settlement of a conflict of Medes and Lydians in the preceding generation and the intransigence of the present generation of Lydians and Persians, the successors to the Medes. The initial statement is then repeated in a slightly different form (1.75.2).

(f) *Croesus' Campaign against Persia* (1.75.2-86.1), a narrative consisting of several sections easily distinguished, is introduced by the closing sentence of the preceding section. Thus, the introductory sentences establish a very close nexus between the campaign and the preceding warning- and *aitiê*-sections. The campaign proper begins with a description of the crossing of the Halys river,[17] a motif commonly associated with aggressive campaigns, and with the conquest of the innocent Pterians in Cappadocia (expansionist motif; 1.75.3-76.2). The next section describes the indecisive battle of Pteria and Croesus' return to Sardis, where he asks his allies to come to him in the following spring. This section ends with the dispersal of Croesus' army and the omen of horses eating snakes (1.76.2-78.3). Characteristically,

---

[17] On the river motif, see *Action* 28, note 22; Ch. VI, 293. Cf. also R. von Scheliha, *Die Wassergrenze im Altertum* (Breslau 1913), with the review by Kahrstedt, *Gnomon* 8 (1932) 165 ff.

both this and the next section begin with Cyrus, who has the initiative. In 1.79.1-80, Cyrus comes to Sardis and, defeating Croesus in battle through the trick of the camels,[18] besieges the city. This section is introduced by a statement on Cyrus' planning (1.79.1). The capture of Sardis is told in two sections: first (1.81-83), Croesus once more asks his allies to come to his rescue, this time immediately, but the Spartans, although victorious against the Argives at home, are not in time; secondly (1.84-85), Sardis is taken through the unexpected discovery of an opening in the city wall, and Croesus' deaf and dumb son saves his father's life during the capture. This section is concluded by a dramatic application of the chronicle formula (Croesus ruled 14 years and was captured in 14 days, 1.86.1).

The three main *logoi* of Croesus' campaign are the battle of Pteria, the battle of Sardis, and the capture of the city. Between them we have a number of stories based on characteristic motifs: the crossing of the river, unmotivated expansion, the omen of horses and snakes, Croesus' call for allies, the words spoken by the dumb son. Unlike other campaigns, that of Croesus lacks a single decisive moment. Instead, it is built upon the repetition of the motif of an unexpected happening, a motif which recurs particularly in the story of the battle and of the taking of Sardis.[19]

(g) *Croesus on the Pyre and his Inquiry at Delphi* (1.86.2-91.6). This famous story consists of a number of short sections not very strongly set apart by framing sentences, and is in the manner of sections describing the aftereffects of battle in other parts of the work. It has no general introduction, but we may perhaps distinguish the story of Croesus on the pyre (86.2-87.2), with Croesus' explanation of Solon's message in the center (86.3-5), from the three conversations between Cyrus and Croesus, the first and last of which make mention of Apollo (87.3-4 and 90.1-4). The second section then culminates in the answer of the Pythia exculpating Apollo (91). The central idea of the whole is Croesus' self-recognition through learning from suffering, as he himself describes it at a later point (1.207.1), a motif underlined by Croesus' repeated periods of silence.[20]

---

[18] On the *apatê*-motif, see Ch. VI, 243.   [19] Hellmann, *Kroisos-Logos* 76; Ch. IV, 159.

[20] Hdt. 1.86.3; 86.4; 88.1. On learning from suffering, see H. Dörrie, *Leid und Erfahrung. Die Wort- und Sinn-verbindung* παθεῖν-μαθεῖν *im griechischen Denken*, Akad. Mainz, Abh. d. Geist. u. Soz. Klasse, No. 5 (1956), esp. 19-20 (Hdt. 1.207.1), and the important review by F. Solmsen, *Gnomon* 31 (1959) 469-75.

The overall structure of the Croesus *Logos* consists of two main parts, which together embody the tripartite pattern of the rise and fall of the ruler. The first part shows a typical parenthetical structure, since the History of the Mermnadae begins with a break after the initial statement on Croesus, but leads without a break to Croesus and the arrival of Solon.[21] Nevertheless, the main division is to be made before the arrival of Solon, since the Solon and Atys stories are warnings of the downfall of Croesus. The actual downfall is an elaborate campaign *logos*, which consists, on the one hand, of a section on planning and preparations, and, on the other, a complex of *logoi* which relate to the campaign proper and its aftereffects, and which begin in 1.71.1 with the announcement of the campaign, before the advice of Sandanis.

Prominent in the Croesus *Logos* are several semi-independent Greek *logoi*. Of these, the story of *Arion and the Dolphin* (1.23-24) is well discussed by Myres,[22] and the relation of the *History of Athens and Sparta* (1.56.2-68) to the corresponding sections in the Ionian Revolt has been analyzed in Chapter I.[23] The latter *logoi* consist of three parts, namely, a short prehistory of Athens and Sparta in the mythical period, followed by the history of each city to the time of Croesus. While the first section is relevant to the history of Athens and Sparta in the work as a whole, the last two supply the background for Croesus' inquiry into the relative strength of the two leading Greek states. The *logos* on Peisistratus (1.59.1-65.1) explains the weakness of Athens as due to tyranny and deals with his three attempts to seize control of the city:

> 1.59.1: Athens "weak and divided" because of Peisistratus' rule at that time.
>
> I. { 59.1-2: warning of Peisistratus' birth, unheeded.
>   { 59.3: birth of Peisistratus.
>
> II.   59.3-60.1: First attempt at tyranny. (Winning of a bodyguard.) First ousting of Peisistratus.
>
> III. 60.1-61.2: Second attempt at tyranny. (Athenians fooled by a tall woman appearing as Athena.) Second ousting.

---

[21] This type of parenthesis (a break at the beginning with close joining at the end) is comparable to the well-known parenthetical *gar*-sentences in Herodotus, for which see Stein on 1.8, line 4, and Fränkel, *Stileigenheit* 87, note 1.

[22] Myres, *Herodotus* 83 f.   [23] 36.

IV.   61.2-64.3: Third and final attempt at tyranny. (Battle of
          Pallene.) Expulsion of Alcmaeonids and others.
   1.65.1: This was the state of Athens at that time.

The *logos* is not primarily an account of the three periods of
rule by Peisistratus, but rather a description of the struggles
leading to revolution and of the renewed disunity after assumption
of power. After a section on the birth of the tyrant, the first two
sections on revolution each begin with party strife (*stasis*), out
of which arises the assumption of power by means of deception,
followed by a brief description of the rule and of his ouster through
renewed factionalism. In the third section, deception is a central
motif of the battle of Pallene, and the high point of rule is the
expulsion of rival factions, causing further divisions among the
Athenian nobility.[24] The last three sections seem to bear a
resemblance to three categories defining the evils of tyranny in
the Persian debate on government (3.80.5), where it is said that the
tyrant perverts the ancestral laws, rapes women, and kills without
trial: in the first accession of Peisistratus, reference is made to the
fact that he did not change the laws (1.59.6), in the second we
have the unnatural relations with Megacles' daughter, and the
third ends with the arbitrary treatment of enemies (1.64.1 and 3).

By contrast with the story of Peisistratus, the Spartan *Logos*
(1.65.1-68.6) describes the gradual increase in power of the
Spartans down to the time of Croesus' inquiry. This *logos* has the
structure of refrain composition:

  1.65.1: At time of Croesus, Sparta has escaped great evils and is
      now superior to Tegea in war.
      65.1: Under former kings Leo and Hegesicles Sparta could
          not defeat Tegea.
I.   65.2: Originally Sparta was worst governed state.
           65.2-5: Lycurgus' *eunomia*.
    66.1-4: The unsuccessful war.
      (Story of the fetters.)
      67.1: Under Anaxandridas and Aristo, at time of Croesus,
II.   Spartans are superior in war to Tegea.
      67.2-68.6: The bones of Orestes.
    68.6: Spartans much superior in this war; most of Pelopon-
      nesus conquered.

[24] The outline given above does not quite agree with such summary phrases as
can be found in this simply told story. Of these, the most important occur before the

Thus, the superiority in the Tegean War proves Spartan power.[25]

The *logos* of the *Spartan War with Argos* over Thyrea is a simple campaign *logos*, not connected with the preceding Spartan account.[26]

3. *Origins of Persia and of Cyrus and Cyrus' Accession* (1.95-140)

The framing statements at the beginning and end of this *logos* have been discussed before.[27] The initial statement does not mention the accession of Cyrus, which is summarized only at the end. The whole *logos* is introduced as an aside from the continuous narrative of the campaigns of Croesus and Cyrus. It thus begins with a marked break, but at the end it is firmly attached to the following campaigns of Cyrus. Nevertheless, the pause in the connecting statement at the end is used for placing the *logos* on the *Customs of the Persians* (1.131-40).

Internally, the *logos* exhibits the same parenthetical structure in its first section, the History of the Median Dynasty (1.95.2-107), ending with Astyages, of whom we are told only the events necessary to understand his downfall and the accession of Cyrus. Thus the structure of this *logos* parallels exactly that of the Croesus *Logos*, and its central figure is Astyages. The second part of the *logos* (1.108-30) consists of a number of sections with their beginnings not always very clearly marked; roughly, there is the

---

two ousters of Peisistratus and before the ouster of the Alcmaeonids: 1.60.1 (οὕτω μὲν Πεισίστρατος ἔσχε τὸ πρῶτον 'Αθήνας); 1.61.1 (ἀπολαβὼν δὲ τὴν τυραννίδα τρόπῳ τῷ εἰρημένῳ); 1.64.1 (οὕτω δὴ Πεισίστρατος τὸ τρίτον σχὼν 'Αθήνας). I would consider these phrases internal repetition in the manner of the mentions of the conquests of Ionia (above, note 14) and base the outline on internal patterning in three episodes. On the *stasis*-theme, see Myres, *Herodotus* 84 and 178; H. Ryffel, *Metabolê Politeiôn* (1949) 57-58, and index, 268; further, Ch. V, note 21.

[25] For the outline of this *logos*, see van Otterlo, *Ringkomposition* 142, note 4, and 143.

[26] Hdt. 1.82-83:

    82.1: Croesus sends to Sparta for help.
        82.1: War of Argos and Sparta over Thyrea.
            82.2:   Cause of the war.
            82.3-4: Arrangement of battle of 300.
                82.4-5: Battle of 300: the three survivors.
            82.6:   Claims of victory.
            82.7:   Full battle and Spartan victory.
                82.7-8: Changes of custom in Argos and Sparta.
                82.8:   Death of Othryades.
    83: Messenger arrives from Croesus, but Spartans are too late.
Cf. also above, Ch. I, note 66.

[27] Ch. I, 21, and Ch. II, 55-56.

dramatic *logos* of Cyrus' birth and discovery, ending with the fictitious story that he had been brought up by a dog (1.108-22); this is followed by the *logos* on the preparations of Harpagus and Cyrus against Astyages (1.123-26), and by the campaign *logos* (1.127-30).[28] The initiative is here much more with Astyages' opponents than with the king, and this perhaps has caused scholars to overlook the parallelism with the Croesus *Logos*.[29]

4. *Campaigns of Cyrus* (1.141-216)

It is convenient to group the three campaign *logoi* together, although Herodotus himself indicates the unity of only the last two (1.177).

(a) *Conquest of Ionia, Caria, Caunia, and Lycia* (1.141-76). This *logos* is attached to the Croesus *Logos* both by the statement that this is "the former argument" (1.140.3, cf. 130.3, etc.), and by the reference to the Persian conquest of Lydia (1.141.1). In several ways its structure is a foreshadowing of that of the Graeco-Persian War campaigns. In the first place, the *logos* begins with Ionian initiative, for they send an embassy to Cyrus asking to be his subjects under the conditions that had obtained under Croesus, a proposal refused by Cyrus (1.141). This is followed by the account of Ionian defensive preparations, including their attempt to form an alliance with Sparta; by an "ethnographic" *logos* on the religious alliances of the Ionian and Aeolian cities; and by a Spartan embassy to Cyrus' court (1.141-53.2). The "ethnographic" *logos* is placed between the Ionian decision to send an embassy to Sparta and the execution of that plan, i.e. between decision and action.[30] The key idea connecting this *logos* with the rest of the preparations section is the lack of unity among the Ionians.[31]

The Greek embassies to Cyrus at the beginning and end of the preparations section balance each other, since Cyrus (who is at this point still in Sardis, the capital of Lydia) is the focal point of this campaign, although he does not participate in it. Cyrus is first

---

[28] The break between the Median history and the birth of Cyrus in 1.108 is marked by the distribution of the two dreams of Astyages in the two *logoi*. At 1.123, Hude's edition wrongly fails to paragraph, although there is a *men-de* sentence (as there is at 1.127 also).

[29] Cf. Ch. IV, 162-64.

[30] The "ethnographic *logos*" contains a reference to the war with Cyrus, 1.143.1.

[31] See Ch. V, 230-31, and Ch. IV, note 111.

shown refusing Ionian overtures by telling them the fable of the
piper (1.141.1-2); then he rejects the Spartans, refusing to be
intimidated by their empty threats (1.153.1-2):

> But afterwards he entrusted Sardis to the Persian Tabalus, and
> the gold of Croesus and the other Lydians he entrusted to the
> Lydian Pactyes to bring after him, while he himself went to
> Ecbatana . . . For Babylon was in his way, and the Bactrian
> people, the Sacae and the Egyptians, against whom he intended
> to campaign in person, while sending another general against
> the Ionians. (1.153.3-4)

On the way,[32] Cyrus hears of the defection of Pactyes, receives
advice from Croesus on how to render the Lydians innocuous, and
appoints Mazares to be general against the Ionians (1.155.1-57.1).
We then lose sight of Cyrus until, after the end of the Ionian
campaigns, we hear, as the introduction to Cyrus' campaigns
proper:

> Harpagus (the successor of Mazares) depopulated Lower Asia,
> but Upper Asia was depopulated by Cyrus himself, who de-
> stroyed every nation, omitting none. (1.177)[33]

Thus Cyrus remains the focal point during the Ionian campaign
in a manner foreshadowing the focal position of Darius during the
Greek campaigns of his generals.[34] In both cases, the scenes
describing the king do not form separate sections of the narrative.

  After the Ionian Preparations Logos (1.141-53.2) there is a kind
of aitié-section (1.154-61)[35] describing the crime of Pactyes and
the complicity of some Ionian cities in harboring him. A single
chapter (1.161) forms the campaign logos of Mazares, who dies
from an illness and is replaced by Harpagus, whose campaign
takes up the rest of the Ionian Logos (1.162-70), ending with two
anecdotes relating the advice given to the Ionians by Bias of
Priene and the earlier advice given by Thales of Miletus, and
illustrating the vulnerability of the Ionian position in Asia as well

[32] Hearing, or doing, something on the road is a common motif in Herodotus: cf.
1.111.5; 1.122.2; 5.92c.2; 9.107.1 and 3; 9.14; 9.113.2; 3.76.2; 1.157.1. This may
derive from tragedy; cf. Soph. OC 553-54 and 303. Similar situations (but not the word
for "road") e.g. in Soph. Ajax 974 ff. (arrival of Teucer) and Eur. Bacchae 1222 ff.
[33] The narrative is attached at a single point: see Ch. II, 59.
[34] Below, 110-11 (European Campaign), 115 (Ionian Revolt), and 105, 120-21,
and 123 (Greek campaigns under Darius).
[35] Causation 265.

as their lack of good sense (1.170). A special section of Harpagus'
campaign *logos* describes the fate of Phocaeans and Teans in their
travels west after their defeat by Harpagus; such escape sections
are common in campaign *logoi* (1.163-68).[36]

The Ionian campaign is followed by *logoi* on the campaigns of
Harpagus against the Carians, Caunians, and Lycians, which are
patterned after the Ionian *Logos* down to a short "ethnographic"
logos for each (1.171-76).

(b) *First Conquest of Babylon* (1.178-200). Chapter 177, whose
first sentence we quoted above, forms a general introduction
to the campaigns conducted by Cyrus in person. Of his exploits,
Herodotus goes on, he will tell only the most significant (Babylon
and the campaign against the Massagetae alone qualify). The
next sentence introduces the Babylonian campaign itself:

> Cyrus, after he had brought the whole continent under his
> sway, attacked the Assyrians. (1.178.1) [37]

After this announcement, and before the campaign proper, there
is a portion of the ethnographic *logos* which deals with the city of
Babylon (considered by Herodotus to be the most important
Assyrian city after the fall of Nineveh), and with the regulation of
the Euphrates by two queens (1.178.2-187), two matters which
are essential to the following campaign.[38] The campaign proper
(1.188-91) begins with a march section, which emphasizes two
contradictory but related motifs: the Persian king drinks only
pure water, and Cyrus punished the Gyndes river for the drowning
of one of his sacred horses. The city is taken by diverting the
Euphrates river. Thus the central motif of the whole expedition
is the river motif. The campaign closes with a reference to this as
the *first* capture of Babylon, thus anticipating its recapture by
Darius. There follows a third section, again dealing with

[36] Escape sections: 3.57-59 and 6.22-25 (Samians); 3.148 (Maeandrius of Samos);
5.124-26 (Aristagoras of Miletus); 6.33.2 (Byzantians); 6.34-41 (Miltiades); 4.147-49
(Theras); 5.42-48 (Dorieus); 6.67-70 (Demaratus); 6.17 (Dionysius of Phocaea);
6.96 (Naxians); 6.97 (Delians); 8.116.1 (king of Bisaltians). Nations and individuals
exhibit in these passages a desire for freedom: cf. also the escape of Democedes from
Persia, 3.133 ff., and of Histiaeus from Susa, 5.35.4, etc. The same idea is broached
in the advice of Bias, 1.170.2, and in Themistocles' threat before Salamis, 8.62.2.
[37] "The whole continent," τὰ πάντα, see Pohlenz, *Herodot* 24, note 4. Pohlenz
rightly points out that the sentence refers to 1.106, where by implication Babylon
appeared as the only region missing for total empire (of the Medes) over Asia.
[38] Pohlenz, *Herodot* 25. Cf. above, Ch. II, 51-51.

ethnographic material, and introduced by a description of
Babylon's wealth as a revenue of the Persian king (her *dynamis*),
but otherwise with the structure of a regular section on customs
(1.192-200). The ethnographic material in this *logos* comprises
fragments of geography, history, and customs.

(c) *Campaign against the Massagetae* (1.201-16). There exists a
striking parallelism in structure between this and the preceding
logos.[39] For the announcement of the campaign is followed by an
ethnographic section on the Araxes river and the Caspian Sea
(1.202-203), and this section stresses the isolation of the Massagetae
and, once more, the river motif. A short *aitiê*-section gives Cyrus'
motivation for the campaign, whereas the wooing of Queen
Tomyris concerns preparations of a sort.[40] The crossing of the
Araxes river (a crucial event in the campaign) is preceded by
Croesus' advice and followed by Cyrus' dream of Darius with
wings overshadowing Asia and Europe. This latter omen
concerns the work as a whole and not only the death of Cyrus in
the campaign.[41] The campaign proper is a highly organized
dramatic *logos* dealing with a mother's vengeance for the murder-
ous slaying of her son,[42] and it closes with a reference to the

[39] Below, note 42.   [40] *Causation* 259.
[41] Egermann, *Geschichtswerk* 249. Below, 129, and note 150 (empire dreams); Ch.
IV, note 41.
[42] Briefly, the outline is as follows:

201:	Announcement of campaign.
	201-204.1: Ethnographic *logos* I: Araxes, Caspian, etc.
204.1:	Campaign restated.
	204.2: *aitiê*-section.
	205.1: Attempt at peaceful conquest.
205.2:	Cyrus goes to Araxes river.
	206.1-3: Tomyris' offer.
	206.3-207.7: Advice of Croesus.
	208: Cyrus' answer to Tomyris.
208:	Cyrus entrusts Croesus to Cambyses and crosses the river.
	209.1-210.3: Dream of Cyrus and conversation with Hystaspes about Darius.
211:	Movement from river and deception of Massagetae.
	212.1-213: Warning of Tomyris and suicide of her son.
214.1-2:	Battle.
214.3:	Death of Cyrus.
	214.4-5: Vengeance of Tomyris.
	215-16: Ethnographic *logos* II (customs).

For the interpretation of this *logos*, see Ch. IV, 166 f. Parallelism with Babylonian
campaign *logos*: splitting of ethnographic material, with the portion put initially of
great importance for the campaign; in each campaign Cyrus fights the son of a woman
who outsmarts him (Nitocris does so in 1.187). This parallelism is meant to underline

beginning of the *logos* on Cyrus' origins.[43] Finally, there is added a short section on customs, corresponding to the last section of the Babylonian Campaign (1.215-16). The parallelism between the two *logoi* underlines the contrast between Cyrus' greatest achievement and his destruction.

5. *Campaigns of Cambyses* (2.1-3.38)

(a) *Campaign against Egypt* (2.1-3.16). The length of the Egyptian Ethnographic *Logos*, which fills the whole of Book 2, may seem to obscure the unified structure of this account. The *logos* is introduced by the announcement of Cambyses' accession and of his campaign against Egypt (2.1), but in addition two other motifs are compressed into this short chapter. The first is the idea of legitimacy, which is incorporated in a short anecdote showing the honor in which Cambyses' mother Cassandane was held by Cyrus. The second concerns the relations of Persia with the Ionians and Aeolians, relations that had been prominent in the Croesus and Cyrus *logoi*. This motif takes the form of the statement that Cambyses considered these peoples his inherited slaves.[44] Thus in both statements the dynastic motif is important. Omitted is the idea (which is nevertheless to be understood)[45] that the war against Egypt was also inherited by Cambyses from his father, who had planned a similar campaign (1.153.4). This short chapter may serve as a model of what I have called elliptic statements in Herodotus, and it is extremely well organized:

1. Cambyses succeeds to the throne,
    being the son of Cyrus and Cassandane.
        1a. Funerary honors for his mother.
    (Framing sentence)
2a. He considers Ionians and Aeolians his inherited slaves.
  b. He campaigns against Egypt, taking Greeks with him.

2a and b are clearly restatements, in an attenuated form, of the two motifs (of East-West relations and of Eastern expansion) which were first stated in the Croesus *Logos*. The statement that

---

the contrast of fortune in the two campaigns: this is a favorite device of Herodotus. It militates against Myres' idea (*Herodotus* 95) that the missing Assyrian *logoi* were intended for the first ethnographic *logos* on Babylon. A certain parallelism also exists with the Scythian Campaign of Darius.

[43] Ch. IV, note 48.   [44] Pohlenz, *Herodot* 14.   [45] *Causation* 260, note 37.

Greeks participated in the Egyptian campaign is of some importance for the campaign itself, and recurs in the Polycrates story,
which forms the next *logos* in the work.[46]

There follows the Egyptian Ethnographic *Logos* (Book 2), after
which the announcement of the campaign (2b) is repeated as an
introduction to the *aitiê*-section (3.1-3), with a renewed emphasis
on the dynastic motif and on Cambyses' mother (1 above).[47] By
contrast, the preparation and march section (here combined,
3.4-9) is introduced by a mere tag:

> The following matter also happened with respect to the invasion.
> (3.4.1)

Phanes, a Greek from Halicarnassus, escaped from Amasis, king
of Egypt, and advised Cambyses to cross the desert by enticing
the Arabian king to furnish water in jars for his troops. The story
balances the anecdote, told in the *aitiê*-section (3.1.1-2), about an
Egyptian doctor who had started a quarrel between Persia and
Egypt. Among such underlings Greeks are important, and the
Phanes story parallels those of Democedes at Darius' court and of
Demaratus, the adviser to Xerxes.[48] The beginning of the
preparations section thus takes up the Greek motif stated in 2.1.
The story of the waterless desert, on the other hand, corresponds
to the river motif at the beginning of other campaigns,[49] a
meaning reinforced by the story of rain in Egyptian Thebes,
an omen that signified the arrival of the Persians in Egypt
(3.10.3). This story closes a short section (3.10) on the preparations of the Egyptians and their royal succession, and we
then return to the Persians, who arrive at Pelusium (3.11.1),
where they fight the battle (11.3). Between the arrival and the
battle is placed the story of Greek and Carian mercenaries taking
vengeance on Phanes' children (a recurrence of the Greek motif
[11.1-3]), and the battle is followed by the account of the
Egyptian and Persian skulls seen by Herodotus at Pelusium and also
at Papremis in Egypt (3.12).[50] The next section (3.13-16) deals
with the aftereffects of the battle and includes the flight of the
Egyptians, the siege of Memphis, the fate of Psammenitus, and

[46] Hdt. 3.44.1, etc.   [47] *Causation* 259-61.

[48] Democedes: 3.129-37. Demaratus: 6.70.2, etc.

[49] Cf. 3.4.3: ὅκως τὴν ἄνυδρον διεκπερᾷ, etc. 3.8 contains the germ of an ethnographic
logos on the Arabians.

[50] For the interpretation of these two stories, see Ch. VI, 242, and note 13.

the burning of Amasis' corpse by Cambyses in Sais. Despite its brevity and the lack of clear framing sentences in some sections, the whole account is clearly organized: (1) aitiê-section, (2) Preparations and march, (3) Preparations of the defender, (4) Arrival of Persians and battle, (5) Aftereffects of victory. Here again is a model of an elliptic account.

(b) Cambyses' attempts to conquer *the Carthaginians, Ammonians, and Ethiopians* form a separate campaign *logos* (3.17-26). The three campaigns, introduced together at the beginning, are evaluated by Herodotus by means of the order in which they are told. The attempt at Carthage (never carried out) is placed between the announcement of Cambyses' plan to send spies into Ethiopia and its actualization (3.19.2-3), and the campaign against the Ammonians (in which the troops were lost in the desert) forms the coda of the Ethiopian campaign (3.26). Thus we have essentially an *Ethiopian Campaign Logos*, in which Herodotus follows the movements of the king himself. That *logos* consists of the visit of the spies (3.17.2-19.1; 20.1; 21-24), to which is attached a very brief ethnographic *logos* on Ethiopia (20.1-2), and the campaign proper, which is a failure (3.25). The visit of the spies has its own themes, which cluster round the idea of the noble savage, and is not connected with the Egyptian campaign.[51]

(c) The final section of the Cambyses *logoi* describes the aftereffects of victory (3.27-38). Despite its weak initial framing, it is clearly a *logos* on *Cambyses in Egypt*, and is in two parts: 3.27-29 describes the wounding of the Apis bull as the cause of Cambyses' madness; 3.30-38, introduced by a strong initial statement, describes his mad crimes, first against his relatives (3.30-32), and then against other Persians, against Croesus, and against Egyptian tombs and sanctuaries (3.33-37; this also is introduced by a strong connecting sentence). The *logos* closes with the anecdote of Darius' investigation of the difference between Greek and Indian funerary customs.

The basic structure, then, is that of a campaign *logos*, with ethnographic account and aftereffects, to which is added a separate campaign against the Ethiopians, inserted between the achievement of victory over the Egyptians and the crimes of Cambyses, i.e. in its proper chronological place.

[51] Cf. M. Hadas, "Utopian Sources in Herodotus," *CP* 30 (1935) 113 ff. A. Lesky, "Aithiopika," *Hermes* 87 (1959) 27-38. Hellmann, *Kroisos-Logos* 84 ff.

It is impossible in this brief space to do justice to the *Ethnographic Logos on Egypt*, although the thematic and structural use of ethnographic material in the work might well receive a separate analysis. Because of the mechanical attachment of ethnographic *logoi*, and because of the peculiar type of inner proemia in the Egyptian *Logos* (they deal, it will be recalled, only with method, not with subject matter),[52] there is no outer connection between this *logos* and the campaign of Cambyses. Therefore, many scholars have held the Egyptian Ethnographic *Logos* to be essentially a separate work that upsets the balance of the remainder of the narrative.[53] We have repeatedly observed, however, that external balance is nowhere a criterion of Herodotean composition. The Egyptian Ethnographic *Logos* has important thematic connections with the campaign of Cambyses, as well as with the remainder of the work. These can only be roughly sketched here. A brief outline of the *logos* follows:

2.1: Campaign of Cambyses.
    2-3:   Experiment of Psammetichus; statement on sources and on avoidance of purely religious subjects.
    4:    Inventions of the Egyptians.
5-34:   THE COUNTRY OF EGYPT.
    5-9:   General.
    10-33:   The Nile.
    34:    Comparison of Nile and Danube.
35-98:   THE CUSTOMS OF EGYPT.
    35-36:   Comparison with customs of other peoples.
    37:    Priests.
    38-48:   Sacrifices and victims.
    49-53:   Greek gods derived from Egyptian.
    54-57:   Divination originated in Egypt.
    58-64:   Festivals derived from Egypt.
    65-76:   Sacred and profane animals.
    77-90:   Secular customs of Egyptians.

[52] Ch. II, 64-65.
[53] So Myres, *Herodotus* 96-97 (he excludes this *logos* from his analysis of internal structure, although he believes that externally it once balanced the Assyrian *logoi*). Pohlenz, *Herodot* 70-71, has a rather unsatisfactory explanation for the inclusion of Book 2. Further bibliography on this question in J. Vogt, "Herodot in Ägypten," Marg, *Herodot* 412, note 2.

The *logos* is set off from its surroundings by the "anaphoric" repetition of the statement on Cambyses' campaign (2.1.2 and 3.1.1). It begins with the story of Psammetichus and with other preliminary matters, some of which are proemial in content.[55] At the end there is no formal conclusion, and the death of Amasis is told concurrently with the arrival of Cambyses' army in Egypt, since it occurred between Cambyses' preparations and his campaigns (3.10.2). Internally the *logos* is very strictly organized in archaic patterns, including, in the section on customs, much linking by intermediate stories (such as the connection between sacred and profane animals as a link between religious and secular customs).[56] The section on customs (*nomoi*) establishes an implicit connection with the campaign of Cambyses, since he comes to be the destroyer of both Persian custom and Egyptian religious practice.[57] Other internal motifs connect the *logos* with the whole work. They are not developed so much in the main sections as in the stories placed in the pauses. The comparison of the Nile with the Danube establishes a relation with the Scythian *logos*, showing a geographical balance* between the continents. The sections describing the derivation of Greek religion from Egypt, as well as the chronology of Greek and Egyptian gods, establish an objective means by which to measure

[54] Ch. I, 26, and Ch. IV, 150-51.
[55] Ch. II, 64.
[56] Cf. Trüdinger, *Studien* 22-24.
[57] This is particularly evident in the story of the god Apis (first mentioned in 2.153; cf. 3.27-29; 33; 64.3). The Cambyses *Logos* ends with the famous illustration of Pindar's statement that "*nomos* is king of all," 3.38. The central idea of the Egyptian *nomoi*-section is contained in the comparison of Egyptian customs with those of other nations, a comparison repeated at strategic intervals in that section (at the beginning: 2.35-36; at the end of the subsection on sacrifices: 2.49-64; at the end: 2.91). On the Pindaric statement and the Herodotean conception of it, see H. E. Stier, "Nomos Basileus," *Philologus* 83 (1927-28) 225-58, esp. 239 f., and M. Gigante, *Nomos Basileus* (Naples 1956), esp. 72 ff. Cf. also M. Treu, *RhM*, n.s. 106 (1963) 193-214.

the beliefs and practices of the Greeks, who are, by contrast
with the Egyptians, a young nation. The motif of the antiquity
of the Egyptians is expressed at the beginning of the *logos* in
the *prôtos*-motif of the Psammetichus story and in the account
of Egyptian inventions. The historical section establishes the true
length of human civilized history and gives, in the accounts of
Egyptian kings, examples of the vicissitudes of national fortunes.[58]
Both as an anthropologist and as a historian, Herodotus finds in
the Egyptian material absolute standards by which to judge
the Greeks, the Persians, and civilization in general.[59]

6. *Spartan War against Polycrates of Samos* (3.39-60)

This short *logos* is the second in the work to show Greek initiative.[60] The unsuccessful forty-day siege of Samos has next to no
pragmatic importance, but the account balances the subsequent
story of the first Persian penetration of Europe (the party of spies
led by Democedes, 3.138.4), and the siege is thus marked as the
first Spartan intervention in Asia (3.56.2). Formally, the *logos*
is a campaign *logos* with double *aitiê*-section and "refrain composition," as I have shown more fully elsewhere.[61] It is attached,
as an afterthought, to the *logos* of Cambyses' campaign by means
of a synchronism in the initial sentence, according to which the
Spartan war took place during Cambyses' campaign in Egypt.
One is tempted to suspect that this synchronism, as well as a later
synchronism, according to which Polycrates was killed during
the madness of Cambyses (3.120.1), are both derived by Herodotus
from the synchronism implied in the second *aitiê*-section of the
logos on the Spartan war, in which Polycrates is said to have sent
troops to Cambyses for the Egyptian campaign (3.44.1-2). The

[58] Nile and Danube: 2.26.2; 2.33.4-34; cf. Conclusion, 316. The same topic
recurs in the Scythian Ethnographic *Logos*, 4.48-50. Relation of Greek and Egyptian
religion: I. M. Linforth in *CalCP* 9, Nos. 1 and 7 (1926), and R. Lattimore in *CP*
34 (1939) 357-65. Chronology of Greek and Egyptian gods: Hdt. 2.142-46. *Prôtos*-
motif: Ch. I, note 43. This motif belongs with the discussion of a nation's origins; cf.
the statement about the Scythians as the youngest nation, 4.5.1. The experiment of
Psammetichus in 2.2 shows that the Egyptians are the oldest people except for the
Phrygians. Egyptian inventions: 2.4. History of Egyptian kings: Ch. I, 26-27, and Ch.
IV, 150-51.

[59] Cf. especially the comparison between Sesostris and Darius implied in the anecdote 2.110; Sesostris surpassed the Persian king, since he had conquered the Scythians.

[60] Ch. I, 40.

[61] Outline in *Samian Stories* 321; cf. *Causation* 267-68. Van Otterlo, *Ringkomposition*
144-45.

three synchronisms are closely related to sections of the Cambyses narrative as we have it: in 2.1.2, Herodotus says that Cambyses took the Ionians with him, and to this the Polycrates story is clearly related; then follow the two sections on Cambyses' campaign and on his madness in Egypt, and for each of these we have a further synchronism. These synchronisms and the structure of parts of the *logos* on the Spartan war, in reverse chronological order,[62] show dependence of this *logos* on the accounts dealing with Cambyses. Thus we may consider the *logos* a minor account placed in a pause, although its relation to the Democedes story and the importance of the motif of Greek initiative show it to be thematically significant for the whole work.[63]

7. *Revolt of the Magi and Accession of Darius* (3.61-87)

This large composition is closely connected with the next *logos*, the *Power of Darius* (3.88-105, our No. 8). The unity of these two groups of *logoi* is not indicated by a general proem or framing sentence, and hence it is necessary to have recourse to the pattern of the ruler, assisted as we are by the fact that the two groups are isolated by two smaller *logoi* placed in the pauses: the Spartan War against Polycrates frames the beginning, and the section on the Ends of the World (3.106-16, see our No. 8), the close. The material covered between these margins clearly corresponds to the *logoi* on origins, accession, and height of power as they are given for Croesus and Cyrus. The separation of the Revolt and Accession from the Power of Darius is thus largely a matter of convenience. At the same time, the Revolt of the Magi and the Death of Cambyses, which form the beginning of the two groups, indicate that Herodotus is dealing with a true crisis affecting the whole course of Persian aggressive imperialism, and not merely with the personal succession of Darius.[64]

The group of *logoi* on the Revolt of the Magi and Darius'

[62] *Causation* 267, note 51.

[63] The *logos* ends (3.60) with the remark that Herodotus has "lengthened" the account of Samian history because of three architectural marvels on Samos, which he goes on to list. This chapter has been much discussed; see e.g. Powell, *Hist. Herodotus* 49, note 1; Jacoby, *RE* Suppl. 2.222 and 429. The marvels are probably the work of Polycrates, cf. *RE*, s.v. Polykrates, 1731, and Herodotus lists them on a par with Samian deeds, since they too are great *erga* (*Ergon* 265, note 10). The phrase "I have lengthened" is proemial and also occurs in the Egyptian *logos*: cf. Ch. II, 64.

[64] *Samian Stories* 314.

Accession is introduced by yet another synchronism with Cambyses:

> While Cambyses the son of Cyrus was lingering in Egypt and had gone mad, there rebelled two Magi who were brothers . . . (3.61.1)

Thereafter, we find only the weakest structural breaks. The story of the Revolt is combined with the Death of Cambyses, which terminates in the standard chronicle notation about the end of his reign (3.66.2). The account of the rule of the Magus (see 3.67.2 ff.) leads directly to the account of his discovery (a slight break occurs at 3.68.1), to the assembly of six of the seven conspirators, and to the arrival of Darius as the seventh. These last sections have no introductory statements at all, so that the narrative is here much more "modern" in the manner of some parts of the last three books.[65] An important feature isolating this group of *logoi* from the preceding narrative is the lack of an explanation for the sudden arrival of Cambyses at Ecbatana in Syria (the place where he dies),[66] and of Darius "from the Persians, where his father was satrap."[67] Such obscurities are characteristic of the relative independence of separate *logoi* and confirm the present analysis.[68]

The account of the Revolt of the Magi and the Conspiracy of the Seven is interrupted after the elaborate debate of the Seven on their plan of action, and before the execution of that plan. The intervening story, placed in the pause, is the Death of Prexaspes (3.74-75).[69] This emphasizes the intellectual (bouleutic) element in the conspiracy and corresponds to the treatment of the same element in the accession story, which contains the famous Debate

[65] The similarity between Books 3 and 7-9 also argues against the idea that the latter differ in style from the rest of the work; cf. Ch. II, note 35.

[66] Some scholars assume that Cambyses was on his way to quell the revolt; see e.g. E. Meyer, *Geschichte des Altertums* 3² (Stuttgart 1937) 192, and generally, Lehmann-Haupt in *RE*, s.v. Kambyses, 1822-23. However, this is not in Herodotus, whose main interest is in the double coincidence of (a) Apis' and Cambyses' wound in the thigh and (b) Ecbatana in Media and Ecbatana in Syria (3.64.3-4). For possible identifications of the latter, see Legrand, Budé 3.84, note 3.

[67] Hdt. 3.70.3. Cf. Ch. I, 32 and notes 50-51.

[68] It should be pointed out, as a matter of principle, that such obscurities are not necessarily inconsistencies, although they are often so taken by modern scholars. It is sometimes possible to supply the missing thought (e.g. that Darius had gone home after the death of Cambyses) and thus harmonize the accounts, although we cannot be sure, in these cases of ellipsis, that we are reconstructing Herodotus' actual thought.

[69] On the question of parallel action here, see Ch. II, note 43.

on Government (3.80-82). The assassination of the Magi by the Seven (3.76-79) is isolated at the end by the story of the festival of the Magophonia. The Accession of Darius (3.80-87) also lacks framing sentences, but is defined at the end by a variant account of how Darius' horse won him his throne.

Within this straightforward narrative, the Death of Cambyses forms both the introduction to the Revolt of the Magi and a separate tragedy, which must, however, be reconstructed by the reader (in the manner of the tragedy of Polycrates), since it is not developed as an independent *logos*. It is noteworthy that this story of the death of Cambyses is separated from the earlier Cambyses *logoi* by a reinterpretation of Cambyses' madness as *atê*, and of his cure as *sôphrosynê*.[70] Another difficult element, the speeches on government, should perhaps be mentioned. Herodotus' belief that these were actually spoken (despite the disbelief of some Greeks, and despite their evidently Greek character) is based on their monarchic, i.e. Persian, conclusion (thus recalling the Persian account of the proem) and on his observation of democratic tendencies in Persia in the period following the Ionian Revolt (6.43.3).[71]

8. *The Power of Darius* (3.88-116, cf. 117)

This *logos*, closely connected with the preceding, is introduced by a statement stressing the result of Darius' accession:

> Thus Darius son of Hystaspes was appointed king, and all peoples of Asia were subject to him, except for the Arabians, (the peoples) having been subdued by Cyrus and later again by Cambyses. (3.88.1)[72]

[70] *Samian Stories* 316.

[71] On the Debate on Government, see now the full discussion by H. Apffel, *Die Verfassungsdebatte bei Herodot* (3.80-82) (Diss. Erlangen 1954) (cf. *AAlt* 14 [1961] 48), and P. T. Brannan, *Traditio* 14 (1963) 427-38. This is not the place to enter into a renewed discussion of this difficult problem. Suffice it to say that the debate owes its inclusion primarily to Herodotus' interest in the origins of national governments. It should thus be compared with the story of Deioces, 1.96-100, and the origin of the Spartan double kingship, 6.52. The story was known before Herodotus (or at least before it appeared in the present work: "some Greeks do not believe it," 3.80.1 = 6.43.3). Disbelievers no doubt based their opinion on the unlikelihood of democratic political currents in Persia; the existence of such was proved to Herodotus by Mardonius' actions in Ionia in 492 B.C. (6.43). One of the central ideas of the debate is the question of freedom in Persia; cf. the Cyrus anecdote in 1.125-26, but the idea continues to be of central importance throughout. The debate explains how it came about that Persia had only external, but not (like the Greeks) internal, freedom.

[72] "Later again": Ch. I, 31. A similar phrase, 7.108.1.

There follows a note on the freedom of the Arabians as friends of
the Persians: they "did not at all obey the Persians in slavery."
Thus, the beginning of this *logos* states the theme of the power of
Darius, and at the same time its limitation, by using the independence of the Arabs as an example.[73] The subsequent items all
support the contention of Darius' great power: his marriages are
dynastic, his statue stresses his accession, and the satrapy list gives
a detailed account of his resources. The theme of the whole *logos* is
stated succinctly after the account of his marriages: "all was full
of power for him" (3.88.3).

At the end of the section dealing with power and revenues
(3.88-96), a series of stories leads gradually to the *logos* on the Ends
of the World. The satrapy list (which is a roster of tribute-bearing
peoples) is followed by a shorter account of peoples bearing
gifts (3.97), and by a *logos* on how the Indians collect the gold they
bring to the king. The Indians are tribute-bearers (cf. 3.94.2), and
thus the Indian *Logos* is an afterthought to the satrapy list, placed
in the pause. The Indian account (amusingly constructed like a
real campaign *logos*, with its own ethnographic section and the
description of the battle with the "fox ants")[74] is linked to the
Ends of the World through the idea of the difficulties which people
of the East encounter in the acquisition of their marvelous
wealth.

The *logos* on the *Ends of the World* (3.106-16) is a model of clear
framing and possesses a lucid internal structure, as has been
shown in Ch. II.[75] Its "digression" on divine providence operating

[73] The idea of Darius' limitation is repeated in 3.97.4 and 3.101.2. Cf. Pohlenz,
Herodot 27, note 1, and Ch. IV, 170.

[74] Brief outline:
    3.98.1:   The Indians collect gold in the following manner.
                    98.2-102.1: Indian Ethnographic *Logos*.
    3.102.1-105: Indian stratagem for battle with fox ants.

[75] The structure of the *logos* is as follows:
    3.106.1: Introductory sentence on parts of world.
            106.2-3:   The East: reference to preceding Indian *Logos* (size of
                            animals, quantity of gold).
            107.1-113.2: The South: Arabia.
                            107.2-110.1: Acquisition of incense in fight with winged
                                        snakes.
                            108.1-109.3: Winged snakes and divine
                                        foresight.
            110:            Acquisition of cassia.
            111:            Acquisition of cinnamon.

in the animal kingdom furnishes an analogy to history in general, and its large section on Arabian wealth and harassment (3.107-13) is linked closely with the Indian *Logos*.[76] Its real purpose, however, is to show how Darius is everywhere enclosed by the limits of a world that does not obey his dictates. This theme is alluded to in the remarkable connecting sentence of the *logos* at the end, where the next story (dealing as it does with the power of Darius in Asia, i.e. at the center of his world) is attached as follows:

> The ends of the world, which *enclose* the rest and hold it within, appear to possess what seems to us the most beautiful and the rarest. And there is a plain in Asia *enclosed* by a mountain on all sides . . . (3.116.3-117.1)[77]

9. *The Five Anecdotes* (3.177-38)

Five stories follow one another in close succession: (a) *The Story of the Plain in Asia* (3.117), (b) *The Death of Intaphernes* (3.118-19), (c) *The Death of Polycrates* (3.120-25), (d) *The Assassination of Oroetas* (3.126-28), and (e) *The Greek Doctor Democedes* (3.129-38). They are here grouped together for convenience, since they form a transition between the *logoi* of Darius' accession and power and those of his subsequent campaigns.[78] The sequence of these stories may be considered from two different points of view. For structurally they are linked to portions of the preceding and following narrative, using the principle of initiating or closing off accounts by a story placed in a pause. Thus the story of the Plain in Asia is an afterthought to the satrapy list, connected with it through the idea of tribute

---

	112:	Acquisition of laudanum.
	113.1:	Concluding sentence: divine odor of Arabia.
	113.1-2:	Long-tailed and broad-tailed sheep in Arabia.
114:		The Southwest: Ethiopia (indirect reference to 3.20 ff.).
115-116.3:		The West and the North: Europe.
	115.1-2:	The Eridanos controversy; tin trade.
	116.1-3:	Gold in North, and Arimaspians.

3.116.3: Concluding sentence on parts of world.
Cf. also Ch. II, 54-55.

[76] Divine providence: 3.108.2; cf. Conclusion, 312.

[77] Herodotus gives a specific location to the plain, but it seems to be fabulous, and so I have kept it anonymous. Cf. How and Wells on 3.117.

[78] *Samian Stories* 314-15 and outline, 321.

(3.117.6, cf. 3.97.5); the story of Intaphernes harks back to the Revolt of the Seven, and the Death of Polycrates to the earlier Polycrates *Logos* contained in the Spartan War; the Assassination of Oroetas, on the other hand, through the agency of Darius, looks forward, as does also the story of the Greek doctor Democedes and the party of Persian spies led by him into Greece (although this last story also balances that of the Spartan war against Polycrates as an invasion of the other continent). Thus, from the structural point of view, the stories hide the break between Darius' Power and his Campaigns in the close connection established between the third and fourth story, i.e. the Murder of Polycrates and the Assassination of Oroetas. From the second, or chronological, point of view, three of the five anecdotes follow one another in a clearly marked sequence. The story of the plain is, it is true, timeless, and thus very closely linked thematically with the preceding *logos*; the story of Polycrates' death is displaced from its proper chronological place during Cambyses' reign; but the Intaphernes story, the vengeance on Oroetas, and the Democedes stories (b, d, and e) carry through a chronological thread beginning right after the accession and ending before Darius' first campaign.[79] It may be observed that the *logos* on the power of Darius is not linked chronologically with this sequence.

The most important section in the Democedes story is the bed-chamber scene of Darius and Atossa, in which the expansionist policy against Scythia and Greece is first developed.[80]

10. *The Campaigns of Darius* (3.139-6.140)

These campaigns form by far the longest string of *logoi* in the work. Their relation is established by the pattern of the rise and fall of the ruler, and at the beginning by the mention of Samos as the first Hellenic or barbarian city conquered (3.139.1). The end is set off by the story of Miltiades' capture of Lemnos and by other Greek stories placed in the pause.[81]

[79] Hdt. 3.118.1 ("right after the revolt"); 120.1 ("approximately at the time of Cambyses' illness"); 126.1 ("not much later . . . after the death of Cambyses and the rule of the Magi"). Cf. subsequently: 129.1 ("when the treasure of Oroetas had arrived, being brought to Susa") and 133.1 ("not much later than this"). Democedes had originally been at the court of Polycrates and was later kept by Oroetas as a slave, among whose possessions he was found at Sardis by Darius (3.131.1-2; 129.3). All these stories precede Darius' earliest campaigns.

[80] On the bed-chamber scene, see *Causation* 271, note 60.

[81] Ch. I, note 23; below, this chapter, 125.

(a) *Conquest of Samos* (3.139-49). Like the Spartan War against Polycrates, this well-articulated *logos* begins with a double *aitiē*-section, which concerns, respectively, Polycrates' brother Syloson and his caretaker Maeandrius.[82] This emphasis on the responsibility of the Greeks is characteristic of Graeco-Persian actions in the work. The campaign includes an escape section, in which Maeandrius tries to get help from Sparta but is refused by King Cleomenes (3.148).

(b) *Second Conquest of Babylon* (3.150-60). This campaign begins with a synchronism with the preceding Samian campaign:

> While a naval armament had gone against Samos, the Babylonians revolted, being very well prepared. (3.150.1)

The *logos* thus begins with a very short section describing the preparations of the defenders and showing their despair and determination. Unlike the Samian campaign, which is led by Otanes (one of the Seven, and general of Darius), the Babylonian conquest is directed by the king in person. The campaign *logos* itself is constructed like a true *logos* of conquest, rather than as the suppression of a revolt. The form of the *logos* is complicated by the story of Zopyrus, where the main themes are loyalty and resulting honor (*timê*).[83] Thus the *logos* expresses the Persian king's relations

---

[82] Outline, *Samian Stories* 321. Cf. *Causation* 268-69. Escape section: above, note 36.

[83] Myres, *Herodotus* 120 (cf. 99), also seems to place Zopyrus in the center of the narrative. My outline is as follows:

3.150.1:	Synchronism with Samian campaign and announcement of Babylonian revolt.
150.1:	Preparations under the Magus and the Seven.
3.150.2:	Announcement of revolt repeated.
150.2:	Further preparations (killing of wives).
3.151.1:	Campaign of Darius: siege.
151.1-2:	Omen of the mules.
3.152:	Anger of Darius, after 19 months of siege.
3.153.1:	In 20th month, omen comes true for Zopyrus.
153.1-2:	Zopyrus deliberates.
3.154.1:	Zopyrus asks Darius how much honor the captor of Babylon would receive.
154.1-2:	Zopyrus plans self-mutilation and (apparent) desertion.
3.154.2:	Zopyrus mutilates himself and visits Darius.
155:	Conversation with Darius: plan for capture of Babylon.
3.156.1:	Zopyrus goes to Babylon.
156.2-157.1:	Speech of Zopyrus: deception of Babylonians; demand of an army.

with his underlings when these relations are at their best—a theme appropriate for the symbolic significance of Babylon as the center of Asiatic power. There is, so far as I can see, no direct thematic connection between the two captures of Babylon, except for the notations that they are the first and the second (1.191.6 and 3.159.1). Herodotus nowhere mentions the third capture of Babylon by Xerxes.[84]

(c) *Scythian Campaign* (4.1-142). Contrary to common opinion, the Scythian *Logos* is not only one of the best-organized accounts in Herodotus, but also one of the most important. Standing midway between the first half of Herodotus' work and the Graeco-Persian actions proper, this *logos* is the main link that safeguards the unity of the work.[85] The following discussion is based

3.157.2-158.2:	Capture of Babylon through trick of Zopyrus (this agrees point by point with his speech before Darius).

3.159.1:	"Thus was Babylon taken for the second time."	
	159.1-2:	Darius' treatment of Babylonians.

	160.1-2:	Honors for Zopyrus.
	160.2:	Zopyrus' grandson Zopyrus, who deserted from Persia to Athens.

The *logos* is clearly a simple campaign *logos*, with two brief preparations sections added for the defender, and with the story of Zopyrus put into the narrative in the place where we expect the account of the method of capture. The rest of the Zopyrus story forms an appendix. The connection between the campaign and the Zopyrus narrative is made by the omen of the mules (there is no inconsistency: see Legrand, Budé 3.110). The main themes of the Zopyrus story are trickery (*apatê*: Ch. VI, 243), loyalty, and resulting honor (*timê*): Ch. IV, note 112. The combination of the last two ideas is stressed by the irony of the ἔργον αἴσχιστον (*Ergon* 270, note 23; cf. Schmid-Stählin 1.2.599 f.) and of the "desertion" (αὐτομολεῖν: 154.2; 155.4; 156.1 twice; contrast the true αὐτομολία of his grandson, 160.2). Note also the emphasis on the intellectual element (deliberations) in Zopyrus' behavior, contrasting with Darius' emotional attitude. Zopyrus is one of a series of loyal Persians (Myres, *Herodotus* 160-61).

[84] There is, however, some indirect reference from the second to the first Babylonian conquest by verbal correspondence. Thus the preparations of the Babylonians for the siege are similar (3.150.1, cf. 1.190.2). Both Darius and Cyrus come to be at their wit's end (3.152, cf. 1.190.2), and Darius even tries the trick by which Cyrus had been successful. In 1.191.1 Herodotus suggests that someone may have proposed that trick to Cyrus; despite the formulaic nature of that phrase one may wonder if Herodotus thought there must have been a person like Zopyrus to make the suggestion to Cyrus. Herodotus' second capture of Babylon does not fit any known revolts, and some scholars assume that it is the revolt of 478 B.C. under Xerxes: see Legrand, Budé 3.178, note 3; How and Wells, 1.300.

[85] For adverse opinions on this *logos*, see Schmid-Stählin 1.2.565, note 2, and 603; Jacoby, *RE* Suppl. 2.345-47. On the inconsistencies in the ethnographic portions, see F. Windberg, *De Herodoti Scythiae et Libyae descriptione* (Diss. Göttingen 1913); Trü-

partly on some excellent observations by J. E. Powell, although this scholar did not himself realize that his remarks were primarily arguments for unity.[86] The importance of the Scythian Campaign is due largely to the fact that it relates the first attempt of the Persians to conquer a part of Europe, the continent for which the Greeks later come to be the champions.[87] Consequently, the Scythian Campaign shows a number of parallels with the later Greek campaigns.

The general structure of the Scythian *Logos* is unique in several respects:

1-4:	Announcement of campaign and *aitiê*-section.	
5-82:	Scythian Ethnographic *Logos*.	
	5-15:	Origins of Scythians.
	16-41:	Country of Scythians and borderlands.
	42-45:	Map of the world.
	46-58:	Nature of Scythians based on country and rivers.
		(Ch. 46 is proemial.)
	59-75:	Customs of the Scythians, continued.
		76-80: Stories of Anacharsis and Scyles.
		81-82: Total number of Scythians.
83-142:	Scythian Campaign of Darius.	
	83-98:	March of Darius from Susa to Danube.
	99-101:	Shape of Scythia.
	102-20:	Councils of Scythians and their neighbors.
	121-42:	Campaign proper.

The *logos* is introduced with a vague chronological reference to the Babylonian campaign, showing that Herodotus did not know its exact date:

---

dinger, *Studien* 18 ff.; Pohlenz, *Herodot* 50, note 2. J. Harmatta, *Quellenstudien zu den Skythika des Herodot* (Budapest 1941), is not known to me. Further, Ph.-E. Legrand, *REA* 42 (1940) 219-26, and Budé 4 (1960) 15 ff. M. A. Levi, *RFIC*, n.s. 11 (1933) 58 ff. J. W. Johnson, *JHI* 20 (1959) 250-57, gives an interesting survey of European ideas about the Scythian. The best literary analysis of the whole *logos* is by Powell, *Hist. Herodotus* 56 ff. For its themes, cf. Ch. IV, 175. See now H.-J. Diesner, "Skythische Religion und Geschichte bei Herodot," *RhM*, n.s. 104 (1961) 202-12.

[86] Powell, above, note 85. Also important are the remarks of Pohlenz, *Herodot* 27-28, on the connections of the Scythian *Logos* with the preceding narrative, in particular the earlier mentions of Scythians and Cimmerians, and the parallel with Cyrus' campaign against the Massagetae.

[87] *Causation* 262, 263, and notes 42-43.

>   After the capture of Babylon, there took place a campaign of
>   Darius himself against the Scythians.[88]

Despite this seemingly casual introduction, Herodotus firmly
connects the beginning of the *logos* with the preceding narrative
through the vengeance motif. For in the *aitiê*-section, which follows
immediately upon the introductory sentence, he says that Darius
fought the campaign in retaliation for a former period of Scythian
rule over Asia.[89] The importance of the motif (which must be
taken seriously) is stressed by the unusual placing of the *aitiê*-section
before the ethnographic *logos*. The remainder of the *aitiê*-section
is largely devoted to the dealings of the Scythians with their
slaves, a story which prefigures the motif of freedom versus
slavery, i.e. the European motif *par excellence*.

The Scythian Ethnographic *Logos* is closely linked with the main
themes of the campaign that follows it. Herodotus here uses a
procedure found also in the campaign of Xerxes into Greece,[90]
which constitutes a kind of "enjambement," with each section
emphasizing a point properly belonging to a later section. Thus, at
the start, the account of the origins of the Scythians stresses the
unknown nature of the far North (4.7.3), a point found again
throughout the campaign.[91] The same motif recurs at the beginning of the section on the Scythian country (4.16). At the
beginning of what is really the first section on customs (despite the
fact that it seemingly deals largely with rivers), Herodotus, in a
short proem,[92] declares that the Euxine coast contains the stupidest
of men, except for the Scythians, who have discovered but one
very wise thing: this is their ability to disappear in the steppes,
i.e. their main strategy in the coming war. The following section
on the rivers of the North is a displaced geographical section, and
it is added at this point in order to prove the feasibility of the

---

[88] "Himself" is added to contrast with campaigns by underlings, either the
preceding Samian campaign or (more likely) the following European, Libyan, Ionian
wars, etc. In fact, Darius fights no more campaigns in person in the *Histories*, until at
the time of his death he is preparing to fight the Greeks and Egyptians.

[89] Jacoby, *RE* Suppl. 2.346, assumed a doublet in the redaction of the beginning
of the Scythian *Logos*; see, however, Pohlenz, *Herodot* 27, note 2. The theme of vengeance
between Scythians and the Asiatic kingdoms begins in the Lydian *Logos* and ends with
Cleomenes; see Pagel, *Aitiol. Moment* 17-20.

[90] Below, 129.

[91] Cf., in the ethnographic part, 4.16; 18.3; 31; in the campaign, 4.83.1; 97.4;
121; 124.2; 125.5; 134.2.

[92] Hdt. 4.46; cf. the first sentence of 59.

Scythian tactic. The remainder of the Scythian Ethnographic
Logos once more follows a standard pattern. The map of the world is
placed between Country and Customs, and at the end an anecdote
shows that the Scythians are numberless.

The campaign proper also has some unusual features. It begins
with a march section which consciously foreshadows the march of
Xerxes in Book 7.[93] At the end of this section, which extends only
as far as the crossing of the Danube, there is a geographical
description of Scythia proper. This is again a displaced geographical section,[94] the purpose of which is to make vivid the
vastness of the country Darius is about to enter. It is placed in the
pause between the March Section and the Council of the Scythians
and their neighbors. This council anticipates the councils of the
Greek defenders in the account of the Persian Wars.[95]

The actual campaign follows the council without a break, since
it begins with the movement of the Scythians to meet the invaders
(4.121.1). The campaign consists of a series of short sections, most
of them initiated by the Scythians and containing thereafter the
reaction of the Persians, as well as a short interpretative passage
in each case, sometimes in the form of dialogue.[96] Since the

[93] Powell, *Hist. Herodotus* 58 f.; Legrand, *REA* 42 (1940) 224 ff.
[94] On this section, see Pohlenz, *Herodot* 50, note 2.
[95] *Causation* 262.
[96] The outline of the campaign is as follows:
 a. 4.121-22.1: Scythians go to meet Persians.
    122.2-123: Persians pursue Eastern army of Scythians.
    124.1: Darius builds eight forts.
 b. 124.2: Scythian Eastern army returns to Scythia.
    124.2-125: Persians pursue Scythian Western army.
    126: Message of Darius to Idanthyrsus.
    127: Answer of Idanthyrsus.
 c. 128.1-2: Scythians send Eastern army to Danube.
    128.2-130: Scythians harass Persians.
    131: Scythian gifts arrive.
    132: Gobryas interprets the gifts.
 d. 133.1-3: Eastern Scythians at Danube: first request.
    133.3-134.1: Western Scythians prepare for battle.
    134.1-3: Incident of the hare; advice of Gobyras.
    135: Darius escapes by night: *apatê*.
 e. 136-39: Second meeting of Scythians and Ionians at Danube. Council of Ionians.
    140-41: Escape of Persians to bridge.
    142: What the Scythians said about the Ionians.
The campaign *logos* begins without a break, since it continues Scythian action subsequent to their deliberations.

Scythian army is split into a Western and an Eastern branch, the narrative follows the Western army and its pursuit by Darius, while, concurrently, the Eastern army moves to the Danube, in an attempt to persuade the Ionians to break down the Danube bridge. This is one of the few places where Herodotus approaches a narrative structure in two parallel actions.[97] The *logos* ends with the opinion given by the Scythians with respect to the slavish nature of the Ionians (4.142).

The end of the Scythian Campaign *Logos* is very closely connected with the narrative leading to the Ionian Revolt, and thus to the Graeco-Persian Wars.[98] The main outer link is the *European Campaign Logos*, supported by stories about Histiaeus, tyrant of Miletus, the transfer of the Paeonians, and, internally, by the role of the Ionians in the Scythian Campaign. It is therefore erroneous to postulate a break before the Ionian Campaign, as Jacoby has suggested.[99]

(d) *European Campaigns of Megabazus and Otanes* (4.143-44 and 5.1-27).[100] On his arrival at Sestus, from Scythia, and before crossing the Hellespont into Asia, Darius appoints Megabazus as "general in Europe" (4.143.1); he is later relieved by Otanes, the son of Sisamnes, and not the conspirator (5.25.1). That this is a proper campaign *logos* results from its introductory statement and from its two introductory anecdotes, one about Megabazus, the other dealing with Greek colonization at the Bosporus and thus foreshadowing the Libyan *Logos* as well. The account of the campaign itself is postponed to the end of that *logos*. In addition, the European campaign is combined with some sections on the relations between Darius and Histiaeus, tyrant of Miletus, and with other matters, so that its structure is somewhat complicated:

4.143-44:   Darius appoints Megabazus; announcement of campaign; two anecdotes.

             4.145-205: Libyan Campaign.

5.1-10:   European Campaign I (Hellespont and Thrace).

---

[97] The account of the actions of the Eastern army is interpolated between the actions of the Western army: 4.128.1-2; 133.1-3; in 136-39, the two branches join. Parallel action: Ch. II, note 43.

[98] Ch. I, 22.

[99] Jacoby, *RE* Suppl 2.328, cf. 342 and 353. Against his idea of a doublet between 5.30 and 5.28, see Pohlenz, *Herodot* 64, note 1.

[100] Cf. *Action* 24.

The whole *logos* is clearly a link between the Scythian Campaign
and the Ionian Revolt, for the campaigns on the European and
Asiatic sides of the Hellespont are an aftereffect of the Scythian
Campaign and at the same time affect the Greeks in northern
Asia Minor. Internally, the Sisamnes anecdote parallels the
anecdote about Megabazus. The central figure is Darius, whose
movements we follow from Scythia via the Hellespont to Sardis
and then to Susa; from here he will supervise the quelling of the
Ionian Revolt and the wars against the Greeks; this is similar to
Cyrus' position in the first conquest of Ionia.[102]

(e) *Libyan Campaign* of Aryandes, satrap of Egypt (4.145-205).
This *logos* forms an interruption of the European Campaign.[103] A
punitive Persian campaign against the Greek city of Barca in the
Cyrenaica is here developed into a great campaign involving
Cyrene herself and indirectly all of Africa. The *logos* has for its
main themes (1) the westernmost penetration of Persian forces
(a variation of the expansionist motif, cf. 4.204), and (2) the
attack upon the Greeks as colonizers of Libya. A strong subsidiary theme of the *logos* is thus the role of the Greeks as colonizers
and their relations with barbarous populations. These ideas are
excellently brought out by the arrangement of material, which
deviates from the normal pattern in several respects:

---

[101] For the importance of the Paeonians, see *Causation* 263-64.

[102] Above, 89-90.

[103] *Action* 24, note 16; *Causation* 269 f. The Libyan Campaign *Logos* is attached to the
European Campaign *Logos* at a single point (4.145.1: activities of Megabazus).

154-56:   Cyrenaean version of colonization of Plataea.
157-58:   Founding of Cyrene.
159-67:   The kings of Cyrene before the Libyan campaign.
167.3:   Statement connecting the history of Cyrene with the Libyan Ethnographic *Logos*.
168-99:   Libyan Ethnographic *Logos*.
168-80:   Eastern Libyans to Lake Tritonis; at the end, story of Jason (179), and Athena festival (180).
181-85:   The Country of Libya: oases.
186-90:   Characterization of Eastern Libyans as distinct from Western.
191-96:   Western Libyans. Mention of Carthage.
197-99: The four nations of Libya; comparison with other continents; harvests of Cyrene.
200-205:   Libyan Campaign.
200-202:   Capture of Barca.
203.1-3:   Two visits of Persian army to Cyrene.
203.3-4:   Recall of army to Egypt.
204:     Statement on westernmost penetration of Persians.
204:     Darius transplants Barcaeans to Asia.
205:     Death of Pheretime.

In this scheme, 4.168-99 forms an ethnographic *logos*, and 145-67.2 is basically a Cyrenaean city history, cut off at the point of contact with the Persians.[104] However, the historical account is presented by Herodotus as an *aitiê*-section, for he tells the history of the kings of Cyrene ostensibly to explain why Pheretime, queen mother of Cyrene, wanted to take vengeance on the city of Barca (4.145.1; 165.3; 167.3). The ethnographic *logos* in turn is attached to the true motive of the Persians in supporting Pheretime against Barca: they wanted to conquer Africa. Hence the famous connecting statement between the History of Cyrene and the Libyan Ethnographic *Logos* must be taken seriously:

[104] It is very likely that Herodotus' account is here based on a written source: see Crahay, *Litt. orac.* 110, note 1, etc.; F. Chamoux, *Cyrène sous la monarchie des Battiades* (Paris 1953) 92 ff., esp. 111; A. J. Graham, *JHS* 80 (1960) 94-111. The same is true of the ethnographic account of Libya; cf. Jacoby, *RE*, s.v. Hekataios, 2731 ff.; Chamoux, *op. cit.* 224.

This (namely Pheretime's request for vengeance) was a mere pretext, and in my opinion the army was sent out to conquer the Libyans. (4.167.3)[105]

The ethnographic *logos* forms the second part of the *aitiê*-section of the Libyan Campaign *Logos*; for such double sections, compare the Samian campaign above.

Internally, the history of Cyrene and the Libyan Ethnographic *Logos* are joined thematically by the idea of the relations between Greeks and natives in Africa. Hence the elaborate colonization stories in the first section, and the unusual organization of the second, in which Herodotus isolates the Eastern Libyans as being closer to both Greeks and Egyptians, and closes his account of them with the Greek stories of Jason at Lake Tritonis and of a native festival to Athena. The geographical section on the oases is placed between the accounts of Eastern and Western Libyans because the native peoples are more important than the geography of the country.[106] In the colonization stories there appears the important motif of cooperation, in sharp contrast with the vengeance motif of the Pheretime story.[107]

(f) *Ionian Revolt* (5.28-6.42). The Ionian Revolt initiates a closely-knit sequence of *logoi* leading directly to the Persian Wars of Darius and Xerxes, and thus to the end of the work. The connection with the subsequent narrative is partly causal, since the participation of Athenians and Eretrians in the revolt, and especially in the burning of Sardis, caused the anger of Darius, which led to Marathon and then to Xerxes' invasion. Hence the Ionian Revolt was, in Herodotus' words, "the beginning of the evil" (5.97.3).[108] This connection is expressed by the elimination from the narrative of nearly all non-Greek campaigns of the Persians, by the sustained reference, in all Graeco-Persian actions, to the figures of Darius and (later) Xerxes, and finally by an

---

[105] This statement has been considered a mere connecting link: Powell, *Hist. Herodotus* 8. However, the connection is natural, since (a) Greek historical *logoi* are to Herodotus comparable with ethnographic *logoi*, and (b) aetiology is likewise a fundamental principle of the work.

[106] The distinction between Eastern and Western Libyans goes back (together with the general scheme of the *logos*) to Hecataeus; Jacoby, *RE*, s.v. Hekataios, 2728; cf. also *FGrH* I, 371-72 and 536. But the geographic section (4.181-85) hardly formed a part of this: see Windberg, *op. cit.* (above, note 85) 64. Cf. also Aly, *Volksmärchen* 134, note 2.

[107] Cooperation motif: 4.152.1 and 5; 158.3; 161.2-3; 167.1. Cf. *Causation* 253.

[108] Cf. *Causation* 265-67 and 272; the passage imitates *Iliad* 5.63 (ships of Paris).

exact chronology according to years, beginning with the first year of the Ionian Revolt, and ending in the detailed description by campaign seasons, with which the work closes.[109]

Thus, the connections at the end of the revolt present no problem, but at the beginning there is a difficulty. The *logos* begins as follows:

> (Otanes) accomplished this much in his campaign, and afterwards there was respite from trouble for no long time, when troubles began once more for the Ionians from Naxos and Miletus. (5.28)[110]

Following what seems to me the best explanation of this difficult sentence, I assume that Herodotus is here connecting the Ionian Revolt with the narrative immediately preceding, in which Otanes was seen subduing the Troad and further regions near the

[109] In Herodotus, time is an aspect of events. Therefore he reckons the early history of the East by kings' rules, but with the Ionian Revolts he begins a series of reckonings by years. This series reaches down to the end of the work (499-479 B.C.), but for the years 480 and 479 it is further amplified by a reckoning by summers and winters; see Pohlenz, *Herodot* 198-99 (who shows that Thucydides' system derives from Herodotus). See further *Tat und Geschichte* 504, note 13, and 512, note 25. Cf. generally the works mentioned in Ch. II, note 40.

[110] The sentence contains several difficulties: (1) "respite": ἄνεως all MSS. except C, which has ἄνεος (cf. *LSJ* s.v. ἄνεω and *add. et corr.*), but this is meaningless. ἄνεσις (respite), de la Barre; ἀνανέωσις (renewal), Gebhardt. Editors rightly prefer the former, although "renewal" would also make sense. ". . . afterwards there was respite from trouble" draws a contrast with the preceding campaign of Otanes. (2) μετά could be connected with οὐ πολλὸν χρόνον (cf. Macan, *IV-VI*, ad loc.): ". . . after not much time there was respite from trouble." This would avoid Herodotus' designating an empty time sequence, which is perhaps against his style (cf. H. Fränkel, "Die Zeitauffassung in der frühgriechischen Literatur," in his *Wege und Formen frühgriechischen Denkens*[2] [Munich 1960] 1-22—unfortunately Herodotus is not treated there). (3) The avoidance of an empty time sequence is the only point in favor of ἀνανέωσις, but this reading would make the clause tautological with the following and destroy the force of καί in the latter ("when": see Stein on 5.28, line 2). Hence ἄνεσις is no doubt correct. (4) The second clause, "when troubles began once more for the Ionians from Naxos and Miletus," is sometimes thought to draw a parallel with Cyrus' conquest of Ionia (Macan, *IV-VI*, ad loc.), but this is erroneous, since that was already the second conquest. τὸ δεύτερον thus refers once more to the campaign of Otanes. Hence the connection established in this paragraph is entirely with the narrative immediately preceding, and no break should be assumed (see above, note 99). (5) As stated in the text, another reason for preferring "respite" is that two passages at the end may contain the same idea, in the manner of ring composition; see 6.42.1: ἐκ τῶν Περσέων οὐδὲν ἐπὶ πλέον ἐγένετο τούτων ἐς νεῖκος φέρον Ἴωσι, and 43.1: καί σφι ταῦτα μὲν εἰρηναῖα ἦν. (6) The true reason for the vagueness of the sentence is Herodotus' uncertainty about the exact chronological relation between the campaign of Otanes and the Ionian Revolt, and thus between the latter and the Scythian campaign as well. Cf. Jacoby, *RE* Suppl. 2.348.

Hellespont and Bosporus. If this is true, then the "respite" (the word itself is a conjecture) concerns all the Greeks of Asia Minor, whereas the phrase "when troubles began . . ." is restricted to the Ionians, including Naxos and Miletus. Essential to the whole passage is the idea of trouble (*kaka*), since Herodotus considered the Ionian Revolt an evil which in turn caused further evils for the Greeks.[111] The sentence corresponds to other statements at the end of the revolt, where it is said that the Persians caused no further harm to the Ionians (6.42.1 and 43.1). At the beginning of the revolt, however, the trouble is said to have been caused by the Ionians themselves, since Herodotus begins the revolt with Ionian initiative; it is, as we have said, the third *logos* so constructed.[112]

The *logos* begins with a complex *aitiê*-section concerning the Naxian affair and the motivations of the two Milesian tyrants Aristagoras and Histiaeus,[113] and a preparations section (5.36-98), which includes Aristagoras' visits to Sparta and Athens—and hence the great *logoi* on Sparta and Athens (see below), which parallel a similar pair of *logoi* in the Croesus story.[114] The revolt itself is described as a campaign *logos* in two sections (5.99-103 and 5.116-6.32), which are separated by the Cypriote revolt (5.104-16.1). The Cypriote Campaign *Logos* is in turn split in two after its *aitiê*-section (104) by some stories that continue the account of Darius' own actions, his anger at the Athenians, and his further dealings with Histiaeus (105-107). The two sections of the Ionian Revolt describe, respectively, Ionian initiative and the subsequent Persian conquest. The second section is constructed, like the Ionian conquest under Cyrus and the "European Campaign" (above, d), as a series of campaigns by a number of Persian generals.[115] The affairs of Histiaeus during the revolt are placed before the battle of Lade (6.1-5) and at the end of the campaign

---

[111] Hence Macan's objection to the repetition of the word "trouble" in the sentence discussed in the last note is not valid. Cf. also above, note 108.

[112] Ch. I, 24.

[113] *Causation* 265-66. On Aristagoras and Histiaeus, see L. Solmsen in Marg, *Herodot* 637 ff.; A. Blamire, *CQ* 9 (1959) 142-54; and J. A. S. Evans, *AJP* 84 (1963) 113-28.

[114] Ch. I, 36.

[115] So already in the Cypriote Revolt (5.108.1), but it does not determine the structure there. The generals are named in 5.116: first comes the campaign of Daurises (5.117-21), then that of Hymeas (5.122), and finally that of Artaphernes and Otanes (5.123); eventually the contingents combine with the navy to attack Miletus (6.6) and fight at Lade. For other campaigns by underlings, see above, note 88.

(6.26-30). There is a section on the flight of the Samians, who go to Southern Italy (6.22-25). Such stories, when used near the end of a *logos*, may be called "escape sections."[115A] The campaign proper closes with the Persian capture of the islands (6.31-32), after which we have the emphatic statement:

> Thus the Ionians were enslaved for the third time, first by the Lydians, and now twice in succession by the Persians.[116]

In the chapter following the Ionian Revolt (6.33) Herodotus returns to the locale of the European campaign, where the Persian navy reconquers those places at the Hellespont which it had previously attacked. A little later, in 6.42, he shows the final after-effect of the quelling of the revolt in the reorganization of Ionia as a Persian province. Between these two chapters on aftereffects is placed the first of the *logoi* on Miltiades (6.34-41). Thus, the Ionian Revolt is framed at each end by action on both the European and the Asiatic sides of the Hellespont (5.26-27 and 6.33).[117]

A large part of the narrative on the Ionian Revolt is concerned with the *History of Athens and Sparta*, told in two separate *logoi* attached to the visits of Aristagoras. The *logos* on the *History of Sparta* (5.39-48) explains why King Cleomenes ruled Sparta at that time; the account of the troubles over succession in one of the Spartan royal houses has little bearing on the immediate situation, although it is important for the whole picture of Sparta in the work.[118] Unlike the Spartan *logos* for the time of Croesus, this account avoids the question of Sparta's power. The following meetings between Cleomenes and Aristagoras show merely that Sparta had by then given up foreign entanglements (5.49-54).

Quite different is the *logos* on the *History of Athens* (5.55-96). The motif of external power is here as strongly developed as it is in the two Greek accounts in the Croesus *Logos*. The *logos* on Athens falls into the following sections:

[115A] Above, note 36.

[116] "Twice in succession" (δὶς δὲ ἐπεξῆς): this is a typical Herodotean statement about a time sequence (cf. above, note 109). It does not mean that the conquests by Cyrus and Darius followed each other closely, but rather that no other nation had conquered the Ionians in the intervening period.

[117] *Action* 24.

[118] Ch. V, 192 ff. and 197-98.

[119] "I have told of the vision in Hipparchus' dream and the origin of the Gephyraeans—the original clan of the assassins of Hipparchus—, and after this I must take up my original argument, how the Athenians were freed from the tyrants." The first part of this sentence summarizes 5.55-61. The question arises how far the stories in that section are pertinent to the *logos* as a whole. The story of the murder of Hipparchus is polemic: it was not this murder which freed Athens; on the contrary, Hippias continued to rule for four years more, and with increased vigor. To this account are added two explanatory notes: (a) the dream of Hipparchus (5.56.1-2), which speaks of the coming murder as vengeance for the crimes of the Peisistratids. This, then, contains the idea that, while ineffective for the future, the murder was an atonement for the past (cf. Pohlenz, *Herodot* 95, and Crahay, *Litt. orac.* 254-55). (b) The origins of the Gephyraeans (5.57-61). This section is in agreement with a general theme of the whole *logos*, by which the noble families of Athens, except for the Alcmaeonids, are shown to be foreign. Just as the Gephyraeans are Phoenicians, so the Peisistratids are Neleids from Pylos (5.65.3), and Isagoras' family sacrifices to Carian Zeus (5.66.1). The Alcmaeonids, however, are "an Athenian clan" (5.62.2), and are "by their descent famous in Athens" (6.125.1). Presumably Herodotus means to contradict, or to hide, the tradition that the Alcmaeonids were also Neleids (How and Wells on 5.62). The section on the Gephyraeans also gives a complete genealogy of the Cadmeans (Cadmus, Polydorus, Labdacus, Laius, Oedipus, Eteocles, Laodamas). Under the last, the Cadmeans were driven out of Boeotia by the Epigonoi and went to Illyria; only the Gephyraeans remained (at Tanagra), and they were later driven out by the Boeotians (cf. Thuc. 1.12, where this invasion is dated 60 years after the Trojan War) and went to Athens. Thus the real purpose of (b) is to give a complete, and dated, genealogical history of the Cadmeans. Compare the more fragmentary genealogical histories of the Alcmaeonids down to Pericles, of the Spartan kings to Archidamas, and of the Persian kings to Artaxerxes: see 126 and Ch. V, 209, and note 56. In this *logos* and others of the sixth book, Herodotus is interested in connecting Greek families and others with their origins, and their succession down to his own time.

I assume that the inscriptions at the Ismenium are cited to support the mythical genealogy, and that the history of the alphabet is added to confirm Herodotus' belief that these inscriptions really were that early. (The whole section is of interest for Herodotus' use of sources, too, since it is presumably derived from different works of Hecataeus: see Jacoby, *RE*, s.v. Hekataios, 2678; *FGrH* I, 323 f. and 342.)

II A. | 66.1-2:   Cleisthenic reorganization of the
                    Attic tribes.
                    67.1-68.2: Similar actions by Cleis-
                              thenes of Sicyon.
      | 69.1-77.4: Reorganization of tribes concluded.
                    Second expedition of Cleomenes;
                    exile of Cleisthenes;[120] Cleomenes
                    driven from Athens; *Athenian embassy
                    to Persia*; Cleomenes' last attempt to
                    oust Cleisthenes; war with Chalcis
                    and Boeotia.

5.78-79.1:   Connecting paragraph: increased power of Athens
              through democracy.[121]

II B. | 79-81:   Alliance of Thebes and Aegina
                    against Athens.
                    82.1-89.1: Origin of old hostility
                              between Athens and
                              Aegina.[122]
      | 89.1-96:   Beginning of war between Athens
                    and Aegina; abortive Spartan
                    attempt to reestablish tyranny in
                    Athens (speech of Socles); return of
                    Hippias to Sigeum;[123] *enmity of
                    Athens and Persia.*

5.97.1:   Framing sentence: Aristagoras of Miletus arrives in
              Athens while Athenians are hostile to Persia and
              Athens is the most powerful city (in Greece).

The subject of the Athenian *Logos* is clearly the external power
of Athens. It begins with some preliminary stories, in a manner
reminiscent of certain ethnographic *logoi*, such as the Egyptian or

[120] In 5.71, in the pause between attempt and execution, the story of Cylon is
added.

[121] Quoted below, 120. After the connecting paragraph, Herodotus continues
(5.79.1): "And they acted as described (οὗτοι μέν νυν ταῦτα ἔπρησσον), but the Thebans..." This formula refers to 5.77, rather than to the chapter immediately preceding
(thus to the war with Chalcis, the fetters, or their dedication); cf. 8.21, which refers
to the end of 8.19.

[122] ἔχθρη παλαιή: see *Causation* 251 and 270.

[123] The problems connected with the structure and chronology of the short *logos*
on Sigeum have been solved by D. L. Page, *Sappho and Alcaeus* (Oxford 1955) 152-58.

Scythian. The story of the murder of Hipparchus explains the harshness of Hippias' last rule, and thus the unpopularity of tyranny in its last four years, and the story of the Gephyraeans parallels the theme of the origins of the other great Athenian houses, most of which (except for the Alcmaeonids) were of foreign origin.[124] The main body of the *logos* falls into two unequal sections, the second and larger of which is in turn subdivided into two parts (II A and B). After the story of the liberation, Herodotus considers the young republic's history in two phases: the first we might call the establishment of the power of the people (*dêmos*) by Cleisthenes (II A), a phase which terminates significantly with the first victory of the young democracy over two external enemies, Chalcis and Boeotia. The second period deals with two major attempts (by Aegina and by Sparta) to attack the new state (II B), but since both attempts misfire, the result is a further strengthening of Athens, so that she can now afford to be openly hostile toward Persia (compare the first and second embassies to Persia). The main portion of the Athenian *Logos* (the history of Athens between the liberation and the Ionian Revolt) is thus not a complete chronological account, but is designed to make a special point: it tells in two phases, one active and the other passive, of what the Athenian people "did and suffered."[125]

The central figure in this account is the Athenian *dêmos*, as distinct from the scions of the noble families. While Herodotus begins the *logos* by saying that "Athens" grew stronger, he goes on to speak of "the Athenians," and this word tends increasingly to denote the Athenian commoners.[126] Thus, in the connecting paragraph separating the active and the passive phases of Athenian growth, he speaks of the benefits of equality and goes on to stress its value for the individual:

[124] Above, note 119.

[125] The phrase is a reminiscence of *Odyssey* 8.490, where Odysseus asks Demodocus to sing of "what the Achaeans did and suffered, and what troubles they had." Here also, Odysseus does not ask for a chronicle of the war, but for significant events. Sections IIA and IIB, if not the whole *logos*, are wrongly taken as a chronicle of Athens by most scholars; see e.g. Jacoby, *RE* Suppl. 2.382; Pohlenz, *Herodot* 36.

[126] Ἀθηναῖοι means all Athenians in 1.60.5; 62.2; 64.3; 5.55; 62.1; 62.2; 65.3; 65.5; 66.2 (*dêmos* mentioned before); 70.2; 71.1; etc. A portion of the Athenians are qualified as the democratic faction in 5.64.2; 69.2; 72.2; 74.1; 76.1 (first occurrence). But in 5.72.4; 73.1; 74.2; 77.1; 78, etc., "the Athenians" are the democracy. Herodotus identifies the *dêmos* with the whole Athenian people after the *dêmos* has won the victory.

Thus the Athenians had been strengthened, and it is clear not only in this respect but everywhere that equality (*isêgoriê*) is a fine thing, if the Athenians under the tyrants were in no way superior in warfare to their neighbors, but when they had been freed from tyranny became by far the first. This proves that when they were held down they fought badly, since they were laboring for a master, but after their liberation each one was eager to work on his own behalf. (5.78)

The account of the active phase of Athenian history after the liberation (II A) stresses the gradual strengthening of the *dêmos* in three stages: first the quarrel between Isagoras and Cleisthenes necessitates the latter's bringing the *dêmos* over to his side;[127] secondly, the new Council of Five Hundred and "the Athenians" drive out Cleomenes after he had sent Cleisthenes into temporary exile; and finally, the *dêmos* wins a victory over Chalcis and Boeotia.

The purpose of both the Athenian and the Spartan *logoi* is to draw a contrast between the aggressive nature of the new democracy, confident in her power, and the increasing reluctance of Sparta, weakened by internal dissensions, to commit herself abroad. On this difference in attitude, Herodotus here passes the judgment that Sparta was wiser than Athens (cf. 5.97.2), for he considered the Ionian Revolt an evil.

The *logos* on *Miltiades' Flight from the Chersonnese* (6.34-41) will be discussed in Chapter V.[128]

(g) *Mardonius' Expedition wrecked at Mt. Athos* (6.43-45), a short campaign *logos*, with preparations and movements perfunctorily indicated. Directed against Athens and Eretria, and at the same time attempting the conquest of as many Greek cities

[127] That is, Herodotus thought of the origin of democracy as a mere matter of power politics. See H. Schaefer, "Besonderheit und Begriff der attischen Demokratie im 5. Jahrhundert," *Synopsis: Festgabe für Alfred Weber* (Heidelberg 1948) 477 ff.; cf. V. Ehrenberg, "Origins of Democracy," *Historia* 1 (1950) 541 ff. Joined with the establishment of democracy was the abolition of the Ionian tribes, an action which Herodotus compares to a similar measure by Cleisthenes of Sicyon, the maternal grandfather of the Athenian Cleisthenes. Here again the question of power is paramount: the Sicyonian maneuver had been intended to strengthen Sicyon in a war with Argos, and the Athenian legislation was also aimed at increasing internal and external strength. It should be recalled that Herodotus considered the Ionians weak (1.143.2), and that the Peisistratids, as Neleids, had a connection with them. Cf. also below, Ch. V, note 54.

[128] See below, Ch. V, 191-92. On the other *logoi* that deal with Miltiades, see Ch. I, 38, and this chapter, below, 125-26.

as possible, the expedition was wrecked by a storm at Mt. Athos and by an attack of the Thracian Brygoi, and is thus reckoned a failure by Herodotus. Mardonius "returns to Asia," a phrase characteristic of the Persian campaigns from the Scythian *Logos* on.[129] In the context of the work, the Mt. Athos expedition foreshadows the campaign of Datis and Artaphernes in several details, and forms an important link between the Ionian Revolt and the Persian Wars.

(h) *Subjugation of Thasos* (6.46-48.1), carried out by a messenger from Darius, and hence not a campaign *logos*.

(i) *Heralds sent to Greece* by Darius to ask for earth and water (6.48.1-49.1).[130] While thus asking for submission, Darius at the same time makes military preparations, which are clearly the preparations for Marathon (6.48.2 and 95.1). The sending of heralds is separated from that campaign partly because the latter is independent of the answers received by the heralds,[131] and partly because a Greek *logos* of great length is attached to this short section. Herodotus tends to list all of Darius' actions as a string of separate events.

The *Aeginetan Logos* (6.49-93) is attached to the demands for earth and water and owes its structure to this fact:[132]

6.49.1:   Aeginetans give Darius earth and water.

49.2:   Athens complains to Sparta.

50:    Cleomenes goes to Aegina to collect hostages, but is hindered by Demaratus, his royal colleague.

    51-55: Origins of Spartan double kingship.

        56-60: Honors accruing to Spartan kings. (A kind of ethnographic *logos*).

[129] A similar expression is used already in 3.137.4, when the Persian party of spies returns to Asia (these Persians had been the first to come to Greece from Asia, 3.138.4). Further: 4.143.1 (Scythian campaign, cf. also 5.12.1); 6.116 (end of account of Marathon); 8.118.1 and 4, and 119 (Xerxes); cf. 8.126.2; 130.1; 9.90.1 (Artabazus). This recurrent phrase merely emphasizes the Europe-Asia motif: cf. Ch. I, note 80. On the Mt. Athos expedition, see H. U. Instinsky in *Hermes* 84 (1957) 477-94 (= Marg, *Herodot* 471-96). Its parallelism with Marathon has made the expedition suspect to many: see H. Bengtson, *Griechische Geschichte*[2] (Munich 1960) 154.

[130] Earth and water: on this motif, see *Causation*, notes 43 and 62.

[131] These heralds are mentioned again indirectly in 7.138.2: see below, 135. The Athenians threw Darius' ambassadors into a pit, 7.133.1, but 6.48.2 shows that he wanted to fight the Greeks even before.

[132] See, generally, Ch. I, 38-39. Cf. G. de Sanctis, "Gli ostaggi Egineti in Atene e la guerra fra Atene ed Egina," *RFIC*, n.s. 8 (1930) 292-99. L. H. Jeffery, *AJP* 83 (1962) 44-54. Myres, *Herodotus* 104 and 125, calls this *logos* "The Tragedy of Cleomenes," but from the structural point of view this is incorrect.

61.1:   Demaratus obstructs Cleomenes at Aegina.

　　61-70: Demaratus dethroned, goes to Persia.

　　　　71-72: Later fate of Leotychidas, Demaratus' successor.

73:      Cleomenes deposits Aeginetan hostages at Athens.

74-84: Madness and death of Cleomenes.

　　The first two reasons given.

　　76-83: Argive War of Cleomenes (the third
reason explained).

　　84:   Cleomenes and the Scythians (the fourth
reason).

85-93:   (a) Aeginetans ask for the return of their hostages.

(b) Speech of Leotychidas: Glaucus' injustice.

(c) War of Aegina and Athens continued (since the
hostages are not returned).

This *logos* is clearly articulated into several sections, framed at
the beginning, in the middle, and again at the end, by the story of
the Aeginetan hostages deposited in Athens. The independence
of the *logos* is shown by its failure to join with the preceding Greek
logoi, and so a significant gap is left in our understanding of
Cleomenes' actions, for he was last seen hostile to Athens (5.90.2),
but now he is doing the Athenians' bidding. In effect, but not
formally, the *logos* continues the story of the relations between
Athens and Aegina before the Persian Wars.[133] Internally, the
logos also continues the story of the quarrels between the two
royal houses of Sparta.[134] The parallel between the eventual
fate of Leotychidas and that of Cleomenes is clearly brought out
in the structure of the *logos*. The speech of Leotychidas parallels
in form the earlier speech of the Corinthian Socles at the end of
the second Athenian *logos* (5.92), in that these are the only
speeches in which Herodotus uses a parable. The speeches complement each other to some extent, for the first deals with internal
politics in the city-state, and the second with Greek international
affairs.

(j) *Marathon* (6.94-120). It has often been remarked that
Herodotus treats the battle of Marathon merely as one item in a
group of Persian actions, and thus fails to emphasize sufficiently
its unique patriotic importance for the Athenians and the Greeks.

[133] On the treatment of these relations, see Ch. V, note 65.
[134] Ch. V, 197-98.

Yet, despite an organization typical of a campaign conducted by underlings of Darius, the *logos* is fairly elaborate and shows a number of unusual features. One of these is the proem previously discussed;[135] it consists of two parts, the first summarizing the preceding narrative, and the second relating the appointment of new generals with their mission to bring the enslaved Athenians and Eretrians before the king (6.94). The *logos* is organized as follows:

6.94.1-2: Proem to Marathon.
6.95-99: Preparations and march of attacker:
    95.1: Preparations.
    95.2: Travel through Aegean.
    96: Attack on Naxos.
    97.1-2: Visit to Delos.
6.98.1: Announcement of attack on Eretria.
    98.2-3: Earthquake at Delos and troubles of Greeks for 100 years.
    99.1-2: Capture of other islands and Carystus.
6.100-101: Eretrian Campaign.
    100: Athenians want to help, but Eretrians are divided.
    101: Siege of Eretria.
6.102: Persians led to Marathon by Hippias.
    103-106: Preparations of Athenians:
    103.1: Athenians go to Marathon under Miltiades.
    103.2-104: Story of Cimon and double escape of Miltiades.
    105-106: Philippides sent to Sparta (meeting with Pan).
6.107.1: Hippias lands Persians at Marathon.
    107.2-4: Hippias' tooth.
    108.1: Athenians joined by Plataeans.
    108.2-6: Origin of Plataean alliance with Athens.
    109-10: Council of Athenian generals; speech of Miltiades to Callimachus; decision.
    111.1: Order of battle.
    111.2: Honors for Plataeans.

[135] Ch. II, 66.

111.3:   Battle plan by accident.
112-13: Battle and pursuit.
114:     Athenian dead.
6.115-16: With loss of seven ships, Persians go to Phalerum;
          Athenians to city; return of Persians to Asia announced.
117.1:   Number of slain on both sides.
117.2-3: Blinding of Epizelus.
6.118:   Return voyage of Persians.
118.1:   Dream of Datis at Myconus.
118.2:   Return of statue to Delos, to be sent back to
         Delium.
118.3:   Fate of the statue.
6.119:   Arrival of Persians in Susa and settlement of Eretrians
         in Ardericca.
120:     Arrival of Spartans *post eventum*.[136]

While some sections are not clearly set off (one misses especially a clear introduction of the battle itself), the major sections are evident from the general pattern of battle descriptions. The arrival of the Persians at Marathon (6.107.1) is isolated before and after by two sections concerning the Athenians, the first regarding their preparations, and the second, the arrival of the Plataeans and the council before the battle. The council scene establishes clearly that the battle was due to Miltiades' initiative. A number of important anecdotes occur, partly in the breaks between sections, but also at the beginning of sections and following the announcement of subsequent action. The latter position, which is very emphatic, is employed e.g. for the earthquake on Delos, the story of Hippias' tooth, and the dream of Datis. The action at Marathon (102-17) is framed by the movements of the Persian fleet, with a second visit to Delos, and by the conquest and disposal of the Eretrians. Both sections thus contain accounts rather favorable to the Persians and in contrast with the proposed treatment of Athens. Despite its brevity, the *logos* gives a very large share to an account of the Greek side, partly because the Athenians were the attackers as well as the victors.

Three Greek *logoi* follow the narrative of Marathon. The first of these, *The Defense of the Alcmaeonids* (121-31), is an explanation

---

[136] Note the separation of the earthquake on Delos from Datis' preceding visit to Delos by the announcement of the campaign against Eretria. Other sections are also introduced by such statements and are framed by anecdotes. Ch. VI, 248 ff.

added to the statement (in the course of the Marathon narrative, 6.115) that the Alcmaeonids were accused of flashing a shield signal to the Persians, an explanation postponed to the end of the account of the battle. The second, *Miltiades' attempted Conquest of Paros and his Death* (132-36), is an independent Greek narrative of the kind found after the Greek victories in the battles of 480 and 479. It follows, then, the pattern of the aftereffects of battle and foreshadows the accounts of the Greek victories later on. The third *logos*, *Miltiades' Capture of Lemnos* (6.137-40), is attached to the mention of the Lemnian victory during Miltiades' last trial shortly before his death (136.2), but as the last *logos* before the Campaign of Xerxes, the story has a special significance, which is underlined by the mention of the Hellespont at the end (6.140.1). The Defense of the Alcmaeonids is followed by a subsidiary *logos* on the prominence achieved by the family, so that the structure of the three *logoi* is as follows:

94-120: *Marathon.*

    121-24: *Defense of Alcmaeonids.*[137]

        125-31: Fame of Alcmaeonids.

            125:       Alcmaeon acquires gold from Croesus.

            126-31.1: Megacles marries Agariste at famous banquet.

            131.1-2: Descendants of the marriage: Cleisthenes and Pericles.[138]

    132-36: *Miltiades' attempted Conquest of Paros, and his Death.*

        137-40: *Miltiades' Capture of Lemnos.*

    7.1.1:   Darius hears of defeat at Marathon . . .

Despite the different levels at which these *logoi* are attached to the narrative that in each case precedes them, they clearly form a group of Greek stories intended to mark an incisive division between the campaigns of Darius and those of Xerxes. This is true also in mood, if I may use the expression here. The Wedding of

---

[137] Despite Pohlenz, *Herodot* 47, note 1, Hdt. 6.122 may well be an interpolation.

[138] Cf. above, note 119. Pericles is here compared to a lion. On the controversy whether this is complimentary or uncomplimentary, see C. W. Dyson, "Leonta tekein," *CQ* 23 (1929) 186 ff.; R. Walzer in *Gnomon* 6 (1930) 581; H. Strasburger, "Herodot und das Perikleische Athen," *Historia* 4 (1955) 16-17. I would agree with Strasburger in taking the lion for a primarily ambiguous symbol. Cf. the lion imagery in the *Agamemnon* (B. M. W. Knox, *CP* 47 [1952] 17-25; below, Ch. VI, note 69). The lion image closes the *logos* with a symbol of greatness (whether good or bad).

Agariste in particular is a kind of mock epic story admirably illustrating the gaiety of an earlier age. The mention of Pericles takes us down to Herodotus' own time and parallels the mention of king Archidamus of Sparta at the end of one section of the Aeginetan *Logos* (6.71.1) and the mention of Artaxerxes and the troubles of the Greek states in the Pentecontaetia, a mention which is attached to Datis' first visit to Delos (6.98.2).[139] Thus we have, in Book 6, and especially at the end, in the accounts of the origins of the first Greek families and their descendants, a series of elements which connect early Greece, the Persian Wars, and Herodotus' own time.

11. *The Greek Campaign of Xerxes and Mardonius* (Books 7-9)

Despite its great length, the Campaign of Xerxes is constructed like an ordinary campaign *logos*. To achieve such a structure, Herodotus had to solve two compositional problems: the preponderance of the Greek narrative over the Persian after Salamis, and the inclusion of Mardonius' campaign within the framework of Xerxes' campaign. The first problem is solved simply by extending the sections I have called "aftereffects of battle" to include the required Greek actions; the second, by a clear subordination of Mardonius' campaign to that of Xerxes. Hence, as we shall see, Xerxes makes a reappearance after Mardonius' campaign. The unity of the last three books is well recognized and has been discussed a number of times before; it will therefore be possible to treat them more briefly. A more detailed account of the five great battles will be found in Chapter VI.[140]

The beginning of Xerxes' campaign *logoi* contains no proper introductory statements announcing the importance of what is to follow. The very nature of the initial break is in question among scholars, but I prefer to make it, with the ancients, at the beginning of Book 7.[141] As in the case of Cambyses, Herodotus deals here very briefly with the question of the legitimacy of succession; this is the occasion for relating the story of the advice given by

[139] This important observation was first made to me by Professor A. W. Allen. Cf. also above, note 119.

[140] 254 ff. The structure of Books 7-9 has been analyzed by Macan, *VII-IX*, Vol. 1, xv ff.; Pohlenz, *Herodot* 120 ff.; Myres, *Herodotus* 105 ff. and 126. Cf. Legrand, *Introduction* 236 f.

[141] Ch. I, 23.

Demaratus to Darius (7.2-3). The unspoken (because evident) connection between the campaign of the father and that of the son is likewise reminiscent of the account of Cambyses. For, since Xerxes inherits the campaign against Greece from his father, who did not live long enough to see it to a conclusion, the *logos* begins with Darius' plans for a new Greek campaign (7.1), and these plans are initiated by Darius' reception of a message about the defeat at Marathon.[142] Thus, in the first four chapters of Book 7, there is no significant break either at the beginning or at the end (where the death of Darius is briefly mentioned),[143] and instead the narrative continues that of Marathon (resuming from 6.120). Nevertheless, the three Greek *logoi* that intervene between the end of the account of Marathon and the message to Darius (6.121-40) suggest a break here, since they are placed in the pause. We have thus both a new beginning and a very close connection with the earlier narrative. This connection is no doubt due to the fact that Darius was already occupied with preparations for the new campaign when he died (7.1.2 and 7.4) and to the fact that this campaign was planned as vengeance for Marathon. Xerxes received from his father the legacy of a war against Greece, as well as that of another war against Egypt, but the focus is upon the Greek campaigns, and the Egyptian campaign is described in only two short sentences (7.7).

The beginning of the Xerxes *logoi* is thus a very clear example of elements belonging to the royal chronicle being subordinated to a historical pattern, in this case the pattern of the campaign *logos*. The legacy of Darius overshadows in importance the question of succession, and his death in 7.4 causes no major break

[142] The connection of 7.1 with the preceding is firm: in 6.116=118.1, Datis and Artaphernes had returned to Asia after the defeat at Marathon; they brought with them the Eretrians as slaves, as Darius had commanded (6.119.1, cf. 94.2). In 7.1.1, how-ever, we return to an earlier period, when Darius receives a message about Marathon (it should be noted that this sentence is merely the second clause of a *men-de* sentence, the first part of which, in 6.140.2, summarizes the capture of Lemnos, another "early" event). Now a message had not been mentioned previously, and Hude's conjecture of the definite article before ἀγγελίη (ἐπειδή CR: ἐπεὶ δέ rell.: ἐπεὶ δὲ ἡ Hude, *alii*) should not be taken in this sense, but rather (as Professor Walton Morris points out to me) in the sense of "the expected message." 5.108.1 is not a parallel here, for there a message had been mentioned: 5.105.1. The message must be understood by analogy to other messages, such as that received by Darius about the burning of Sardis, which event is actually referred to here (see 5.105=108.1), or the messages sent by Xerxes to Persia before and after his defeat at Salamis. It is also to be understood that Darius now desires to campaign in person: above, notes 88 and 115.

[143] Ch. I, 23.

in the narrative. Hence we may group 7.1-4 with the following narrative, which clearly forms a section on causation and motivation.

(a) *Aitiê- and Planning Section* (7.1-18). After the *Legacy of Darius and Succession of Xerxes* (7.1-4), the following section on *The Persuasion of Xerxes by Mardonius, the Aleuadae, and the Peisistratids* (7.5-6) is attached to the former by the motif of Xerxes' initial unwillingness to fight Greece, a motif which later develops into that of Xerxes' ambivalence. The persuasion section combines the motifs of expansionism and vengeance, in the speech of Mardonius, with that of Greek provocation, in the entreaties of the Aleuadae and Peisistratids. In this combination of motivating factors Herodotus follows his own well-established causation pattern.[144] In addition there is here the first mention of the important motif of the joining of continents by the bridging of the Hellespont (7.6.4).[145]

After the mention of the Egyptian campaign (7.7), Xerxes holds a *Council of Persians* (7.8-11).[146] The scene duplicates the previous persuasion scene, and its connection with the preceding narrative is weak. Its real importance lies not in the discussion of the advisability of the Greek campaign, but in the description of Xerxes' motives and the summary of Persian historical ambitions in general. In a sense, therefore, the scene gives a complete description of the causes of the Persian Wars, and from this point of view it is a summary of the whole work.

The Council Scene is introduced by the following statements:

> Xerxes . . ., when he was about to undertake the campaign against Athens, called a council of his Persian nobles, in order to hear their opinions and to speak out his wishes before all. (7.8.1)

The peculiarity of this statement lies in the inconsistency that Xerxes wants to announce his campaign, while at the same time he asks for advice. His speech before the council thus combines planning with a mention of preparations, which properly belong in the following section. We have here an "enjambement" similar to that noted in the Scythian *Logos*.[147] At the end of his

[144] *Causation* 273.
[145] *Action*, 19-27.
[146] For the interpretation of the Council, see *Action* 30 ff., and *Causation* 274 ff.
[147] Above, 108.

speech Xerxes asks his nobles to be ready to come with an army at a time yet to be specified, and he promises prizes to the best-prepared commander (7.8d.1). The motif of the awarding of prizes is later used to frame the preparations section.[148]

The Dreams of Xerxes and Artabanus (7.12-18) complement the Council, to which they are attached by the motif of Xerxes' ambivalence. Having decided not to fight Greece, Xerxes is now forced by a dream figure to go on the campaign.[149]

(b) *Preparations Section* (7.19-26.2). This section begins with yet another dream by Xerxes, in which he sees himself crowned with an olive wreath, branches of which reach over the world, when the whole wreath suddenly disappears. This dream does not belong with the preceding group, but is one of a series of "empire dreams" which recur throughout the work.[150] Next we hear that the Persian nobles return to their homelands, eager to win Xerxes' prizes (7.19.2), and this statement is followed by a general description of the four years of preparations, in the form of an internal proem (7.20-21) that stresses preparations especially at the end.[151] The main feature of the section is the digging of the Mt. Athos canal (7.22-24). At the end, there is a brief account of the preparation of cables for Xerxes' bridges, and of food depots in Thrace and Macedonia (7.25).

The section shows a strong enjambement with the next, or march, section. Some preparations (no doubt contemporaneous with the first stages of the march) are left for the next section, among them the building of the Hellespontine bridges (7.33-37.1).[152] That section itself overlaps, as it were, with the preparations section, for the beginning of the march ·is mentioned before the reference to prizes (7.26.1-2). Despite this peculiarity of arrangement, the initial sentence of the march section demands our starting Xerxes' march at Critalla in Cappadocia rather than, as is sometimes done, at Sardis (i.e. in 7.41). The initial sentence reads as follows:

> While these were accomplishing their prescribed task, at that time the whole army, gathered together, traveled with Xerxes to Sardis, having started from Critalla in Cappadocia. (7.26.1)

[148] Hdt. 7.19.2 and 26.2.
[149] For the interpretation of the Dream Scene, see *Action* 33 ff.
[150] *Tat und Geschichte* 523, note 48; above, 92, and note 41.
[151] Ch. II, 63-64. Similar topics, Thuc. 6.31.1-3 (Sicilian Expedition).
[152] *Tat und Geschichte* 506, note 15.

Between the end of the preparations and the beginning of the march there is thus the unusual phenomenon of parallel action for a short stretch. The idea (and no doubt the actual fact) of the arrangement is that preparations are still being carried out until the moment of Xerxes' departure from Sardis.

It may be noted in passing that the internal proem (7.20-21) contains a comparison of the expedition of Xerxes with former campaigns, stressing vengeance and mutual warfare between Asia and Europe, and further that it emphasizes the river motif, which is then taken up by the story of the Mt. Athos canal and by the bridging of the Hellespont.[153]

(c) *The March of Xerxes to the Confines of Greece* (7.26.1-130). This gigantic section, one of the best compositions in Herodotus, is based, as is natural, entirely on the principle of the paratactic series with irregular interruptions. These latter nevertheless achieve a certain balance by a number of internal correspondences. Following the principle of accounting, wherever possible, for the whereabouts of the king (a principle used consistently for Eastern campaigns),[154] Herodotus shows us the separate stages of Xerxes' march, and follows the movement of both army and navy in great detail throughout the last three books. As we shall see, these later sections are of great importance for the overall organization of the narrative that deals with the Persian Wars. The outline of the march section from Cappadocia to Therma is as follows:

I. 7.26-32: March of army from Critalla to Sardis.
    27-29: First meeting with Pythius the Lydian, at Celaenae in Phrygia.
    30-31: March from Celaenae to Sardis.
    32: Sending of new heralds into Greece to ask again for earth and water.
II. 33: Announcement of march to Abydus.
    33-37.1: Building of bridges at Hellespont.
        (33: Story of Artayctes, a reference to the end of the work, 9.116).
        (35.2: The lashing of the Hellespont, a reference to the river motif).[155]

[153] See also Ch. II, 63-64.
[154] Above, notes 34, 88, and 115.
[155] On the lashing of the Hellespont, see *Action* 28. Herodotus moralizes a tale that perhaps referred to a magic ritual: H. J. Rose, *CQ* 34 (1940) 83.

37.1-43: March from Sardis to Abydus.

    37.2: Omen (eclipse of the sun).

    38-39: Second meeting with Pythius the Lydian, at Sardis.

    40-41: Order of march, foreshadowing the order of troops crossing the Hellespont, 7.55.

    42.2-43.2: Xerxes at Ilium and panic of army (cf. Artabanus' warning, 7.10e).

III. 44-53: Viewing of navy and boat race (cf. Darius at the Pontus, 4.85.1).

    45-52: Conversation of Xerxes and Artabanus (cf. Artabanus and Darius, 4.83.1-2).[156]

    53: Xerxes addresses his generals.[157]

IV. 54-57: Crossing of Hellespont.

    56.2: Saying of a Hellespontine.

    57: Two omens, the second told in retrospect and connected with Xerxes' stay at Sardis.

V. 58-105: From the Hellespont to Doriscus in Thrace.

    58: First distinction between itinerary of navy and army.

    59-100: Review of army and navy (roster of forces):

        61-83: infantry,

        84-88: cavalry,

        89-99: navy,

        100: review.

    100-104: First conversation between Xerxes and Demaratus (valor and poverty of Spartans).

VI. 105-27: March to the confines of Greece (from Doriscus to Therma). This falls into two main sections:

a. 106-20: March to Acanthus.

    106: Story of Mascames, governor of Doriscus (cf. Darius' pride in Megabazus, 4.143.2).

---

[156] *Action* 41 ff. For the parallelism between the Scythian campaign and this section, see Powell, *Hist. Herodotus* 56 ff.

[157] Another general's speech is that of Themistocles before Salamis, reported in summary in 8.83.1-2; see below, Ch. VI, notes 91 and 127.

The individual subdivisions of the march are clearly separated in most cases by initial statements, but the real unity of the narrative is achieved by the incidental stories with their multiple themes and cross references.[159] The measured stages of the march are articulated by static pictures which have a symbolic significance. Thus the arrival at Celaenae is followed by the first meeting with Pythius, and the arrival at Sardis, by the second sending of heralds, as well as by the more elaborate complex of the building of the bridges at the Hellespont. The march from Sardis to Abydos begins with an omen and with the second meeting with Pythius, and it ends with the elaborate complex of the viewing of the armament and the conversation with Artabanus. The crossing of the Hellespont introduces the march from Abydos to Doriscus,[160] but is itself kept distinct from it by an anecdote and two further omens. The great step from Asia into Europe is thus not very clearly isolated, but is nonetheless underlined by a change in advisers (Artabanus is left behind in Asia and Demaratus replaces him), by repeated mentions that the march is from then on directed against Greece (7.105; 108.1), and by the parallelism of the viewing of the armament before the crossing and the review of army and navy at Doriscus. At the Hellespont, the navy joins

---

[158] On the triple route, see How and Wells *ad loc.*

[159] *Action* 21 f.

[160] *Ibid.* 23.

Xerxes' army, and from now on Herodotus carefully traces the course of each. After Doriscus, the march sections are more liberally interlarded with significant stories (such as the stories of underlings loyal to the king), but here also we have static pictures at the end of each stretch of the march. The arrival at Acanthus is followed by the feeding of the army, and the arrival at Therma by Xerxes' visit to Pieria. Leaving aside minor detail, we may say that the basic structure comprises march sections alternating with static pictures. The stories contained in the static sections are remarkable not only for their interconnections, but also for their relations with other portions of the narrative, especially with the preceding parts, and thus they show the weight of tradition upon Xerxes.

(d) *Greek Preparations Logos* (7.131-78). As was mentioned in Chapter I, the internal structure of this *logos* is entirely dependent on the connection with Persian action.[161] The arrangement thus makes vivid the effect upon the patriotic Greeks of Xerxes' impending arrival.

The initial connection with the preceding *logos* is made very skillfully, but there are also some difficulties of interpretation. The March of Xerxes ends with Xerxes' visit to Pieria, after which he returns to Tempe (7.130.3); it is at this point, while Xerxes is standing at the threshold of Greece, as it were,[162] that Herodotus adds the Greek Preparations *Logos*. In 7.131 he returns to the visit in Pieria, with the first of a series of short statements and stories:

1. (Xerxes had) spent a good many days in Pieria . . ., and the heralds who had been sent into Greece with the request for earth and water had returned, some of them empty-handed, others bringing earth and water.[163]

[161] Above, 39. On the Greek Preparations *Logos*, see Macan, *VII-IX*, Vol. 2, 188 ff.; Pohlenz, *Herodot* 134 ff.; Legrand, Budé 7.129 ff. (but I do not think that the arrival of the heralds precedes the stay in Pieria, *ibid.* 131, note 1); Myres, *Herodotus* 231 ff.

[162] Thessaly is the traditional boundary of Greece: cf. Hdt. 7.172.2, and e.g. M. Cary in *CAH* 3.598.

[163] Xerxes' stay in Pieria is here referred to again, in repetition of 7.128.1-130.3. The purpose is to connect the Greek Preparations *Logos* with the March of Xerxes, cf. Ch. I, 39. At the end, the *logos* is once more connected with the stay in Pieria by a synchronism between the latter and the movement of the Greek troops to Artemisium and Thermopylae (7.177). The length of Xerxes' stay in Pieria should probably be estimated at no more than eight or nine days, and perhaps less. The total time spent on the journey from Therma to Thermopylae (Malis) was 14 days: see the chart in

Thus Xerxes was met by his heralds while sightseeing in Pieria. A series of stories now shifts the field of attention from the Persians to the Greeks:

2. List of Greek states which gave earth and water. (132.1)
3. Oath of the Greeks (Herodotus gives no date for it) against medizing Greeks. (132.2)[164]
4. Xerxes had sent no heralds to Athens and Sparta, since these cities had killed Darius' heralds. (133.1)
5. For this crime, no vengeance was taken by the gods on the Athenians, but Sparta suffered. (134-37) (This story also stresses the theme of freedom vs. slavery.)
6. Herodotus returns to his "former argument." (137.3)

The precise point of attachment is here the return of the heralds from Greece and the mention of medism (7.131 and 132.1): this parallels the attachment found earlier in the Aeginetan *Logos* (6.48.2-49). But what is the "former argument" to which Herodotus is now (7.137.3) returning? According to the principles of ring composition, it can only be one of the first three points listed above, probably the mention of the heralds (No. 1).[165] For Herodotus continues:

7. And (*de*) the campaign of the Great King was nominally directed against Athens, but actually pertained to all of Greece. (7.138.1)

This statement, recalling a number of similar statements at the

---

Grundy, *Great Pers. War* 320, repeated by How and Wells 2.372-73, section A, except that the fleet's arrival at Aphetae should fall on day 16. Myres, *Herodotus* 255-56, follows Macan, *VII-IX*, Vol. 2, 275, but that is a reconstruction. Of the 14 days, I should estimate a minimum of five or six for the actual travel (25-30 miles per day, for 150 miles, plus the horse race of 7.196), leaving the rest for the stay in Pieria. I mention this in order to show that the stay in Pieria, although a convenient literary motif, is clearly a part of Herodotus' actual chronology. There is, nevertheless, a subtle dramatic use of time, for between the return of the heralds and the Greek movement to Thermopylae there can be but a week at most.

[164] In modern times, the oath has been variously dated: see How and Wells on 7.132.2. Further, Hauvette, *Hérodote* 328 ff.; L. Robert, *Études épigraphiques et philologiques* (1938) 311; G. Busolt, *Griechische Geschichte*[2] 2 (Gotha 1895) 654. It is this passage that has given rise to the idea that the whole section (7.131-44) observes no chronology. However, nothing in Herodotus' narrative prevents making the oath contemporary with the return of the heralds to Pieria, and Herodotus may have thought it so. See also below, note 169.

[165] For the different possibilities, see Macan, *VII-IX, ad loc.*, and Vol. 2, Appendix III. Van Groningen, *Comp. litt.* 51, thinks the reference is to the march of Xerxes (i.e. 7.128.1, at the latest?).

time of Darius' attacks on Greece,[166] should probably be understood as an explanation of why Xerxes and Darius had sent
messengers into Greece. Herodotus then turns to the period before
Xerxes' invasion, when the Greeks first heard about it:

8. At that time those that had given earth and water (to Darius)[167]
   were "of good cheer," the others were afraid. (7.138.2)
9. Herodotus' own judgment on the roles of Athens and Sparta
   in the conflict. (139)
10. The oracles given to Athens before the invasion, and the role
    of Themistocles. (140-44)[168]

This is followed by the actual beginning of the Preparations
Logos. Thus we find here a number of stories, not all in chronological order,[169] but on the whole leading from Xerxes' stay in
Pieria back in time to the Greek preparations. The Greek stories
depend on two statements concerning the Persian narrative: (1) the
heralds returned to Xerxes, and (2) the campaign affected Athens

---

[166] Hdt. 6.44.1; 6.48.2; 6.94.1, cf. 7.1 and the speeches in the Persian Council
(*Causation* 274-75). The demand for earth and water is symbolic of subjection to the
Persian World Empire, and thus belongs with the phrase "pertained to all of Greece."
Note that the Athenians had thrown Darius' messengers into a pit, while the Spartans
had drowned in a well those sent to them, and thus the King received "earth and water"
(7.133.1; G. de Sanctis, *RFIC*, n.s. 8 [1930] 295). Cf. now K. Kraft, *Hermes* 92 (1964)
144-53.

[167] Macan, *VII-IX*, on 7.138, line 4, argues that Herodotus has here revised his
narrative, since it does not agree with 7.131, but our passage should be compared with
7.133.1, the mention of the early embassy under Darius.

[168] Herodotus clearly puts the oracles, and with them the whole section from 7.138
(second sentence) to 7.145.1 (a section which he says deals with events that happened
πρὸ πολλοῦ of Xerxes' invasion), in 481 B.C., while Xerxes was still in Susa; see
Rev. Crahay 209, and J. Labarbe, *La Loi navale de Thémistocle* (Paris 1957) 111, note 1.
I cannot here discuss the question of the Herodotean date of 7.144.3, which Professor
M. Jameson assumes to be a reference to the purported Themistocles decree; cf.
Hesperia 29 (1960) 201 f. and 204. It seems that this paragraph must also be dated to
481 B.C., whereas the decree has the dramatic date of early summer, 480.

[169] The relative chronology, however, is clearly marked: A. *Stay of Xerxes in Pieria*;
arrival of heralds; list of medizing states (our Nos. 1 and 2). With this may belong
No. 3 (see above, note 164). B. The killing of Darius' heralds, and subsequent events
down to the time of the Peloponnesian War (Nos. 4 and 5). C. The "*former argument*"
(our Nos. 6-7). D. The πρὸ πολλοῦ section (Nos. 8, 9, and 10), including 7.144.3 (see
last note). From 7.145.1, the sequence is chronological down to the stay of Xerxes in
Pieria again (7.177). Consequently, from D onward, we have an orderly sequence
(as appears from the outline in the text above); C is then a repetition of A, occasioned
by the story of the killing of the earlier heralds, i.e. B. It is evident that much confusion can be avoided if we do not follow those who would start the Greek Preparations
Logos with 7.128.

and all of Greece. This double connection has caused some apparent obscurity in the narrative.

The Preparations *Logos* proper (145 ff.) deals with the councils of the Greeks at the Isthmus in several phases:

(7.131-37: Introduction to *logos*.)

(7.138-44: Athenians consult Delphic oracle, while Xerxes is in Susa.) PHASE I

7.145.1-2: First Council of Panhellenic League,[170] while Xerxes is in Sardis. PHASE II

146-48.1:   Spies sent into Asia.
              147.2-3: The grain ships at Abydos.

148.1-153.1: Embassy to Argos.
              150-52:   Other stories about Argive medism.

153.1-167: Embassy to Gelo of Syracuse.
              163.2-164: Cadmus, the emissary of Gelo.
              165-67:   The battle of Himera.

168:         The same embassy calls on Corcyra.

169-71:   Embassy to Crete.
              170-71:   Minos in Sicily, and depopulations of Crete.

7.172-74: Greeks called by Thessalians to defend Thessaly, while Xerxes is crossing the Hellespont. Change of plans and return to Isthmus. PHASE III.

7.175-78: Second Council at Isthmus, and plan to defend Thermopylae and Artemisium, while Xerxes is in Pieria. PHASE IV.

178.1-2:   The Delphic prayer to the winds.

After the introductions (7.131-44), the *logos* describes two councils of the Panhellenic League at the Isthmus; these are in three stages that are synchronized with the march of Xerxes from Sardis to the Hellespont and thence to Pieria. The last section of the introductions, dealing with the Athenian consultation of the oracle, although not expressly synchronized, should be connected approximately with the sending of the heralds and thus with

---

[170] Herodotus says only, "When those Greeks who held the better counsel for Greece had been assembled in the same place . . ." Despite Pausanias 3.12.5, where the meeting is said to have taken place in Sparta, I assume that this sentence looks forward to 7.172.1, where the Panhellenic Council at the Isthmus is mentioned. See Ch. II, 52, on Herodotus' manner of having a vague reference refer forward to a more precise one. Cf. also Stein on 7.145, lines 2 ff.

Xerxes' stay in Susa.[171] The main theme of the *logos* is the contrast, under the pressure of Xerxes' advance, between patriotism and medism, the first embodied in the Athenian reaction to the oracles and the story of the spies, and the second, in the Greek embassies.

The story of the Delphic prayers to the winds (178) closes the *logos* and is to be connected with other stories in the account of the campaign of Xerxes which emphasize the winds as helpers on the side of the Greeks.[172]

(e) *March of Xerxes from Therma to Thermopylae and Artemisium* (7.179-200). This continuation of the great March Section is not unified, but consists of two separate *logoi*, the first of which gives the itinerary of the Persian navy from Therma to Aphetae (7.179-95), while the second sketchily traces the march of the army from Therma to the Malian gulf, i.e. to the battle position at Thermopylae (7.196-200). The second section in turn shows "enjambement" in that it emphasizes primarily the arrival of Xerxes and describes in detail the geography of the Malian area. Herodotus' compositional problem at this point is to bring the navy to the fore, since the fate of Greece (according to his interpretation) was decided on the seas. We have seen earlier that the distinction of land and sea forces begins with the joining of the two at the Hellespont. In the March Section that contrast is still of minor importance; now, with the approach of the great sea and land battles, the distinction becomes the means for setting the five great battles in their proper relation and for giving to each its correct interpretation. The two themes of land and sea mentioned by Artabanus to Xerxes before the crossing of the Hellespont (7.49.2) are in fact basic to the structure of the last three books.

Salamis was to Herodotus the central battle of the Persian Wars, and therefore he stresses the approach of the Persian navy more than that of the army. Indicative of this preference is the placing of the itinerary of the navy before the march of the army, despite the fact that the army left Therma eleven days before the navy (7.183.2). We have seen earlier that the *logos* of the advance of the navy centers upon the storm off Magnesia.[173] This storm

---

[171] Above, note 168.

[172] The winds: *Tat und Geschichte* 515. Cf. also the winds at Salamis, which brought about the fulfilment of an oracle (8.96.2). The winds at Salamis are discussed by N. G. L. Hammond, *JHS* 76 (1956) 49-50. Cf. also Instinsky in Marg, *Herodot* 490 ff.

[173] See the outline, Ch. II, 72.

parallels that during the battle of Artemisium (8.12), and the present naval section is thus in effect an introduction to that battle. In Herodotus' account, the sea action of Artemisium and its antecedents frame the battle of Thermopylae, which is thus isolated from the rest of the action. A further element that connects the advance of the navy with the following battles is the reckoning, prior to the account of the storm at Magnesia, of the totals of Xerxes' sea and land forces (7.184-87). Detached from the army and navy list in the great March Section (7.61 ff.), where it would have had its proper place, this computation is remarkable for reversing the order of army and navy so that it is foremost a totaling of naval forces, and thus it introduces Artemisium before introducing Thermopylae.[174]

The march of the army (7.196-200) is in turn an introduction to Thermopylae. At the beginning we find Xerxes already at Malis, so that a case could be made for beginning the *logoi* on Thermopylae here rather than later in 7.201, as I have done. The initial statement reads:

> The barbarian navy, except for the fifteen ships which I have said Sandoces was commanding, arrived at Aphetae, but Xerxes and the land army, having traveled through Thessaly and Achaea, had invaded Malis three days before. (7.196)

Particularly striking is the omission of any reference to the actual departure of the land army from the Thermaic gulf. Thessaly and Achaea are mentioned to introduce two stories in this section, the contest of Thessalian and Persian cavalry, and the human sacrifice at the sanctuary of Laphystian Zeus at Halus. This is followed in turn by a lengthy account of Malian geography (7.198-200), which should be connected with the description of Thermopylae proper during the Greek Preparations *Logos* (7.176).

The main function of the two *logoi* is thus to bring the attacker to the field of battle. The naval section is presently continued with the roster of Greek forces at Artemisium (8.1), and the march of the land army is likewise continued by a roster of Greek forces at Thermopylae (7.202). Thus the two battles really begin at 7.179 (Artemisium) and 7.196 (Thermopylae), but I have adopted a simpler division, by which each battle begins with the account of the defending Greeks.

[174] Ch. VI, 254 ff.

(f) *Battle of Thermopylae* (7.201-39). The account of the battle is a group of *logoi* arranged in a circular composition, with Leonidas' decision to forfeit his life as the central part.[175] This account is framed by the second and third conversations of Xerxes with Demaratus, and it ends with the earlier message of Demaratus from Susa to the Spartans, warning them of the impending invasion (7.239).[176] The second conversation, before the battle, stresses Spartan law, but the third looks forward to Salamis in the discussion of possible naval action against Cythera (7.235).[177]

(g) *Battle of Artemisium* (8.1-26). The complicated structure of this group of stories, which describe three separate minor engagements, and their relation to the narrative of Thermopylae, will be discussed in Chapter VI. The battle is framed by two tricks of Themistocles, the first, the bribery of his colleagues with Euboean money (8.4.2-8.5), and the second, the announcement of his plan to bring the Ionians over to the Greek side (8.19.1). At the end, the Persian navy visits the battlefield of Thermopylae (8.24-25), and the whole group is separated from the following march section by the story of the celebration of the Olympic festival (8.26).

(h) *March of Land Army from Thermopylae to Boeotia, and to Delphi* (8.27-39). This short section is a filler which connects Artemisium and Salamis. It is not fully developed at the end, since the arrival of the Persians at Athens is told in the Greek section before

---

[175] Myres, *Herodotus* 112 and 129. Ch. VI, 259 ff.

[176] The chapter has been much criticized. Stein on 7.239 thinks it a later addition by Herodotus, not brought into connection with the preceding narrative, and he brackets the first sentence. Macan, *VII-IX ad loc.*, How and Wells, and others, follow Krüger in considering the whole chapter an interpolation. Jacoby, *RE* Suppl. 2.457, considers 239 genuine in substance, but thinks with Stein that 238 is a later addition by Herodotus. Pohlenz, *Herodot* 68, note 1, and 141, note 3, successfully defends the received text. Cf. also Myres, *Herodotus* 254-55. Powell, *Translation*, considers both 239 and 220 later additions. The truth of the matter is that the anecdote is postponed, being shifted from its proper place to the end of the *logos* in the same manner as the defense of the Alcmaeonids (6.121 ff., cf. 115); see also Ch. II, 61 ff. 7.238 is also unexceptionable, although we must add, as Stein indicates, a particle (δέ, δή, ὦν, or the like) after δῆλα.

[177] The occupation of Cythera (or more generally the harassment of the Peloponnese by sea) is a commonplace of Athenian strategic thinking even before the Peloponnesian War (see How and Wells on 7.235.2), but here the conversation has the function of turning the reader's attention to the following naval actions, and specifically to the fact that the Athenians at Salamis saved the Peloponnese from Persian naval attack. This last had been stated by Herodotus in 7.139.3-4; cf. also 9.9.2 and Thuc. 1.73.4.

Salamis (8.50, with a reference to 8.34). Likewise, the movement of the navy is told only in connection with the battle of Salamis (8.66.1, with a reference to 8.25.3). The change in structure, which begins with the narrative of Salamis, thus disturbs, at this point, the orderly description of the advance of the army and navy.

At the beginning, the march of the Persians is introduced by a lengthy account of hostilities between Thessalians and Phocians, which leads to a Thessalian offer to guide the Persians through central Greece (8.31); only at this last place is there an announcement of Xerxes' march. The march of the main army is carried only as far as Panopeus in Phocis, where a detachment is sent to Delphi (8.34-35.1). The remainder of the *logos* is devoted to a Persian attempt to capture Delphi, thus continuing the Delphic motif of the end of the Greek Preparations *Logos* (7.178).

(i) *Battle of Salamis* (8.40-125). In this remarkable composition, the battle description itself is quite short (84-96), but before and after, Herodotus has made use of every device to build up a large picture. Like the battles of Thermopylae and Artemisium, this battle begins with a Greek *logos* (8.40-64) on battle preparations, which contains a number of councils. This is followed by a *logos* on Persian battle preparations (8.66-70), with the omen seen by Dicaeus and Demaratus at Eleusis placed in the pause (8.65). A second Greek section (8.70-83) describes further Greek vacillation, further councils ending with the forced decision to fight, and an address by Themistocles to the troops (8.83).[178]

The aftereffects of the battle consist of alternate Persian and Greek sections. Xerxes' plan to take flight (8.97-107) is followed without a break by the Greek siege of Andros (8.108-112), a section that parallels Miltiades' ill-fated attack on Paros after Marathon (6.133 ff.). Xerxes' flight (113-20) is carried as far as the return crossing of the Hellespont. The final section (121-25) deals with the awarding of prizes among the Greeks and ends with an anecdote about Themistocles.

This splintering of the sections on the results of Salamis is determined by the necessity of describing pursuit as well as retreat, the affairs of the victors as well as those of the vanquished. It is the direct result of the about-face of the narrative at Salamis.

(j) *Return of Artabazus from the Hellespont to Mardonius* (8.126-29). The section is introduced as follows:

[178] On this speech, see above, note 157.

This happened (in the manner described above), and Artabazus son of Pharnaces, a Persian of some account previous to this, but after the battle of Plataea of even greater account, accompanied the king to the straits with six thousand of Mardonius' chosen troops. (8.126.1)

The remainder of the *logos* is concerned with Artabazus' return to Mardonius, with two campaign notices detailing his capture of Olynthus and his attempt to take Potidaea. His failure in the latter place is seen as a punishment by Poseidon (129.3).

This short *logos* on a person not hitherto prominent[179] clearly looks forward, since it mentions Plataea and connects the retreat of Xerxes with the coming campaign of Mardonius. Artabazus later appears in the battle of Plataea (where he refuses to participate), and his return to Asia closes the account of that battle (9.89). Thus, the *logos* of his return to Mardonius may be said to initiate the account of Plataea, but the break is a weak one, since Mardonius' campaign is seen by Herodotus as an event of definitely lesser importance than the campaign of Xerxes himself.

(k) *Movements of the Persian and Greek Fleets between Salamis and Mycale* (8.130-32). The Persian fleet winters in Cyme, and in the spring it moves to Samos, where it guards Ionia (8.130). Concurrently, the Greek fleet moves to Aegina and is persuaded by the first Ionian embassy to proceed as far as Delos. We leave the two fleets at Samos and at Delos: "thus fear guarded the interval between them" (131-32). The further movement of the Greek fleet introduces the narrative of Mycale (9.90), with the account of Plataea intervening.

The two short *logoi* (j and k) outlined above are all that Herodotus gives us as an introduction to the campaign of Mardonius. Both are clearly related in form to patterns applied previously to the great battles. The Return of Artabazus is a short march section (his campaigns are subordinated to that idea) connecting Xerxes' campaign with that of Mardonius. The Movements of the Fleets connect Salamis with Mycale in such a way that the land battle of Plataea is framed by naval action. Thus the relation between Plataea and Mycale is exactly the same as that between Thermopylae and Artemisium. As has been pointed out by previous scholars, the accounts of the five battles exhibit a symmetrical arrangement, with Salamis at the center. In this scheme naval

[179] Artabazus had been mentioned only once, 7.66.2.

operations are used to frame the operations on land.[180]

(1) *Actions of Mardonius in the Spring of 479* (8.133-9.18). I group under this heading three short *logoi* or sections, each beginning with Mardonius' initiative, and all preparatory to the battle of Plataea. Here again we note the lack of an incisive break at the beginning of Mardonius' campaign. The sections connect the end of Book 8 with the beginning of Book 9, and between them there is such a strong parallelism that the book division in this place is rather unfortunate.[181]

i. At the beginning of spring, Mardonius sends a messenger to consult a number of Greek sanctuaries, and then dispatches Alexander of Macedon to Athens with an offer of alliance (8.133-44). Herodotus was somewhat embarrassed about the exact connection between the consultation and the message to Athens (since he did not know the text of the oracle given to Mardonius), but he had no doubt that there was such a connection (136.1 and 3). The offer brought by Alexander resulted in the double consultation of the Athenians with Alexander and with the Spartans (whose arrival was also motivated by an oracle, 141.1), including the great Athenian patriotic speech.[182] Between Alexander's departure from Mardonius and his arrival at Athens there is a *logos* on the origins of the Macedonian dynasty, which should be compared with one of the stories about the origins of the Scythians (137-39, cf. 4.5-6).

ii. Mardonius now reoccupies Athens and sends a second message to the Athenians, who have taken refuge on Salamis (9.1-11). This results in the stoning of the Athenian Lycidas (who was in favor of heeding Mardonius' message), and in an Athenian embassy to Sparta, whose citizens are finally persuaded to assist by sending an army. The pattern in these two sections is very similar, since they both end with consultations among Sparta and Athens for the conduct of the war. Thus the Greek preparations are here split up and attached to actions by Mardonius.

iii. Mardonius' march from Athens to Thebes (9.12-15.3).

[180] On the symmetrical scheme, see Ch. VI, 254 ff.

[181] Cf. above, note 2. Note especially the parallelism between sections i and ii below. Cf. also L. Solmsen in Marg, *Herodot* 650 ff.

[182] The debate may well have been the model for the speeches at the Spartan assembly in Thuc. Book 1. Jacoby, *RE* Suppl. 2.494, however, compares it rather with the debate of the Corinthians and Corcyreans; cf. A. Deffner, *Die Rede bei Herodot und ihre Weiterbildung bei Thukydides* (Diss. Munich 1933) 29.

This section is prefaced, as it were, by the warning on the approach of the Spartans, sent by Argos to Mardonius (9.12), a message which determines Mardonius' departure from Athens to meet the Greeks in Boeotia. The advice has no introductory statement (they are missing in a number of these short sections). The structure of the account (Greek initiative and then the main movement of the Persians) parallels the March of Xerxes' Army from Thermopylae to Boeotia (h, above). The further movements of Mardonius are determined by two further messages: he is clearly losing the initiative.[183]

After Mardonius' arrival at Thebes, the section closes with the banquet of Attaginus, where the Persian defeat at Plataea is fore-told (9.15.4-16), and with Mardonius' mock battle with the Phocians,[184] the latter event stressing the motif of Persian cavalry versus Greek, an element which is important in the battle of Plataea with its cavalry skirmishes.

(m) *March of Greeks to Cithaeron* (9.19 and 20-24). The brief description of the march of the Spartans to Athens and of the combined forces to Cithaeron is followed immediately by the first in a series of cavalry skirmishes. In the first skirmish the Persian Masistius is killed, to the grief of the Persians. It would be possible to begin the group of battle *logoi* with the section containing this skirmish. However, Herodotus uses the skirmish primarily to motivate the advance of the Greeks to Plataea, and therefore I prefer, perhaps arbitrarily, to begin the battle *logoi* with the next section, which opens with the Greek movement to Plataea. This seems preferable, despite the fact that the present *logos* is the first independent Greek action in the Plataean narrative.[185] Again, the vagueness of the breaks is characteristic of the account of Mardonius' campaign. The problem here is similar to the beginning of Thermopylae (see e, above).

(n) *Battle of Plataea* (9.25-89). This difficult group of stories, of

---

[183] There are, all told, three messages: 9.12.1 (Argives); 14 (source not specified); 15.1 (source also not specified).

[184] Hdt. 9.17-18. The exact meaning of the mock battle is obscure (it was in fact obscure to Herodotus, 18.2), but stories in support of a "cavalry motif" abound in the work: e.g. 1.80 (Lydian horse and Persian camels in the battle of Sardis); 4.128.3 (Scythian campaign); 6.112.2 (Marathon); 7.84-87 (Persian cavalry); 7.196 (Persian and Thessalian cavalry in contest); 8.28 (Phocians and Thessalians). This motif finds its climax in the account of the battle of Plataea; see Ch. VI, 291. Cf. also A. E. Wardman, *Historia* 8 (1959) 56 ff.

[185] See Ch. VI, 290.

which the battle description itself is only a relatively small part (9.58-65), will be fully analyzed in Chapter VI.[186]

(o) *Battle of Mycale* (9.90-113). The battle *logoi* are introduced by a clear introductory statement:

> (Artabazus) returned to Asia, and on the very day on which the defeat at Plataea took place, there also happened to take place (the other) at Mycale in Ionia. (9.90.1)

The structure of this battle is much simpler than that of Plataea. We have first the movement of the Greek fleet from Delos to the Samian Heraeum, a movement requested by the second Ionian embassy; to this is immediately attached the movement of the Persians to Mycale (9.90-97). The battle account itself is short (9.100-105). Introduced by the account of the rumor concerning the battle of Plataea and the coincidence of the existence of sanctuaries of Demeter at Plataea and at Mycale, it follows a standard pattern and ends with praise of the best men. The aftereffects of the battle consist of a short section on the Greeks who, after a council on the fate of the Ionians, depart for the Hellespont (106), and another on the return of the Persians (107).

It is to the return of the Persians that a number of Persian stories are added, one of which concerns Xerxes. On the way home a quarrel takes place between Masistes, brother of Xerxes, and a certain Artayntes (9.107.1-3); after their arrival at Sardis, we rejoin Xerxes, who proceeds to destroy his brother Masistes out of love for the latter's wife (9.108-13). The account of Xerxes thus frames both the campaign of Mardonius and the battle of Mycale. In the course of the story Xerxes returns to Susa and finally sends an army to the East, where the actual murder takes place.

(p) *The Greeks at Abydos and Sestus* (9.114-22). The last *logos* of the work describes the further pursuit by the Greeks of their victories, and is thus simply a development of the aftereffects of battle added to the account of Mycale. The islands and the Hellespont, as Herodotus had said before the battle of Mycale, were the prizes of that battle (9.101.3). After Mycale, the Athenians win a point over the Spartans in admitting the Ionian islands to the Hellenic League (106.4), and then the entire navy proceeds to the Hellespont. This last *logos* begins with their arrival at Abydos (114.1), where they find the bridges destroyed.

[186] 289-99.

At that point the Spartan contingent returns home, but the Athenians besiege Sestus, the European bridgehead at the Hellespont. The *Siege of Sestus* (9.114.2-122) is a regular campaign *logos* which starts, after its announcement, with the defenders' preparations, among which occurs the story of Artayctes and his mistreatment of the sanctuary of the Greek hero Protesilaus, who had participated in the Trojan War. The aftereffects of the successful siege are primarily the capture of Artayctes and his crucifixion at the Hellespont, and the return of the Greeks with the remnants of the cables to be dedicated in their sanctuaries. The two unequal sections of this *logos* (the arrival of the Greeks at Abydos, and the siege of Sestus) are thus held together by the motif of the cables. Since the cables were not found at Abydos, having been brought by a Persian to Sestus, they fell to the victors when Sestus was taken.[187]

The *logos* closes with the remark that "in this year" (i.e. 479 B.C.) "nothing in addition to these things happened," a formula employed elsewhere by Herodotus.[188] After this, the work closes with the famous anecdote about the advice given by Cyrus the Founder to the Persians right after the establishment of the Persian empire. This anecdote is attached to the preceding *logos* much as the Arion story is attached to the Croesus *Logos*; the interlocutor of Cyrus was grandfather of Artayctes, the person treated prominently in the Sestus campaign. We have seen many examples of anecdotes closing an account by being placed in the pause. Both with his chronological notation and with his final anecdote, Herodotus treats the end of the work as if it were a pause. This has led many to suppose that the work is in fact unfinished, but it is very doubtful that any other conception of the end of the work was possible for Herodotus, since epilogues were apparently not customary in early prose and poetry.[189]

---

[187] *Action* 26, note 20. In 9.115, ἐνθαῦτα ἦν κεκομικώς refers to Sestus (so rightly How and Wells, whereas Macan and Rawlinson refer it to Cardia).

[188] Much has been written about this innocuous statement. Some have deleted it as an interpolation (Macan; Powell, *Hist. Herodotus* 80). Others have conjectured ἐπί for ἔτι (Werfer, etc.). The sentence is the first half of a connecting sentence, such as are found in 9.41.1; 9.107.3; and especially 6.42.1. The second half of the sentence is missing, of course, since the work comes to an end here: how else should Herodotus have put this idea? On the controversy, see the discussions of the state of completion of the work: above, Introduction, note 17; Pohlenz, *Herodot* 164; Schmid-Stählin 1.2.595 ff.

[189] The lack of epilogues in early Greek literature is discussed by van Groningen, *Comp. litt.* 70 ff. Cf. also Fränkel, *Stileigenheit* 84 and 85.

The two closing features, however, are not chosen arbitrarily. The chronological notation owes its inclusion to the fact that Herodotus had ended his *Histories* by giving a complete account of two full years (480 and 479 B.C.). The Cyrus anecdote recalls the very beginning of Persian rule (and in particular the anecdote in which Cyrus shows the Persians the difference between hard work and the luxury of freedom, 1.125-26),[190] and thus may be said to close the whole story of Persia's rise and expansion. Such closing anecdotes are characteristic of the work. I shall not deal here with the further implications in this story, since they have been discussed by various scholars.[191]

Other elements in the last *logos*, while not formally isolated like the final anecdote, nevertheless close portions of the work by implicit backward references. Among these are the Hellespontine cables, first emphasized in connection with the building of the bridges, the story of Artayctes, first mentioned in the introduction to the same account of the bridges (9.116, cf. 7.33), the council on the Ionians (9.106), which closes the account of Ionian weakness, the reappearance of Xerxes just before this *logos*, the indirect reference to the Trojan War in the mention of Protesilaus (the Trojan War is referred to in the proem, 1.3-4), and finally the repetition of the statement, also made in the proem, that Asia is thought by the Persians to be their own (9.116.3, cf. 1.4.4). In view of these correspondences, and for reasons stated earlier, I may record here once more my opinion (it cannot be more than an

[190] The reader should not be confused by the fact that the meaning of the two stories is nearly contradictory; for in 1.125-26 the Persians choose wealth and leisure, while in 9.122 they are advised against luxury. It is a key idea of Athenian imperial democracy that freedom brings with it rule as well as leisure. That this is a danger is a commonplace of conservative criticism of such imperialism. The two anecdotes thus illuminate a single problem from two different points of view, a method altogether characteristic of Herodotus.

[191] The following is a brief bibliography on this chapter: Jacoby, *RE* Suppl. 2.375-76. H. Fohl, *Tragische Kunst bei Herodot* (Diss. Rostock 1913) 82-84. K. Glaser, "Das Schlusswort des Herodot," *Commentationes Vindobonenses* 1 (1935) 12-20. Schmid-Stählin 1.2.597. L. Weber, *SFIC*, n.s. 11 (1934) 193 ff. Bischoff, *Warner* 73 ff. (=Marg, *Herodot* 670 ff.). W. Schadewaldt, *NJbb* 9 (1933) 249. Pohlenz, *Herodot* 175 ff. A. Lesky, *Gesch. d. griech. Lit.*[2] (Bern and Munich 1963) 488, compares the words of Penia in the *agôn* of Ar. *Plut.* 487 ff., and he contrasts (348) the imperialism of Xerxes in 7.8. L. E. Lord, *CJ* 18 (1922) 73 ff. Van Groningen, *Comp. litt.* 70. Cf. also A. R. Burn, *Persia and the Greeks* (London 1962) 61. T. Sinko's paper on the prologue and epilogue of the *Histories*, *Eos* 50 (1959-60) 3-20, is known to me from the abstract in *BCO* 6, fasc. 2 (1961) 117-19.

opinion) that we have in the last chapters of the work the original ending as Herodotus conceived it.[192]

[192] See above, Ch. I, 43, and Introduction, 8-10. Also this chapter, notes 188 and 189. Herodotus ends his work with the full accounts of two campaign years. Since the Delian League is now thought to have been organized as early as 478 B.C. (see *ATL* 3 [Princeton 1950] 192-93; Hammond, *Hist. Greece* 256), one wonders how Herodotus would have introduced this completely new subject into his work, had he added a whole campaign year (as he would have been obliged to do).

Chapter IV

THE PATTERN OF HISTORY: THE EAST

I

In the preceding chapters, elements of repetition, patterning, and mechanical structure in the *Histories* have been stressed heavily, in the hope that such observations could form the basis for observing similar patterns in Herodotus' understanding of history itself. The form is not an arbitrary creation, but the arrangement of the work embodies Herodotus' perception of repetition, patterning, and structure in the sequence of historical events: history becomes intelligible only when individual happenings are viewed together as parts of an orderly process. Thus the work of Herodotus mirrors reality not only in the individual *logos*, but fundamentally also in the perception of the relations between single *logoi*.

The pattern of history (i.e. the order in which events tend to follow one another) should be seen by the historian in all the events treated in the *Histories*, and not only in the Persian or the Greek accounts. Despite the obvious differences existing between Europe and Asia, between Greeks and barbarians, the two pictures should complement each other in such a way that together they constitute a unified image of human history. Hence we are forced to reject theories that postulate a fundamental difference between Herodotus' description of Asia and his characterization of Greece.[1] The differences are, as we shall see, merely relative, and lie in each case in a change of emphasis on certain aspects of the development of world history. These aspects are present everywhere, though not to the same degree. The next two chapters, the one concerned with the East, the other with the West, are thus simply two parts of a single argument.

The arrangement of *logoi* furnishes Herodotus with a peculiar method of distinguishing periods in history, as is evident in the restriction of subject matter, for the work as a whole, to the period

[1] Cf. Schmid-Stählin 1.2.584-86.

from Croesus to the defeat of the Persians. From the point of view of an ever-present expansionism of the Oriental empires, the establishment by Deioces of the power of Media, and the enlargement of the Median empire by Deioces' successors, constitute the beginning of an era (1.96 ff.). A similar phenomenon occurred, almost simultaneously, in the growth of the Mermnad dynasty in Lydia (1.7 ff.). In this process, Herodotus found in the figure of Croesus the single point where expansion first involved the Greeks. Thus he isolated that period of Oriental expansionism which affected the Greeks. At the end of the period, such a problem did not exist, since the defeat of Xerxes by the Greeks could be interpreted as the final blow to Asiatic expansionism as a whole.

Now within the whole picture of Croesus' rule (the subject covered by the Croesus *Logos*) his relations with the Greeks are only one element, and they differ from later East-West relations by being hostile only in part. The characteristic method of Herodotus is to maintain the integrity of a *logos*, while stressing the element unifying the *logoi* in framing sentences that have a tendency (but not more than a tendency) to generalization. This shows an awareness on his part that periods in history affect only some of the relations between individual units. In Herodotus' work, there are no absolute breaks between periods of history, and so Herodotus himself has no conception of what we call universal history. The historian always follows particular connections between events, not because of his individual whim, but because historical events have only particular relations with one another. If we insist on speaking of the universality of history in Herodotus, we should think of it as universality of viewpoint rather than of subject matter.

Thus one effect of the arrangement of *logoi* is the proper apportionment in each account of what is unique and what is of general significance because it is related to other accounts. Framing sentences stress the interrelationships of events by external connections, but within a single *logos*, events may also acquire meaning by their similarity to those described in other accounts—a similarity expressed through the repetition of *logos*-structure and *logos*-pattern. One of the great merits of Herodotus as a historian is the fine balance his work maintains between the particular and the general, the individual and the pattern. No other ancient historian, it has been claimed, exhibits so much awareness for individuality.[2] I would amend this to say that no other ancient historian shows such fine feeling for the individual within the framework of the typical.

Periods are defined by specific events, such as accession and downfall, alliance and war, which serve to emphasize the beginning and end of a *logos*. These stories always express a definite change (*metabolê*), which is usually a change of fortune.[3] An example is the change which, after Croesus' downfall, his advice to Cyrus brings about in the character of the Lydians (1.155-56). The historian, whose vision extends over long stretches of history, is thus faced by a spectacle of well-marked alternation between greatness and decline. The function of the idea of the wheel of fortune (1.207.2), when applied to the work, is the perception of the unity of historical periods. We have seen that the history of Egypt consists of four periods of alternate prosperity and decay, following one another in irregular alternation.[4] Thus a change of fortune does not always result in extinction. Egyptian history shows the continuity of a country's history through several cycles. Such continuity is expressed (somewhat allegorically) in a story told to Herodotus by the Egyptian priests:

> In this period of time (i.e. during the entire 11,340 years of human kingship in Egypt) they said the sun had changed four

[2] R. G. Collingwood, *The Idea of History* (Oxford 1951) 20-21; 28-31; 42 ff.

[3] H. Strohm, in *Gnomon* 23 (1951) 145, note 1, sketches the early uses of the concept of μεταβολή. The idea is best known from the latter part of the fifth century onward, especially in connection with constitutional changes (cf. H. Ryffel, *Metabolê Politeiôn: Der Wandel der Staatsverfassungen* [Bern 1949]). It has, however, a much wider application, notably in Euripides (changes of fortune in *Iphigeneia in Tauris*, e.g. 1117 ff., cf. *Her.* 1291-93, frs. 15-17 Nauck[2]; changes of mind and character in *Iphigeneia in Aulis*, e.g. 343 ff., 500, etc.), as well as in Thucydides (cf. Ryffel, *op. cit.* 240-41). Herodotus is not affected by the new emphasis on *tychê*, and therefore uses the word *metabolê* in the more archaic meanings outlined by Strohm. It is true that changes in climate and in living conditions are twice mentioned as unfavorable (2.77.3 and 8.117.2), but more often *metabolê* is not hostile; cf. e.g. the eclipse of the sun (1.74.2) which brought about peace, or changes of customs (cf. 5.58.1 and 87.3; differently, however, 1.157.2 and the passage in 1.155-56 as cited in the text). Principally, *metabolê* in Herodotus refers to ethnic and political changes, usually favorable or at least neutral, but almost always of exceptional significance. These changes include changes of ethnic names (1.57.3; 7.62.1; 73; 74.1; 164.1; 170.2) or important political changes (1.65.2 and 66.1; 5.68.1 and 2; 69). Besides these, changes in allegiance or in planning are less important (see Powell, *Lexicon* s.v. μεταβάλλω). Mutability in Herodotus is a part of the general process of nature, and is not necessarily hostile to man. Cf. also Conclusion, note 34.

[4] See above, Ch. I, 26-27.

times the accustomed regions for its rise, rising twice where it now sets and setting twice where it now rises. And by this nothing in Egypt had been altered, neither the products of the earth nor of the river, neither illnesses nor deaths. (2.142.4)

The human condition, the priests say, was unaffected by the double change of the sun's course from east to west and west to east. More properly historical is Herodotus' remark on the periods of hostility and collaboration between Sparta and Athens:

> (The Spartans withdrew from Eleusis), this being the fourth arrival of Dorians in Attica. They had entered it twice for war, and twice for the benefit of the Athenian people: first at the time they also founded Megara—this expedition is best placed at the time of Codrus, king of Athens—secondly and thirdly when they arrived from Sparta to drive out the Peisistratids, and in the fourth place at this time, when Cleomenes entered Eleusis with a Peloponnesian force. Thus this was the fourth time that Dorians had entered Athens. (5.76)[5]

It may not be too fanciful to compare the existence of such periods with the four invasions of Asia and Europe mentioned by Herodotus in connection with the campaign of Xerxes.[6] Elsewhere, alternation between peace and war, or between cooperation and hostility, is presupposed rather than expressly mentioned.[7]

[5] The interpretation of this chapter is complicated by the fact that Herodotus' narrative provides five, not four, Spartan invasions of Attica, for in addition to the mythical invasion he mentions four others at the time of the establishment of democracy: 5.63, Anchimolius; 64-65, Cleomenes drives out the Peisistratids; 72, Cleomenes drives out Cleisthenes' adherents; 74 ff., Cleomenes at Eleusis. Of the four, the third is omitted from the reckoning as having been a private affair between Cleomenes and Isagoras (at least it is so considered by Herodotus; cf. 5.63.1, where private expeditions are mentioned beside public ones). Nevertheless, the balance of the four remaining invasions is highly contrived; yet it is typically Herodotean in that the first and last of the invasions correspond with each other in their hostile intent, so that history shows neither progress nor regression. The order is thus ABBA. Cf. also How and Wells, and Stein, ad loc.

[6] Hdt. 7.20.2. Here also there are two groups, but in the order AABB, for the two more recent invasions are motivated by mutual vengeance, whereas the two legendary expeditions are not.

[7] In several cases, Herodotus contrasts an earlier period of cooperation between nations with a later period of strife. See e.g. the peaceful settlement reached between Lydians and Medes (1.74), as contrasted with the relations between Croesus and Cyrus; or the peace between Alyattes and Miletus (1.22), as contrasted with Croesus' conquest of Ionian cities. Cf. further the cooperation motif mentioned in

There is in these alternate periods, as they are observed by
Herodotus, no special regularity. We are not told how long each
solar period lasted in Egypt; the Spartan interferences in Athens
follow no particular order; and the wars between East and West,
while following a strict pattern of double correspondence, are a
selection. The observation of balance between acts of aggression,
stated in the proem and so important for the work as a whole,[8]
does not imply an orderly sequence of time. The patterns of rise
and fall, or of cooperation and war, are thus irregular patterns,
when seen as historical time sequences, rather than as moral or
religious patterns of crime and punishment or the like. Each pattern is an individual one, and it does not necessarily coincide with
other patterns, although there is sometimes a partial connection.

Herodotus does not work with large cycles in universal history;
he is not a cyclical historian. The unity of history does not, for
him, consist in the overlapping of individual cycles to form larger
patterns. The only connection between individual cycles is the
fact that action corresponds to reaction, and victory to defeat.
Thus it is true that the downfall of Lydia is identical with the
unification of Asia under Persia, and the defeat of Xerxes, with
the growth of Athenian power. Apart from this linking at individual points, however, there is no overall patterning except for
the observation of constantly recurring irregular cycles. It is not
to be thought that Herodotus contrasted an earlier period of
cooperation with a later overall increase in hostility. Wherever
he contrasts cooperation with hostility, he does so on a purely
individual basis.[9] Herodotus' picture of the world is thus not
comparable to the Empedoclean, with its overall increase in
strife for a whole period of world history, but rather to the
Heracleitan, in which strife and cooperation would coexist at all
times, combining in manifold individual patterns.[10]

Causation 253. Such harmony is mentioned in different periods, e.g. the Trojan (e.g.
7.171.1) and Lelantine Wars (5.99.1), the period of the colonization of Libya, and the
time of the tyrants. Hence it must not be thought that these periods of cooperation
are contemporaneous with each other. Herodotus does not use such instances to construct a world picture of alternate phases of cooperation and strife.

[8] For the concept of balance (τὸ ἴσον), mentioned in the proem of the *Histories*
(1.2.1) and thus a major theme of the work (cf. especially 3.108-109, below, 172),
see Pagel, *Aitiol. Moment*, esp. 29-40; *Causation* 244, note 3; Conclusion, 312-13.

[9] Above, note 7.

[10] This is not the place to enter into a discussion of the significance of Heracleitus
and Empedocles for ancient historiography. Broadly speaking, in Heracleitus we find

Another principle in which Herodotus is found to agree with Heracleitus is that of the coincidence of opposites, by which fortune and misfortune may be identical actions affecting the two parties to a dispute in different ways. It is in this sense that we should understand the statement at the end of the proem, although it is expressed in a more archaic manner as the movement of fortune from place to place:

> For (the cities) that once were great have mostly become small, and those that were great in my time, had formerly been small. Thus (I know) that human prosperity never remains in one place. (1.5.4)[11]

The movement of prosperity from place to place is irregular, and the balance which exists between greatness and decline is not connected by Herodotus with the idea of justice, as it is in earlier ethical thought. The quotation above, therefore, refers to the rise of one country and the eclipse of another either through a direct victory or by a simple shift in international politics.

The cycle of growth and decay is primarily a principle of individuation. If we want to know who Croesus was, we can do so only by knowing his rise to power and its end. Each unit—be it a city, a country, or an individual—can be identified only by a particular configuration of the cycle of growth and decay. It is thus a transient part of a permanent historical world that maintains its constancy in alternations of growth and decay. In themselves, the changes that take place are aimless and repetitive. Progress applies only to individual units and not to the whole course of history. Only the totality of history is permanent, since the principle of individuation is permanently operative. Herodotus thus nowhere speaks of the origins of mankind.[12] While it is true

coexistence of opposites, whereas in Empedocles we have succession of opposites. The Empedoclean view leads to periodicity in history, while the Heracleitan view implies constant opposition of factors, whether they be contemporaneous or follow one another in time.

[11] The movement of prosperity from place to place occurs at the end of Solon's so-called *Elegy to the Muses* (fr. 1 Diehl³, lines 75-76); cf. Fränkel, *Dichtung und Philosophie* 271 f.

[12] The phrase "from the time when the race of men originated" in 2.15.3 shows that Herodotus, following Greek mythological tradition, postulated a beginning of mankind; he thought that the Egyptians had been in existence since that time. Yet this statement receives a correction, however slight, from the story of Psammetichus,

that he contrasts civilized and savage peoples, he rarely describes how the one develops into the other.[13] He is concerned only with civilized history, which he treats as permanent, since it is to him simply a variety of nature (*physis*) following the natural pattern of growth and decay.

Individual uniqueness within a fixed pattern is expressed by Herodotus through the simple rule that, for each state or individual, *the very conditions that give rise to greatness are also the conditions of downfall*. This principle can also be reversed: the conditions that keep an individual or state down at one time may also operate to bring about greatness. For it is possible to isolate a portion of the curve of prosperity either from trough to trough or between two crests. Eastern history is seen by Herodotus mainly in the former pattern, and Greek history partly in the latter. Since the work deals primarily with the East, it is easier to observe the rise and fall of Eastern kings than the growth of the Greek states. The Greek development has to be pieced together from a number of small *logoi*, while Eastern history furnishes the great portraits of Oriental kings and Oriental empires. Hence we shall consider the Orient first.

II

The figure of Croesus is treated in so much detail by Herodotus that it seems to typify, in the manner of a parable, the whole fate of man. Unfortunately, the commentators are not agreed on the contents of the message thus conveyed.[14] Some have stressed the element of fate, by which Croesus' downfall was the inexorable result of the crime of Gyges, as predicted by the Delphic oracle. Others have stressed rather Croesus' own folly and the lesson derived therefrom: the divine punishes those who think of themselves too highly because they have risen too high in fortune. As I have attempted to show elsewhere, we must consider these two points of view in combination.[15] The Croesus story has also been understood as a demonstration of divine government, and as an

---

who discovered that the Phrygians alone had preceded the Egyptians, since they spoke the original language of mankind (2.2). Cf. also in general K. von Fritz, "Herodotus and the Growth of Greek Historiography," *TAPA* 67 (1936) 329 f.

[13] However, certain Libyan tribes acquired civilization from the Egyptians (4.168, etc.).

[14] See especially Hellmann, *Kroisos-Logos* 1 ff. (= Marg, *Herodot* 40 ff.); *Action* 38.

[15] *Action* 36.

expression of the primitive belief in divine jealousy. A precise answer to these problems at once involves the commentator in controversy.

A consideration of the precise conditions under which Croesus rose to greatness may perhaps assist in solving these conflicts. The Mermnad dynasty had, from the beginning, been bent on conquest, but these aggressions had been of a limited kind. The attacks against Greek cities had been mere raids (*harpagai*), and the Greeks, prior to Croesus, had remained free (1.6.3). Alyattes, the father of Croesus, had been compelled, because of an oracle, to give up his projected conquest of Miletus; he had also been induced by an eclipse of the sun to make peace with the Medes. In both cases alliance had succeeded war, and conquest had been limited, on the one hand, by accepting the freedom of the Ionian cities, and on the other, by establishing a fixed boundary, at the Halys river, between Western and Eastern Asia. Croesus' own conquests were at first limited by a similar policy. He conquered the Ionian cities, but listened to the advice of a wise man who urged him to forego the conquest of the Ionian islands (1.27). His conquests of native peoples originally respected the Halys boundary, so that his achievement, in Herodotus' eyes, was the consolidation of Western Asia. At the end of his early reign his empire was secure, and his wealth enormous, because his aspirations had been limited by the policies of his predecessors. Croesus thus represents a type of ruler morally superior to the Persian kings, and one on whom Herodotus looks with more favor, following therein the bias of Greek tradition.[16]

The dominant characteristic of Croesus at the time of Solon's visit to Sardis (a visit coinciding, it will be recalled, with Croesus' high point in fortune) was his secure wealth, or prosperity (*olbos*). *Olbos*, in early Greek thought, is true (that is, lasting) prosperity, as reflected in external fortune and possessions; the word has a very strong concrete connotation.[17] Herodotus uses the concept

[16] For the Greek traditions about Croesus, see e.g. Weissbach in *RE* Suppl. 5, s.v. Kroisos (1931).

[17] On the concept of *olbos*, see O. Regenbogen, "Die Geschichte von Solon und Krösus," in Marg, *Herodot* 389-90, and W. Jaeger, *Paideia: The Ideals of Greek Culture*, tr. by G. Highet, 1² (Oxford 1945), index, s.v. "wealth," especially 70, 144, and 201 f. Further, Cora Mason, *The Ethics of Wealth in Early Greek Thought* (Diss. Harvard 1944); E. Fraenkel, Commentary on Aeschylus' *Agamemnon* (1950), lines 928 f.; A. W. Allen, "Solon's Elegy to the Muses," *TAPA* 80 (1949) 51.

emphatically in the Solon-Croesus story, but only rarely in the rest of the work.[18] Thus the discussion between the Oriental king and the Athenian wise man turns on Croesus' basic condition.[19] The emphasis on Croesus' wealth was traditional in the Greek world, because Croesus was well known for his gifts to the oracle at Delphi.

In the Solon-Croesus story the king's treasury is the outer manifestation of his *olbos*, and the relation between visible wealth and prosperity is comparable to that implicit in the story of Darius' treasury as a manifestation of Persian royal power.[20] When Solon has inspected Croesus' treasure, the king asks him, "Who is the most prosperous?" Solon's well-known answer comprises, in summary, three related ideas of early Greek wisdom literature: (1) prosperity (*olbos*) is insecure, (2) man is at all times liable to accident, or as Solon phrases it, he is "wholly accident (*symphorê*)," and (3) observe the end (*horâ to telos*). Since accident tends to prevent prosperity from having any permanence, one must consider the completed life of a man before one can judge him to have been truly prosperous. The particular importance of the notion of the end (*telos*) is that it turns Solon's description of the human condition into a prediction of the dangers that might befall Croesus. Therefore, the idea of the end furnishes the structure of the whole conversation. Solon, it will be recalled, gives three answers to Croesus' repeated question on who is the most prosperous. In the first he praises the Athenian Tellos. The very name of this unknown person stresses, in the manner of ancient etymology, the notion of *telos*.[21] The story of

[18] The noun ὄλβος occurs only in the Croesus *Logos* (1.32.9 and 1.86.5). ὄλβιος is more common. It means "rich" in 6.24.2; 61.3 (*pace* Powell, *Lexicon*); 8.75.1. The meaning "fortunate" occurs only in 1.216.3 and 5.92e.2 (the latter passage is an oracle). Cf. L. Radermacher, *Gnomon* 14 (1938) 296.

[19] On the Solon-Croesus episode, see especially O. Regenbogen, "Die Geschichte von Solon und Krösus," *Hum. Gymn.* 41 (1930) 1 ff. (= Marg, *Herodot* 375 ff.). Further, A. Alföldi, "Der Philosoph als Zeuge der Wahrheit und sein Gegenspieler der Tyrann," *Scientiis Artibusque* (*Collectanea Academiae Catholicae Hungaricae*) 1 (1958) 7-19, esp. 16. J. Audiat, "Apologie pour Hérodote (1.32)," *REA* 42 (1940) 3-8. O. Gigon, *MH* 3 (1946) 5. K. Hönn, *Solon: Staatsmann und Weiser* (Vienna 1948). K. Nawratil, "Solon bei Herodot," *WS* 60 (1942) 1-8. K. Wehrli, *Lathe Biôsas* (Leipzig 1931). A. E. Zimmern, *Solon and Croesus* (London 1928). M. Miller, "The Herodotean Croesus," *Klio* 41 (1963) 48-94, esp. 89 ff.

[20] Hdt. 1.30.1; 50-52; 54.1; 92; cf. 3.96.2.

[21] *Tellos* is a hypocoristic form of a Greek proper name such as *Telenikos*, *Telesidromos*, or the like: cf. *RE*, s.v. Tellos. This person is rightly assumed to be a historical figure, cf. e.g. F. Jacoby, "*Patrios Nomos*," in his *Abhandlungen zur griechischen Geschichts-*

Tellos ends with a reference to his glorious funeral. In the second answer, Solon praises the Argives Cleobis and Biton, and at the end of this story we read once more a description of a marvelous death: "this end (*telos*) befell them." Solon's third answer is a speech on the human condition consisting of three parts, each of which ends in a reference to "the end" in some form.[22] Thus we may isolate, by means of "refrain composition," three main sections of Solon's great speech, the first of which answers the king's question in general terms, while the second establishes the distinction between wealth and fortune, and the third establishes the doctrine of balance in human life and shows that the end of life is an integral part of that balance. The final reference to *telos* is then linked with *olbos*:

> In every matter one must mark the end how it will result; for the god has quite uprooted many to whom he had (previously) shown prosperity. (1.32.9)

The idea that "man is wholly accident" is less fully developed in the remarks of Solon. Its full import becomes apparent only when we consider the following story of the death of Croesus' son Atys in its obvious relation with the Solon-Croesus episode.[23] The death of Atys by the innocent hands of the Phrygian Adrastus, whom Croesus had entrusted with his son's safety, was an accident *par excellence*, and Herodotus uses the word *symphorê* as a link between the two stories.[24] At the same time, another link is established between the two stories through the name Atys and

---

schreibung, ed. H. Bloch (Leiden 1956) 275 f. and note 32. It is of course possible that Tellos was his real name, but it may be that Herodotus (or his source) used a hypocoristic variant of a full name, in order to make an etymological point about τέλος, *end*: for such double names, see E. Fraenkel in *RE*, s.v. Namenwesen, 1628 ff. The doubling of the consonant is regular for nicknames and constitutes no obstacle to the etymology, since the ancients frequently assumed additions and subtractions of letters in making their etymologies; see e.g. Plato, *Cratylus* 394 B 1-6.

[22] The first part of Solon's speech ends with the answer to Croesus' original question as to who was the most prosperous: "that which you ask me I do not yet call you, until I have heard that you have ended your life well" (1.32.5). The second part compares prosperity and luck, and ends with another reference to Croesus' eventual death (1.32.7). The third section establishes the doctrine of balance in human life and shows that the end of life is a necessary part in such balance (1.32.9, cited in the text).

[23] For bibliography on this story, see Ch. II, 71 and note 71.

[24] συμφορή occurs once in the Solon-Croesus story (1.32.4), and no less than six times in the Atys story (1.35.1; 35.4; 41.1; 42.1; 44.2; 45.1). Cf. also βαρυσυμφορώτατος at the end of the story (1.45.3). See Hellmann, *Kroisos-Logos* 58 ff. and *passim*.

the notion of the blindness (*atê*) of Croesus.[25] Thus the Atys story supplements the Solon-Croesus episode by supplying the idea that misfortune, although seemingly accident, is actually due to blindness, and further that this blindness allows an inescapable fate to take its course. We shall see shortly that the combination of these ideas prefigures the story of the fall of Croesus.

Solon proves the thesis of the insecurity of prosperity by first introducing a distinction between mere wealth (*ploutos*) and true prosperity (*olbos*):

> The very wealthy (*plousios*) man is not more prosperous (*olbios*) than he who has only enough for the day, unless fortune follow him so that he dies while all is (still) in good shape. (1.32.5)

Solon goes on to say that the wealthy man is superior to the lucky man in only two respects: he can fulfill his desire and he can bear disaster more easily; but the lucky man is superior to the wealthy man in many respects: he is uninjured, healthy, does not suffer, has children, is good-looking (cf. 1.32.6). In short, the wealthy man is superior only in what is under his control, but the lucky man is superior in the much larger area of what man cannot control. Thus the appearance of mere wealth is deceptive, and true prosperity is primarily the gift of fortune. Croesus' *olbos* is only *ploutos*.

The Solon story stresses the specific condition of Croesus' greatness, (seemingly) secure wealth based, as we know, on the limitation of his conquests to Western Asia. Starting with this specific condition, Solon develops several other themes (in particular those of accident and of the importance of the end) that help to place Croesus' downfall into a more general framework showing the fate of all great rulers.

Croesus originally decided to attack Persia because he was afraid of her growing power (1.46.1), but this defensive motivation soon changed into the opposite motivation of an unlimited expansionism. In the preparations for the campaign and in its conduct, Croesus' wealth and his confidence in continued pros-

[25] Atys, the son of Croesus, is properly the man of misfortune (*atê*), but since the same word also means "blindness," there is here a reference to Croesus' own blindness as well, a blindness shown in the Solon-Croesus story. For the double meaning of *atê*, see E. R. Dodds, *The Greeks and the Irrational* (Berkeley 1951) 2 ff., 18, and 37 ff. The term *atê* occurs only twice in Herodotus, both times in the same section of Solon's speech (1.32.6). Adrastus' name ("he who cannot escape"—his fate) is also an omen: see Hellmann, *Kroisos-Logos* 62.

perity play a significant part. The gifts he sent to the Delphic oracle were intended to propitiate the Delphic Apollo (1.50.1). Here was a use of his gold that would surely bring good fortune. However, the answers of the god were not, like Croesus' gold, genuine, but deceptive or "spurious" (*kibdêla*).[26] Thus the wealth of Croesus contributed greatly to his downfall, since his reliance upon the correctness of the oracles that were given to him made him confident in his alliance with Sparta and the success of his campaign. When, after his defeat by Cyrus, he thought that the god had played him false, he accused him of ingratitude (1.90.4). Yet Apollo, although unable to prevent Croesus' defeat, had nevertheless saved his life when the flames had been about to consume him (1.87.1-2), thus showing that Croesus' gifts had been of some profit to him by making him "a man beloved by the gods." Croesus' wealth has then two opposite effects on his life: it contributes to a false sense of security which makes him lose his empire, but it also saves his life. We have here once more the idea of a moderate destruction corresponding to the moderation shown by Croesus in the conduct of his previous life.[27]

The concepts of accident and blindness leading to destruction are also developed in the story of the downfall of Croesus. As Hellmann has shown, the campaign itself hinges on a series of unexpected happenings.[28] Croesus could not have known that Sparta would be involved in domestic warfare just when her Lydian ally needed her; he expected his army to be sufficiently large to defeat Cyrus in the battle of Pteria; he thought Cyrus would not arrive in Sardis as soon as he did; and Sardis was taken quite unexpectedly when a breach in her walls was discovered by accident. The final anecdote of the campaign section, in which Croesus' dumb son suddenly finds his speech, well illustrates the theme of foiled hope and expectation. Here again, false expectation, besides destroying Croesus' empire, is also

---

[26] κίβδηλος means literally "alloyed." It is used of misleading oracles only here (1.75.2) and shortly before (1.66.3, in a different context). 5.91.2 is not comparable, since there the reference is to forged oracles. On the idea of misleading oracles, see Daniels, *Rel.-hist. Studie* 72, and Crahay, *Litt. orac.* 153.

[27] A similar contrast exists between the favorable picture of Croesus' wealth used for offerings at Delphi (e.g. 1.50-52) and the unfavorable one of the wealth acquired upon accession (1.92).

[28] For the *elpis*-motif (false expectation), see the excellent analysis by Hellmann, *Kroisos-Logos* 73 ff.

instrumental in saving his life; the dumb son, by speaking out,
prevents a Persian from killing his father (1.85).

The motifs of accident and blindness are less indicative, however, of the specific situation differentiating Croesus from other
royal portraits in Herodotus, than they are typical of the situation
of rulers in general. For in addition to his special situation, Croesus
is also the typical ruler, showing emotion (*thymos*), rashness, and
blindness to fortune.[29] The *symphorê* motif thus represents the
general pattern rather than the specific character of Croesus'
downfall.

The end (*telos*) of Croesus is not his death (which is not reported
by Herodotus, since it occurred, in the tradition he follows,
considerably later than the loss of empire),[30] but his capture by
Cyrus. Sitting on a pyre, where Cyrus intends to burn him alive,
Croesus remembers Solon:

> He said that in the beginning the Athenian Solon had come,
> who upon seeing his whole wealth (*olbos*) had made light of it—
> telling them in what way he had done so—; also how every-
> thing had turned out for him as Solon had stated it, speaking
> not only with respect to himself (Croesus), but for the whole
> human race and especially for those who were of the opinion
> that they were prosperous (*olbioi*). (1.86.5)

Thus, after the event, Solon's statements, like the famous letter
of Amasis to Polycrates, turn out to have been predictions.[31] The
main point of the Solon story is now found to be his explanation
of the uncertainty of *olbos*, and more particularly the danger
implicit in thinking oneself prosperous when one is merely wealthy.
Hence, clearly, Herodotus is saying that Croesus' confidence in
prosperity (the basis of his existence as king), even more than his

---

[29] Croesus' passion (θυμός) appears first in the Solon story, when the questions he
asks of Solon are described as dictated by whim (νῦν ... ἵμερος ἐπειρέσθαι μοι ἐπῆλθέ σε,
1.30.2); secondly, when he asks "sharply" (ἐπιστρεφέως) why Solon is praising
Tellos, 1.30.3; thirdly, when he gets angry (σπερχθείς, 1.32.1) after the praise of Cleobis
and Biton. The same passion (ἵμερος) appears when Croesus wants to attack Persia
(1.73.1).

[30] Croesus survived into the reign of Cambyses (3.36), and his death is not mentioned by Herodotus. At the time of Cambyses' Egyptian campaign he must have been
an old man, by Herodotus' reckoning: see Weissbach in *RE* Suppl. 5.465. According
to Oriental sources, Croesus was killed by Cyrus; hence the Greek tradition is pure
legend.

[31] Hdt. 1.86.5 should be compared with 3.125.4. Cf. also *Samian Stories* 318.

wealth as such, caused Croesus' downfall. At the same time, as we have observed in regard to the ideas of prosperity and accident, the idea of the end (which is the presupposition of Croesus' speaking of Solon at all) also has its positive aspect. The mention of Solon arouses Cyrus' pity, and he attempts to save Croesus from the pyre, an attempt afterwards carried to completion by Apollo.

In summary, we may say that the Croesus story, while based on a very wide framework of general ideas applicable, in Croesus' own words, "to the whole human race," shows also a specific pattern applicable only to Croesus himself. In the former category belongs all that can be said about the curse placed on the Mermnad dynasty at the time of Gyges, according to which Gyges' crimes had to be punished in the fifth generation (1.13.2), as well as Croesus' character and role as a despot whose fall is due to his own blindness and to accident. In this sense the Croesus story is a parable. Its specific features are the role of wealth in his downfall, and the moderate character of both his early expansion and his destruction at the end. These individual characteristics lend a certain inevitability to his downfall, for Croesus cannot, as king of Lydia, escape his wealth. So long as he is king he cannot, therefore, escape the belief in his own prosperity. It is only because he did not die when losing his empire that he was able to learn from what had happened and to change character completely, ending his days as the wise adviser to the Persian kings.[32]

III

If wealth is the main characteristic of Croesus, Cyrus' fate derives from the fact that he is the founder of the Persian empire.[33] The story of Cyrus' accession may be analyzed from two different points of view. Formally, it is the *logos* of the overthrow of Astyages, king of the Medes, who resembles Croesus in losing his empire to the new Persian nation ruled by Cyrus. At the same time, the story includes the Founder's Myth of the miraculous birth, exposure, survival, and discovery of the child Cyrus. The story of

[32] On the standard patterns of learning from suffering, see above, Ch. III, note 20. Learning from a tragic experience is found in Croesus (see especially 1.207.1), in Astyages, who shows a certain wisdom after his defeat (1.129), in Psammenitus after his defeat by Cambyses (3.14), and in Cambyses himself (3.65), but is absent from many of the major tragic figures, such as Cyrus, Xerxes, Cleomenes, and others.

[33] Cf. also *Causation* 259.

Cyrus the Founder resembles the old myth of the "divine child" so well known all over the world.[34] Now Herodotus, as he tells us at the beginning of the Accession *Logos* of Cyrus, knew, all told, four versions of his origins, and he chose among them the version told by those "who did not magnify the affairs of Cyrus" (1.95.1). He means, perhaps, that he selected the account in which the divine element in Cyrus' accession was least prominent, but this cannot be maintained with certainty.[35] At any rate, the essential feature of the account he gives us is its rationalization of the divine element, so that the story is primarily a human one.

The external structure of the account, as we have said, derives from the overthrow of Astyages. Like Croesus, Astyages had to come to a bad end, as shown by the two dreams concerning his daughter Mandane before the birth of Cyrus. Astyages' failing is his excessive cruelty (he is *pikros*, 1.123.2 and 130.1). He attempts to outwit fate by marrying his daughter, not to a Mede, but to a subject Persian, yet his plans misfire. His downfall is accomplished by the gods clouding his senses (he is *theoblabês*, 1.127.2), and he becomes a wise man only after the event. Like Croesus he escapes death, and continues to live at the Persian court.[36] Possibly Herodotus thinks of Astyages as "the leader of the city," whose city (i.e. country) is destroyed.[37] He is destroyed by Harpagus,

---

[34] Cf. E. Norden, *Die Geburt des Kindes. Geschichte einer religiösen Idee* (Leipzig 1924). M. Delcourt, *Œdipe, ou la Légende du conquérant* (Liège 1944). C. Kerényi and C. G. Jung, *Essays on a Science of Mythology. The Myth of the Divine Child and the Mysteries of Eleusis*, tr. by R. F. C. Hull (New York 1949). J. Laager, *Geburt und Kindheit des Gottes in der griechischen Mythologie* (Winterthur 1957). G. Binder, *Die Aussetzung des Königskindes. Kyros und Romulus* (Meisenheim/Glan 1964).

[35] The problem is what meaning we are to give to σεμνοῦν, to magnify. The verb occurs in only one other passage in Herodotus: ἄλλως . . . σεμνοῦν, "to assert falsely" (3.16.7). Stein on 1.95, line 5, assumes that Herodotus has in mind his own version of the story of the dog that suckled Cyrus, a version which reduces the divine element (1.122.3). How and Wells, however, assume that Herodotus is following an anti-Achaemenid source; see J. Wells, "The Persian Friends of Herodotus," *JHS* 27 (1907) 40.

[36] Cyrus' saving of Astyages balances his own survival after his discovery by the latter. It is due, however, to Persian custom, for according to Herodotus the Persians do not usually kill conquered kings (cf. the story of Psammenitus, 3.14 ff.).

[37] Astyages' city, Ecbatana, is mentioned only once in the *logos* (1.110.2), but is referred to in the first dream concerning Mandane's child as "his own city" (1.107.1), and later as "the city of the Medes" (1.128.2); cf. also the description of Ecbatana in 1.98.3 ff. The repeated emphasis on "the city" may be due to the etymology of Astyages' name, although this must remain uncertain. That Herodotus gave Greek etymologies of foreign names is likely from 2.52.1, where we find a Greek etymology of the "Pelasgian" word θεός (Pelasgian speech was probably non-Greek: 1.57), and

"the robber," a Mede whose son Astyages has cruelly slain and fed to the father, and by Cyrus, "he who succeeds," in alliance with Harpagus.[38] The three main characters of the story thus each represent one aspect typical of a change of dynasty: Astyages is the tragic ruler, Harpagus, the bringer of vengeance, and Cyrus, the fortunate new prince.

The figure of the divine founder is thus only one element of three in the accession story, but it is the one most heavily emphasized. Cyrus' own story begins with the two dreams that concern his mother Mandane, dreams typical of the advent of a ruler, and as such frequently employed in the work.[39] The first dream occurs before Mandane is married and shows her inundating Astyages' own city and then all of Asia. The second, which occurs after her marriage to Cambyses the Persian, and before the birth of the child, shows a vine growing from her genitals and overshadowing all of Asia (1.107.1 and 108.1). The two dreams differ from each other primarily in the imagery employed. Mandane's urine is a pollution of the land, and this dream uses the idea of Persian reverence for pure water, a motif related in Herodotus to the river motif.[40] The vine overshadowing Asia represents the beneficent aspects of royal power and should be connected with the wine motif of Cyrus' campaign against the Massagetae, to be

---

from 6.98.3, where (as the text stands) the Greek translations of the names Darius, Xerxes, Artaxerxes, contain the sounds of the names Xerxes, Darius, and (Karta)-Xerxes. See also the name Atys, above, note 25.

[38] The etymology of Harpagus (the most certain of the three etymologies here proposed) is stressed by the alliteration of *pi* and *rho* in the first sentence of 1.108.4 and again in 1.109.2 (Harpagus' answer to his wife). A similar play upon the name Prexaspes occurs in 3.62.2; cf. Aly, *Volksmärchen* 98. The etymology of Cyrus is less clearly implied in the narrative. The word-stem of κυρεῖν, *to succeed*, occurs only twice in the *logos*, although in rather significant contexts (1.112.3 and 119.2), but note the alliteration in 1.122.3: ὡς ἐκκείμενον Κῦρον κύων ἐξέθρεψε, and the repeated emphasis on Cyrus' change of name (1.113.3; 114.4; etc.). On such alliterations, see W. B. Stanford, *Aeschylus in His Style* (Dublin 1942) 82.

[39] Cf. Agariste's dream about Pericles, 6.131.2 (above, Ch. III, note 138), and the dreams presaging future empires (above, Ch. III, note 41). Other omens of the birth of rulers are found in 1.59.1-2 and 5.92.2-3. The duplication of the dream seems to be unique in Herodotus (7.12-18 is somewhat different); it may have been in the Eastern tradition about Cyrus, for duplicate dreams are common there; cf. C. H. Gordon, *Before the Bible* (New York 1962) 64. Yet the dreams are not mere doublets: see K. Reinhardt, "Herodots Persergeschichten," in Marg, *Herodot* 339.

[40] The impurity of urine is mentioned twice in the *logos* on Persian customs (1.133.3 and 138.2: Persians do not urinate into rivers). Reverence for pure water is further stressed in 1.188, where it is stated that the Persian king drinks water only from the Choaspes river. On the river motif, see above, Ch. III, note 17, and below, Ch. VI, 293.

discussed presently.[41] Mandane's marriage to an inferior (a motif representing the idea of the defective ancestry of the divine ruler)[42] is motivated as an attempt of Astyages to forestall the meaning of the first dream. The same rationalistic explanation is given for the exposure of Cyrus, which is Astyages' answer to the second dream. Thus the original primitive meaning of the dreams is replaced by purely human motivations.

Herodotus employs human motivation throughout this story to explain the (to him) archaic features of the Founder's Myth. He is following a tradition that we can still see reflected in Attic tragedy, a tradition hostile to great rulers, and one which explains the original divine features of the myth by reducing them to ordinary human events.[43] Thus Cyrus is saved by Harpagus and a shepherd, whose elaborate reasoning is quite in the manner of tragedy. The birth, by the shepherd's wife, of a dead child at the very moment such a baby is needed as a substitute for Cyrus, who was to have been killed, is not divine interference, but a co-incidence.[44] The eventual recognition of the child is based on natural features and the child's royal nature, which we may think of as inherited on his mother's side.[45] Astyages brings a thank-offering to the gods for the "change of fortune" by which Cyrus has survived (1.118.2). The key word of the story is *periesti*, "he has survived," which thus emphasizes once again the element

---

[41] The Persians were great wine drinkers: 1.133.3; 212.2; 126.2; 3.34.2 (Cambyses); 3.22.3. When Sandanis, in 1.71.3, says that the Persians drink no wine, but only water, this refers to the pre-empire period, and does not contradict 1.133.3: see 1.126.2, where Cyrus teaches the Persians to drink wine, as it were. The famous golden vine given by Pythius the Lydian to Darius (together with a golden plane tree, 7.27.2) overshadowed the king's couch (Ath. 12.539 D) and was proverbial in antiquity (see Macan, *VII-IX*, on 7.27, line 9). That the particular images of growth have symbolic significance is strongly suggested by the Sophoclean imitation of an empire dream in *Electra* 417 ff., where Agamemnon's scepter grows a shoot, i.e. Orestes. Cf. Jebb *ad loc.* and, in general, Aly, *Volksmärchen* 42, note 1.

[42] Cf. Hdt. 5.92b.1 (Labda, the mother of Cypselus). See also Kerényi and Jung, *op. cit.* (above, note 34) 38 ff.

[43] See Crahay, *Litt. orac.* 206-207, 231-33, and 281 ff., but the point of view put forward there is exaggerated.

[44] Herodotus says that it happened κατὰ δαίμονα (1.111.1), but the phrase means little more than "by coincidence." Stein on 1.62, line 15, lists examples of similar expressions, but in some instances he overstresses the providential aspect. Cf. *Rev. Crahay* 206 (on Hdt. 1.62.4). At best we may say that such coincidences have religious overtones, since they reveal processes of nature; for the corresponding phenomenon in Sophocles, cf. H. D. F. Kitto, *Form and Meaning in Drama* (London 1956) 73-75.

[45] Cf. Xenophon, *Anab.* 1.9, on the royal nature of Cyrus the Younger.

of chance rather than that of fate.[46] The Magi, when questioned
about the meaning of the original dreams in the light of the new
developments, answer by saying that Cyrus has shown his royal
nature "without anyone's foresight," i.e. by accident (1.120.3).
Hence, Astyages, in saying to Cyrus that he has survived "by his
own fate (*moira*)," means merely that luck alone has been responsible for Cyrus' survival.[47] The divine element is reduced (a)
to a general necessity, which appears only at the beginning of
the story in the two dreams, and (b) elsewhere in the *logos* to a vague
good fortune, by which the dreams are fulfilled.

At the end of the story Cyrus returns home to his parents and
tells them that he was saved by a shepherd and his wife. The
parents, "in order that the Persians might think their son's
survival more divine," invent the tale that he was suckled by a
dog (1.122.3). The ancient motif of the suckling of the ruler by a
totemistic animal, a story also used by Livy to magnify the divinity
of Romulus, is thus rationalized out of existence, and instead of a
truly divine origin we have the mere appearance of divinity.
This belief in his survival by divine will is carefully implanted in
Cyrus by Harpagus. In a letter to Cyrus urging him to revolt from
Astyages, Harpagus says that the gods supervise Cyrus, as is
shown by his luck; and further that he has survived because of the
gods and Harpagus (1.124.1-2). Cyrus accepts this version of his
survival, and later says to the Persians: "I expect to (revolt
successfully) since I am born under a divine fortune" (1.126.6).
It is this belief that eventually causes Cyrus' destruction.

There is a close correspondence between Cyrus' accession and
the campaign against the Massagetae, in which he finds his death.
The correspondence is based on the idea that the conditions of
his rise to kingship arouse in Cyrus a false belief in his more than
human greatness, and that this belief causes his death. The
stories of accession and death are connected by the repetition of
the statement that Herodotus has chosen the most reasonable
account of Cyrus' life,[48] as well as by the motivation of Cyrus'
campaign against the Massagetae:

[46] περίεστι or the like occurs seven times in the story: 1.112.3; 118.1; 120.2;
120.3; 121; 122.3; 124.2.

[47] Hdt. 1.121. For this loose use of *moira*, cf. 3.142.3; 4.164.4; and also 3.64.3
(καιρίη = *mortally*, see Stein on 3.64, line 13). Cf. Pohlenz, *Herodot* 108, note 2.

[48] Hdt. 1.214.5: "With regard to the end of Cyrus' life, while many accounts are
given, I have told the above as being the most likely," should be compared with 1.95.1:

> ... many things incited and aroused him, first his origin, the belief that he was more than a mere man, and secondly the luck he had had in warfare, since wherever Cyrus directed his campaigns that nation was unable to escape him. (1.204.2)[49]

Croesus, who accompanies Cyrus on the campaign against the Massagetae, refers to the same motif in his advice to Cyrus before the crossing of the Araxes river:

> "If you believe that you are immortal and rule over an army of immortals, it is not necessary for me to give you advice. But if you know that you too are a man and are ruling over men, then learn that there is a cycle of human events ..." (1.207.2)

Cyrus, however, does not cease to believe in his privileged position, as he shows in the words spoken after his dream about Darius:

> "The gods care for me and they show me everything that comes to me." (1.209.4)

He is, of course, at this very moment, misinterpreting the dream.

Finally, both dreams concerning Mandane find their ironic solution in the campaign against the Massagetae. The river motif (and consequently the idea of the purity of water) is stressed both in Cyrus' Babylonian Conquest and in the Massagetan Campaign.[50] In the Babylonian Campaign, the punishment of the Gyndes river contrasts with the story of the purity of the water drunk by the Persian kings, and the capture of Babylon by diverting the Euphrates is also hybris. In the campaign against the Massagetae the crossing of the Araxes differs from this in being advised by the wise man Croesus. From the point of view of Cyrus' individual fate, it is again hybris, but from the point of view of the safety of the empire it is a wise move.[51] The wine motif (connecting as it does with the vine of the second dream) is the central motif of the Massagetan Campaign. Like the water motif, it contrasts with certain other statements in Herodotus, namely that the Persians are great wine drinkers.[52]

"As some of the Persians say who do not want to magnify the affairs of Cyrus, but to tell the true story, according to them I shall write it down, although I could relate three other ways the *logos* of Cyrus goes." Cf. above, note 35.

[49] Cf. *Causation* 259 and note 35.

[50] For the Babylonian Campaign, see Ch. III, 91-92.

[51] For the interpretation of Croesus' advice to Cyrus, see Ch. II, 75.

[52] Above, note 41.

While such statements are clearly favorable to the Persians, the wine metaphor in the present campaign is unfavorable to Cyrus. In the deceitful stratagem suggested by Croesus, wine is used to inebriate Spargapises, the son of Tomyris, queen of the Massagetae, and this leads to his capture. Tomyris chides Cyrus for this use of wine:

> "Bloodthirsty Cyrus, do not rejoice in this event, that with the fruit of the vine (with which you fill yourselves up and go mad, so that as the wine goes down into your bodies evil words come up), that with this poison you deceived and conquered my child, rather than in a test of strength in battle." (1.212.2)[53]

In this speech the wine motif is combined with the expansionist motif, since Cyrus is desirous to drink not wine, but blood. The yearning to drink blood becomes Cyrus' undoing when the queen holds his severed head in a wineskin filled with human blood (1.214.4). Thus the vine, a life-giving plant, becomes symbolically the instrument of Cyrus' death. The imagery shows how Cyrus' original conditions turn against him and cause his destruction. This agrees with the use of the other motifs of the divinity of the ruler in this campaign.[54]

IV

Cambyses, who received the kingship from his father before the campaign against the Massagetae,[55] and who also inherited the

---

[53] Tomyris accuses Cyrus of deception (*apatê*); this is a recurrent motif (arranged in patterns of retaliation) in the Cyrus stories; cf. e.g. the deception of Harpagus by Astyages (1.118-19), and the two deceptions of Astyages by Harpagus (1.109 ff. and 1.123). On *apatê*, see further Ch. VI, 243 and note 17. In the present passage, Tomyris acts the part of the noble savage who is critical of civilization; cf. the stories of the king of the Ethiopians (Ch. III, note 51).

[54] The unity of the Cyrus *logoi* discussed here is further reinforced by the differences in the picture of Cyrus which is developed here and elsewhere in the work. In 1.86.6, Cyrus attempts to save Croesus from the pyre because he realizes that "he too was a mere man and was delivering another man . . . to the flames." This stands in absolute contrast to the Massagetan *Logos*, as do also passages where Cyrus appears as the wise founder of Persia (3.75.1; cf. 3.82.5; 3.89.3; 3.160.1; 9.122). Such inconsistencies between major *logoi* (but not within a *logos*) are characteristic of Herodotus' dramatic technique.

[55] See Ch. I, 21-25. For the successor motif in Herodotus, compare especially 7.2-3 (Xerxes), and see *Action* 25, note 19 (contrast of great and petty generations). Other examples: *Causation* 258, note 30, and below, note 76 (Gobryas and Mardonius). For the idea of an "inherited" war, see *Causation* 260, note 37. Plato, *Laws* 3.693 D ff., may be following Herodotus in praising Cyrus and Darius, while judging their successors to be inferior. Cf. also below, note 95, and Ch. I, 40.

campaign against Egypt, derives both his greatness and his decline from the idea of legitimate succession. Loyalty to his dynasty and respect for custom (royal succession is a matter of custom, as is seen in the story of Xerxes' succession at the beginning of Book 7) are Cambyses' original attitudes. He reverses both, and his end is due to his disrespect for Egyptian custom, while the end of his family's rule is caused by his murder of relatives.

The first motif of the Campaign *Logos* of Cambyses is thus the dynastic motif, which is central to the *aitiê*-section of that *logos*.[56] It finds its clearest expression in Croesus' answer to Cambyses' question as to how he compares with his father:

> "To me, son of Cyrus, you do not appear the equal of your father, since you do not as yet have a son such as he left behind in you." (3.34.5)

Instead of producing a son, Cambyses destroys his relatives. The murder of his brother Smerdis actually makes possible the Revolt of the Magi, and the murder of his wife (especially if, as one version has it, she was pregnant) results in his death "without any male or female offspring whatever"(3.66.2). Because of the importance of the destruction of offspring for the whole course of Persian empire, Herodotus has underlined this motif by adducing in Book 3 many stories dealing with the destruction of children.[57]

The second great theme of the Cambyses story is the destruction of custom, which as we have seen is the main idea connecting the Egyptian Ethnographic *Logos* with Cambyses' campaign.[58] In burning and dishonoring Amasis' corpse, Cambyses acts contrary not only to Egyptian but also to Persian custom, since neither Persians nor Egyptians cremate their dead (3.16.3). The reversal of Cambyses' attitude is so violent that it could only be understood as madness. Cambyses had had epilepsy from childhood; this "sacred disease" turned into a frenzy of destroying custom, and

---

[56] Above, Ch. III, 93-94.

[57] Emphasis on family and children: 3.1.1 (an Egyptian doctor sent away by Amasis from wife and children); 3.3.1 (the tall and handsome children of Cassandane); 3.11.2 (Phanes' children killed before their father by Greek and Carian mercenaries); 3.14.2 and 4 (Cambyses dishonors Psammenitus' daughter and kills his son); 3.19.2 (the Phoenicians refuse to fight their "children," the Carthaginians); 3.32 (Cambyses kills his wife-sister; note the dog's "brother" in one version, and the wife's pregnancy in the other); 3.35 (Cambyses kills the son of Prexaspes); 3.36.1 (Croesus chides Cambyses for killing the Persians and their children). See also *Samian Stories* 316.

[58] Above, Ch. III, 97.

the offenses committed against Egyptian religion resulted in a final
blossoming of insanity directed against Cambyses' own people.[59]
At the same time, this illness is nothing but an extreme form of the
natural characteristics of tyranny. For the tyrant, as a speaker in
Herodotus says elsewhere, perverts the ancestral laws, rapes
women, and kills without trial.[60] In this sense, the self-destruction
of a petty ruler is a form of blindness. In a later section of the
narrative, Cambyses, shortly before his death, reinterprets his
former actions as the excessive precautions of a cautious ruler, and
in understanding their futility he comes to his senses.[61] This does
not quite agree with the picture of the mad Cambyses as the
destroyer of custom and of his own dynasty, as shown in the
Campaign *Logos*.

V

The fifth-century Greek tradition, as reflected in the *Persians*
of Aeschylus and the *Histories* of Herodotus, considers Darius the
embodiment of Persian character at its highest, and thus draws
his portrait in a very generalized form. Although the picture of
Darius in Herodotus differs considerably from that in Aeschylus,
this differentiation does not result in a highly individualized
portrait, and thus the unity of conception is less transparent here
than is the case for the other royal biographies in the *Histories*. A
further problem is that the prosperous state of Persia at this
time presented Herodotus with particular difficulties in applying
to Darius his scheme of the rise and fall of the ruler. The main
difference between Aeschylus and Herodotus is, however, that in
the former Darius appears as the wise king, while Herodotus clearly
presents a more unfavorable view. We shall find that the
Herodotean principle noted for the other Persian kings, namely,
that their fall is due to the conditions of their rule, applies to Darius
as well.[62]

[59] Cambyses' illness was related to the complex of diseases described in the Hippocratic treatise *On the Sacred Disease*.

[60] Hdt. 3.80.5; cf. above, Ch. III, 87.

[61] Ch. III, 101.

[62] On the picture of the wise Darius in Aeschylus' *Persians*, see B. Snell, *Aischylos
und das Handeln im Drama, Philologus*, Suppl. 20, No. 1 (1928), 75, and more fully
K. Deichgräber, "Die Perser des Aischylos," *NGG*, Phil.-hist. Klasse, 4 (1941) 183 ff.
Further, Swoboda in *RE*, s.v. Dareios No. 1, 2199 (1901). The idealized picture of
Darius reappears in Plato, *Laws* 3.696c 6 ff. and *Ep.* 7.332a. Daniels, *Rel.-hist. Studie*
173-76, wrongly insists that Herodotus gives to Darius no pattern of rule.

The essential characteristic of Darius is the extent of his power. This is the reason for his greatness and it becomes the main reason, not of course for his downfall, but for frustration in conquest. Hence the limitation of power is the central idea of the Darius *logoi*. It holds together the three principal groups of *logoi* dealing with this king: the accession story, the description of the extent of his power, and his campaigns. In the course of this narrative, Darius develops from the clever usurper into the great and prosperous ruler, and finally into the frustrated and tyrannical king of the campaign *logoi*.

The young Darius of the Accession *Logoi*, who appears unexpectedly on the scene to join the six conspirators at the moment they have discovered the fraud of the two Magi, is not represented as of royal blood, a treatment which appears to contradict the list of Xerxes' ancestors in Book 7.[63] Darius is here merely the son of the Achaemenid Hystaspes, of the highest nobility, but not a descendant of kings.[64] He should be compared with other usurpers in Herodotus who begin a new dynasty, for example Gyges, Deioces, Cyrus (to an extent), the Egyptian kings Psammetichus and Amasis, and the Greek tyrants Peisistratus and Polycrates. These usurpers use trickery to gain the throne, and thus Darius gives us his famous defense of lying, contradicting thereby the customary truthfulness of the Persians.[65] Usurpers are also activists, and Darius' success is based on his decisive urge for immediate action, both in the council preceding the assassination of the Magi and

[63] Otanes, in 3.71.3, addresses Darius merely as a young nobleman, and Darius himself implies the same when he justifies easy admittance to the king (3.72.2). The whole manner of Darius' election to the kingship also presupposes this. Hence Darius' coup d'état represents a genuine change of dynasty; cf. also Cyrus' dream about Darius (1.209). All this gives the appearance of contradicting the list of ancestors given by Xerxes in 7.11.2 (cf. Lehmann-Haupt in *RE*, s.v. Kambyses, 1810-11 [1919]), but Xerxes does not imply that all his ancestors had been kings. He means: I would not be the son of Darius the Achaemenid, if I did not take vengeance on the Athenians. Also, this list is not inconsistent with 1.111.5, where Cyrus' father and grandfather are given as Cambyses and Cyrus, for Herodotus could not have thought them identical with the much earlier Cyrus and Cambyses listed in 7.11. Hence in 7.11 the immediate ancestry of Cyrus the Great is not given; the list is similar to the genealogy of Leotychidas in 8.131.2-3, where the immediate ancestry of Demaratus is not included. In actuality, Darius was of course of royal blood; see Olmstead, *Hist. Pers.* 107 ff. Cf. also Ch. I, 31-32.

[64] Hdt. 3.70.3: παραγίγνεται ἐς τὰ Σοῦσα Δαρεῖος ὁ Ὑστάσπεος ἐκ Περσέων ἥκων· τούτων γὰρ δὴ ἦν οἱ ὁ πατὴρ ὕπαρχος.

[65] Hdt. 3.72.4; contrast 1.136.2 and 138.1. On *apatê*, see below, Ch. VI, 243 and note 17, and this chapter, note 53.

in the assassination itself. At the same time, the divine participates
from the beginning in his success. In Cyrus' dream Darius' rule
had been foretold as a necessary event; on the way to the Magi
an omen of hawks and vultures strengthens the determination of
the Seven; when Darius' horse neighs, a thunderclap confirms
his election as king.[66] Darius' luck is also shown in a number
of fortunate coincidences: he arrives on the scene just at the right
time; the conspirators are admitted to the palace "by good luck";
and Darius in thrusting his sword at the Magus, kills him and
not his friend Gobryas, who is wrestling with the Magus.[67]
Darius' accession is the result of human cleverness, divine fortune,
and luck. The relation of these elements is well brought out in the
story of the neighing of the horse, in which the cleverness of
the groom is accompanied by signs of divine favor (3.85-86).[68]
This is, then, a story of the clever usurper and his helper.

By contrast, the main emphasis in the description of Darius'
power is on legitimacy. Darius is said to have inherited an empire
built by Cyrus and Cambyses, and he strengthens his claim to it
by marriages. His main accomplishment is the organization of the
satrapies as tribute districts, for his power consists in his revenues.
The satrapy list therefore closes with the graphic description of
Darius' treasury and the conversion of the tribute into bullion,
available to the king at all times (3.96.2). Darius is a huckster
(kapêlos, 3.89.3), who owns an inherited empire. We have seen in
Chapter I that this view of Darius at the beginning of his reign is
highly stylized.[69] At the end of this group of logoi Herodotus
returns to the same picture in the story of the Plain in Asia (3.117).
This plain is surrounded by mountains, but rivers, breaking

[66] Cyrus' dream: 1.209. Hawk omen: 3.76.3. Thunderclap: 3.86.2. Cf. also
Causation 261.
[67] Arrival: above, note 64; cf. συνήνεικε, 3.71.2. Admission to palace: 3.77.1
(θείη πομπῇ χρεωμένους, cf. Rev. Crahay 206). Stabbing: 3.78.5.
[68] The accession of Darius may also be considered as a part of a roughly sketched
composition describing the accession, rule, and destruction of the Magus Smerdis and his
brother Patizeithes: for the accession, see 3.61 and ff.; for the rule, the short notice (it
is rather favorable) in 3.67.2-3; and for the destruction, the whole Accession Logos of
Darius. This recalls the accession stories of Gyges and Cyrus, in that Darius is here
strictly speaking only one element in a total situation comprising (a) the "hero," i.e.
the false Smerdis, (b) the avengers, i.e. the conspirators and Prexaspes, and (c) the
fortunate usurper, i.e. Darius. Differently Aly, Volksmärchen 97 ff.
For a more theoretical (and somewhat eccentric) interpretation of Darius' accession, see S. H. Rosen, "Herodotus Reconsidered," GM 18 (1963) 205-13.
[69] Above, Ch. I, 33.

through five passes, were used to irrigate the surrounding land until the Persian king closed them. Now the plain is inundated, and the water is made available to those who need it the most, for a tax in addition to the tribute. The Persian king is here shown to be just in his apportionment of water, but also greedy for revenue.

Thus far Darius is depicted as successful and in control of his empire. But other material added to the narrative on the power of Darius contradicts this picture. The Arabians, who bring gifts rather than tribute, show that not all peoples obey the Persian king in equal measure, and this idea is developed, in the description of the Ends of the World, into a general picture of a world in which Darius' empire is surrounded by regions he does not control.[70] At the same time, the Ends of the World contains the notion of a balance in the world, a balance both between the outer margins and the center of the earth, and between luxury and labor.[71] This idea is expressed in a short passage (3.108-109) that describes the role of divine providence in the animal kingdom. The dangerous winged snakes of Arabia are reduced in number by difficulties in reproduction, and are confined to Arabia by the ibises that stand guard at the border of Egypt and prevent the snakes from entering (3.107.2 = 2.75). The lioness gives birth to only one cub in a lifetime, but rabbits are plentiful, since that animal is able to conceive while pregnant. Thus weak animals are numerous and strong animals scarce, because of the foresight of the divine. This passage has been rightly applied to history by Pagel, for it furnishes an analogue, in the realm of nature, to the historical process.[72] But the passage is likewise clearly applicable to Darius' specific situation. Herodotus implies that the process of nature will control Darius' aspirations to excessive growth by limiting them in some way. The description of Darius' power contains at the same time elements which deny the unlimited extension of that power.

It is true, nevertheless, that the pictures of Darius as usurper and as legitimate monarch are on the whole rather favorable to him. The despotic element in his character, alluded to in the story of the plain, comes to the fore in the campaigns. Yet even

[70] Above, Ch. III, 102-103.
[71] Above, Ch. II, 54-55.
[72] Above, note 8; below, Conclusion, 312-13.

there we must make a distinction between Darius and Xerxes, in that Darius is more moderate and wiser than his son, although they both contribute to the unfavorable portrait of Persian tyranny. The basic situation in the campaign *logoi* is that Darius controls Asia firmly and is able to put down all revolts, but that he is defeated whenever he tries to expand the empire. The only exceptions to this are the Indian campaign (which, however, Herodotus does not describe in detail) and the European campaign, by which Darius gains a firm foothold in the Hellespont. It is evident, however, that Herodotus looked upon the latter campaign as a minor event rather than as a true conquest. The two main themes of the campaigns of Darius are thus the picture of the tyrant and the frustration of the conqueror.

The anecdotes following the story of the Plain in Asia show Darius' suspicious nature when he punishes one of the Seven Conspirators, Intaphernes, and his family, for an offense against royal prestige and in fear of a plot (3.118-19). When he saves the brother of Intaphernes' wife, he shows a certain superior justice combined with cruelty, and this combination is characteristic of him from now on.[73] Darius likewise combines generosity in rewarding the services of inferiors with a certain arbitrariness in dealing with them,[74] and a high regard for defeated enemies with

[73] On the Intaphernes story and its relation to the passage in Sophocles, *Ant.* 904-20, see Jacoby, *RE* Suppl. 2.232 ff., with whom I am in substantial agreement. Further, Powell, *Hist. Herodotus* 34, and recently: I. Errandonea, *SO* 32 (1956) 22-34 (with long bibliography); R. E. Wycherley, *CP* 42 (1947) 51-52; A. Lesky, *Die tragische Dichtung der Hellenen* (Göttingen 1956) 102, note 3. I. Errandonea, *Humanidades* 7 (1955) 59-69, is not known to me. For the combination of justice and cruelty in the figure of Darius, cf. also 3.159.1-2 (killing of 3000 Babylonians, and provisions for survivors); 3.117.3-6 (distribution of water). Similarly of other Persians, e.g. Otanes at Samos (3.147.1), and even of Xerxes (7.27-29 and 38-39), although more stories are told of Xerxes' cruelty, as well as that of the Persians, than about that of Darius; cf. 7.114.1; 7.180-81; below, Ch. V, 190; 9.108-13. Darius exhibits the noblest traits of Persian character. In the Intaphernes story, Darius' suspicion is no doubt aroused by the similarity between Intaphernes' behavior and his own when approaching the palace of the Magus. Nevertheless, his suspicion is characteristic of the tyrant (cf. Lang, *Biogr. Patterns* 76 ff.), his fairness, of the Persian king.

[74] In the *logos* on Persian customs, Herodotus says that the Persian kings never punish for single misdeeds, but reckon up services against disloyal acts (1.137.1). Cambyses' treatment of Sisamnes contrasts strongly with this (5.25), as do several of Xerxes' actions (e.g. his treatment of Pythius, 7.38-39, and of the Phoenicians at Salamis, 8.90.3). Here also Darius shows his superiority over Xerxes: the assassination of Oroetas was well deserved (3.128.5); Democedes (3.130.4), Syloson (3.140.4), Zopyrus (3.160.2), Megabazus (4.143.2), Coes and Histiaeus (5.11), Scythes (6.24), and Metiochus (6.41) were all well treated. An instance of cruelty is the murder of

typical Oriental cruelty.[75] In all these respects he is similar, but superior, to his son Xerxes. This superiority appears most strongly in the adviser scenes, where Darius (especially in the Scythian campaign) accepts good counsel more frequently, and with better grace, than does his son.[76] Darius typifies the Persian empire at a higher level of conduct than does Xerxes.

The frustrations of Darius stem from his dissatisfaction with the mere dominion over Asia as he received it from his predecessors. At the beginning of his rule Queen Atossa strengthens his desire to increase Persian rule by the projected conquests of Scythia and Greece (3.134). The motives she puts forward are illuminating: Darius must show himself a man and he must avoid revolts. The second reason refers to the theme of Darius' limitation to Asiatic empire, while the first is based on his greatness as an individual. We shall see later that this motivation contrasts with one put forward by Xerxes, in which he wishes merely to be the equal of his ancestors.[77]

Darius is successful in putting down revolts: Babylon, Ionia, Media (as related in a short reference by Herodotus), and the revolts at the beginning of his reign.[78] He does not live to subdue the revolt of Egypt, but that is successfully accomplished by Xerxes. His Indian campaign was also a success, but Herodotus makes nothing of this. All campaigns outside of Asia (with the exception, mentioned above, of the European campaign) are failures. The two most instructive *logoi* in this respect are the Babylonian and Scythian, which follow each other as do the Babylonian and Massagetan Campaigns of Cyrus, an obvious

---

the children of Oeobazus (4.84.2), a case of arbitrary killing is the death of Aryandes (4.166.2). Most characteristic is perhaps the story of Sandoces, governor of Aeolis, whom Darius crucified for having given wrong judgment, but whom he liberated after reckoning up his good deeds against his crimes (7.194.2).

[75] Regard for defeated enemies is mentioned indirectly in 3.15.2-3. Cf. the treatment of the Ionians after the Revolt (6.20 and 42 f.), and of the Eretrians after Marathon (contrast 6.94.2 with 6.119). Cruelty toward defeated enemies: 3.159.2.

[76] Note especially Darius' reaction to the advice of Gobryas during the Scythian campaign, 4.134.2 ff. The advice of Gobryas' son Mardonius, also accepted by Xerxes, was of a quite different nature (7.5, etc.); cf. above, note 55. Darius was well advised by Zopyrus also (Babylonian campaign, 3.153 ff.), by Coes (Scythian campaign, 4.97.2 ff.), and by Megabazus (European campaign, 5.23.2 ff.). He was deceived by Democedes (3.133 ff.) and by Histiaeus (5.106-107), and he did not accept the advice of his brother Artabanus before the Scythian campaign (4.83.1-2). Cf. Myres, *Herodotus* 160-61.

[77] Cf. also *Causation* 261 and 274. Below, 178 ff.

[78] Media: 1.130.2. Beginning of reign: 3.126-28.

parallelism underlined by certain resemblances between the Massagetae and the Scythians in the narrative.[79] The two major themes of the Scythian Campaign are European freedom as contrasted with Asiatic despotism, and the scorched earth policy of the Scythians, as based on the unlimited extent of their northern country. As we have seen, the idea of the limitless is introduced in the Scythian Ethnographic *Logos* and is the main element of strategy in the campaign.[80] This motif ties together the Scythian Campaign as a whole with the picture of Darius' power as developed by Herodotus. Darius, who could not accept the limitation of a purely Asian empire, is thus literally defeated by the limitless. In all other respects, his conduct in this campaign is excellent and quite different from the behavior of Xerxes in Greece.[81] Darius is defeated in Scythia only by his unlimited desire for expansion.

The other failures of Darius bear different explanations. Some are due to failures of his underlings. The Libyan failure occurs in a campaign not authorized by Darius in the first place. The disasters at Mt. Athos and at Marathon are, in Herodotus' description, merely the beginnings of subsequent actions against the Greeks. With Marathon, there begins the theme, already prefigured in the Scythian Campaign, of the superiority of Greek freedom to Asiatic despotism. Nevertheless, the decisive motif in Darius' relations with Greece is contained in the statement added to the notice of his death, that "he did not succeed in taking vengeance either on the rebelling Egyptians or on the Athenians" (7.4 = 7.8b.2). Darius dies before he can complete his conquests, and thus is frustrated in his ambitions.

The picture of Darius given in the campaign *logoi* corresponds closely to most of the numerous mentions of him elsewhere in the

---

[79] Cf. Pohlenz, *Herodot* 28, and note 1. Cf. above, Ch. I, note 48, and Ch. III, note 42.

[80] Above, Ch. III, 108.

[81] Darius shows folly and *hybris* in disregarding Artabanus' advice at the beginning, in murdering the children of Oeobazus, and in twice boasting of the size of his armament (4.87.1 and 92); the words that "he brought all he ruled" are ominous (4.87.1). Yet he showed sense during the campaign: he admired nature twice (the Pontus: 4.85.1 ff.; the river Tearus: 4.90-91), he followed the advice of Coes and of Gobryas (4.97-98 and 134.2), and he retreated before he was defeated. He was also lucky in his trust of the Ionians (4.137.2-3). On balance, he thus comes out much better than his son Xerxes; nevertheless, his portrait is not idealized to the extent that it is in Aeschylus and Plato.

narrative. Among these, the comparison in Book 2 of Darius with the early Egyptian king Sesostris is particularly noteworthy (2.110.2-3). There, the great Persian king is compared to the Egyptian conqueror Sesostris and is found wanting because he did not conquer the Scythians as Sesostris had done. At the same time, Darius is depicted as abiding by the priest's decision which forbade him to put his own statue in front of that of Sesostris, and thus he shows once more a certain moderation superior to that of Xerxes in similar situations.[82] Herodotus is aware of the ideal picture of Darius in the Greek tradition, but he has added to it certain unfavorable traits, as well as the concept of limitation as the specific explanation of his failures.

VI

When we compare the picture of Xerxes with the portraits of the preceding kings, it becomes apparent that they are in a sense the preparation for the full development of the figure of this last Persian king discussed by Herodotus. Hence Xerxes exhibits traits common to all other royal portraits. He shares with Cambyses the derivative nature of his rule as well as certain destructive tendencies, and with Croesus his excessive wealth. Even the divine guidance apparent in the affairs of Cyrus recurs in Xerxes' speech before the Persian nobles, when he says of the Persian tradition of conquest, "A god leads us thus" (7.8a.1). The main similarity, however, is with his father Darius, as we have had occasion to mention before. The portrait of Xerxes is the most complex royal portrait in the work, and we must consider not only his specific traits but also those generic features that are characteristic of royalty as a whole.

Xerxes, even more than Darius, is for Herodotus the typical Persian. During his description of the march into Greece, Herodotus changes back and forth from the description of the Persians to that of the king himself, and the Greek war is equally a war of the Persian nation and Xerxes' own private affair.[83] Stories told of Xerxes can

[82] Cf. the treatment of the priest and statue of Bel in Babylon, a story in which Darius is contrasted with Xerxes (1.183.3).

[83] E.g. in the March Section of Xerxes' campaign (7.26 ff.) the subject of the sentences changes from the Persians to Xerxes and back. In 7.22, προετοιμάζετο is middle voice, not passive (as Powell, *Lexicon* 318, has it), despite the fact that the sentence concerns the preparations at Mt. Athos, where Xerxes was not present; this interpretation results clearly from 7.25.1 (ταῦτα μέν νυν οὕτως ἐποίεε, etc.); cf. also 8.24.1 (προετοιμάσατο).

be paralleled by stories about the behavior of the troops during the Greek campaign. When Persian marines kill the first Greek they capture (his name was Leo), they act in a manner similar to Xerxes, when he disfigured the body of Leonidas after Thermopylae.[84] Characteristic of this relationship is the description of Xerxes on the march:

> Among these thousands of men there was none who, for beauty and stature, was worthier than Xerxes himself to hold such power. (7.187.2)

Xerxes is the typical Persian in an extreme form, both in magnificence and in cruelty.

In addition, Xerxes is the typical tyrant. His behavior is throughout motivated by passion rather than by reason, a fact particularly noticeable in the frequent adviser scenes, where Xerxes usually listens only to what he has already agreed on beforehand. His reactions to others are due to pleasure or anger to a higher degree than are those of any other king.[85] His outstanding characteristic is his pride in his magnificence (*megalophrosynê*) and no one is permitted to outdo the king.[86] In several places, Xerxes is compared to Zeus, and he himself wishes to make his empire "coterminous with Zeus' sky." [87] These ironical comparisons illuminate the excessive pride of this ruler. Xerxes is all appearance: his untold possessions result in a pride of luxury that is illustrated in the description of his tent and equipment, which are found by Pausanias after Plataea (9.82.1-2). These features are examples of *hybris* and blindness (*atê*), and thus are

---

[84] Hdt. 7.180; cf. 7.238.1.

[85] Pleasure (ἡσθείς, etc.): e.g. 7.28.3 (Pythius); 7.44 (ship contest); 8.69.2 and 103 (advice of Artemisia); twice in the Amestris story (9.109.1 and 2); 8.101.1 (advice of Mardonius). The word describes a typical reaction of kings to their advisers, e.g. 1.27.5 (Croesus). Anger (θυμωθείς, etc.): 7.39.1 (Pythius, contrasting with 7.28.3); 7.11.1 (advice of Artabanus); 210.1 (stubborn Spartan resistance); 238.2 (stubbornness of Leonidas). This is also characteristic of kings generally, e.g. 3.32.4 and 34.3 (the mad Cambyses). In his *thymos* Xerxes greatly resembles Cambyses.

[86] In 7.136.2 Xerxes says ὑπὸ μεγαλοφροσύνης that he will not equal the Spartans by murdering their emissaries. This is usually translated "magnanimity," but comparison with 7.24.1 (where the word clearly means "pride") shows that here also Xerxes is boasting and wants to show himself superior to the Spartans. The same motif is more clearly stated in the two parts of the story of Pythius the Lydian (cf. 7.27-29 and 39.2), and it also recurs in the viewing of the corpses at Thermopylae (8.24.2 ὑπερβαλέεσθαι).

[87] Hdt. 7.8c.1. Other comparisons with Zeus: *Action* 20-21, and note 10.

perfectly conventional. Xerxes is an extreme example of the typical great ruler whose pride leads to his fall.

Within this framework we find other features more specifically due to Xerxes' particular circumstances, and thus characteristic of Xerxes alone. Two elements are of special importance for the character of Xerxes: one is the fact that he is the legitimate successor of Darius and hence a scion of tradition; the other, that he lives at the moment of decision for the Persian empire, as Herodotus saw it.

It is true that Xerxes did not inherit the empire automatically. There had been another candidate for the throne, but his mother Atossa and the Greek exile Demaratus persuaded Darius that the succession was rightly his (7.2-3). Thus Xerxes "rose quickly" to power (7.14: the dream figure is speaking); and yet he acts throughout as Darius' legitimate successor, especially in the Persian Council, where he recites his entire pedigree with pride (7.11.2). Two other motifs depend from the idea of legitimate succession. The first of these, the inheritance of the war against Greece, parallels Cambyses' inheritance of the Egyptian war. It is characteristic of Xerxes, however, that he did not want to fight this war; we shall have to return to this point shortly. Another aspect of the idea of an inherited war is the resulting comparison of father and son, in which the son is found to be inferior to the father. This inferiority lies not so much in failure (for Darius had had his failures too), but in an excess of folly and crime. Particularly damaging to Xerxes is the comparison of the Scythian campaign of Darius with Xerxes' Greek Campaign, a comparison stressed in numerous ways in the work.[88] For Darius in Scythia had behaved with a certain reasonableness, which is altogether lacking in Xerxes. Therefore, Darius had been able to save his army, while Xerxes loses his. Symbolic of this contrast is the fact that Gobryas is a better adviser to Darius in the Scythian campaign than his son Mardonius is to Xerxes in the Greek war: in both cases the sons are inferior to their fathers.[89] Another aspect of Xerxes' inferiority is expressed early in the work in the anecdote that Darius refrained from stealing the statue of Bel in Babylon, while Xerxes, in order to abduct it, killed the priest (1.183.3). Thus Xerxes is also morally inferior to his father.

[88] See *Causation* 262-63 and note 43; 271, note 60; 272, note 62.
[89] Above, note 55.

Besides the inheritance of the war, the emphasis on Xerxes' youth also depends on the idea of succession. In actual fact Xerxes was old enough to have a son of marriageable age at the time of the Greek invasion.[90] Cambyses, whose youth is also mentioned by Herodotus, had been regent of Babylon for eight years before his accession (although Herodotus may not have known this).[91] The youth of Xerxes, and possibly also the youth of Cambyses, are thus not features of historical tradition, but rather natural inferences from the idea that these kings were the sons of famous fathers. Actually, Darius was much younger, when he came to the throne, than either Cambyses or Xerxes, but his youth is not an important element in the account of his accession, and when it is mentioned by Atossa, this is to make him confident of military exploits (3.134.2). By contrast, Xerxes' youth is the explanation of several unfavorable character traits. Xerxes himself refers to his youth in excusing his changes of mind about the Greek campaign, as well as his anger at Artabanus. Artabanus in turn tells him in effect that because of his youth he listens to false counsel.[92] Thus the result of Xerxes' youth is lack of steadfastness, a motif that we shall find to be central to Herodotus' picture of him.

As a successor, Xerxes is naturally concerned with his own succession, but the stories about his precautions show his insecurity in this respect. When Cyrus was about to cross the Araxes river into the country of the Massagetae, he gave his kingdom to Cambyses and left Croesus as his adviser (1.208). When Darius was about to invade Greece, he chose Xerxes as his successor (7.2-3). Xerxes made no such arrangements, but he left Artabanus behind as his viceroy. During the campaign, however, he shows an even greater fear for the security of his own person than for the dynasty as such. After Salamis, he sends his bastard children back to Asia (8.103)[93] and immediately heeds Artemisia's advice to save himself and, in his person, the empire.[94] Xerxes

---

[90] Hdt. 9.108: his name was Darius.

[91] See Olmstead, *Hist. Pers.* 86 ff. Cambyses' youth is mentioned to him by Croesus, 3.36.1. On the topic of the rashness of youth, cf. also E. R. Dodds, *Euripides: Bacchae*² (Oxford 1960), Commentary 197 (on lines 973-76).

[92] Hdt. 7.13.2 and 18.2 (cf. 16a.1 and b.2).

[93] On the Hermotimus story (which is associated with Xerxes' concern for his children), see below, Ch. VI, 284-85.

[94] Hdt. 8.102.2. Stein rightly brackets the phrase περὶ οἶκον τὸν σόν as a gloss on the preceding words ἐκείνων τῶν πρηγμάτων; without it the sentence has a more personal application.

equates his empire with his person. In the final story about
Xerxes, he is seen destroying his brother and his brother's family
somewhat in the manner of Cambyses; such behavior might call
forth the destruction of Xerxes' own family.[95] Did Herodotus
know—and did he motivate it in this story?—that the succession
from Xerxes proved eventually not to be regular? Xerxes was
murdered by a certain Artabanus (not his uncle), who then
persuaded Xerxes' own son Artaxerxes to murder his elder
brother Darius, whom he falsely accused of Xerxes' murder.[96] In
the oblique remarks on Xerxes' own succession, the theme
is handled ironically, so as to show the insecurity of Xerxes'
rule.

Xerxes the successor has inherited his father's wars. He thus
lives at the time of decision for the empire and the world in
general, since the war against Greece is at the same time a war
for world domination. This view of Herodotus is a matter of
interpretation rather than of historical fact, for Herodotus was
quite aware, as he shows in several places, that Xerxes' empire
survived the war and continued to cause troubles for the Greeks.[97]
However, the cumulative build-up of Persian world aspirations
throughout the work forces the reader to accept Xerxes' campaign
as a decisive event of world-wide importance. Xerxes himself

[95] Hdt. 9.108-113. Actually, the main destroyer is Xerxes' wife Amestris, on whose
character see 7.114.2. For Cambyses' crimes against his family, see above, 168, and
Ch. III, 95.

The question of succession arises when the Persian king leaves the country on a
campaign: according to Persian *nomos*, a successor must then be appointed (7.2-3).
As stated in the text above, this was done by both Cyrus and Darius, but Cambyses
(who had no children) merely appointed the Magus Patizeithes as caretaker of his
house (3.61.1), and Xerxes left Artabanus behind as viceroy (7.52.2). (Darius, on the
Scythian campaign, seems to have disregarded the Persian *nomos* entirely.) After
Salamis, Xerxes showed great concern for his illegitimate sons (8.103), but nothing is
said about his legitimate children, of whom Herodotus mentions Artaxerxes several
times (6.98; 7.106; 151; 152) and Darius, the eldest, once (9.108). Since Darius was
of marriageable age in 479 B.C., he must have been old enough in 480 B.C. to have
been appointed successor (*pace* Macan, *VII-IX*, on 8.103). The only mention of the
question of succession—and an indirect one—is thus the Artaynta story, 9.108-13, in
which Masistes, the brother of Xerxes, is killed, as Smerdis had been killed by
Cambyses. The disregard of the Persian *nomos* of succession, shown by the Persian kings
in some instances, is typical of their destructive tendencies.

[96] Olmstead, *Hist. Pers.* 289-90. Cf. E. Wolff, "Das Weib des Masistes," *Hermes*
92 (1964) 51-58, esp. 53 ff.

[97] In 8.102.3, Artemisia says to Xerxes after Salamis: "If you and your house
survive, the Greeks will continue to fight many battles on their own behalf." Cf.
6.98.2, where Herodotus himself mentions the same fact.

calls the Greeks the last obstacle to world dominion (7.8c.3), and in committing his total resources to the campaign (resources which are described as almost wholly lost in the defeat), he shows his awareness of the decisive nature of the struggle ahead. This decisive moment is the inevitable result of a long Persian tradition, as Xerxes himself explains to the council of Persian elders and again to Artabanus at the Hellespont. The same inevitability is expressed in the dreams of Xerxes and Artabanus, in which Xerxes is forced to go on his campaign.[98] The idea of an inevitable decision based on tradition is one of the most characteristic elements in the portrait of Xerxes, and it distinguishes him from all other kings.

Xerxes' reaction to this situation is uncertainty and vacillation. According to a view found both in the Attic dramatists and in Herodotus, hesitation and ambivalence are typical reactions to the necessity for decisive action. In the *Libation Bearers* Aeschylus fills much of the play with the emotional as well as the rational ambivalence of Orestes and Electra, and in Herodotus the same attitude prevails among the Greeks before Salamis, and with Xerxes during the whole of the campaign. Xerxes' ambivalence is his outstanding characteristic, because it is the expected reaction to the situation he has to meet.[99] A decision is not simply a rational problem, but the situation it is meant to resolve contains irrational and daemonic elements, and so cannot be solved without divine participation. Xerxes' ambivalence manifests itself primarily in his changes of mind about the advisability of the Greek campaign, and later by his emotional instability when faced by defeat. Its psychological explanation is Xerxes' youth, but its significance lies in its relation to decisive action.

Two particular elements of Xerxes' situation thus help to defeat him. The first is legitimacy of succession, which causes an excessive fear for his own person and is to be contrasted with the insecurity of his own line of succession. The second consists of the necessity for decisive action: for this necessity causes an ambivalence that results in Xerxes' flight after the first defeat. A further element is perhaps of even greater importance, since it directly involves the Greeks. Xerxes, the despot, is defeated by the representatives of freedom. Absolute control over his forces—

[98] *Action* 33 ff.
[99] *Ibid.* 41.

again the consequence of a long tradition—is shown to be a fundamental weakness.

The motif of Xerxes' mastery over his forces is stressed throughout the Greek Campaign. Of all the Oriental kings, Xerxes is the one who most wants to see and supervise everything for himself. He views his armament twice, once before and once after the crossing of the Hellespont. He visits Thessaly to see for himself how the natural obstacle of the Vale of Tempe could be overcome (7.128.1). He attributes the lack of success at Artemisium to the fact that he did not personally supervise his navy in that battle, and he expects his subjects to fight much better at Salamis under his personal surveillance. During the battle of Salamis he writes down the names of all those he sees fighting well, but he is constantly in error and has to depend on information from others. In his first conversation with Demaratus he claims that people fight well only under a master, but later Salamis disproves this contention.[100] Both at Thermopylae and at Salamis Xerxes is shown that the Greek city states, quarrelsome but free, are superior in valor to nations ruled by a single master.

These three features (reliance on legitimacy of succession, the necessity for action, and despotism) best illustrate how Xerxes' basic conditions and attitudes turn against him. But they are merely examples of a more general aspect of Xerxes' character, in which he touches upon the very principles of Herodotus' own conception of the world. In all his complexity, Xerxes is primarily a contradictory character, in whom opposite qualities balance each other throughout. Thus, Xerxes' magnificence is balanced by weakness, his courage by fear, his nobility by baseness. Xerxes' contradictory attitudes are exemplified by a large number of anecdotes, the most famous of which are the two stories about Pythius the Lydian, who, when offering all his gold to Xerxes, is outstripped by him in generosity, but when asking for a favor, is cruelly punished (7.27-29 and 38-39). In a similar manner Xerxes rewards and punishes his own subjects to excess.[101] He

---

[100] Viewing of armament: 7.44 and 7.59.2 ff. Surveillance at Artemisium and Salamis: 8.69.2 and 86. Cf. K. Reinhardt in Marg, *Herodot* 360-61. List of names: 8.90.4. Fight under a master: 7.103.4.

[101] Rewards: 7.106-107; 7.19.2 and 26.2; 8.90.4. Punishment: 7.35.3 (Phoenician and Egyptian builders of Hellespont bridges); 7.56.1 (Xerxes watches his army driven across the bridge under the whip; cf. his words to Demaratus, 7.103.4); 8.15 (Persian

honors and respects certain sanctuaries but destroys others.[102]
Like his father Darius, he admires nature at the Hellespont, but
he does so after having treated the strait shamefully, as if it were
his slave.[103] A similar antithetical relation exists in Xerxes'
fortunes, with their sudden reversal at Salamis, as is shown in the
sending of the two heralds to Susa, the hunger of his army on the
return from Greece, and the weakness of his excessive armament.[104]

Thus we may say that in Xerxes all character traits turn into
their opposites and help in various ways to destroy him. It is
therefore not a question of any single characteristic that causes
his downfall: his whole kingly existence brings about his ruin.
This ambiguity in the characterization of Xerxes presents us, I
think, with a conception of the tragic hero peculiar to Herodotus.
The portrait of Xerxes is the most fully developed in the work.[105]

---

admirals afraid of X., cf. 8.86); 8.90.3 (Phoenicians decapitated); 8.118.4 (ship
captain decapitated); 9.113.2. Xerxes' cruelty is directed principally against his non-
Persian subjects; cf. Herodotus' remark, 8.119.

[102] Xerxes shows respect for Athena's temple at Troy (7.43.2), and the temple of
Zeus at Halus (7.197). He destroys the sanctuary of Apollo at Abae (8.33), attempts
the destruction of Delphi (8.35-39), and destroys the Acropolis at Athens (8.53.2),
although on the next day he orders sacrifices there (54). Cf. Macan, *VII-IX*, Vol. 1,
part 2, 529, on 8.109, line 15.

[103] The relation of man to nature is a theme appearing both in Darius' Scythian
Expedition and in Xerxes' Greek Campaign; cf. above, note 81, and *Action* 42 and note
46. Characteristic of Xerxes are attempts to change nature: he cuts the Mt. Athos
peninsula apart (7.24; one might compare the oracle of Apollo to the Cnidians forbidding such an enterprise, 1.174.3-6) and inquires into the possibility of inundating
all of Thessaly, which was created by Poseidon (7.130.1-2). He honors a plane tree
(7.31), but mistreats the Hellespont (7.35), while later sacrificing to it (7.54.2-3).
The last instance has a connection with the river motif, which is prominent in the
campaign (Xerxes' army drains nearly all Greek rivers—another perversion of nature,
7.21.1, etc.); likewise connected is the theme, stated by Artabanus at the Hellespont,
that both sea and land are Xerxes' enemies (7.49.2, etc.).

[104] Heralds: 8.54 and 98-99. Hunger of army: 8.115.2 ff.

[105] Some scholars see in Mardonius, rather than in Xerxes, the principal hero of
the Persians in the war of 480-79 B.C. See Macan, *VII-IX*, Vol. 1, part 2, 518 (line 13)
and 541 (line 11). Myres, *Herodotus* 78 and 216. Yet the "unheroic" waverings of
Xerxes are deliberate and conform to the Herodotean conception of the hero (see
Action 40 ff.). Cf. also W. Marg in Marg, *Herodot* 619 ff. Xerxes is the hero of the
Persian Wars because Salamis, and not Plataea, is the central battle (see below, Ch.
VI). Mardonius is a derivative figure: his motives and actions can be paralleled
elsewhere in the work. His basic desire to become satrap of Greece recalls earlier
Persians in 3.120.3 and 5.31 ff. (Aryandes of Egypt is also comparable, cf. 4.166.)
His reason for remaining in Greece after Xerxes has decided to depart is largely fear
of punishment (cf. Aristagoras' reason for starting the Ionian Revolt, 5.35.1). His plan
to conquer Greece originated with Darius. Mardonius' campaign in Greece imitates
that of Xerxes: cf. e.g. the second capture of Athens to impress Xerxes, 9.3.1; the

VII

The biographies of Croesus and the four Persian kings find their individual differences, as well as their cohesion, in the pattern of the rise and fall of the ruler, through the simple principle of stressing for each king a different aspect of this single pattern. Cyrus the Founder, Cambyses and Xerxes the Successors, Croesus and Darius the Powerful Monarchs, are individual creations that are at the same time typical manifestations of royal power as such. Individual character is thus not the result of any accidental traits of human nature, but is strictly connected with typical situations. Croesus differs from Darius because the limited Lydian empire is better exemplified in a moderate king; Xerxes differs from Cambyses because of his special position at the end of a long Persian development. In Herodotus Man and Situation are closely tied to each other by means of a pattern that represents the typical and recurrent aspects of events.

The four great Persians also fit together in the overall cycle of Persia's growth and decay. In this picture their individual failures (such as Cyrus' campaign against the Massagetae or Darius' Scythian expedition) are less important than their general achievements. Only Xerxes' defeat is also the defeat of Persian greatness as such. We have in the work a picture of the general rise of Persia to its highest point at the time of Darius, where it finds its limits, as is shown by Xerxes' defeat. In this view, the Persians are identified with Asia, as the Greeks are identified elsewhere with Europe, and the Persian conception of freedom as external independence and mastery over others is the Asian way of life *par excellence*.[106] Oriental despotism was thus based on a free decision of the Persians and their kings. Before Cyrus revolted from the Medes, he put before the Persians the alternatives of hard and slavish work, or wealth acquired through mastery of others (1.125-26). In choosing the latter, the Persians embarked on the road to empire.

In considering the Persians as a nation, we may again ask what specific factor or factors brought about their rise and their

flight of troops after Plataea, as after Salamis, 9.89.4 (cf. 8.115). The gold in the tent at Plataea is Xerxes' (9.82). What Mardonius principally lacks, when compared with Xerxes, is magnificence. I do not deny, of course, that he is also a figure in his own right; for that reason something is made of the disappearance of his body after Plataea (9.84). See also below, Ch. VI, 298.

[106] Above, Ch. I, note 80.

decline. Persian national character is best described in the *logos* on Persian customs (1.131-40), a section that shows a remarkable consistency with the portrait of the Persians in the rest of the work.[107] A keynote of this *logos* is the feeling of unity that exists in Persian society. When sacrificing, a Persian does not pray for himself, but for all the Persians, including the king, for he feels that he himself is included among all Persians (1.132.2). This social cohesion takes, however, special forms; for mutual honor depends on one's station in life and is thus on a graduated scale of values. The Persians honor a man's birthday, but the actual display at the birthday meal depends upon one's station (1.133.1). Their communal deliberations during meals are a further sign of unity. Rank is honored by different forms of greeting on the streets. Among nations, rank is determined by proximity: one honors most those nearest to oneself, and gradually reduces honor proportionately to the increase in distance. Hence the Persians believe themselves to be the best of men and think of those living farthest as the worst (1.134.2). Thus internal cohesion with a corresponding respect for rank may be considered the main characteristic of Persian rule over others. This feeling for rank was inherited by the Persians from the Medes, who (as Herodotus seems to say in a somewhat obscure statement) had formed an empire in which each nation ruled over its nearest neighbor, with the Medes themselves at the top of the pyramid.[108] The Persians (who ruled of course more directly over each

[107] For the analysis of the *logos* on Persian *nomoi*, see in general How and Wells; Pohlenz, *Herodot* 71 ff.; E. Wolff, "Das geschichtliche Verstehen in Tacitus' Germania," *Hermes* 69 (1934) 157 ff. (= Marg, *Herodot* 404 ff.). Wolff discusses well the idealizing tendencies of the portrait of the Persians in the *logos* itself, but he does not discuss in detail the relation of this portrait to the characterizations in the rest of the work, and these relations are more complex than he apparently sees. Further, Trüdinger, *Studien* 24-26; Myres, *Herodotus* 148-50. My remarks above are not an analysis of the structure of the *logos*, which to an extent follows a standard pattern: gods—sacrifices—meals—social intercourse—dress—sex and family—education—justice—morality (the end of the *logos* is less traditional).

[108] Hdt. 1.134.2-3, a difficult and much discussed passage (see the commentaries). Without going into detail, I believe the general meaning to be as follows: (1) The Persians honor their neighbors in inverse proportion to the distance they live from them, thus considering themselves in the center, and consequently the best of all nations. (2) Under the Medes, this system had pertained to government, each nation ruling over its nearest neighbor, with the Medes at the apex. (3) The system was taken over by the Persians, but applied by them to honors only, not to government (see Stein), since the Persian nation progressed gradually through both direct and indirect rule. (4) Generally speaking, the Persians accept foreign customs easily, etc.

nation) transformed this type of government into a mere code of ranks, with honors accruing from rank. Asiatic autocracy is a proportional system. It is for this reason that Persian kings have to ask who those Greeks are who come from afar to make repeated demands of them.[109]

Another theme mentioned in the *logos* on Persian customs is the easy acceptance of foreign customs by the Persians. This should be connected with Persian love of luxury, shown in the Persian choice of a life of wealth and leisure when Cyrus proposed it to them. This love of luxury is a danger of empire, against which the same Cyrus warned the Persians after they had acquired it (9.122): luxury is both a motivation for empire and its greatest liability. The *logos* on customs presents the Persian belief in wealth as their love of gifts, and their belief in numbers as encouragement of large families. Both motifs are then developed in other parts of the *Histories*.[110]

The end of the *logos* stresses a number of further themes characteristic of the Persians in the work. Foremost among them is the final statement that Persian magnificence is reflected in their proper names, all of which, according to Herodotus, end in the consonant -s. This statement is symbolic of the external magnificence, as well as the unity, of the Persians.[111] Secondly, there is the stress on purity and cleanliness, features which have a religious basis and are connected with the Persian respect for purity of water and with the river motif. With this cult of purity goes love for truth and a great emphasis on honor (*timê*). Honor and

---

[109] Hdt. 1.153.1 (Cyrus at the occasion of a Spartan embassy), 5.73.2 (Artaphernes, of an Athenian embassy), 5.105.1 (Darius, of the Athenians). Cf. 5.13.2 (Darius, of the Paeonians). Croesus also did not originally know anything about the Greeks (1.56.1-2). Cf. Aeschylus, *Persians* 231.

[110] Love of gifts: 3.84.1 (cf. 3.20.1); 3.160.2; 7.116; cf. Stein on 3.84, lines 5 ff. Belief in numbers: cf. the Persian army lists and especially the warning of Artabanus, 7.47.2 ff.

[111] Hdt. 1.139 The passage is in agreement with ancient ideas of etymology. The statement that the names of the Persians are similar to their persons (σώμασι, see Stein) and to their magnificence should refer to the length and peculiar sound of the names, not to their meaning. The statement that all Persian names end in -s (which is true of the Greek forms only—Herodotus knew no Persian: see H. Diels, "Die Anfänge der Philologie bei den Griechen," *NJbb* 13 [1910] 17 ff.) symbolizes national unity. All this is based on the idea that the sound of a word is somehow connected with its meaning.

With this passage contrast 1.148.2, where the unity of the Greek names of festivals (all of which end in -a) contrasts with the disunity of the Ionians (so Herodotus wants us to understand). Both passages occur at the end of a *logos*. Cf. below, Ch. V, 231.

loyalty, as we have seen, are the key concepts in the relations between the kings and their underlings.[112]

The ideas of national unity, rank, love of wealth, magnificence, purity, and loyalty are confirmed in the rest of the work wherever we observe the Persians at their best, but they are also often contradicted by individual actions of the Persian kings and their subjects. This contradictory attitude of the Persians is climaxed in the Greek campaigns, where it corresponds to the contradictory character of Xerxes.[113] It finds its best symbolic expression in the paradox that the Persian troops, while men, are acting like women.[114] This theme is last stated in the story of the murder of Masistes by Xerxes, in which Xerxes is himself ruled by a woman (9.108 ff.). Thus we see the Persian nation deteriorating by a reversal of the great qualities described in the *logos* on Persian customs at the beginning of the history of the Persian kings.

If one is to name one basic condition of Persian greatness that also causes their downfall, this would be an excess of unity, both internally and in the structure of their empire. The conquest of Asia, as Herodotus describes it, proceeded at a rapid and un-hindered pace, with the result that all Asia was soon unified under the rule of the single person of Cyrus the Founder. Hence there was not in the East that multiplicity of forces characteristic of Greece. The Oriental rulers were able to deal with their external enemies by and large on an individual basis. Within their kingdoms the Persian kings also had only single enemies, and these primarily in time of crisis, such as at the beginning of Darius' reign. It is true that Herodotus had found in the traditions about Persia certain pro-democratic tendencies, but these did not affect the overall cohesion of Persian governmental structure. The nature of the Eastern form of government is symbolically expressed

[112] On loyalty (δικαιοσύνη), see e.g. 6.24.1; 7.51.2-3. Justice is a matter of mutual give-and-take (cf. 2.147.3 and 151.1; 7.52.1). See also above, Ch. III, note 83. Loyalty is especially important in the Darius stories (3.128; cf. Democedes, Gillus [3.138], Histiaeus, and Zopyrus).

[113] Cf. e.g. 7.180-81, where Persian marines (or perhaps Phoenician sailors) first kill Leo, and then greatly honor Pytheas of Aegina.

[114] Artemisia, tyrant of Halicarnassus, shows herself superior to the men in Xerxes' forces, and she herself points out that Greek sailors are as superior to Persian sailors as men are to women (8.68a.1). At Salamis, Xerxes finds that his men are women, and his women men (8.88.3). The theme may find its first expression in the omen of the mule born with male over female organs (7.57.2; contrast the first line of the oracle in 6.77.2). It is last mentioned (9.107.1) in, as well as implied throughout, the Masistes story, with its superiority of Queen Amestris over Xerxes (cf. above, note 95).

by the palace walls with which the Mede Deioces surrounded himself after assuming the empire, and by the court ceremonial he created.[115]

Excessive unification within and without made Persia into an autocracy desiring unlimited expansion. Unification is of course the basic force establishing any historical entity, be it a king's rule or that of a dynasty. In this sense, unification is the basis of individuation. However, when conquest is unopposed, the result is an excessive concentration of power, and a single entity in the total world of history tries to behave as if it were that totality. This is the excess to which the Orient fell prey. Instead of considering itself merely one state beside others, Persia tried to grow beyond the confines of Asia (its natural province) and comprise the whole world. It was thus a natural process of history that prevented such excessive growth, and in the decline of Asiatic power the plurality of historical forces was re-established.

[115] Hdt. 1.98.3-99.1.

Chapter V

THE PATTERN OF HISTORY: THE WEST

I

Whenever Herodotus arranges events to follow the general historical pattern that is dominated by the cycle of fortune, he is describing the actions of individual units in isolation. The pattern is thus not confined to the Eastern monarchies; it is, however, most clearly exemplified there, since the work's major *logoi* deal with the East. The pattern also appears in the shorter accounts which concern various fragments of Greek history, wherever Herodotus shows us the general development of individuals and states. It is here sometimes harder to discern, partly because the Greek accounts are elliptic, but principally because this pattern is overlaid, as will be shown in this chapter, by another, which is based upon the multiplicity of Greek city states. Some scholars believe that Herodotus draws a clear distinction between East and West in this respect, in the sense that the Greeks, by virtue of their moderation and civic excellence, are exempt—or at least protected—from the cycle of fortune. It will become apparent that this is an erroneous view, for Greek states and Greek individuals are just as liable to growth and decay as is the East.[1]

We have noted earlier, using the example of the Greek Ameinocles of Magnesia, Herodotus' fondness for completing the life stories of certain individuals simply because their full lives reveal a change of fortune. Ameinocles, it will be recalled, collected untold wealth, but this did not prevent the death of his son.[2] Certain obscure mentions of individuals (Greek or Oriental) find their probable explanation in the idea of change of fortune.

[1] For the distinction between Greeks and barbarians, see J. Jüthner, *Hellenen und Barbaren* (1923), and Helen H. Bacon, *Barbarians in Greek Tragedy* (New Haven 1961). Further, Schmid-Stählin 1.2.585, and Regenbogen, *Werk* 226 ff. (=Marg, *Herodot* 84 ff.) and similarly Regenbogen, "Die Geschichte von Solon und Krösus," *Human. Gymnas.* 41 (1930) 1-20 (=Marg, *Herodot* 375 ff.). Recently, *Fondation Hardt: Entretiens sur l'antiquité classique* 8 (1962): *Grecs et Barbares*; the contributions by H. Schwabl, H. Diller, and H. C. Baldry concern our period.

[2] Above, Ch. II, 76 and note 83.

When the Persian Oroetas sends a messenger to the court of
Polycrates to entice the tyrant to visit him, the messenger's name
Myrsus is given for no apparent reason. Myrsus, son of Gyges the
Lydian, may owe his inclusion to some notoriety of which we are
not now aware, or to the fact that his name, as well as that of his
father, recall early Lydian kings of different dynasties.[3] The same
Myrsus is mentioned only once again, namely in the narrative of
a battle during the Ionian Revolt:

> . . . the Persians themselves were killed, as well as their generals
> Daurises, Amorges and Sisimaces. With them also died Myrsus
> the son of Gyges. (5.121)

This is all we know about Myrsus: his name, his participation in
a mission, and his death.

Somewhat more transparent is the story of a third individual,
Pytheas, the son of Ischenous of Aegina, who participated in the
battle of Salamis. Before Artemisium, we are told, this Pytheas
was captured by a Sidonian vessel of the Persian navy and was
saved by the enemy because of his outstanding bravery (7.181.1-2).
At Salamis the Sidonian ship was captured by Pytheas' com-
patriot Polycritus, whose father Crius had been a hostage in
Athens because of the medism of Aegina (8.92, cf. 6.50.2-3 and
73.2). Thus Pytheas miraculously survived the capture of his
vessel and miraculously retained his freedom. Now while Pytheas
perhaps belonged to an illustrious Aeginetan family known to us
from Pindar and Bacchylides,[4] the function of this person in the
work is to underline three changes of situation: his survival after
capture illustrates the contradictory behavior of the Persian
marines, who had wantonly killed another Greek before they came
upon Pytheas; his survival at Salamis stresses the change of
fortune of that battle; and his deliverance at the hands of a fellow Aeginetan illustrates the change of attitude of the Aeginetans
toward the Persians. In this instance the changes of fortune of a
single individual are intimately connected with changes of much
greater importance.

[3] How and Wells on 3.122.1.

[4] He cannot be identified with any known members. In 9.78-79, Herodotus tells a
story about Lampon, son of Pytheas, of Aegina, perhaps the father of the Pytheas
famous for athletic victories celebrated by Pindar and Bacchylides; see How and
Wells, and B. Snell (ed.), *Bacchylidis Carmina cum fragmentis*[7] (1958) 44* f. Our Pytheas
is hardly the father of Lampon (differently *RE*, s.v. Lampon No. 2); he may be of a
collateral branch of the family, but this is conjecture.

The personal lives of the Greek tyrants and other great men contain further examples of changes of fortune, and more particularly of the pattern of the ruler. Of the three outstanding examples, Polycrates, Miltiades, and Cleomenes, one is a Greek tyrant, the other an Athenian aristocrat, and the third a Spartan king. Among them, Polycrates in particular is treated exactly like a Persian ruler.[5] According to Herodotus, Polycrates rose to power by treachery. He killed one of his brothers, exiled another, and deliberately mistreated his friends. He later attempted to enlarge his rule to the point of founding a Greek maritime empire in the Aegean. His death was caused by this expansionist policy and by the treachery of the Persian Oroetas, who laid a trap for him when he invited him to discuss a plot against the king of Persia. Thus two basic conditions of Polycrates' rule may be said to have caused his downfall.[6]

Miltiades, the descendant of a powerful family in Athens, is considered by Herodotus something of a tyrant also, since he ruled on the Chersonese as an autocrat and had been accused of tyranny at Athens. In his family, a series of narrow escapes and violent deaths forms a characteristic pattern as Herodotus tells the story. His uncle, the elder Miltiades, was saved by Croesus from death at the hands of the Lampsacenes (6.37.2); his father Cimon had been killed by the sons of Peisistratus in the Prytaneum (6.103.3); and his brother Stesagoras was murdered in a prytaneum too—one in the Chersonese (6.38.2). Our Miltiades himself was subject to similar violent changes of fortune. As tyrant of the Chersonese he had to escape twice, first from the Scythians and shortly afterwards from the Phoenician navy at the close of the Ionian Revolt (6.40.1-41.1). During the second flight, his son Metiochus was captured, but escaped death through the leniency of Darius (6.41.2-4). Back in Athens, Miltiades escaped death twice more, when he was accused first of tyranny and later of betraying the Athenian people (6.104 and 136).[7] Miltiades' heroism at Marathon is thus framed by his two trials, and this was perhaps the reason for the stress Herodotus placed on the

---

[5] On the pattern of the Polycrates story, see Daniels, *Rel.-hist. Studie* 160-63 and 174; also H. Fohl, *Tragische Kunst bei Herodot* (Diss. Rostock 1913) 66-68. I have not seen J. Diesner, "Die Gestalt des Tyrannen Polykrates bei Herodot," *AAntHung* 7 (1959) 211-19.

[6] Cf. *Samian Stories* 317 f.

[7] Cf. Hdt. 6.104.1: "having escaped a double death . . ."

escapes and violent deaths in the account of the other members of the family. However, Miltiades shows other tyrannical traits. One of his arguments for attacking the Persians at Marathon was that a victory would make Athens the foremost city in Greece (6.109.6). After Marathon he attacked Paros because of a personal grudge and, in committing a religious crime during the siege, he hurt his thigh, somewhat in the manner of Cambyses (6.133 ff.). This wound, rather than his last trial, brought about his death. The history of Miltiades and his family follows a particular pattern of fortune and impiety, since that family had risen to greatness by the good fortune of having the tyranny of the Chersonese offered them through an oracle (6.34 ff.).[8]

The story of Cleomenes forms, as Myres has shown, a particularly vivid account, despite the fact that it has to be pieced together from separate *logoi*.[9] The central motif of the stories of Cleomenes is his impiety; for the Spartan kings, as Herodotus of course knew, were religious leaders, and the Spartans in general, as we shall see, were considered by Herodotus a particularly religious people. Cleomenes' acts of impiety were largely committed during his campaigns: his greatest crime lay in his disregard for Spartan moderation in conquest as practiced in the late sixth and early fifth centuries.[10] Cleomenes' birth and accession had both been irregular: his father, without children by his first wife, had taken a second wife against Spartan custom (5.40.2), and from her he had had Cleomenes as his first-born son. When the first wife subsequently gave birth to three children, Cleomenes remained the candidate for succession, although the eldest of his half-brothers, Dorieus, would have been a better king.[11] Cleomenes in turn acted against custom by eliminating Demaratus, the incumbent of the other royal house (6.61 ff.).

[8] The tyrannical picture of the Philaids is developed by Herodotus without any reference to their friendly relations with the Peisistratids (cf. 6.35 and 103). Cf. Hammond, *Hist. Greece* 183.

[9] Myres, *Herodotus* 77, 104, 125, and 174 f. However, Cleomenes is not in any sense the central hero of the narrative of Books 5 and 6, any more than Mardonius is the hero of 7-9 (cf. above, Ch. IV, note 105).

[10] In this, Cleomenes' behavior contrasts with his refusal to support the schemes of Maeandrius of Samos (3.148) and of Aristagoras of Miletus (5.50-51), but these two stories are outside the main *logos*, as it were. Cf. the discrepancy between the Cyrus accounts, above, Ch. IV, note 54.

[11] Dorieus, the foremost of the sons of Anaxandridas (5.42.1), left Sparta to found a colony without consulting the Delphic oracle (5.42.2), and his attempt at colonization

The story of Cleomenes' religious crimes[12] begins with his disregard, during one of his invasions of Attica at the time of the overthrow of the Peisistratids, of the true meaning of the warning by the priestess of Athena on the Acropolis, that Dorians were not allowed in the sanctuary. The omen came true when Cleomenes had to leave Attica shortly thereafter (5.72.3-4). Further, he bribed the Pythia at Delphi to help him oust Demaratus (6.66.2-3 and 75.3), and he defiled a number of sanctuaries: that of Demeter at Eleusis, and at Argos the sanctuaries of the hero Argos and of Hera (6.75.3 and 79-81). When Cleomenes had gone insane and had committed suicide, most Greeks blamed his illness and death on his impiety: some ascribed them to his bribery of the Pythia; the Athenians, to the sacrilege at Eleusis; and the Argives, to the crime against their hero Argos. Herodotus stresses the theme of impiety by telling the Argive version in great detail, but he himself considered Cleomenes' death the punishment for the expulsion of Demaratus (6.84.3), while the Spartans themselves gave an altogether different version in claiming that his insanity was caused by his habit of drinking unmixed wine, a habit acquired from the Scythians when he was plotting revenge on the Persians (6.84.1-3). The common Greek versions thus stress Cleomenes' impiety, while Herodotus blames his violation of the royal succession, and the Spartan story refers to Cleomenes' expansionist interests. Together, these three motifs explain the rise and the fall of Cleomenes.[13]

---

in Africa was unsuccessful. On his second expedition, he did consult the oracle, but he did not follow its advice and so perished (5.45.1), according to one version. His companions all perished in Sicily. Here also the religious motif is paramount: Dorieus' impatience (cf. 5.48) led him to impiety. See in general Daniels, *Rel.-hist. Studie* 68. On the Spartan kings, see below, 197-98.

[12] I mean the story as told by Herodotus, for Cleomenes' Argive expedition may have preceded the expulsion of the Peisistratids, although it is reported at the end of his reign. For the date, see E. M. Walker in *CAH* 4 (1926) 164, and cf. How and Wells, 2.352, and Hammond, *Hist. Greece* 196.

[13] In 5.48, Herodotus makes the well-known statement that Cleomenes did not rule for a long time, but died childless, leaving only a daughter, Gorgo. This statement conflicts with the known length of Cleomenes' reign (about 520-490 B.C.). However, Stein on 5.48, line 3, may be right in suggesting that Herodotus is thinking of his early accession, his violent death, and the youth of his brother Leonidas when he succeeded him. Herodotus' statement parallels another made a little earlier, that one of Dorieus' companions ruled over Selinus for only a short time, and was killed at an altar by the Selinuntians (6.46.2). Therefore, in both cases, the prime meaning may be religious (cf. above, note 11), in that the life of an impious leader is cut short as a punishment.

Herodotus does not give single independent *logoi* to the Greek kings and tyrants,[14] but the examples cited suffice to show that he has nevertheless included enough particulars in his narrative to present in each case an exact portrait of a powerful individual. He was also aware that Greek autocracy as such gave a rough unity to the sixth century B.C. His descriptions of the Corinthian Cypselids, the Athenian Peisistratids, and the kings of Sparta and Cyrene are fragmentary histories of individual dynasties of a kind, and they achieve a unity similar to that found in the accounts of individuals. The story of the Cypselids is told as a parable in the speech of the Corinthian Socles before a Peloponnesian audience intent on restoring the Peisistratids to power in Athens at the very end of the sixth century (5.92). The aim of the speaker is to dissuade the audience from this venture by pointing out the evils of tyranny. His speech summarizes the main traits of tyranny at a time when tyranny was disappearing from the Greek scene, and the portrait it gives of the rise and fall of a whole "dynasty" of tyrants is at the same time a summary of tyranny as the characteristic form of government of a past age. This speech is an excellent example of the application of the pattern of rise and fall to a Greek subject.

The story of the birth of Cypselus recalls the Cyrus story and the birth of the divine child. Cypselus rises from a lowly origin: his mother, a descendant of the noble house of the Bacchiads, was lame (whence she was called Labda, for one of her legs was shorter than the other), and she was married to a man of inferior origin. The marriage was childless, and the oracle, when consulted, promised a son. The text of the oracle (as well as that of an earlier one given to the Bacchiads) bristles with etymologies and symbols of royalty, such as the eagle and the lion, and the predicted "birth on the rocks" recalls divine births on mountain tops. Tyranny is implied to be an honor in the etymology of the name of Eetion, father of Cypselus, as "he who is greatly honored."[15] The Bacchiads (the relatives of Labda, who were at

---

[14] E.g. for Gelo of Syracuse, Herodotus gives only the rise to power (7.153-55), for Periander, a number of typical stories (see below, note 18); similarly for Cleisthenes of Sicyon (5.67-68; 6.126 ff.).

[15] Compare the lowly origin and weak nature of the first Battus, in the Theraean version (4.155.1), and Battus the Lame, father of the notorious Arcesilaus III (4.161.1). This type of story is also familiar from the accession story of king Agesilaus of Sparta (Xenophon, *Hellcn.* 3.3.2 ff.). In Herodotus, the Macedonian dynasty also has a low

that time ruling in Corinth) try to kill the baby, but the child survives by smiling at the assassins; the smile of the divine child is a well-known feature of this type of myth.[16] A further attempt at assassination is prevented by hiding the child in a chest (*kypselê*). The imagery of the birth of the divine child is more fully developed here than in the Cyrus story, and the development is particularly poignant, because it contradicts the intention of the speaker, who wants to show the horrors of tyranny rather than its greatness.

The speaker's anti-tyrannical bias appears first in the statement that tyranny was a necessary evil for Corinth (5.92d.1). A third oracle, which precedes the assumption of tyranny, while describing Cypselus as a "blessed king," ends in the ominous words:

"You and your children, but no longer your children's children."

The predicted limitation of the length of reign is common in Herodotus, and is to be assumed, I believe, for all dynasties.[17] The subsequent account of Cypselid rule is not a complete history of the family, but stresses their increasing cruelty and perversion, especially in the figure of Periander, who is to Herodotus the tyrant *par excellence*.[18] The speech ends with the story of Periander's relations with his dead wife as the utmost in tyrannical perversion. Thus, the speech tells of the growth and nature of tyrannical power as such by drawing a vivid contrast between a glorious birth and later wickedness.

---

origin (8.137 f.), contrasting with the divine, or heroic, origins of the Scythian and Spartan dynasties (4.5 ff. and 6.53). Labda was married to a Thessalian, not to a Bacchiad (5.92b.1). The motif of the questioning of an oracle περὶ γόνου derives (in Herodotus) from myth and tragedy. For births on mountain tops, cf. C. Kerényi and C. G. Jung, *Essays on a Science of Mythology. The Myth of the Divine Child and the Mysteries of Eleusis*, tr. by R. F. C. Hull (New York 1949) 70, 73, and 82-88; J. Laager, *Geburt und Kindheit des Gottes in der griechischen Mythologie* (Winterthur 1957) 29, 58-60, 154-55, 167-68, and 174, etc. Cf. also above, Ch. IV, 161 ff. and note 34.

[16] Vergil, *Ecl.* 4.60. Cf. E. Norden, *Die Geburt des Kindes: Geschichte einer religiösen Idee* (Leipzig 1924) 59 ff.

[17] See *Causation* 262, note 41 (allotment of time). Cf. especially the oracle predicting eight generations of kings in Cyrene (4.163.2), and another predicting fifty years of Ethiopian rule over Egypt (2.139.3; cf. above, Ch. I, note 37). From these instances it would seem to follow that plain indications of lengths of rule should be interpreted as involving divine limitations, even where divine punishment is not involved, as it is in the famous limitation of the Mermnad dynasty to five generations (1.13.2). In all these cases, Herodotus shows that the end of rule involves a "necessity," which usually takes the form of punishment for a crime.

[18] *Samian Stories* 320 and note 14 (on the three Periander stories, 1.23 f., 3.48 ff., 5.92z, as illustrating the general course of tyranny as such).

The history of Peisistratus and his sons is given in a much more
fragmentary form. The first element recalling Oriental dynasties
is the omen of the birth of the ruler, when the tripods boil over
without fire during a sacrifice performed at Olympia by Peisistratus' father (1.59.1 ff.), an omen interpreted as a warning by
the wise Chilon of Sparta. Then follows the story of Peisistratus'
three accessions to tyranny, a story which is important within the
context of Athenian history as such,[19] but which from the point
of view of the "dynasty" of Peisistratus may be compared with the
accessions of Polycrates and Darius. The story of the trick played by
Peisistratus upon the Athenians when he had himself introduced into Athens by Phye ("the Well-grown One") representing Athena,
plays, I think, upon the etymology of Peisistratus ("the Persuader
of the People"), although Herodotus does not specifically say so.[20]
Herodotus does not give the history of Peisistratus and his sons
in any detail, but he clearly intends to contrast an early munifi-
cence with later cruelty, directed primarily against other noble
families.[21] Thus, the picture of the Peisistratids is drawn with
reference to the whole picture of the Athenian development, with
its change to democracy through the efforts of a noble family, the
Alcmaeonids. To Herodotus, the family of Peisistratus was
essentially a divisive force in Athens.

The history of the kings of Cyrene, depending as it does quite
literally on a specific Cyrenaean source, which was possibly
written, has less to teach us about the cycle of fortune than do
other Greek accounts, although here also Herodotus develops
briefly some individual reigns, and sketches a segment of royal
history as far as his special purposes allow.[22] The accounts dealing

---

[19] Above, Ch. III, 86-87, and below, 208-209.

[20] Hdt. 1.60.3-5. The fact that Peisistratus had been named after the son of Nestor
(5.65.4) does not exclude the etymological pun here. στρατός originally means
"people."

[21] On the structure of the Peisistratus *logos*, see above, Ch. III, 86-87. Herodotus
begins the *logos* with the statement that Athens was "weak and divided" under
Peisistratus, a statement followed by the omen at Olympia presaging an evil tyrant.
All this refers to the last period of Peisistratus' rule, for concerning the first tyranny
Herodotus praises Peisistratus' good government (1.59.6): contrast with this the last
sentence of the *logos* (1.64.3), which is an explanation of the introductory sentence.
Therefore, the *logos* describes at least two stages in the moral degeneration of tyranny;
a third is mentioned later, after the murder of Hipparchus: it is the worst (5.55). Thus
the development corresponds to that of the Cypselids (see above, note 18).

[22] For the source of Herodotus' account of Cyrene, see above, Ch. III, note 104.
Brief development of individual reigns: the murder of Arcesilaus II by his brother

with the Spartan kings, on the other hand, form a most interesting series. Here too Herodotus follows a specifically local motif—the Spartan idea of irregular marriages—which undoubtedly has a connection, in Spartan mythology, with the rape of women.[23] This motif is joined from the start with another, the hatred of the two royal houses of Sparta for each other. Eurysthenes and Procles, the ancestors of the two houses, were twins, and the question of which twin was the elder was settled by watching the mother handle them (6.52.2 ff.). The prerogatives established in this manner between the two houses led to an undying hatred, which contributed much to the weakening of Sparta.[24] It is true that at an early period, down to the time of Croesus, Spartan royalty, restricted in its power by the *eunomia* of Lycurgus, appears in a favorable light (1.65 ff.), but the picture changed thereafter, when king Anaxandridas, a member of the more honored house of the Agiads (descendants of Eurysthenes), was compelled because of childlessness to marry a second wife, against Spartan custom (5.39 ff.). Cleomenes, as we have seen, was the son of this second marriage and the first-born of Anaxandridas: Dorieus, Leonidas, and Cleombrotus were born later from the first marriage. In the inferior house of the Eurypontids (descendants of Procles) a parallel event occurred: King Aristo married a third time (abducting his wife from a friend), and Demaratus was born, it was rumored, less than ten months after his mother's new marriage, a fact used by Cleomenes to oust Demaratus and to replace him by Leotychidas, a member of a collateral branch of the Eurypontid

---

(4.160.4) and the death of Arcesilaus III (4.164.4) are two examples of the cycle of fortune. More important is the overall sketch of the dynasty, although Herodotus gives us only that segment that leads to the death of Arcesilaus III, since the *logos* gives one reason (*aitiê*) for the Persian invasion; see above, Ch. III, 112. However, he has in mind the whole dynasty, as he shows by citing the oracle of the eight generations (4.163.2), and by the fact that the death of Arcesilaus III appears as a pure accident caused by his own wickedness. Arcesilaus "wittingly or unwittingly" failed to understand the oracle of the oven (4.164.4), and he had acted contrary to the democratic settlement of Cyrene, which had been sanctioned by the Delphic oracle (4.161.3). This combination of crime and folly caused his downfall; hence, when Herodotus says that Arcesilaus "fulfilled his destiny" (4.164.4), this means no more than that he ended his life. Arcesilaus' death and the end of the dynasty are not connected in any way. Nevertheless, in the segment related by Herodotus there is both loss of power and increase in wickedness (note the democratic settlement and the characters of Arcesilaus III and Pheretime). See also above, note 15.

[23] So in the story of Helen and in the earlier story of the Leucippidae. Cf. especially Alcman, fr. 1. On the Spartan "Raubehe," cf. R. Merkelbach, *Philologus* 101 (1957) 22.

[24] On the thematic importance of strife, see below, 198.

house (6.61 ff.). Three times Herodotus stresses the importance of the mother, and twice the irregularity of marriage leading to the accession of individuals who did not expect to rule. This last motif is used with great effect during the Persian Wars, when Leonidas and Pausanias appear unexpectedly as the great Spartan leaders.[25] The history of the Spartan kings (whom Herodotus treats like true royalty and makes responsible for Sparta's fortunes) shows a continuous development: on the basis of an original hostility between the two houses, irregular matrimony (after a period of strength) leads to disturbances in royal succession; these irregularities result in two bad kings coming to power in the persons of Cleomenes and Leotychidas, and in two heroes, Leonidas and Pausanias, appearing during the Persian Wars. The dangers of royal succession are the same in Sparta and in Persia, and Herodotus in several places compares the two Spartan royal houses with the Persian.[26]

II

The examples cited may suffice to show the applicability of the pattern of the ruler to Greek tyrants and "dynasties." We turn now to the discussion of another pattern in Greek history, which (as mentioned earlier) is based on the multiplicity of forces in the Greek world. This is the pattern of disunity and strife, and, like the pattern of the ruler, it will also be found to be applicable to the East, but to a lesser degree. The distinction between East and West is a matter of emphasis rather than of complete divergence. In the East, power was developed more freely than in the West, since internal and external strife was restricted to a few crucial periods. In Greece, on the other hand, power could not grow unhindered, because states were engaged in constant competition with one another. The restrictions placed upon the acquisition and maintenance of power may be self-imposed and thus moral (we shall later find at least one case of true moderation in politics), but more commonly they are forced upon states and individuals from the outside. Hence injustice between historical agents is an important subsidiary theme in Herodotus.

[25] Leonidas: 7.204-205.1. Pausanias: 9.10. Mention should also be made here of Gorgo, daughter of Cleomenes and wife of Leonidas, who appears in two stories as a woman superior to men (5.51 and 7.239).

[26] Hdt. 6.59 and 7.2-3.

The significance of these modes of interaction, if I may so call them, lies in the fact that for Herodotus history itself consists of just this constant opposition of forces which, in fighting and obliterating one another, create alternate periods and individual cycles in the same manner as observed earlier for the pattern of the ruler. From an overall point of view, such cycles balance each other, despite their irregularities. The total result of the vicissitudes of the historical process is the stability of history as such. However, states or individuals operating within the framework of competitive strife are better able to withstand, or avoid, changes of fortune, because they are closer to the historical process itself. When seen individually, disunity, strife, injustice, and vengeance may work for evil as well as for good, and the same is true of their counterparts, unity, justice, and cooperation. It is when we look at the whole picture, as Herodotus does in his work, that we see restricted power triumph over absolute power, and for this the Persian Wars are the prime example.

Herodotus, using the ideas and principles just mentioned, develops as one of the main themes of his work the contrast between Athens and Sparta. Despite the lack of a unified account for these two cities, both emerge with clear individual features. The comparison is initiated by a passage preceding the first Athenian and Spartan *logoi* at the time of Croesus' preparations for war against Cyrus (1.56-58). There Herodotus derives the Athenians from the pre-Greek Pelasgians and the Spartans from the Dorians, saying that the Pelasgian people have never left their original abodes, but that the Dorians have been "much driven about." The Athenians joined the Greek nation only later, by changing their language, in a process consisting of definite stages, which are described by Herodotus elsewhere (8.44.2). The characterization of Athens and Sparta in Herodotus differs greatly from that given by Thucydides, to whom Sparta is sedentary and Athens revolutionary.[27] But Herodotus, dealing as he does with an earlier period,

[27] Thuc. 1.2.5 actually agrees with Herodotus on the sedentary nature of the *early* Athenians, but he attributes to it their strength rather than their weakness. Since he subsequently develops the power of Athens from her naval effort, he is basically describing a situation later than the Persian Wars. Thucydides differs from Herodotus in his judgment on the energy of land powers, and thus his judgment of Sparta in the *Archaeology* does not agree with that of Herodotus, except with respect to the effect of the Spartan constitution (Thuc. 1.18.1). He restricts his analysis of power to sea power, while Herodotus (for both Sparta and Athens) considers equally the land and the sea,

is aware that Sparta, before the Persian Wars, was a more active (although frustrated) power than Athens, which began to come into conflict with other Greek states on a large scale only after the establishment of democracy, namely in the war against Chalcis and Boeotia, in the Ionian Revolt, and in the Aeginetan Wars.[28] The aggressive policy of Athens was an effect of the Persian Wars, as Herodotus well knew.[29]

The brief account of the origins of Athens and Sparta thus sets the tone for the further accounts regarding the two states. In all of these, the main emphasis is on external relations rather than on internal history *per se*, so that both states are seen in their intimate connection with the affairs of Greece and with the Orient as a whole. The history of the Spartan kings is given in some detail because the kings were Sparta's leaders in war, and the constitutional development of Athens is important in the work because Athens was weak under the tyrants and became strong under democracy.

III

The history of Sparta, as related by Herodotus, begins with the institution of the *eunomia* by Lycurgus (1.65.2-66.1). Previous to that change, Herodotus says, Sparta had been the worst governed Greek state and had had no relations with foreigners.[30] The

at least before the Persian invasion (see Ch. VI, 255-56). Land and sea, in the fifth century, have political and even moral significance. Cf. e.g. the imagery in Aeschylus, *Ag.* 990-1002, with the comments by George Thompson (Vol. 2 [1938] 107).

[28] Unlike modern scholars, Herodotus gives comparatively little space to the foreign relations of Athens under the Peisistratids. He stresses principally the Peisistratid alliances with other states (1.61; 5.63; 5.90; 5.94; 5.96.1, etc.), but makes little of their foreign conquests. The capture of Sigeum is described in a highly elliptical account (5.94-95; cf. Ch. III, note 123); that of Naxos is mentioned in a parenthesis (1.64.2). The elder Miltiades' acquisition of the Chersonese is not presented as a Peisistratid measure (6.36). The Peisistratids are interested primarily in security of rule (1.64.1-2): for this, compare Thucydides' judgment on the tyrants, 1.17. Cf. also below, note 58.

[29] Athenian aggressiveness develops in the following stages: Miltiades' Parian adventure after Marathon (6.133.1) is attributed by Herodotus to private motives, although he also alludes to Athenian greed (6.132). Themistocles' Andrian expedition after Salamis (8.111-12) is more strictly presented as an "imperialist" venture, although there is an allusion to Themistocles' greed too (8.112.1). The last account has been compared to Thucydides' Melian dialogue: cf. Aly, *Formprobleme* 99, and M. Gigante, *Nomos Basileus* (1956) 136, note 1 (=Marg, *Herodot* 273, note 13). The imperialist line of action is continued in the Athenian liberation of Ionia and especially in the campaign of Sestus (9.106 and 114 ff.).

[30] As How and Wells point out on 1.65.2, the early hostility toward foreigners conflicts with the acceptance of the Minyans (4.145). I would suggest that the period of

effects of the change were an increase in the strength of the newly organized state and the opening up of foreign relations both hostile and friendly. This resulted in imperialism of an Oriental kind:

> Because of the excellence of their country and the large number of men, they at once shot up and flourished, and consequently they were no longer content to keep quiet ... (1.66.1)[31]

Sparta's history, however, differs from Oriental history in that her expansionist tendencies were at once checked by the divine, whereas in the East a check was more commonly imposed at the end of a longer period. The first object of Sparta's lust for power was Arcadia, but the Delphic oracle forbade its conquest except for the capture of Tegea. The Tegean war in turn contains several features that recall Oriental wars of conquest. The Spartans at first fail, because of overconfidence in an obscure oracle,[32] but later they succeed through the cleverness of Lichas, who practices deceit on the smith of Tegea and abducts the bones of the hero Orestes.[33] The principal difference between Sparta and the East lies ultimately in her relation with the divine: after forbidding total conquest, and subsequent to the obscure oracle, Delphi finally assisted in the conquest of Tegea by advising Sparta to acquire the bones of Orestes, an act whereby Sparta became superior to Tegea. The result was an increase in power:

> From this time on, whenever (the Spartans and the Tegeans) made trial of each other, the Spartans were much superior in warfare; and they had already conquered most of the Peloponnesus. (1.68.6)

---

bad government and hostility to foreigners must be thought of as immediately preceding Lycurgus, and not as extending to the mythical period. Herodotus seems to accept the Spartan tradition that placed Lycurgus about four generations after the conquest of the Peloponnese (1.65.4; cf. 7.204).

[31] The combination of a good constitution, fertile land, and numbers leads to imperialism. Nature arranges matters in such a way that military strength and occupancy of a rich country do not coincide; cf. 1.32.8 and especially 9.122.3: "the same land does not grow a marvelous crop and men brave in warfare." The early Persians lived in a notoriously poor country (1.71.2); so did the Spartans, according to a statement by Demaratus (7.102.1, speaking of all the Greeks; cf. Conclusion, 308); and the same topic is known from Athenian patriotic oratory. "They ... shot up" (ἀνέδραμον) is a metaphor from the growth of plants; see Stein *ad loc.* and Powell, *Lexicon*, s.v. Not content "to keep quiet" (ἡσυχίην ἄγειν): this expression is used with respect to the Oriental kingdoms; cf. 7.11.2; 8.14.1; 8.108.3. However, the more poignant expression is οὐκ ἀτρεμίζειν (see Powell, *Lexicon*, s.v. ἀτρεμίζω).

[32] On the meaning of κίβδηλος, see above, Ch. IV, note 26.

[33] Trickery and deceit: above, Ch. IV, 167 and below, Ch. VI, 243.

This passage reads like a comment on an Asiatic dynasty, but the situation differs in that Sparta did not fully conquer Tegea and the rest of the Peloponnesus. Thus her conquests did not develop into a true Peloponnesian empire.

The idea of limited success is continued farther in the story of Sparta's relations with Croesus. When advised that (because of the victories just mentioned) Sparta was the most powerful state in Greece, Croesus concluded an alliance with her, an agreement which was eagerly accepted by the Spartans because, as Herodotus says, they were pleased that Croesus had recognized their eminence (1.70.1). But the alliance came to naught when the Spartans, called upon by Croesus in his war against Cyrus, arrived too late to be of help, since Sardis had already fallen. Contemporaneously, Sparta is shown to be engaged in a domestic war with Argos over the region of Thyrea in the Peloponnesus. In this war she was successful; thus, while Herodotus does not yet show Sparta's being prevented by domestic difficulties from engaging in foreign wars, he nevertheless points a contrast between her domestic and her foreign commitments, an idea that comes to be important later on. At this moment we find Sparta engaged in warfare with two Peloponnesian states.[34]

Sparta's participation in international politics is erratic and inconsistent. After Cyrus' accession she warned him "not to destroy any city on Greek soil, as they would not tolerate it" (1.152.3), but she did not define whether that meant only the mainland of Greece or Greek Asia Minor as well. In fact, Sparta refused at that time to come to the assistance of the Ionians (1.152.2), just as she later refused Maeandrius of Samos and Aristagoras of Miletus, in two scenes described with an obvious parallelism (3.148 and 5.49-51). This attitude reappears at the end of the Persian Wars, when Sparta refuses to support Athens in defending the Ionians (9.106.2-4).

Herodotus means to draw a contrast between Sparta's reluctance to commit herself abroad in the late sixth and early fifth centuries, and an earlier desire to do so. Her alliance with Croesus and the sharp words spoken to Cyrus should be compared with her aggressive war against Polycrates, an overseas war undertaken

[34] On the Thyrean war, cf. Ch. I, note 66, and Ch. III, note 26. The principle of carrying the history of a Greek event only so far as its contact with the East derives ultimately from ethnographic *logoi*; cf. Ch. I, 34 ff.

ostensibly to repay certain Samians for help previously rendered to Sparta, but perhaps actually to punish Samian piracy (3.47.1).[35] Yet this was also a half-hearted war, and on the whole we have in Sparta a power whose actions are inconsistent, because her plans of conquest cannot be fully carried out. This attitude also reappears during the Persian Wars.

The relations between Sparta and Athens at the time of the overthrow of the Peisistratids give us a similar picture. In two expeditions the Spartans helped the party of Cleisthenes, because they understood that the Delphic oracle demanded the expulsion of the tyrants, for "they honored the Divine more than human affairs" (5.63.2). In two further expeditions Sparta opposed Cleisthenes. The first of these was a private venture of Cleomenes, who was motivated by friendship with Isagoras of Athens, and perhaps even by relations with Isagoras' wife (5.70.1-72.4). This expedition thus falls outside the series of official Spartan invasions of Attica.[36] The second invasion was intended as a punitive expedition against the Athenian *dêmos* for the treatment Cleomenes received during the preceding private venture (5.74-76). Still another attempt by Sparta to interfere in Athenian internal affairs came to nothing because of the opposition of the Corinthians (5.90-93). Here the Spartan motives were (1) annoyance when Sparta found out that the Delphic oracle's demand for the expulsion of the Peisistratids was a fraud; (2) a feeling of having betrayed the Peisistratids without receiving any gratitude from the Athenians; and (3) fear of the growing power of Athens, a fear reinforced by certain oracles predicting future Athenian hostilities against Sparta (5.90-91.1). Here again we find a motive reminiscent of Eastern monarchs in their fear of a growing rival;[37] Sparta, however, is not intent on the destruction of her opponent, but merely on restoring the Peisistratids. Sparta's attitude toward Athens is no more consistent than her relations with the East, and she is not motivated by real expansionism.

Thus, the portrait of Sparta includes features of imperialism,

---

[35] Cf. also, for the early period, Sparta's colonization of Thera (4.147 f.) and her relations with Amasis (3.47.1).

[36] Above, Ch. IV, note 5.

[37] Fear of a growing rival: see *Causation* 251 and note 15. Cf. also 3.1.2 (Amasis and Persia); 1.163.3 (Arganthonius and Persia); 1.190.2 (Babylonians and Persia). Thus the motif is connected primarily (but not exclusively) with Persian imperialism. Cf. Pohlenz, *Herodot* 202 and note 1.

especially at the beginning of her history, while later her aspirations become restricted in scope by troubles with her neighbors in the Peloponnesus, by an insular attitude that keeps her from foreign entanglements, and by quarrels between the two royal houses and irregularities in the succession. The main factor, however, that operates in favor of a quieter policy is Sparta's high moral and religious sense (I am here describing Herodotus' picture, and not ours), and these admirable traits thus have both beneficial and harmful effects. Taken together, these factors combine to offset an early "restlessness" (1.56 and 1.66.1), as can best be seen from the Spartan rejection of the arguments of Aristagoras of Miletus when he tries to induce them to join the Ionians in fighting Persia:

> "In the region of the Choaspes river (he said, pointing to a map) is Susa, where the Great King lives, and there are his treasures of money: if you take this city, you may confidently compete with Zeus in riches." (5.49.7)

The Spartan answer, delivered by Cleomenes, was that Persia was too far from the sea. Elsewhere, of course, Cleomenes is the opposite of the moderate Spartan, and his aggressive policy contrasts with Spartan custom in the same manner as the behavior of the Eastern kings conflicts with the customs of their native countries.

Sparta's conduct during the Persian Wars agrees with the general development outlined by Herodotus. Although she remained the leader of the Panhellenic League throughout the invasion of Xerxes and Mardonius, the conduct of the war was primarily determined by others, especially by the Athenians. The typical representative of Spartan policy is her general Eurybiades, who is forced into action by Themistocles.[38] Her failure to send troops to Marathon and to Thermopylae is attributed by Herodotus to her strict observance of religious

---

[38] The hegemonic position of Sparta is affirmed in the speeches before Gelo of Syracuse (7.159 and 161), further in 8.3 (below, 220-22), at Plataea in the speeches of the Athenians and the Tegeans (9.26-27), and elsewhere. Themistocles' initiative at Salamis: 8.58 ff., etc. Also characteristic is Spartan procrastination in engaging the enemy at Plataea (9.47-48). Eurybiades is bribed by Themistocles at Artemisium (8.5), agrees to fight at Salamis because he fears the Athenians might leave (8.63), but later reverts to his original lack of initiative (8.74.2), and opposes the attack on the Hellespont after Salamis (8.108.2). He received, of course, the crown of victory in Sparta (8.124). Further, below, Ch. VI, 286.

festivals.[39] More fortunate were the irregularities in royal succession, in that they brought forth Leonidas and Pausanias. Sparta's moral strength found its purest expression at Thermopylae and in the final victory at Plataea, as well as in the heroism of her citizens in combat,[40] but it did not win the war. The greatest weakness of Sparta in the Persian Wars was her insular character. The symbol of this attitude is the Isthmian Wall, the mentions of which constitute an important motif in the narrative of Xerxes' invasion. Herodotus' famous judgment on the comparative merits of Athens and Sparta during the Persian Wars includes the following passage:

> Even if many rows of walls had been laid across the Isthmus by the Peloponnesians, the Spartans would have been betrayed by their allies, not willingly, but out of necessity when the allies were captured one by one by the Persian navy, and thus the Spartans would have been left alone, and in isolation they would have died nobly accomplishing great deeds of valor ... (or) they would have made a pact with the Persian ... For I cannot discover what use the Isthmian fortifications would have been had the Persian controlled the sea. (7.139.3-4)

The Panhellenic Council met at the Isthmus before the arrival of Xerxes and decided to defend the pass at Thermopylae (7.172 ff.). When the Persians arrived there, the first thought of the Greeks was to return to the Isthmus, where they could defend the Peloponnesus (7.207). When the Athenians had brought the Greek fleet to Salamis, they found to their dismay that the Peloponnesian land force was busy fortifying the Isthmus, so that Attica was left undefended (8.40), and it took the persuasion of Themistocles, and finally his trick of communicating with Xerxes, to keep the Peloponnesian navy from joining their compatriots (8.49.2, etc.), especially after the Persians had moved toward the Peloponnesus (8.71-74.1). All during the fall of the year 480 B.C. the Isthmian wall was being built, and although it was not continued during the winter, because of an eclipse in October (9.10.2-3), the spring of the following year saw further work on it while Mardonius was reoccupying Athens (9.8.1).

[39] Hdt. 6.120 (Marathon); 7.206.1 (Thermopylae). Herodotus does not state that the reasons given were mere pretexts, as some scholars think.

[40] Many of the *aristeiai* which Herodotus appends to his battle descriptions concern Spartans: 7.226-32 and 9.71-72.

Therefore, Herodotus concludes that it was really finished only at that time. The completion of the wall made all the difference in Sparta's attitude toward the war, for while they had previously been anxious to keep the Athenians on their side, they now no longer cared:

> I cannot tell the reason why at the time of the embassy of Alexander of Macedon to Athens they were very anxious to keep the Athenians from medizing, but now they cared not at all, unless it was that the Isthmian fortification was now complete and they thought they no longer needed the Athenians. (9.8.2)

Nevertheless, the Spartans eventually sent an army to help the Athenians against Mardonius, when Chileos of Tegea pointed out that the Isthmian wall was no defense against an Athenian navy on the side of the Persians (9.9.2). It was no doubt the behavior of the Spartans at this time that called forth Herodotus' comments in 7.139. Insularity, and not any moral weakness, also determined the conduct of the Spartans at the very end of the war, when they suggested the transfer of the Ionians to the mainland (9.106.3) and later refused to participate in the capture of Sestus at the Hellespont (9.114.2).

IV

A conscientious morality, traditional valor and piety, and royal competition thus operate in the development of Sparta primarily in a negative way, so that she is capable only of isolated accomplishments. In the characterization of the rise of Athens in the *Histories*, similar factors frequently have an opposite effect, and Athens, while at times less virtuous, yet proves in the end to be more effective than Sparta.

Central to the understanding of Herodotus' picture of Athens is his concept of power (*dynamis*). Familiar from Thucydides as the main force behind Athenian imperialism, the notion is on the whole employed differently in Herodotus, in the sense that power is to him a static quality characterizing royalty and empire.[41]

[41] As Dr. A. L. Peck has shown, the notion of *dynamis* undergoes a change in the late fifth century in the medical writers; instead of denoting a static quality it comes to mean an active force (see his Introduction to the Loeb edition of Aristotle, *De part. animal.* [1955] 30-32). Analogically, the same difference seems to appear in Herodotus

The word *dynamis* occurs frequently in the common meaning of troops, wealth, and territory,[42] i.e. as a quantity measurable in external possessions. Thus, the power of Darius consists of his revenues when collected in the form of bullion in enormous vats (3.96.2), and that of Babylon in the gold she contributes to that treasury (1.192.1 ff.). Hecataeus of Miletus, in trying to warn his countrymen against undertaking a war with Persia, recounts "all the nations over which Darius rules, and his power" (5.36.2), no doubt on the basis of a list similar to Herodotus' own satrapy list, as is commonly assumed.[43] In Herodotus, power is possession and thus something a ruler can be stripped of,[44] while in Thucydides it is an abstract force and identical with activity. The main difference between Herodotus and Thucydides[45] is that in the latter *dynamis* is a direct causal factor for historical action, whereas in Herodotus it is possible for a ruler to enjoy his power while "sitting still," to use a phrase commonly employed by the historian.[46] The activism of states in Herodotus is due not to power as such, but to *hybris* in some form, and thus a moral judgment is always implied.

It is interesting, however, to observe that Herodotus did anticipate Thucydides in the use of the activist concept of power, albeit in a restricted sense. In some places, as we have noted, Herodotus

---

and Thucydides. Cf. also W. Miller, "Dynamis and Physis in *On Ancient Medicine*," *TAPA* 83 (1952) 191, note 26 (on the notion of *dynamis* in the fifth century). For the historical (or historiographical) concept of *dynamis*, see e.g. H. Frisch, *Might and Right in Antiquity*, tr. by C. C. Martindale (Copenhagen 1949) 11 ff. J. Vogt, "Dämonie der Macht und Weisheit der Antike," *Die Welt als Geschichte* 10 (1950) 17 ff. For Thucydides' concept of power, see e.g. D. Grene, *Man in his Pride* (1950), Ch. V; J. de Romilly, *Thucydide et l'impérialisme athénien* (Paris 1947) 79 ff.; Schmid-Stählin 1.5.33 f.; K. Reinhardt, "Thukydides und Machiavelli," in his *Vermächtnis der Antike* (Göttingen 1960) 184-218 (first published in his *Von Werken und Formen* [Godesberg 1948] 237-84).

[42] Herodotus has *dynamis* in its physical meaning in 2.19.3 (Nile) and 2.87.3 (properties of cedar oil in embalming). Troops: see Powell, *Lexicon*, s.v. δύναμις no. 2. Wealth: 7.9a.1. Territory: 3.88.3 (Darius' power consists in large part of his satrapies); cf. below, note 43.

[43] See How and Wells, and E. H. Bunbury, *A History of Ancient Geography*² (1959 [1883]) Vol. 1, 134 ff. The work of Hecataeus was accompanied by a map: the speech of Aristagoras in Sparta gives a good idea of the relation between map and list in the early geographers (5.49).

[44] So in 1.4.3; 1.46.1; 2.151.3.

[45] Above, note 41. The idea of *dynamis* is developed in the *Archaeology* of Thucydides (1.2-19) as perhaps the major theme of the work, since *archê* (empire) is only the outward manifestation of *dynamis*.

[46] Above, note 31: ἡσυχίην ἄγειν and ἀτρεμίζειν.

speaks of the growth of power both in the East and in Greece,[47] and in the accounts of internal struggles in the Greek states he speaks frequently of powerful individuals.[48] A more consistent picture of power as growth develops naturally in the story of Athens, which rose from small beginnings to the position of the greatest Greek naval power in the Persian Wars. Although the word *dynamis* is not used to describe the growth of Athens, the underlying idea is clearly similar to Thucydides' basic concept.[49]

Sparta's growth of power, as well as her lust for conquest, were checked early, as we have seen, by her sense of religious and secular obligation and by strife within and without. Athens, however, profited by similar factors to become the foremost power (in fact, if not in name) during the Persian Wars. At the beginning, Athens was weak, not only while still a Pelasgian nation (1.57.3 and 58), but also under the Peisistratids, when she is described as "disunited and held down" by tyranny (1.59.1). The keynote of the story of Peisistratus' accessions is *stasis*—civil strife—between three factions representing noble families of Athens, each heading a separate section of Attica.[50] When Peisistratus finally won the upper hand, he eliminated his rivals by death and exile (1.64.3). At the time of the overthrow of tyranny, the triple division of factions reappears in different forms: first Hippias, Cleisthenes, and the Athenian *dêmos* (the last is to Herodotus originally a faction in the Athenian state),[51] and later Cleisthenes, Isagoras, and the *dêmos*.[52] Thus we have at Athens a disunity similar to that prevailing in Sparta, but it is based on a triple division rather than merely a double one, and it leads to increased

[47] Above, note 37. Growth is a frequently mentioned aspect of power (αὐξάνεσθαι); see Powell, *Lexicon*, s.v. The term occurs in the passages cited in note 37; however, it is not confined to the East but is a general imperialist phenomenon, e.g. 3.39.3 (Polycrates); 5.78 and 5.91.2 (Athenian democracy); 6.132 (Miltiades' position). The term is also Thucydidean, e.g. 1.2.6; 1.16; 1.69.4, etc.

[48] *Dynamis* in the sense of political power occurs already in Solon, fr. 5 Diehl³, line 3, and it is a common term in Theognis, as well as in fifth-century Attic literature: see M. C. Lane's *Index to the . . . Elegiac and Iambic Poets*, and *LSJ*, s. vv. δύναμις, δυναστεύω, δυνατός. In Herodotus, see e.g. 5.66.2 (Cleisthenes and Isagoras ἐστασίασαν περὶ δυνάμιος; 6.132 (cf. note 47); 7.5.1 (Mardonius).

[49] Cf. Pohlenz, *Herodot* 124 (Persian and Athenian imperialism in Herodotus, Euripides, and Thucydides).

[50] Above, Ch. III, 87.

[51] For the meaning of δῆμος, see above, Ch. III, 119-20.

[52] Hippias, Cleisthenes, and δῆμος: 5.62.2 and 64.2. Cleisthenes, Isagoras, and δῆμος: 5.66.1-2 and 69-70.

strength rather than to weakness. The strengthening of the Athenian people did not lead to the tyranny of the *dêmos* (as Thucydides and others later had occasion to present it),[53] because the power of the noble families remained strong throughout the period preceding the Persian Wars. The overthrow of tyranny was due, in Herodotus' eyes, to rival noble families and the foreign intervention of Sparta, and not to the *dêmos*. Democracy arose when Cleisthenes needed the Athenian people in order to overthrow his opponents, and thus added them to his party (5.66.2). To strengthen them further he severed their connection with the Ionians through his reorganization of the tribes.[54] The origin of democracy is therefore seen by Herodotus as a question of internal power politics. The rise of the young democracy prior to the Persian Wars is described in turn from the point of view of external power, as we have noted in Chapter III.[55] In all this, the central idea is the self-interest of factions in the state, of private individuals, and of the state itself.

The notion of a balance between contending factions remains constant in Herodotus' account of Athenian affairs, except for the very end of the work, and is especially striking in the sections connected with Marathon. In sketching the history of Athenian noble families from their origins to his own day (these families include the Gephyraeans, the Peisistratids, the Alcmaeonids, and the families of Isagoras and Miltiades),[56] Herodotus emphasizes the fact that Marathon was won by the Athenian people under the leadership of aristocrats, whom he treats in a manner reminiscent of the Spartan kings.[57] At the time of Xerxes' invasion, we have a

[53] E.g. Thucydides 2.63.1; 8.68.4; especially the Old Oligarch (Ps.-Xenophon, *Ath. Pol.* 1.8), and also Aristophanes, Plato, and Aristotle.

[54] See above, Ch. III, note 127. Herodotus says that Cleisthenes despised the Ionians (as Cleisthenes of Sicyon had despised the Argives). This sentiment should not be criticized for its superficiality, as do How and Wells, and K. Wüst, *Politisches Denken bei Herodot* (Diss. Munich 1935) 30 ff. The passage conforms to Herodotus' view that the establishment of democracy in Athens was the work of aristocrats. See C. Hignett, *A History of the Athenian Constitution to the End of the Fifth Century B.C.* (Oxford 1952) 156. Despite V. Ehrenberg, "The Origins of Democracy," *Historia* 1 (1950) 540 ff., I believe this view to be essentially correct.

[55] Above, 119.

[56] Above, Ch. III, 125-26. H. Berve, "Fürstliche Herren zur Zeit der Perserkriege," *Antike* 12 (1936) 1 ff.

[57] Herodotus deals with the origins of the Spartan kingship in 6.53-55 and describes their honors in life and death in 6.56-60, comparing them once with the Persian kings (59). The pattern is basically the same for the Athenian nobles, although it is more

similar account of factionalism in the relations between Themistocles and Aristeides, who make peace only before Salamis (8.79-80). In the account of Sestus, however, the Athenians appear as a unified power, but one may wonder if their very determination to continue the Persian War did not, in Herodotus' eyes, expose them to the dangers of aggressive expansionism.

Power and strife, in combination with injustice, are the key concepts underlying Herodotus' account of Athens' external history before the Persian Wars. While he tells little of her wars prior to the overthrow of tyranny (for Athens was, in his opinion, a weak state at that time),[58] he emphasizes the war of 506 B.C. against the Chalcidians and Boeotians as the first proof of the increasing strength of the Athenian democratic state (5.77-78). Athens' main foreign enterprises before the Persian Wars are for him the participation in the Ionian Revolt and the conflicts with Aegina. Both events, to be sure, had an influence upon the Persian Wars, the Ionian Revolt by angering Darius, and the Aeginetan Wars by forcing Athens to build a navy later used to good purpose at Salamis.[59] Yet both events were also characteristic of a young and growing state. The participation in the Ionian Revolt could not be fully explained by Persia's support of the Peisistratids, and it showed, in Herodotus' opinion, the folly of the *dêmos* in the assembly.[60] The wars with Aegina (an obscure series of events about which Herodotus was not well informed)

---

sketchily applied, and they are of course not comparable to the Persian kings. The noble families were undoubtedly among Herodotus' principal informants: see Jacoby, *RE* Suppl. 2.413. Themistocles and Aristeides, the representatives of Athenian democracy, are treated quite differently (7.143.1; 8.79.1 and 95).

[58] Above, note 28. The capture of Sigeum (5.94-95), the conquest of Naxos (1.64), and the conquest of the Chersonese (6.34 ff.) are all told as chapters in the personal history of the tyrants and nobles, and not as "Athenian" enterprises. Myres, *Herodotus* 178, is certainly wrong in claiming that Herodotus presents Peisistratus as the founder of an Athenian empire.

[59] Participation in the Ionian Revolt: 5.97.3; 99.1, etc.; 5.105; 6.94.1; 7.1.1. Aeginetan wars: 5.80 ff.; 6.49 ff.; 73; 85; 87 ff.; 7.144.1-2.

[60] Hdt. 5.97.2. This much criticized passage expresses a common anti-democratic criticism by contrasting the wisdom of one man (the Spartan king Cleomenes) with the folly of thirty thousand Athenians. Cf. Heracleitus, fr. 49 Diels-Kranz[10], and Plato's criticism of democracy. The underlying assumption of the passage is that a democracy is more liable to engage in imperialist schemes than are conservative governments: the arguments used by Aristagoras to persuade the Athenians were the same (5.97.1) imperialist arguments he had used in Sparta. The imperialism of democracy is an outstanding phenomenon in the fifth century. See also above, Ch. III, 120.

showed, on the other hand, how international injustice could bring about the greatness of a nation.[61]

Herodotus describes the hostilities between Athens and Aegina in three separate stages, preceded by an ultimate cause in the form of an early struggle that led to a permanent hostility.[62] That early struggle (5.82-89.1) originated over two cult statues, made by the Epidaurians from olive wood furnished by Athens and later abducted by the Aeginetans from Epidaurus. When Epidaurus thereupon ceased to send the offerings to Athens as agreed, the Athenians tried unsuccessfully to remove the statues from Aegina, but were worsted by thunder and lightning, and also (or so the Aeginetans claimed) by Aeginetan and Argive troops. The story is based on the twin ideas of justice as an international obligation and of piety as an obligation toward the gods. Aegina, by starting with injustice, freed the Epidaurians from their obligation toward Athens and her gods: the Epidaurians, says Herodotus, proved to the Athenians that they were "not unjust" in refusing to bring offerings since they no longer had the statues (5.84.1).[63] The Athenians in turn committed a religious crime in trying to abduct the statues from Aegina, and were punished for it. These mutual acts of injustice caused the later wars of Athens and Aegina.

The first Aeginetan war was started by the Thebans in retaliation for the defeat of Chalcis and Boeotia by the young democracy (5.79 ff.). Calling upon the Aeginetans, who gladly acceded to their demand, "being spurred on by great wealth and recalling their old enmity against Athens" (5.81.2), they used their navy to raid the Attic coast in an "unheralded war." The religious element is strong here also, for the Thebans were told by an oracle to borrow the statues of the Aeacids from Aegina, and the Athenians, when attacked, were told to found a sanctuary of Aeacus and to wait with reprisals for thirty years. Disregarding this last piece of advice (and thus once more showing disrespect for the divine), they were nevertheless saved from their own folly by a threatened Spartan invasion of Attica, so that they

---

[61] On the difficult chronology of the wars of Athens and Aegina, see recently N. G. L. Hammond, *Historia* 4 (1955) 406 ff.; id., *Hist. Greece* 210 ff.; L. H. Jeffery, *AJP* 83 (1962) 44-54.

[62] On the meaning of ἔχθρη παλαιή, see *Causation* 251 and 270.

[63] Aegina was a colony of Epidaurus (8.46.1): hence the Aeginetans were breaking religious as well as secular bonds; for the latter, see 5.83.1.

did not at once retaliate against Aegina. The second Aeginetan
war (if I may call it that) found the Athenians as the aggressors
when they complained of Aegina's medism before Sparta and
acquired hostages from Aegina, whom they later refused to
surrender despite the representations of King Leotychidas of
Sparta (6.49.2 ff.).[64] The account of this war centers on the idea
of injustice, and is thus not to the credit of Athens. Finally, there is
a brief mention of a third phase of the Aeginetan war, from which
Themistocles derived the arguments for increasing the Athenian
navy by two hundred ships (7.144): this phase, which is specifically
called the war that saved Greece through the newly built ships,
cannot be identical with the second. While undoubtedly the three
episodes form a single sequence of extended hostilities, it is
characteristic of Herodotus to break the series into three separate
parts.[65] The third phase is the one which is concluded by a truce
as part of the general truce between Greek states prior to the
Persian invasion of 480 B.C. (7.145.1).

From very scanty historical material, Herodotus here created a
clear picture of the roles of impiety and injustice in the international struggles between city states. The ever-changing combinations between nations are based on the desire to take vengeance

[64] Above, Ch. III, 121-22 (Aeginetan *Logos*).

[65] The second war is clearly represented by Herodotus as having started before
Marathon, regardless of when modern scholars want to place it; see Macan, *IV-VI*,
Appendix VIII, and the bibliography listed in note 61, above. Herodotus carries the
description of it down to the time when Darius got ready for Marathon (6.94.1), but
indicates that the war had not yet ended (συνῆπτο). He says nothing about any
further actions. In 7.144 he mentions Themistocles' naval decree (the 200 ships),
giving as its reason "the Aeginetan war," and then continues: "this war having
broken out (συστάς) saved Greece at that time (τότε)," namely at Salamis. Miss
Jeffery, *AJP* 83 (1962) 46, rightly emphasizes that the aorist συστάς must refer to the
outbreak, not to the continuance, of an Aeginetan war. Therefore, two possibilities
suggest themselves: (1) Herodotus believed that there had been three distinct Aeginetan
wars: in 505 B.C. (Hdt. 5.79 ff.), in 491/90 B.C. (Hdt. 6.49 ff.), and *ca.* 483/82 B.C.
(Hdt. 7.144). In that case the references in 7.144 are not to the war last mentioned in
6.94.1, but to a new war, i.e. the current war mentioned by Themistocles in his
proposal. (2) Herodotus believed that there had been two wars, the latter one forming
two phases, one of 491/90 B.C., the other of 483/82 B.C. In this case συστάς refers to
491 B.C., and the following τότε, to 483/82 B.C. In favor of the second alternative is
the fact that Herodotus specifically mentions that the new Athenian ships authorized
in 483/82 were not used against Aegina prior to Xerxes' invasion; presumably, this
last phase was merely a continuing state of war, without overt action. Hence I have
adopted the latter alternative in the text, although I am not sure that the first is
incorrect. In neither case is there an inconsistency in the Greek, as Miss Jeffery and
others assume.

for one reason or another, and in these combinations injustices are committed by both sides. Religious crimes are both the cause and the effect of such warfare, but the divine is curiously inconsistent in helping now one side and then the other. The ultimate effect of impiety and injustice is the growth of Athens, which enables her to fulfill her decisive role at Salamis; there the collaboration of Aegina and Athens is symbolized in the arrival from Aegina of the statues of the Aeacids to fight the battle on the side of the Greeks. Thus, in this case, the ultimate effect of strife and injustice is the good of Greece.

In the course of telling the antecedents to the second Aeginetan war, Herodotus gives to Leotychidas a speech that, like the earlier speech of Socles, summarizes the leading ideas of the narrative by telling a parable (6.86). The speech has been severely criticized as irrelevant to the situation, since its ostensible purpose of persuading the Athenians to return the Aeginetan hostages has seemed to some ill-served by the parable of Glaucus of Sparta, an unknown individual whose private affairs have no connection with history.[66] This criticism overlooks the exact parallel between the situation of Glaucus and that of the Athenians, as well as the possibilities of symbolic connections in Herodotus' narrative. Glaucus had received a deposit of money from a Milesian, but when the man's children came to ask for its return, he claimed not to remember and put them off for four months. He then went to the Pythia at Delphi asking whether he could keep the money by swearing a false oath, and was told that the very intent of committing such a crime would mean the end of his line of descent. The story parallels exactly the Athenian situation, for the Athenians had received the Aeginetan hostages from the Spartans as a deposit, and this involved an obligation to return them.[67]

[66] See How and Wells on 6.86.1; Aly, *Volksmärchen* 155 ff.; Crahay, *Litt. orac.* 97-99. On the structure of the speech, see Myres, *Herodotus* 83.

[67] Deposit ($\pi\alpha\rho\alpha\theta\eta\kappa\eta$, or, as some MSS have it in some places,$\pi\alpha\rho\alpha\kappa\alpha\tau\alpha\theta\eta\kappa\eta$, the latter the Hellenistic word for "bank deposit"): 6.73.2 and 86.1, etc.; the word recurs throughout the speech. Why had the Athenians approached Sparta, and why had Sparta deposited the hostages with the Athenians? Sparta had a right to collect hostages, since Aegina was a member of the Peloponnesian League (cf. H. Busolt, *Griechische Geschichte²* 2 [Gotha 1895] 572, note 3; Hammond, *Hist. Greece* 210). However, the complaint of the Athenians and the deposit of the hostages at Athens were both based on Sparta's informal position as Leader of Greece ($\pi\rho\sigma\tau\acute{\alpha}\tau\eta\varsigma$ $\tau\hat{\eta}\varsigma$ $\dot{E}\lambda\lambda\acute{\alpha}\delta\sigma\varsigma$); so already G. Grote, *A History of Greece*, 5.34 ff. (Everyman's Library). This last position has primarily religious sanction; cf. Oliver, *Demokratia* 14 ff., and H. Schaefer in *RE* Suppl. 9, s.v. *prostatēs*, 1300 (1962). The legal position of the Leader of Greece

Whereas Glaucus tried to cheat the children of the Milesian, the
Athenians claimed that the deposit was made by two Spartan
kings (meaning Cleomenes and Leotychidas), so that they now
could not return them to Leotychidas alone. Glaucus is punished
primarily for having thought of breaking an oath, and we must
supply a similar binding agreement between Sparta and Athens.
The parable illuminates the themes of the Aeginetan wars in
several ways. First, its underlying idea is that justice in international relations corresponds to justice in private relations, in
that both are a give-and-take based on mutual trust.[68] Secondly, it
connects the idea of injustice with the notion of impiety in the
statement that the gods punish even the thought of impious
action.[69] The parable thus underlines the idea that in the Aeginetan wars the Athenians, as well as the Aeginetans, were unjust.
At the same time, the parable is used ironically, not only with
reference to the speaker, who acquired the throne by fraud
and later came to a bad end,[70] but also in respect to the Athenians,
who do not anywhere receive punishment from the gods for
refusing to hand over the hostages. It is an important observation
of Herodotus that Athens was not punished in his own lifetime
for her religious crimes.[71] This is tantamount to saying that in
Athens' case injustice led to success, whereas in other instances

and of a friendly power, with regard to hostages, is thus very similar to that of two guest
friends with regard to a deposit of money.

By a remarkable coincidence, the only other instance of the occurrence of
παρακαταθήκη of a guest friend in a prominent place is at the end of the speech of
Socles of Corinth, 5.92h.2, a speech which parallels that of Leotychidas in being the
only other speech containing a story as *exemplum*. For the relation of these two speeches,
see above, Ch. III, 122.

[68] For justice (δικαιοσύνη) as give-and-take, see above, Ch. III, note 83, and
Ch. IV, note 112.

[69] This last idea is Delphic: see M. P. Nilsson, *Geschichte der griechischen Religion* 1²
(1955) 647 f. However, Plato, *Rep.* 2.363 D 2-4, mentions as a teaching of the Orphics
a central point in the Glaucus story, namely that the ὅσιος and εὔορκος leaves behind
good issue (cf. Nilsson, *op. cit.* 688 f.; the scholion to Plato on this passage mentions
the Herodotean connection: cf. J. Adam, *The Republic of Plato* 1 [Cambridge 1905]
79). This would suggest a more individualistic ethical meaning of the passage than
Nilsson (647) assumes. For the connection of injustice and impiety in our story, cf.
also Leotychidas' remark that the return of the hostages would be ὅσια (6.86a.1).

[70] The end of Leotychidas: 6.72. He was exiled after an accusation of bribery
following the Persian Wars; Herodotus considered his death a punishment by the gods
for his crimes against Demaratus.

[71] The two main instances where punishment was to be expected were the disregard
of the oracle commanding the Athenians to wait thirty years before they attacked
Aegina (5.89.2) and the treatment of the Persian heralds (7.133.2).

punishment had followed the crime. In the story of Glaucus Herodotus comes very close to defining injustice as the very condition of historical action, a view that recalls the famous first fragment of Anaximander.[72]

As we have seen, the growth of Athens resulted from factors similar to those that arrested the growth of Sparta. The divine was more lenient with Athens; external and internal strife led to greatness instead of frustration; Sparta, and later Corinth, assisted the young democracy; and injustice resulted in the acquisition of a navy and in victory in the Persian Wars. In all this, the moral position of Athens is perhaps inferior to that of Sparta, so that morality has little to do with the acquisition of power. It is only in the exercise of power during the Persian Wars that Athens' moral position became a problem for Herodotus.

Athens' role as a sea power during the invasion of Xerxes is seen by Herodotus from the vantage point of the fifth-century development of the Athenian empire and the beginnings of the Peloponnesian War, which Herodotus lived to see. The commonplaces of the criticisms and defense of Athens at that time are well known from Thucydides and the dramatists, and later from the orators. Athens is praised for her role as liberator of other Greek states, for her espousal of Panhellenism in the Persian Wars, and she is condemned as a tyrant city enslaving others and as restlessly imperialist.[73] In Herodotus, Athens' early role as liberator plays only a minor part. In defending the Athenian title to the hegemony of the fleet before Gelo, tyrant of Syracuse, the speaker points only to the strength of the Athenian navy and the antiquity of Athenian descent (7.161.3). In defending the title to the leadership of the left wing of the Greek forces at Plataea, the Athenians point to the help given the Heracleidae (thereby showing themselves to be friends of the Spartans), to their support of the sons of the Seven against Thebes (showing their respect for religious burial rites), and finally to their wars against the Amazons, Trojans, and Persians, but they do not claim to be the liberators of Greece

---

[72] For the fragment of Anaximander, see Pagel, *Aitiol. Moment* 29-30; G. S. Kirk, *CQ*, n.s. 5 (1955) 21-38; G. S. Kirk and J. E. Raven, *The Presocratic Philosophers* (Cambridge 1957) 117 ff.

[73] On this double aspect of the fifth-century image of Athenian imperialism, see recently H. Strasburger, "Thukydides und die politische Selbstdarstellung der Athener," *Hermes* 86 (1958) 17-40.

(9.27.2-5).[74] When heeding the appeals of the Ionians, Athens is simply fulfilling her role as mother country of the Ionian colonies, rather than a Panhellenic one.[75] It is the Spartans who, when they are afraid of an alliance of Athens with Mardonius (8.142.3), call the Athenians liberators of men, but the force of the compliment is weakened by its being coupled with the accusation that the Persian Wars are really the fault of Athens.[76]

The Athenian claim to have served the Panhellenic cause is treated more intensively. In their answer to the Spartans at the occasion just mentioned, the Athenians, in a famous speech, express their strong devotion to the Panhellenic cause (8.144.2). The reason for this difference in emphasis is primarily that in Herodotus' view the liberation of other states ill accords with Athenian self-interest, but Panhellenism is more easily reconciled with it.

The moral problem existing in Herodotus' judgment of Athens' role in the Persian Wars is thus the adjustment of her self-interest with her Panhellenism. It is not to be thought that Panhellenism in Herodotus is a pious fraud (as it clearly is in much of Thucydides) practiced by Athens in her own interest. Both attitudes are genuine, and the principal difference between Athens and Sparta, for Herodotus, is the fact that Athens combined both attitudes, whereas Sparta decidedly did not, although she had been from of old the "Leader of the Hellenes." Athens was able to combine them by pursuing her own interest strongly, while refraining from certain actions (such as the assumption of leader-

[74] Note the absence, in Herodotus, of the Athenian claim that Marathon was fought in the service of Greece; see below, Ch. VI, note 38.

[75] The relations between Athens and the Ionians differ in various periods: In 5.97, Aristagoras of Miletus persuades the Athenians to send the twenty ships, but they do not remain long in Ionia. In 8.132.1 (Ionians at Aegina) and 9.90-91 (Ionians at Delos), the Ionians address themselves to the Panhellenic League rather than to the Athenians. In the messages written on the rocks of Euboea, Themistocles appealed to Ionian relations with the mother country, meaning perhaps Greece as a whole, and not Athens only (8.22.2). Thus the motif of Athens as protector of her Ionian colonies is strong only at the end of the work, when the Athenians (after Mycale) take on the protection of the Ionians against the wishes of the Spartans (9.106.3). Contrast also Cleisthenes' contempt for the Ionians (5.69.1).

[76] Differently Macan, VII-IX, on 8.142, line 8, who cites Plataea, the Ionians, and Marathon as services to Greece. For Marathon, however, see above, note 74; Plataea and the Ionians occur later than the passage here considered. For the text of 8.142.2, see J. C. Kamerbeek's attempt to defend the reading of the MSS, Mnemosyne, ser. 4, 11 (1958) 252-53—but the parallel phrasing in 8.22.2 still seems to me to require, in 8.142.2, the conjecture usually accepted, ἀρχῆθεν.

ship in the Panhellenic League) in the interest of the other Greeks.

The question of the relation of these elements is dealt with in five passages in the work: (1) Herodotus' own judgment on the roles of Athens and Sparta in 7.139; (2) the account of the preliminaries to the battle of Salamis (8.40 ff.); (3) the negotiations conducted by Alexander of Macedon on behalf of Mardonius, which we have just mentioned, and the subsequent negotiations at Sparta (8.136-9.11); (4) Herodotus' statement on the antecedents to the formation of the Delian League (8.3); (5) the last section of the work, where we see Athens pursuing the war against the wishes of the Spartans. The points of view expressed in these sections differ, but I believe that they can be reconciled.[77]

The first passage (7.139) is a summary judgment based upon Herodotus' observations on the course of the war, and is thus in strict accord with the rest of the narrative. Herodotus praises the patriotic choice of the Athenians in the war, defending them against the envy of the Greeks of his time, and shows that instead of fighting the Persians as they did, they had open to them the alternatives of leaving their country or coming to terms with the enemy. The first alternative had been discussed by Themistocles in the assembly that dealt with the oracle about the wooden wall (7.143.3), and is later mentioned by him as a threat before the admirals of the Greek fleet at Salamis (8.62.2); the second is an important motif in the negotiations conducted with Mardonius and Sparta before Plataea (passage No. 3 above). Herodotus then goes on to condemn Sparta for her insular attitude, again judging her from the same negotiations before Plataea, as we have seen.[78] In the final analysis, Herodotus' preference for Athens originates with his Panhellenic point of view. The statement

---

[77] Much has been written concerning Herodotus' point of view with regard to Athens. See especially Jacoby, *RE* Suppl. 2.352 ff.; Meyer, *Forschungen* 197 ff.; H. Kleinknecht, "Herodot und Athen," *Hermes* 75 (1940) 241-64 (=Marg, *Herodot* 541-73); Pohlenz, *Herodot* 167-75 and 187; Legrand, *Introduction* 30 f. and 104 ff.; Wells, *Studies* 151 ff.; H. Strasburger, "Herodot und das Perikleische Athen," *Historia* 4 (1955) 1-25. For other recent discussions, see P. MacKendrick, *CW* 56 (1962-63) 271.

[78] See above, 205. The only item that has no correspondence with other parts of the narrative (despite Macan, *VII-IX*, on 7.139, line 16) is the idea that Sparta might have medized. However, Herodotus knew that Sparta had made overtures to Persia at the beginning of the Peloponnesian War (7.137). The motif of voluntary exile vs. medism is first applied to the Scythians (4.118.2). In general, see H. Kleinknecht, *op. cit.* (see last note) 263, note 57 (=Marg, *Herodot* 571, note 57).

"they chose for Greece to remain free" describes an almost superhuman effort, and the imagery used in this passage recalls the divine.[79]

The Athenian behavior before Salamis contrasts with this judgment by adding the theme of self-interest. The Athenians brought the Greek fleet to Salamis primarily to protect their own people. When the council of generals decided to withdraw to the Isthmus and join the land army there, Themistocles argued against it with vigor. Now Themistocles had been counseled by his teacher Mnesiphilus[80] to oppose the withdrawal to the Isthmus, on the grounds that once the navy left Salamis the allies would all return to their several cities, and thus the fight would no longer be "for a single fatherland" (8.57.2). This Panhellenic line of reasoning was employed by Themistocles in speaking to Eurybiades alone, but in the subsequent council of the generals he had to use other arguments for fear of offending the allies. Consequently, Themistocles used largely tactical arguments in the council, such as the suitability of the straits of Salamis and the presence of the Megarians and Aeginetans, who would not go to the Isthmus (8.60a). He further stressed Athenian self-interest in mentioning the women and children who had been brought to Salamis from Athens, and referred to the safety of the Peloponnesus if the sea battle were won. Finally, he gave the assembly an ultimatum: the Athenians would leave for Siris in Italy, unless the allies remained to do battle at Salamis (8.62.2). Hence Eurybiades, for fear of losing the Athenian contingent, acceded to Themistocles' plea. It is interesting to observe, in this debate, how Themistocles gradually changes from the Panhellenic point of view to the idea of the self-interest both of the allies individually and of Athens in particular.

We have had occasion previously to refer to the important negotiations of Mardonius (through Alexander of Macedon) in Athens, and to the subsequent negotiations of the Athenians in Sparta, preceding the battle of Plataea.[81] In sending a message to Athens with the offer of an alliance, Mardonius was interested in bringing over to his side both the land army and the navy of

[79] Panhellenic point of view: Pohlenz, *Herodot* 175 and 187. Imagery: *Action* 37. The passage referred to in the text is quoted at the end of Ch. VI, 305.

[80] His teacher, according to Plutarch, *Themistocles* 2, etc.

[81] See also Ch. III, section eleven (1), i-ii, 142-43.

the Athenians. Sparta, as we have mentioned earlier, argued through her ambassadors that Athens should continue to oppose the Persians, but characteristically, she did not offer to send an army outside the Peloponnesus, suggesting instead that she care for the women and the infirm of Athens in the Peloponnesus (8.142.4). The Athenians answered Alexander and the Spartans in two separate speeches. Their speech for Mardonius stressed only Athens' own desire for freedom and her trust in her own gods:

> "So long as the sun continues on its present path, we shall never make an agreement with Xerxes." (8.143.3)

The speech addressed to the Spartans is one of the finest expressions of Panhellenism:

> "Many things prevent (our making common cause with the Persians), first and foremost the burned and destroyed images and sanctuaries which we must avenge to the utmost, rather than uniting with those who have done this; secondly the Greek nation, which is of one blood and one tongue, the common places of worship and sacrifices, as well as our common customs, which Athenians cannot properly forsake." (8.144.2)

Once more, the Athenians distinguish between their own injuries and the Panhellenic cause, but the main emphasis is on the latter. The Athenians then ask for an army to be sent from the Peloponnesus before Mardonius approaches Athens.

When this army failed to arrive, the Athenians again evacuated their people to Salamis, and while Mardonius was in Athens, they sent an embassy to Sparta, having refused a second offer from Mardonius to become his allies (9.1 ff.). The Athenian ambassadors were specifically empowered to recall Mardonius' offer and to threaten Athens' defection to the enemy (9.6). Their review of the Persian offer in Sparta recalls verbally Alexander's speech in Athens, although they actually refer to Mardonius' second offer.[82] The Athenians lodge a complaint with Sparta as

---

[82] Compare 9.7a.1 with 8.140a.2, but Mardonius' first embassy was sent from Boeotia, while in the present speech he is in Athens (9.7b.2); it was from Athens that Mardonius had sent his second embassy (9.4.1). For the "Hellenes" (by whom the Athenians feel betrayed) as the Panhellenic League, see *ATL* 3.97, note 12; differently P. A. Brunt, "The Hellenic League against Persia," *Historia* 2 (1953-54) 135-63. The Spartans are here addressed as leaders of the Panhellenic League.

the leader of the Panhellenic League, by whom they feel betrayed. Hence they say that they refused Mardonius' offer "out of regard for Zeus Hellenius."[83] When the Spartans delay the ambassadors (meanwhile secretly sending out an army on the advice of Chileos of Tegea), the Athenians make another speech, in ignorance of Spartan compliance with their request to send an army. At this point they make the ultimate threat that Athens, betrayed by the Spartans, will now join the Persians, the very thing they had sworn never to do so long as the sun kept its present course. The speeches in Sparta are clearly the counterpart of the earlier speeches in Athens. Athens' Panhellenism lasted only so long as she felt sure of Hellenic support. When betrayed by her allies, she realistically prepared to do the best for her survival.[84]

Herodotus' contemporaries argued hotly that the establishment of the Delian League was from the beginning an Athenian im-perialist scheme. Herodotus gives his own opinion on this point in some remarks connected with the roster of ships at Artemisium (8.3). Explaining why the commander-in-chief was the Spartan Eurybiades rather than an Athenian, he says that the allies from the very beginning (before the embassy had been sent to Gelo of Syracuse)[85] refused to campaign unless led by a Spartan. Athens had yielded in order to avoid Greek civil strife, for she laid great store on the survival of Greece:[86]

> ... the Athenians did not offer opposition, but gave in until (the allies) needed them badly, as they proved by the following event: when the allies had driven off the Persian and were fighting over his own country, they cited openly the *hybris* of Pausanias and took the leadership away from the Spartans. (8.3.2)[87]

[83] On Zeus Hellenius as the Panhellenic god who had an altar at Sparta, see Oliver, *Demokratia* 14-15 (but I do not believe that the passages in Herodotus refer specifically to this Spartan Hellenium). Cf. also Aly, *Volksmärchen* 146, note 1.

[84] The Athenian threat was not a mere rhetorical device: Chileos of Tegea pre-vailed over the Spartans by using the same argument (9.9.2).

[85] The reference is to the debate about the hegemony in the coming war with Persia, in 7.161, etc.

[86] In its phrasing 8.3.1 corresponds to 7.139.5.

[87] The common rendering of the passage is quite different. Rawlinson, for example, translates: "The Athenians ... did not push their claims, but waived them, *so long as they* (the Athenians) were in such great need of aid *from the other Greeks*. And *they* afterwards showed their motive: for at the time when the Persians had been driven from their own country, *they took occasion* of the insolence of Pausanias to deprive the

In this passage, as rendered above, Herodotus agrees with
Thucydides, who says that the origin of the Delian League lay in
the hatred felt by the allies of the Penhellenic League for Pausanias.[88] Herodotus does not, however, speak of the formation of the
Delian League itself, as is commonly assumed, but only of the
transfer of hegemony in the Panhellic League from Sparta to
Athens, an event which, it is true, led almost at once to the
withdrawal of Sparta and the formation of the Delian League.[89]
The main subject of his statements are throughout "the allies,"
i.e. the membership of the Panhellenic League. As Pohlenz has
shown, Herodotus here praises Athens for her moderation in
yielding the hegemony to Sparta during the Persian Wars, and he
imputes no imperialist motives to her. It was purely a moral

Lacedaemonians of their leadership." (Italics and the parenthesis mine.) Here the
subject of the paragraph is throughout the Athenians, and if thus read, the passage
clearly (but I believe falsely) attributes to them that self-interest which in Thucydides'
view was one motive for the existence of the Athenian empire (Thuc. 1.75.3). That
μέχρι ὅσου means "until," rather than "so long as," and that the subject of the phrase
"they needed them badly" is the allies, and not the Athenians, was suggested by
K. W. Krüger, Ἡροδότου Ἱστορίης Ἀπόδεξις (Berlin 1856), and has been proved by
Pohlenz, Herodot 170 ff., whom I follow despite the recent objections voiced by H.
Strasburger, op. cit. (above, note 77) 20, note 4, and by H. D. Meyer, "Vorgeschichte
und Begründung des delisch-attischen Seebundes," Historia 12 (1963) 405. I differ
from Pohlenz only in the translation of κάρτα ἐδέοντο, which in Herodotus always
seems to mean "they needed badly," and not "they demanded strongly" (see Powell,
Lexicon, s.v. δέω, B 1); thus δέομαι is here used differently from the passages which
Pohlenz cites from Thucydides. It is clear that after the hybris of Pausanias the allies
needed the Athenians badly, since they had no other leader. They used this hybris as
a prophasis, i.e. they cited it openly (the term does not necessarily mean "pretext";
cf. Causation 246). Having thus cited it, the allies deprived the Spartans of the hegemony
and gave it to the Athenians; the latter had of course no authority to do so themselves.
Thus Herodotus, in this passage, says nothing unfavorable about the Athenians, but
describes their assumption of the hegemony of the Panhellenic League (he does not
refer here to the Delian League) as a gift handed to them by the allies.
    There are two possible objections to this interpretation: (1) the abruptness of the
change of subject in κάρτα ἐδέοντο (Strasburger), and (2) the fact that the allies of
478 B.C. mentioned in this part of our passage are not the same states as the allies at
Artemisium, mentioned just before in 8.2.2 and 8.1. However, both objections can be
met by the same argument that Herodotus is here using the technical vocabulary of the
Panhellenic League. "The allies," οἱ σύμμαχοι, are throughout the members of that
League, whoever they may be at any one time (see the reference to ATL in note 82
above). The whole passage deals primarily with the allies, not the Athenians, and thus
the reader will have them in mind when the subject changes.
    [88] Thuc. 1.75.2; 95; 130.2. (But Herodotus describes a slightly earlier stage.)
In the OT of Sophocles, Oedipus also says that he received the rule as a gift, and had
not sought it (384); see B. M. W. Knox, Oedipus at Thebes (New Haven 1957) 66.
    [89] For the chronology of the years 478-477 B.C., see Ch. III, note 192.

decision, and perhaps the only case in the *Histories* of true morality in international politics.[90]

At the end of the work, Athenian strategy appears in a somewhat different light. At Mycale, the Athenians fight better on land than the Spartans,[91] and as a result of the victory they decide, against the wishes of the Spartans, to continue the war. When the Spartans withdraw, the Athenians become *de facto* leaders of the Panhellenic League in the capture of Sestus under Xanthippus, the father of Pericles. Their interest in the fate of the Ionians shows the beginnings of an Athenian policy of self-interest, for the Hellespont had been an Athenian sphere of interest since the elder Miltiades, and Sestus herself was an old Athenian possession.[92] It should be noted that Herodotus does not impute such motives to the Athenians directly. However, in capturing Sestus, the Athenians came upon Artayctes, the Persian governor of that region, and nailed him on a plank in view of the Hellespont, killing his son in front of him, in reprisal for Artayctes' defilement of the sanctuary of Protesilaus, a hero of the Trojan War (9.120.4). The stress on vengeance at the end of the work raises the question of possible Athenian transgression against the Persians in the future.[93]

In summary, Herodotus' portrait of Athens consists of a number of contradictory traits. On the one hand, her growth is explained by injustice, good fortune, and strife with her neighbors. Less admirable than Sparta in her actions toward men and gods, she is less seriously punished for her transgressions. During the Persian Wars her self-interest was best served by a genuine interest in Greece as a whole, although, when driven to extremes, she was of course willing to put her own interests first, even to the extent of considering an alliance with Persia.[94] On the whole, Herodotus

[90] In 8.3.1 and 2, Herodotus uses the word εἶκον, "they yielded." This attitude recalls the restraint of great rulers placed upon them by wise men (cf. *Action* 37 ff. and note 39). In important situations, the advice of wise men is preponderantly negative; the verb used is ἐπέχειν, to "hold back." Cf. Conclusion, 310.

[91] Herodotus follows in part a pro-Athenian version of the battle of Mycale; cf. Jacoby, *RE* Suppl. 2.466 (line 64)-467. Cf. Ch. VI, note 186.

[92] Herodotus does not give the history of Sestus, but it is clear from 6.34 ff. (esp. 6.36.2) that it was an Athenian possession in the time of Peisistratus. By the time of Darius' Scythian expedition it seems to have been lost to Athens (4.143), and it continued as a Persian possession (7.33 and 78) until its recapture in 479 B.C. (9.114 ff.).

[93] Cf. *Action* 27.

[94] Herodotus mentions the embassy to Sardis after the final return of Cleisthenes *ca.* 508 B.C., but is careful to avoid implicating the Alcmaeonids in it (5.73). This

does not attribute to Athens imperialist motives during the Persian Wars, although I believe that he hints at such at the end of his work. Athens is truly exalted not only because of her espousal of the Panhellenic cause, but even more by her refusal, for purely altruistic reasons, to make an issue of the hegemony.

The foremost characteristic of Athens is, however, her adaptability, an indication of which is the favor she receives from the divine. The representative of adaptability and good fortune is Themistocles, the trickster who comes out on top in any situation. Much has been written on the supposedly unfavorable picture of this statesman in Herodotus.[95] It is true that Themistocles was represented in a partially unfavorable light by Athenian sources reflecting contemporary party traditions, on which Herodotus depended. The portrait he derived from these traditions, however, has the function of exemplifying the Athenian character: Themistocles compares to the Athenians as Croesus compares to the Lydians, and Darius to the Persians. The main characteristics of Themistocles are therefore his egotism, his adaptability, his patriotism, and his good fortune.

Themistocles is introduced into the work with a Homeric flourish that was later imitated by Xenophon in the *Anabasis* with reference to himself,[96] and we hear first of his political cleverness in interpreting the oracle of the "wooden wall" to suit his own purposes, as well as his creation of the new Athenian navy (7.143-44). At Artemisium, Themistocles was bribed by the Euboeans to keep the fleet there for battle, and in turn he bribed the captains of the

attempt to conclude an alliance with Persia should be contrasted with the definite hostility established soon afterwards (5.96), with which Herodotus concludes his *logos* on the Athenian democracy. Herodotus also rejected the story of Alcmaeonid medism at Marathon (6.121 ff.), and on the whole has so little to say about pro-Persian parties at Athens that the proposals of Mardonius seem to have little historical reality. However, it was sound practice for the Persians to separate Athens from the rest of Greece, and Mardonius was no doubt following established policy. On the relations of Athens and Persia in this period, see K. J. Beloch, *Griechische Geschichte*² 2.2 (Strassburg 1916) 130 ff.; Grundy, *Great Pers. War* 166 ff.; A. T. Olmstead, "Persia and the Greek Frontier Problem," *CP* 34 (1939) 312 ff.; F. Schachermeyr, "Marathon und die persische Politik," *HZ* 172 (1951) 1-35 (cf. above, Introduction, note 13); Olmstead, *Hist. Pers.* 151 ff.; M. McGregor, "The Pro-Persian Party at Athens from 510 to 480 B.C.," *HSCP* Suppl. 1 (1940) 71-95; A. W. Gomme, *AJP* 65 (1944) 321 ff.; C. A. Robinson, Jr., *ibid.* 66 (1945) 243-54.

[95] See e.g. Schmid-Stählin 1.2.576; How and Wells, 1.42 f. and 2.272. Recently, C. Guratzsch, *Klio* 39 (1961) 48 ff.; W. den Boer, *Mnemosyne*, ser. 4, 15 (1962) 225 ff.; C. G. Starr, *PP* 17 (1962) 321 ff.

[96] Cf. Pohlenz, *Herodot* 69.

other contingents: having made a good profit from this, he also
served the Greek cause (8.4.2-5.3). After the battle he extricated
the Greeks by a trick (8.19) and wrote inscriptions on the rocks
of Euboea inviting the Ionians in Xerxes' army to join the Greek
cause (8.22-23.1). Of his speeches at Salamis we have already
spoken: he followed there the advice of Mnesiphilus, and it is often
thought that this is meant to detract from his greatness; but in
Herodotus it is not a sign of weakness to accept the advice of
another.[97] His two secret messages to Xerxes before and after the
battle of Salamis show once more a typical combination of
patriotism and self-interest: for the first message was sent to force
the Greeks to fight at Salamis (8.75), and the second to ingratiate
himself with the king of Persia (8.110.2-3). Themistocles is clearly
the hero of Salamis, as Herodotus shows by a number of means:
his conversation with his enemy Aristeides (8.79-80)—where
patriotism is the central motif—, the summary of his address to
the troops (8.83), his participation in battle, and the prizes he
received afterward, even from the Spartans.[98] When his plan to
pursue Xerxes to the Hellespont was rejected by the Greeks, he
adapted himself quickly to circumstances (8.108 ff.), and eventually made a big profit from the islanders:

> Themistocles did not stop the pursuit of wealth, and sent
> threatening messages to the other islands (for he had been
> unsuccessful at Andros) asking for money through the same
> messengers that he had employed for his message to the Persian
> king,[99] (and) announcing that if they did not give what he asked
> for, he would bring the Greek army and destroy them by siege.
> (8.112.1)

And further:

> Themistocles, starting out from Andros, acquired money from
> the islanders without the knowledge of the other generals.
> (8.112.3)[100]

[97] See above, Ch. II, note 78.

[98] Participation in battle: 8.92. Prizes: 8.124.2-3. On the theme of disunity
expressed in the last-mentioned chapter, see Ch. VI, 285-86.

[99] The phrase "that he had employed for his message to the Persian king" is
deleted by Macan, perhaps rightly; in that case the messengers were the same as those
employed by Themistocles at Andros.

[100] Themistocles did not, as Miltiades had done, use patriotic reasons to enrich
himself, but rather used the opportunity of enriching himself while punishing medizing
states; he was thus not unpatriotic. Cf. above, note 29.

The last mention of Themistocles in the work well expresses his relation to Athens, namely in the famous anecdote in which he tells a political enemy that he is famous both as an Athenian and as Themistocles.[101]

V

An important aspect of the contrasting portraits of Athens and Sparta derives, as we have seen, from the history of their interactions in the period covered by the *Histories*. As Herodotus says in a passage already cited,[102] Sparta had been alternately the friend and the enemy of the Athenian people. Although this statement refers to the Athenian *dêmos* only, it can be applied to all relations between Athens and Sparta. Both states were hegemonic powers, and neither tried to suppress the other in the periods under discussion. Their collaboration was broken at certain times when Sparta feared the growing power of her rival, and the work ends with a disagreement on the further conduct of the Persian Wars, a disagreement which was to have grave consequences, but which Herodotus treats merely as one phase in the series of their previous disputes.[103]

The story of the relations of the smaller Greek states with one another gives a similar picture of irregular alternations of friendship and hostility. I shall not here go into details about these states and their mutual quarrels.[104] The most vivid characterization of the disunity of the Greek states is given in the *logos* dealing with the Greek preparations against Xerxes (7.131-78). Each state is there characterized individually: Argos medizes because of her bitter hostility to Sparta; Gelo of Syracuse refuses to assist the Greeks against the Persians mainly because of a quarrel over the

[101] Quoted in full, Ch. VI, 286. This is the last mention of Themistocles, since 9.98 is an interpolation.

[102] Above, Ch. IV, 151.

[103] In the period following the four Spartan invasions of Attica mentioned in 5.76, Herodotus refers to one other plan to reinstate the Peisistratids (5.90 ff.), which was not carried out, but otherwise he gives a picture of rather friendly relations. Cf. 6.49, etc. (Aeginetan hostages), 6.105-106 (Marathon), 8.3, etc. (Persian Wars). In 480/79 B.C. Sparta failed at times to support Athens, but real disagreement arose only at the end of the war, and over the treatment of the Ionians (9.106.2 ff.). Thus, during the Persian Wars, we find a kind of antagonistic cooperation between the two states. Cf. also Ch. VI, note 101.

[104] E.g. Corcyra and Corinth, 3.53.7 and 48.2. Samos and Aegina, 3.59.3-4. Thessaly and Phocis, 7.176.4; 8.27 ff.; 31 ff.; 9.17.4 ff.

leadership of the Greek forces; Corcyra brazenly lies to the Greek
ambassadors and, like Gelo, decides to wait and see which way
victory will turn; Crete is told by Delphi not to risk devastation
for the fourth time in her history, and she thus abstains from the
war;[105] and finally the Thessalians are forced to medize by
their rulers and their geographical position. The central episode in
this *logos* contains the speeches by the ambassadors of the Panhellenic League and of Gelo, with their quarrels over the leadership of the Greek forces.

   Among the smaller states in the *Histories*, the most outstanding
mainland states owe their importance to their relations with
either Athens or Sparta. In the Peloponnesus, the principal
antagonists of Sparta are Tegea and Argos. As representatives of
the pre-Dorian population, the Tegeans are the bitter enemies of
Sparta, and they base the claim to lead the left flank at Plataea
specifically on their hostility—and this even before the Spartans
as judges (9.26). Despite their early wars with Sparta, the
Tegeans participate in the Persian Wars in a distinguished
manner, and this participation is not presented as a result of
Spartan conquest, but as patriotism.[106] We have, in the end,
between Tegea and Sparta a kind of antagonistic cooperation.

   The case of Argos differs widely from this. Herodotus has
something to tell of the greatness of Argos in the mythical period
and under Pheidon, but in the period covered by the *Histories* she

   [105] Herodotus inserts into the story of the troubles of the Cretans what by his
own admission is a "digression" (παρενθήκη: cf. Introduction, note 34) that deals
with the slaughter (in 473 B.C.) of Tarentines and Rhegians by the descendants of
those Cretans who had gone to Sicily after the death of Minos and had become
Messapians (7.170.3-4). Pohlenz, *Herodot* 137, note 2, says that this digression has
nothing to do with the punishment of the Cretans by Minos. It is, however, a typical
sequel to the main *logos*, in that it shows a reversal of fortune by which Greeks are
defeated by the descendants of those Cretans who had themselves earlier been
obliterated from Crete. The Western additions to the work repeatedly demonstrate
that these countries were the seat of great troubles for the Greeks. Cf. 1.166 (Phocaeans);
5.43-47 (Dorieus); 6.17 (Dionysius of Phocaea); 6.22-24 (Samians).
   [106] The conquest of Tegea is the subject of the first Spartan *logos* in the work
(1.66-68). Later the Tegeans accept fugitives from Sparta (the seer Hegesistratus,
9.37.3-4; Leotychidas, 6.72.2). Herodotus also refers to the battle of Tegea, which may
be dated about 472-470 B.C. (How and Wells *ad loc.*; Hammond, *Hist. Greece* 262),
and which shows an almost immediate renewal of hostilities between Sparta and
Tegea after the Persian Wars (9.35.2). However, in the Persian Wars themselves, the
Tegeans fought beside their enemy (Thermopylae, 7.202; Plataea, 9.26 ff.), and in
479 B.C. Chileos of Tegea persuaded the Spartans to join in the fight against Mardonius
(9.9).

is shown to be exhausted by strife with her neighbors.[107] Of this Herodotus tells a number of characteristic stories: the change of hair style after the sixth-century war with Sparta (1.82.7-8), the lengthening of women's brooches after a war with Athens (5.88.2), the war with the slaves after the defeat by King Cleomenes (6.83). Argos refused to participate in the Persian Wars, citing an oracle and her losses in the war with Cleomenes, but actually she feared that by joining the Greek alliance against Persia she would be brought under Spartan rule (7.148 ff.). Accused by some Greeks of having made an agreement with the Persians, the Argives did in fact warn Mardonius of the approach of the Spartans before Plataea.[108] Argos put her hostility to Sparta above the Greek cause, since she had preserved a greater independence than most states, and thus she forms a counterpart to Tegea.

A similar contrast exists between Thebes and Aegina in their relations with Athens. Less important in the historical than in the mythical period, Thebes appears as the champion of Boeotia and enemy of Athens soon after the Athenians established their democracy, while earlier she had been on friendly terms with the Athenian and other tyrants. The Theban hegemony is not explained by Herodotus, but he clearly understood it to be basic to Thebes' medism and her hatred of Athens (and especially of Plataea, the Athenians' Boeotian ally) during the Persian Wars. Herodotus knew many stories of the servile behavior of Thebes during the campaigns of both Xerxes and Mardonius, and he characterizes her freely as a power whose local commitments and animosities triumph over any thought of national conscience.[109]

---

[107] Greatness in the mythical period: 1.1 (story of Io); 5.57.2=61.2 (expedition of the Epigonoi). The Argive origin of the Macedonian dynasty is mentioned twice (8.137.1 and 5.22.2). Pheidon of Argos: 6.127.3. Wars of Argos in the sixth and fifth centuries: 1.82 and 6.76 ff. (Sparta); 5.67 f. (Sicyon); 5.86.4 ff., cf. 6.92 (Athens). But the Argives had been friends of the Peisistratids (1.61.4 and 5.94).

[108] Hdt. 9.12. See above, Ch. III, 142-43, and Ch. VI, 289.

[109] Originally friendly with the Peisistratids and with Cleisthenes of Sicyon (1.61.3; 5.67.2), but not then an important power, as she had been in the mythical period (5.59), Thebes stirred up trouble for the young Athenian democracy after the overthrow of the tyrants (5.79-81=6.87), and suddenly appears in the work as the champion of Boeotia (6.108), but the origins of her hegemony are not mentioned by Herodotus. Her friendship with Persia is first alluded to during Datis' second visit to Delos after Marathon, during which he left a statue to be given to the sanctuary of Apollo at Delium in Boeotia (6.118.2). The Thebans gave earth and water to the Persians (7.132.2) and were forced by Leonidas to fight at Thermopylae, where they were branded as Persian slaves (7.205.2-3; 222; 233). Thebes was responsible for

We have already spoken of Aegina and her old quarrel with Athens, which resulted in intermittent warfare until shortly before the invasion of Xerxes. Herodotus mentions several instances of Aegina's early power, but he nowhere indicates that it diminished in the period covered by his work, so that he is able to present the competition of Aegina and Athens during the battles of 480 B.C. as a contest between equals, culminating in the awarding of the prize of valor to the Aeginetans at Salamis.[110] As a counterpart to the Thebans, the Aeginetans illustrate a change from hostility to peaceful competition. Herodotus does not explain the causes of this change, but merely describes the phenomenon.

A similar, but opposite, change is indicated, again without an ultimate explanation, in the case of Corinth. Herodotus relates much of her greatness in the period of the tyrants, and he also documents the active opposition of Corinth to tyranny later in the sixth century.[111] In this period, and down to Marathon, Corinth was friendly to Athens. In the late sixth century, she settled a war between Thebes and Athens over Plataea in favor of Athens; after the overthrow of the Peisistratids, she twice refused to attack Athenian territory; and shortly before Marathon she assisted Athens against Aegina, "being great friends with (the Athenians)

Xerxes' sack of Thespiae and Plataea (8.50.2), and was of much assistance to Mardonius, who made her his headquarters before Plataea (8.134 f.; 9.2; 15.2; 16; 31.2; 40 and 69; cf. 67). Important is the story of Attaginus and Timagenidas, leaders of Thebes on Mardonius' side; in Attaginus' house the famous banquet was held during which a Persian predicted Mardonius' defeat (9.15.4 ff.); both leaders were later delivered to the Panhellenic League, and Attaginus alone escaped death (9.88). The cause of Theban medism (her hostility toward Athens) is fully explained by Herodotus, when he tells the story of Athens' defense of Plataea in 519 B.C., but the position of that story in the narrative of Marathon rather minimizes the causal connection (6.108).

[110] Aegina's early strength is hinted at in 2.178 (founding of Naucratis); 3.59.3-4 (war with Samos); 3.131 (Aegina hires the famous doctor Democedes). For the wars with Athens, see above, 211-12. Symbolic of the change from war to peaceful competition is the taunt that Polycritus of Aegina directed at Themistocles during the battle of Salamis (8.92): for Polycritus was the son of Crius, who had been held as a hostage at Athens for medizing (6.50 and 73.2). The Aeginetans won the *aristeia* at Salamis (8.122).

[111] The Cypselids are the prime example of tyranny in Herodotus; see above, note 18. Cf. also the treasury at Delphi: 1.14.2; 50.3; 51.3; 4.162.3. Later fame: 3.134.5 (Atossa wants handmaidens from Sparta, Argos, Attica, and Corinth). 7.154.3: Corinth and Corcyra intervene in Sicily against Hippocrates, tyrant of Gela, and on behalf of Syracuse, early in the fifth century. Earlier Corinth had participated in the Spartan war against Polycrates (3.48.1).

at that time."[112] All this had changed by the time of the invasion of Xerxes, although Herodotus gives no explanation of the change. Corinth participated in the Persian Wars, but her role as Herodotus describes it (and he knew there were other accounts) was an inglorious one. When the question of the defense of the Isthmus was brought up before Salamis, she was of course on the side of Sparta, and her general Adeimantus insulted Themistocles. During the battle Adeimantus left the Greek forces and was chided by an apparition: this, at least, was the Athenian account, which Herodotus gives in detail, although he knew that according to the Corinthian and common Greek accounts the Corinthians distinguished themselves at Salamis.[113]   The history of Corinth falls into two separate periods: in the first, which comprises both the period of the tyrants and the remainder of the sixth century down to Marathon, Corinth is distinguished and powerful. In the campaign of Xerxes she appears in a much worse light. We are not concerned here with the fact that the later picture is clearly Athenian propaganda. Instead we note once more the lack of an explanation for a change in attitude. Corinth, like Aegina, but in a different sense, is a prime example of the mutability of attitude in a nation. Such mutability is an analogue to, and is sometimes accompanied by, a change of fortune.

If of the five powers cited, Argos and Tegea are seen in relation to Sparta, and Thebes, Aegina, and Corinth largely in relation

[112] Settlement of Plataean quarrel: 6.108.5. Refusal to attack Athens: 5.75.1 and 5.92 (speech of Socles defining Corinth's hostility to tyranny). Help against Aegina: 6.89.

[113] Herodotus' treatment of the Corinthians at Salamis is notorious: see e.g. Jacoby, *RE* Suppl. 2.459; Plutarch, *De Herodoti malignitate* 870 B ff. At Plataea, the role of Corinth is equally inglorious (9.69.1); at Mycale it is only slightly better (9.102 and 105). Adeimantus: 8.5 (Artemisium); 59 and 61 (before Salamis); 94 (flight at Salamis). Herodotus knew that Adeimantus' son was later killed by the Athenians (7.137.3). Thus the friendship of Athens and Corinth prior to the Persian Wars comes to contrast strongly with their antagonism during the wars, an attitude reconstructed by Herodotus' informants from the known hostility of Corinth and Athens in the period of the Athenian empire. However, it seems to me that this picture cannot be explained solely by the bias of Herodotus' informants. I suspect that he developed it out of the support given by the Corinthians to the defense of the Isthmus, both by sea (Adeimantus) and on land (8.72). The Council of the Panhellenic League, which presumably met at the Isthmian sanctuary of Poseidon (G. Glotz and R. Cohen, *Histoire grecque* [Paris 1925-38] 2.58, note 80), is twice intimated by Herodotus to have had headquarters in Corinth (7.195, end, and 9.88, end): but Corinth's attitude was to him anything but Panhellenic, although he notes her claim, supported by other Greeks, that it was (8.94.4). Cf. also H. Strasburger, "Herodot und das Perikleische Athen," *Historia* 4 (1955) 18 f. (= Marg, *Herodot* 599 f.).

to Athens, this relationship suggests that Herodotus has a clear picture of the changing patterns of mainland alignments. The role of the Ionians in the work is, on the other hand, a different one, for here we find not so much a change of character and of active alignment as a fairly static picture of weakness and disunity, with changes of character and of political position imposed by other powers and the events they initiate. Outside of Athens and Sparta, no other Greek nation is followed with such consistency in the work as are the Ionians.[114] They differ from other Greek states in their lack of independence and power, for the work begins with Croesus' conquest of Ionia, and only at the very end are the Ionians freed by the Panhellenic League. The main themes in the portrait of the Ionians are thus freedom and slavery, and the disunity of the Ionians among themselves.

Herodotus does not ask the question (as he does for the colonies in Libya) of the justification for the colonization of Asia by the Greeks, since this took place long before the time at which he begins his work.[115] His account of their plight falls into four phases. The three Asiatic conquests (one by Croesus and two by the Persians) are clearly numbered as a series, as are their two liberations, the first, temporary, in the Ionian Revolt, and the second at the end of the Persian Wars.[116] The Lydian dynasty before Croesus had raided the Ionian cities one by one, and there is no mention of any concerted Ionian defense. Miletus was assisted by Periander of Corinth rather than by her compatriots, and when Croesus attacked Ephesus, there was again no combined effort.[117] But when, right after his overthrow of Croesus, Cyrus threatened to attack, the Ionians met at the Panionium to consult about their common safety (1.141.4 ff.). The *logos* on the Ionians, placed by Herodotus at this point (142-48), stresses

[114] On the picture of the Ionians in Herodotus, see Pohlenz, *Herodot* 9 ff.; G. Nenci, "Le fonti di Erodoto sull' insurrezione ionica," *RAL*, ser. 8, 5 (1950) 106-18; Lenschau in *RE*, s.v. Iones (1916). On the Ionian Revolt, add now H. Bengtson, *Griechische Geschichte*² (Munich 1960) 149-54, and on the early history of Ionia, Carl Roebuck, "The Early Ionian League," *CP* 50 (1955) 26-40; *Ionian Trade and Colonization* (New York 1959) 24-41; and "Tribal Organization in Ionia," *TAPA* 92 (1961) 495-507.

[115] Cf. Pohlenz, *Herodot* 11-12. In Book 4 Herodotus answers the question of the justification of colonization by showing that the colonization of Africa was commanded by Apollo.

[116] Three conquests: 1.6.2 and 1.92.1, etc.; 1.169.2; 6.32. Two liberations: 5.37.1; 9.105.1.

[117] Miletus and Periander: 1.20. Ephesus: 1.26.

Ionian disunity throughout. The Ionians speak four different dialects, he says, and thus have no common language;[118] they are a mixture of races from the mainland of Greece, and they intermarried with Carian women and took on local kings. The twelve cities that united in the Panionian League did so not from a position of strength but out of weakness. Stronger Ionian powers (such as Athens) spurn the name "Ionian" (we have seen how Cleisthenes severed connections with the Ionian tribes)[119] because they are ashamed of it. Ionians are united in name only: the Panionium is not a league of "all the Ionians."[120] The disunity of the Ionians is symbolized by the endings of the names of their festivals, which (as Herodotus tells us at the end of the Ionian "ethnographic" *logos*) all end in the same letter (namely alpha), as do names of Greek festivals in general, "like the Persian proper names."[121] However, the difference between Persians and Ionians is precisely the fact that the Persians are truly united, while the Ionians are united only in name.[122]

Cyrus' war against the Ionian cities shows a divergence in behavior among the members of the confederacy, with some cities more patriotic than others.[123] Miletus is not involved, since she has a special treaty with Cyrus. The Chians are cowards, and impious to boot: they appear in a quite different light during the Ionian Revolt (6.15, etc.). The main heroes of this war are the Cymaeans and the Phocaeans: the latter prefer escape to slavery and are thus the precursors of the Samians later on.[124] On the

[118] Herodotus' conception of the nature of dialects as expressed in this passage (which occurs in the same *logos* as his remark on the forms of Greek festivals, cf. above, Ch. IV, note 111) is puzzling, although it is usually cited with approval in modern dialect studies, e.g. A. Thumb and A. Scherer, *Handbuch der griechischen Dialekte* 2 (Heidelberg 1959) 246 f.; H. Diels, "Die Anfänge der Philologie bei den Griechen," *NJbb* 13 (1910) 14 (Diels thinks Herodotus refers more to accent and *Satzmelodie*). Language is of course a main feature of ethnic identity to Herodotus, cf. 8.144.2. It is possible that he was thinking of differences in vocabulary, since that is his main linguistic interest.

[119] Above, note 54.

[120] Hdt. 1.148.1; compare 1.143.3 and 147.1.

[121] Hdt. 1.148.2; see above, Ch. IV, note 111.

[122] The exclusiveness of the Asiatic Ionians is paralleled by the exclusiveness of Dorians and Aeolians in Asia Minor: see 1.144.3 and 150.1.

[123] Pohlenz, *Herodot* 17, note 1, has shown (against E. Howald) that Herodotus has great respect for patriotism. Yet when he explains (6.13.1) the Samians' behavior at the battle of Lade, the very awkwardness of Herodotus' sentence betrays his embarrassment. Cf. also *Samian Stories* 321.

[124] *Samian Stories* 320-22.

whole, the Ionians fought well (1.169.1). Therefore, Herodotus' unfavorable judgment in the Ionian *Logos* is based not on their record in this war, but in general on their behavior throughout the *Histories*. We may say that at this time the Ionians still had a spark of freedom left in them, which was later lost. The character of the Ionians as a whole is liable to change, as is the character of individual Ionian cities.[125]

Under the Persians, the Ionian cities are ruled by tyrants who, unlike the tyrants in the mainland cities of Greece, are described as hirelings. Their power, as Histiaeus points out to his colleagues during the Scythian campaign (4.137.2), is based on Persian might. The Ionian Revolt against Darius is therefore considered by Herodotus a slave revolt, and he has little sympathy for it.[126] The Scythians, upon finding that the Ionians have let Darius flee across the Danube on the bridge they were guarding, accuse the Ionians of slavish behavior (4.142). The theme of the Ionians as runaway slaves is brought out most clearly, however, at the battle of Lade (6.7-17), where the Ionian sailors cannot bear discipline and declare openly that they prefer slavery to such conditions. The cowardice of the Ionians results in a breakup of the alliance, whence the Milesians are besieged and conquered (Herodotus tells no deeds of bravery here).[127]

The work closes, as it began, with the freedom of the Ionians. During Xerxes' invasion they fought on his side, and despite the attempts of Themistocles to win them over, they contributed nothing to the Greek cause.[128] Only after the Greek victory at Salamis did the Ionian cities awake. In the following spring

---

[125] Although helped only by Chios, Miletus defended herself well in the war with Alyattes, but later she entered into an alliance with Lydia and Persia (1.18.3; 141.4; 143.1). Chios held out longer: 1.18.3; 6.2.2, etc.; 15-16. In the Ionian Revolt she was severely treated by fate (6.16), as well as by the Persians (6.31), but she was among the first Ionian islands to support the Greek cause in the Persian Wars (8.132.2; 9.106.4). Some of the stories about Chios characterize her as motivated by egotism (e.g. 1.160.4-5). Some scholars have seen a connection between the crime of the Chians in 1.160 and the disasters reported in 6.27 (cf. also 6.16 and 31): see Daniels, *Rel.-hist. Studie* 83, note 2, and Crahay, *Litt. orac.* 100. Herodotus, however, does not state this, and it is more likely that the stories about Chios express simple changes of fortune. For Samos, a more fortunate state, see above, note 123.

[126] *Causation* 266.

[127] On the battle of Lade, see below, Ch. VI, 246-48.

[128] Cf. Herodotus' remark on the behavior of the Ionians at Salamis, 8.85.1. The same topic was later used by Euphemus at Camarina to justify the Athenian empire (Thuc. 6.82.4).

some Chian expatriates, because of their hatred for the tyrant of Chios, asked the allies to sail to Ionia (8.132). A second embassy, sent by the people of Samos in their fight against the Samian tyrant and the Persians (9.90-92), was successful in bringing the allies to Mycale. Thus, in both embassies, the internal disunity of the Ionian cities is the prime motive. At the battle of Mycale, Leotychidas, the commander of the allied forces, was successful in persuading the Samian and Milesian contingents of the Persian army to revolt, and they both distinguished themselves in the battle.[129] Nevertheless, the account of Mycale shows clearly that the Ionians could not have freed themselves, and therefore the Spartans suggested transplanting the Ionians to mainland Greece (9.106.3). Athens, in taking on the cause of the liberation of all Ionian cities, now entered the aggressive phase of the Persian Wars, with which Herodotus does not deal.

The Ionians are a major unifying element in the *Histories*. Originally free, they still showed some spirit individually during their battles with Lydia and with Cyrus. The Ionian Revolt is the low point of their fortunes and patriotic valor. The Persian Wars are a return to their original condition of independence, but their disunity and dependence on foreign powers remain unchanged.

VI

Athens, Sparta, and the Ionians are the three principal forces in the Greek world whose affairs are related to the Eastern empires, while most of the other mainland states arrange themselves in some well-defined relation to one of these three. Seen as a whole, the function of the Greeks in the work is first and foremost their role in causing a change of fortune in the East through the Persian Wars. Greece thereby rises from helplessness to a position of superior strength, but her rise in fortune is limited by the internal and external conflicts that characterize European freedom in contrast to Oriental monarchy. We can still see, from some casual remarks of Herodotus, what he considered to have been the result of this limited increase in power for the Greece of his own time. He clearly distinguished between the repulse of the invader from Europe and the subsequent fight for his own homeland

---

[129] Hdt. 9.98.2-3 (the meaning of the passage is not affected by the excision of the interpolation 9.98.4); 9.99, etc.

(8.3.2), and he considered the Pentecontaetia a period of struggles with the Persians and among the Greek states (6.98.2), so that a clear-cut victory was not achieved by any one Greek state. The period which followed the liberation of Greece from the Persian invasion ended, not in the annihilation of Persia, but in the Peloponnesian War.[130]

The motif that binds the Greek accounts together is therefore disunity. The Greek states, forming the Panhellenic League under the threat of invasion, achieved a defensive victory through peaceful competition. This was possible because the antagonism of the Greek city states took place within the framework of Greece as a unified region. In many places Herodotus defines what Greece, or "the Greeks," means to him: the unity of Greece is in the first place ethnic, i.e. the Greeks share a common language, common inherited customs, common institutions, and common gods.[131] Secondly, their unity is moral: as champions (*promachoi*) of Europe, the Greeks are fighters for freedom in a sense unknown to the East.[132] Athens surpasses all other Greek states in knowing both external and internal freedom. But Greeks do not share a common history: both in the mythical period and later, Greek history proves the divisiveness rather than the cohesion of the Greek people.[133]

In Herodotus we observe the struggle of the Greek mind to conceive of Hellas as one.[134] The two main symbols of Greek

[130] For Herodotus' references to the beginning of the Peloponnesian War, see Jacoby, *RE* Suppl. 2.231.

[131] See Hdt. 8.144.2.

[132] For the idea of Europe, see above, Ch. I, note 80. For the European notion of freedom, see Pohlenz, *Herodot* 205 f. and *Griechische Freiheit* (Heidelberg 1955) 14 ff. The Greeks appear as fighters for this kind of freedom primarily in the conversations of Xerxes and Demaratus.

[133] For the divisiveness of the Greeks, see above, 198 ff., and below, Ch. VI, 267 ff. In Herodotus the Trojan War is in the first instance a symbol of the hostility of Greeks and barbarians (Asia and Europe); but it is also a symbol of Greek disunity. For the former meaning, cf. Hdt. 1.4.2-3; 7.20; 7.33 and 9.116.1; for the latter, cf. the story of Cretan participation in the Trojan War and their neglect of Minos, 7.171. The story of Helen in Egypt gives an unfavorable picture of the Greeks in this war, 2.113 ff. On the other hand, 9.27.4 expresses a Panhellenic point of view. Thus the Trojan War forms an exact parallel to and analogue of the Persian Wars.

[134] For the Panhellenism of the time of Herodotus, cf. J. de Romilly, *Thucydide et l'impérialisme athénien* (Paris 1947) 91, note 3. W. Jaeger, *Paideia: The Ideals of Greek Culture*, tr. by G. Highet, 3 (Oxford 1943) 306, note 3. Pohlenz, *Herodot* 175 and *passim*, seems to me to exaggerate the Panhellenism of Herodotus. There exists in his work a kind of polarity between Greeks and barbarians, to which corresponds a polarity of unity and strife in Greek history. The corollary to this conception is

unity are Delphi and, to a lesser extent, Olympia. At Olympia, Herodotus tells us, only Greeks were allowed to compete (5.22), and when Xerxes was about to move toward Athens after Thermopylae, he heard that the Greeks were even then celebrating the Olympic festival, where the prize was not money but an olive wreath given for valor (8.26).[135] The main use of Olympia in the work is to make manifest the valor of individuals and noble families.[136] The Panhellenic character of the festival is stressed in the story of the advice given an Elean embassy by the Egyptians, who said that the fairest procedure in the games would be to allow all Greeks to compete, except for the local Eleans, who would otherwise always win the prize (2.160).

Herodotus' relations with Delphi are so complex, and his accounts of the sanctuary and its oracles fill so much of the work, that it is not possible to mention here more than a few salient features.[137] The Delphic oracle is most prominent in the Croesus *Logos* and in the account of the campaign of Xerxes, i.e. at the beginning and end of the work. In the Croesus story, Delphi is seen mainly in its international relations, and it shows a moral superiority over the Eastern rulers when it announces the limit of the Mermnad dynasty (1.13, etc.). On the other hand, in the Persian Wars the sanctuary represents the Greek world fighting the barbarians, and acts on a par with the other Greek gods. Between these extremes, Delphi is seen in various relations with Sparta, Athens, the Corinthian Cypselids, the Ionians, and other Greek states,[138] but its principal appearance here is in the history

Herodotus' notion of the composition of his public, by which he addresses himself to individual local audiences, while at the same time having in mind a Panhellenic one. On Herodotus' references to his audience, see Pohlenz, *Herodot* 208 ff., and Jacoby, *RE* Suppl. 2.278.

[135] The same festival had kept the Peloponnesians from sending their main army to Thermopylae (7.206.2 and 8.72).

[136] Hdt. 5.47.1 (Philip of Croton); 5.71.1 (Cylon of Athens); 6.36.1 (the elder Miltiades); 6.70.3 (Demaratus); 6.103.2-3 (Cimon, father of the younger Miltiades); 6.122, perhaps interpolated (Callias of Athens); 6.125.5 (Alcmaeon of Athens); 6.126.2 (Cleisthenes of Sicyon). The list is basically a roster of great sixth-century personages, and (characteristically) the items all occur in Books 5 and 6. Cf. above, note 57.

[137] On Delphi in Herodotus, see e.g. Jacoby, *RE* Suppl. 2.272; Pohlenz, *Herodot* 97 ff.; Crahay, *Litt. orac.*; Daniels, *Rel.-hist. Studie.* For a recent survey of Delphic studies, see M. P. Nilsson, *Historia* 7 (1958) 237-50. On the Panhellenic role of Delphi, cf. Oliver, *Demokratia* 136.

[138] Delphi's relations with the several Greek states play a major role in the first Spartan *logos* (1.65 ff.), the history of the liberation from the tyrants in Athens (5.55 ff.),

of Cyrene, where the oracle functions as the supporter of Greek colonization and hence in a Panhellenic role (cf. 4.159.2-3).

In its manifold dealings with individual states certain fixed rules appear. Delphi often predicts the end of absolute rule for individual dynasties, and when supporting one Greek state over another, counsels moderation. The oracle's activities, often concerned with peacemaking and the establishment of good government, encourage unity among the Greeks. When Delphi predicts the destruction of a client, it adduces moral grounds.[139] The unifying function of the oracle in Greek politics is based on its morality, about which Herodotus tells a good many stories. In the Pythia's answer to Croesus (1.91), Apollo establishes a relationship between fate and human responsibility; in the story of Glaucus of Sparta, he punishes the mere thought of dishonesty (6.86c); and elsewhere he explains the divine use of human failings to further religious ends.[140] The Delphic concern with individual Greek states and with Greece as a whole is the main theme of the story of its participation in the Persian Wars. Like other Greek states, Delphi was attacked by the Persians, but Apollo defended his sanctuary (8.35 ff.). When the Greek states inquired individually whether they should oppose the Persian, the oracle answered by painting for some a frightening picture of the Persian host and advised the weak states against resistance, not out of sympathy for the Persians, but as a realist. Thus, Sparta was told that either she or her king must perish (7.220.3), but she was also encouraged to fight at Plataea (8.114). In Herodotus' view not only did the oracle not medize, but it collaborated with other local gods in the war and helped to win the victory, e.g. at Salamis.[141] Delphi's role in the Persian Wars symbolizes Greek cohesiveness.

Herodotus' general scheme for representing the Greeks in the

---

the history of the Cypselids in the speech of Socles (5.92), the Aeginetan *Logos* (6.49 ff.) and generally in the accounts of the relations between Athens and Aegina (5.82 ff.), the fall of Miletus in the Ionian Revolt (6.18 ff.), and in the famous responses given during the Persian Wars.

[139] E.g. the destruction of Miletus, 6.19.2, line 1.

[140] E.g. the priestess Timo at Paros, to punish Miltiades, 6.135.3. Cf. Evenius in Apollonia, 9.93.4.

[141] Cf. *Rev. Crahay* 209-10. Cf. the oracle of the winds given to the Delphians, 7.178. Apollo's demand for a dedication from the Aeginetans after Salamis apparently implied that the god had helped them; see How and Wells on 8.122. The idea that Delphi medized during the Persian War is un-Herodotean and in fact modern. Cf. also H. W. Parke and D. E. W. Wormell, *The Delphic Oracle*, 1 (Oxford 1956) 176 ff. and 180.

work corresponds to their position in the structure, which is of a subordinate kind and does not lead to large independent Greek *logoi*, because the Greeks are not the overt protagonists of the *Histories*. The importance of the Greeks for the work does not lie in their internal history, and therefore not in the pattern of rise and fall, but in their external relations with one another and with the East. Thus Herodotus' prime concern is to explain how the individual Greek states succeeded and failed through cooperation and mutual hostility. This treatment differs radically from the treatment of the East in major *logoi* and in corresponding phases of growth and decline. The two concepts can, however, be reconciled, since they are merely two aspects of the general process of history, in which individual units grow and decay both by an inner law of their own and through mutual interaction. The cycle of fortune governs the individual person and state, while strife in one form or another governs the relation of individual units. Of the two processes, the second is superior in that it renders states and individuals better able to cope with fortune. In this difference lies the superiority of the Greeks over the East.

If this explanation of the unity of Herodotus' own conception of history is correct, then we should find its two aspects used both for the West and for the East, and this is in fact the case. At the beginning of this chapter we saw that the pattern of the ruler is equally applicable to the Greek tyrants and kings. A corresponding use is made of the concepts of justice and injustice among the Persians. There is strife in Asia for the overlordship of the continent, and strife within dynasties for succession. Herodotus had even discovered that in Persia the question of freedom was also debated, not only as regards independence from a foreign master, but also true internal freedom within the state.[142] The difference between the East and West is thus one of the relative proportion of these various factors. Together they make up a single world of history as a part of nature.

[142] Hdt. 3.80 and 83 (Otanes); 6.43.3 (Mardonius in Ionia).

Chapter VI

THE GREAT BATTLES OF THE PERSIAN WARS

In the first chapter of this study we saw that the work of Herodotus is organized, for the most part, according to the course of Persian aggressive action, and that its subject is therefore the history of Asiatic expansionism. In the fourth chapter this expansionist desire was further shown to be based on the excessive unification of the East under autocracy. The pattern of the rise and fall of the ruler appeared as the law of development of individual units in history. Thus the work finds its climax in the account of the great defeat of Xerxes' invasion, through which Persia's aspirations to world empire were foiled.

Since history is to Herodotus primarily the history of action, the battle descriptions stand necessarily at the spiritual center of his work. Seen from the point of view of the aggressor, the battles of the Persian Wars are the turning points in the tragic pattern of rise and fall. The cumulative weight of Asiatic tradition, which gives the work its external unity, finds here its fulfillment and solution. In this sense, Herodotus' account of Salamis has exactly the same function as the description of Salamis in the *Persians* of Aeschylus.

At the same time, the battle description is the place where the subsidiary line of the work, the story of the several Greek nations, also reaches its climax, and in this sense Herodotean battle descriptions differ from that in the *Persians*. In the Herodotean battle, attacker and defender face each other on an equal footing, and the historian develops from the conflict not only the fate of the defeated party, but also that of the victor. Thus, in the great battles of the Persian Wars we see the individual Greek states, and particularly the Athenians, acquire a new position of power; we see Sparta's withdrawal from the exercise of leadership, and the beginning of a solution of the Ionian Question. The battle descriptions are therefore also the climax of the themes described in Chapter V. Herodotus' work, which uses tragic patterns to such a large extent, is thus not a tragedy in the ultimate analysis, since it combines the tragic view with another, more properly historical, view that embraces the growth of nations as well as their downfall. The central point at which these two views intersect is the battle description.[1]

In order to understand the importance of the battle scenes in Herodotus, we must distinguish between different kinds of action, in particular between pragmatic and symbolic action.[2] An example of this distinction occurs, I believe, in the messenger speech of the *Oedipus Tyrannus* of Sophocles. Oedipus has found out everything; he rushes into the palace demanding, we are told, a sword and his wife (1255-56); but he does not get the sword, because a "daimon" shows him his wife already dead and hanging from the rafters. It is then that he puts out his eyes with her brooches (1268 ff.)—a purely symbolic act contrasted with the intended pragmatic use of the sword.[3] In a similar manner, Herodotus has comparatively little interest in military action *per se*; instead he uses tactical situations to characterize people and events. Thus what really keeps him from fully describing military situations is his interest in the dramatic and symbolic aspects of strategy. Paradoxically, Herodotus, a "nonmilitary" historian, puts great emphasis on battle descriptions.

The form of the battle *logos* has been discussed in Chapter II,[4] where it was defined as a circular composition forming the climax of a campaign *logos*. Its circularity is often due to the fact that in

---

[1] I do not enter here upon a discussion of the development of the battle description as a fixed literary topic, the study of which has been somewhat neglected. Most general treatments of Herodotean battles deal with tactics and strategy. See e.g. How and Wells 2.397 ff. (Appendix XXIII); Hauvette, *Hérodote*; Grundy, *Great Pers. War*; and several recent papers by W. K. Pritchett on the topography of the battles in the Persian Wars (*AJA* 61 [1957] 9-28: Plataea; *ibid.* 62 [1958] 203-13: Thermopylae; *ibid.* 63 [1959] 251-62: Salamis; *CalCA* 4, No. 2 [1960] 137-90: Marathon). In matters of fifth-century strategy, the best general guide is perhaps G. B. Grundy, *Thucydides and the History of his Age*[2] 1 (Oxford 1948), Part V, 240-314. Recently, J. de Romilly, in her brilliant book *Histoire et raison chez Thucydide* (Paris 1956), has opened up a new field of investigation by her analyses of Thucydidean battle descriptions: see esp. her Ch. 2, 107-79. Cf. also Jacoby, *RE* Suppl. 2.489, and H. Deffner, *Die Rede bei Herodot und ihre Weiterbildung bei Thukydides* (Diss. Munich 1933) 15. A. E. Wardman, "Tactics and the Tradition of the Persian Wars," *Historia* 8 (1959) 49-60, has some interesting observations on bow and lance, and on sea battles versus land battles, in the Persian Wars.

[2] See *Action* 16-17 and note 1, on Karl Reinhardt's idea of "meaningful gestures."

[3] I am not aware of any comment on the importance of Oedipus' sword in the literature.

[4] Above, 68-69 and 71-72.

any battle, in addition to the element of human planning and responsibility, there is an element of external fortune. At other times, circularity is a vehicle for symbolic thought and conveys a central idea not otherwise apparent from the direct account of the action: at the center of the composition stands a static picture.[5] The typical Herodotean battle scene is composed of short sections, usually not set off formally by framing sentences. Among these are anecdotes or other static accounts—geographical descriptions, rosters of troops, lists of persons who distinguished themselves (*aristeiai*)—which are combined with council scenes and their lengthy speeches. The battle action proper is often short, or falls into separate sections, important not so much for their inter-connections as for their value as anecdotes.[6]

The character of Herodotean battle compositions is due partly to the nature of Herodotus' sources, which consisted mainly of oral traditions, fragmented as to their information and anecdotal in character.[7] Such stories were biased and mutually contradictory, since many fundamental questions about the Persian Wars were hotly debated in the fifth-century tradition. These disagreements were ultimately based on value judgments: was Marathon as important as Salamis, and had it been won by Miltiades or by Callimachus? Was Salamis or Plataea the decisive action of the Persian Wars—i.e. was Sparta or Athens the victor, or in Athens, Themistocles or Aristeides? What part of valor should be assigned to the actual fighters: Aegina, Corinth, Athens, and Sparta—or Thebes?[8] The originality of Herodotus consisted largely in the

[5] External fortune: e.g. nightfall (1.76.4); an eclipse of the sun (1.74.2); fate of the Chians at Lade (6.15.2 and 16.2); appearance of camels (1.80); encirclement at Thermopylae. Similarly, the weak center at Marathon, the storms at Artemisium, the accidents in the ship contests at Salamis, and the interference of the divine at Plataea and Mycale. All of these incidents are discussed below. Central idea: see *Action* 18.

[6] On the anecdotes in Herodotean battle descriptions, see also de Romilly, *op. cit.* (above, note 1) 113 f.

[7] On the oral nature of Herodotus' sources, see above, Introduction, note 15. Cf. also Jacoby's survey of sources, *RE* Suppl. 2.392-467, and his *Atthis* (Oxford 1949) 163 f., 183 ff., etc. Further, *Rev. Crahay* 208.

[8] It is not possible here to do more than give a few brief indications concerning fifth-century controversies about the Persian Wars. In Aeschylus and Herodotus, Marathon is definitely less important than Salamis, but in the later fifth century this judgment changes: cf. especially the praises of the Marathon fighters in Aristophanes, as well as Thucydides 1.73.4 and 2.34.5. Cf. Macan, *IV-VI*, Vol. 2, 182 ff. A similar evaluation is implied earlier in the Marathon painting by Micon in the Stoa Poecile; cf. R. E. Wycherley, *Phoenix* 7 (1953) 27-29. In this picture, the dying Callimachus was prominent: Pausanias 1.15.3 and *RE*, s.v. Kallimachos. On the question of the

preservation and arrangement of the elements of tradition in such a way that a unified interpretation resulted. For Herodotus, unlike Thucydides, believed strongly in the ultimate value of traditions.[9]

II

The importance of the battles in the campaign of Xerxes (Books 7-9) is prepared for by a similar emphasis on battles in the preceding six books with their long campaign *logoi*. For the early periods covered by his work—i.e. for the times for which there were no longer any eyewitnesses—Herodotus had only very sketchy material; perhaps one or two salient facts were known, in the form of anecdotes, for any battles before the early fifth century. Yet the brevity of many battle descriptions is due not only to this lack of information, but also to Herodotus' lack of interest in pragmatic action as such. Events which have no special meaning for the interpretation of history, i.e. for moral and psychological history as Herodotus understood it, are slighted.

Thus we find that in several cases there is no battle description at all,[10] or that a decisive battle is mentioned, after a lengthy preparation, in but a single sentence. Croesus' first great battle against Cyrus, in Pteria, is described in a formula:

> When a fierce battle had taken place and many on both sides had fallen, they separated at nightfall without either side having won the victory. (1.76.4)

What interests Herodotus here is not the battle itself, but Croesus' reaction to it, which follows: Croesus blamed the insufficient

---

importance of Callimachus and Miltiades in that battle, see esp. the so-called Callimachus dedication in *GHI* 1², No. 13; B. B. Shefton, *BSA* 45 (1950) 140 ff. Question of Salamis versus Plataea: the Serpent Column (*GHI* 1², No. 19) presupposes that Plataea was the decisive battle in the Persian Wars, as is shown by its heading. Cf. also Wardman, *Historia* 8 (1959) 49-60. Themistocles and Aristeides: in Herodotus, Themistocles is clearly the hero, but Aeschylus in the *Persians* mediates between them by giving a larger part to the occupation of Psyttaleia than does Herodotus (Aesch. *Pers.* 447 ff.).

The rival claims of the individual Greek states, as well as the judgment of their contemporaries, are in part documented by Herodotus himself: e.g. Aegina at Salamis, 8.92.2 and 122. Corinth: 8.94.4 (cf. above, Ch. V, 229). Athens and Sparta: 7.139 (above, Ch. V, 205 and 217). Thebes: Ch. V, 227. It is well known that Plutarch dealt much with this question in his essay *De Herodoti malignitate*.

[9] *Causation* 276 ff. Introduction, 6-7.

[10] Cf. e.g. the wars of Sparta with Tegea down to the time of Croesus (1.66.4 and 68.6) and the first Persian conquest of Ionia under Cyrus (1.169).

size of his army and returned to Sardis, in the mistaken belief that he had enough time left to call his allies.[11] In other instances, battle descriptions are enlarged by the addition of significant anecdotes, and in some cases (such as the feuds between Sparta and Tegea) they are completely replaced by them.[12] Even where the battle is mentioned, anecdotes are apt to overshadow it. When Cambyses has entered Egypt, the decisive battle of Pelusium is mentioned in a formula similar to that used for Pteria (3.11.3) and framed by lengthy and important stories, one stressing the participation of Greeks on both sides, the other, the physical differences between Egyptians and Persians.[13]

In another type of battle description, the anecdote invades the narrative of the battle itself. A curious instance of this is found in the description of a very early (585 B.C.) battle between Alyattes of Lydia and Cyaxares of Media (1.74.2). This battle was famous because of an eclipse which Thales had predicted. Herodotus, in his brief description, uses an idea originally expressed by Archilochus in reference to an earlier eclipse, namely that day had been turned into night, and thus he calls the battle "a night battle of a kind"—a description that has given rise to much misunderstanding.[14] The sudden change in the natural order

[11] For the *elpis*-motif, see above, Ch. IV, 159-60 and note 28.

[12] Above, Ch. III, 87. The first anecdote is the story of the fetters (1.66.2-4), which expresses the idea of lack of power, since power is the main theme of the *logos*. The second anecdote concerns the recovery of the bones of Orestes, through which this power is re-acquired (1.67 f.). A similar use of fetters: 5.77.3.

[13] Before the battle, Greek and Carian mercenaries slaughter the children of Phanes and drink their blood (3.11.1-2). The story stresses the motif of the destruction of offspring, as well as the participation of Greeks on both sides; on the former, see also Ch. IV, note 57. Herodotus is hardly aware of the original ritual significance of the act. After the battle, the story of the differences in skull thickness between Egyptians and Persians (3.12) develops certain ideas of the Egyptian Ethnographic *Logos*, showing that the Egyptians differ from other nations physically, as well as in their customs; custom in fact here brings about a change in *physis*.

[14] A similar phrase: 7.37.2. How and Wells declare the night battle to be different from the battle during the eclipse, and strictly speaking the chronology mentioned by Herodotus (according to which the night battle took place during the first five years of the war, and the eclipse battle in the sixth) seems to exclude the identification of the two battles. I believe, however, that the figure six is a Herodotean "correction" (cf. E. Fraenkel, *Aeschylus: Agamemnon* 3 [1950] 805; cf. also Introduction, note 30), and that the battles are thus identical (cf. also Stein on 1.74, line 6). In 1.74.2, first line, the particle δέ stands for γάρ; cf. Powell, *Lexicon*, s.v. δέ, 79, No. III, and J. D. Denniston, *The Greek Particles*[2] (Oxford 1954) 169. (In 1.108.1 we should read ἐδόκεε δέ οἱ with **a**: cf. 3.65.2 and 6.131.2.) On the eclipse, see A. R. Burn, *Persia and the Greeks* (London 1962) 31, note 16.

brings about a change in the minds of the combatants, who agree on peace.[15] Furthermore, night and day are important symbols in battle descriptions, especially in the account of Salamis, as we shall see later.

Elsewhere the anecdotal element is more transparent and repetitive. At the battle of Sardis between Croesus and Cyrus, victory is achieved when the Lydian horses cannot stand the sight and smell of Cyrus' camels (1.79 ff.); the story prefigures the fear which Darius' donkeys and mules show of the Scythian horses (4.128 ff.). When the Carians, during the Ionian Revolt, decide to fight with their backs to the Marsyas river (5.118 ff.), the reader is reminded of the discussion between Cyrus and Croesus at the Araxes (1.207). The animal anecdotes stress the unexpected fortunes of war, and the river stories, the futility of human planning.[16] Another element in the anecdotal style is the emphasis on deception or trickery (apatê), perhaps the single most common motif in Herodotean military accounts, especially for sieges.[17] Here trickery is purely human—in Herodotus divine deception is not a major motif. An ancient idea in Greek literature, deception on a divine level occurs already in Homer and in Hesiod, and it is still found in Aeschylus. With Sophocles purely human trickery comes to the fore, and Herodotus' view of apatê is similar to that of Sophocles in that it shows the weakness of man when beset by misfortune—it arouses sympathy for the sufferer.[18]

[15] Herodotus likes to contrast an earlier peaceful settlement with later belligerence; cf. Ch. IV, 152.

[16] Similar anecdotes: e.g. the field mice of Sanaharib's army (2.141); the story of the hare in the Scythian campaign (4.134).

[17] For the apatê-motif, see above, Ch. IV, note 53. Examples are: Alyattes' war against Miletus (1.17, wasting of land; cf. also the manner of concluding peace, 1.21). The scaling of the walls during Cyrus' siege of Sardis (1.84). At Babylon, Cyrus diverts the river (1.191), and Darius is helped by Zopyrus' trickery (3.153 ff.); see Ch. III, note 83. Trickery may develop into treachery, e.g. the Persians at Barca (4.201.2-3) and the Paeonians at Perinthus (5.1.2-3). See also H. R. Breitenbach, *Historiographische Anschauungsformen Xenophons* (Diss. Basel 1950) 57-59 (on the use of μηχανήματα in war).

[18] The statements above are based on the interesting essay by K. Deichgräber, "Der listensinnende Trug des Gottes," in his book by the same title (Göttingen 1952) 108-41. However, I do not believe that the dreams of Xerxes and Artabanus in Herodotus indicate divine trickery: see *Tat und Geschichte* 523-29; differently Deichgräber, *op. cit.* 29, and "Die Perser des Aischylos," *NGG*, Phil.-hist. Klasse, 4 (1944) 170, note 1. Croesus was not betrayed by Apollo (1.91), nor by Zeus, as he had thought when his son was killed (1.44.2): in each case fate took hold by means of his own actions. On *mêchanêmata*, see further Schmid-Stählin 1.3.763; F. Solmsen, "Zur Gestaltung des Intrigenmotifs in den Tragödien des Sophokles und Euripides," *Philologus* 87 (1932) 1-17; W. Zürcher, *Die Darstellung des Menschen im Drama des*

This motif of trickery also occurs in battle descriptions.[19]

A certain number of battles are more fully treated, but here too the realism of the earlier descriptions is suspect. The battle between Sparta and Argos over Thyrea at the time of Croesus' war with Cyrus (1.82.1-7) owes its pattern (the arrangement of an equal struggle between chosen contestants) ultimately to the old epic and folklore story of the duel as opposed to the people's battle, a famous example of which is Livy's story of the Horatii and Curiatii.[20] The seeming realism of Cyrus' battle against the Massagetae is likewise unconvincing (1.214). This is the battle, it will be recalled, in which Queen Tomyris seeks vengeance for the capture and death of her son, and in which Cyrus meets his end. Herodotus had heard that it had been the fiercest battle ever fought by barbarians, and he proceeds to describe it:

> For it is said that first they shot arrows at each other from a distance, and then, when their missiles had given out, they joined forces and fought with spears and daggers. The battle raged for a long time and neither side attempted to flee. Finally the Massagetae won. (1.214.2)[21]

In all probability Herodotus knew nothing specific of this battle (which is presumably legendary), but only the general manner of barbarian fighting, without hoplite equipment and the sword. It amazed him that with the more primitive weapons a close contest could be fought just as well. The description is immediately overshadowed by the account of the death of Cyrus

---

Euripides (Basel 1947), index, s. vv. μηχαν-. It is not surprising that Herodotus' conception of trickery is most similar to that of Sophocles. However, we must not forget that *apatê*, in addition to its importance in fifth-century thought, is also a very old and primitive motif and draws its persistence from being a basic mythical pattern, as is evident e.g. in Hesiod's *Theogony*.

[19] Several battle descriptions resemble sieges in being depicted as won by deception: see 1.63.1-2 (Peisistratus at Pallene); 1.211 (capture of Tomyris' son by Cyrus) and 4.135 (similar ruse employed by Darius to withdraw from Scythia); 5.63 (Anchimolius of Sparta fooled by Thessalian cavalry) and 6.78 ff. (Cleomenes fools the Argives by the sound of a trumpet). That much of Greek warfare consisted of such tricks is evident from Thucydides and the *Stratagemata* of Polyaenus; but in Herodotus there is also a larger meaning.

[20] Livy 1.25; cf. also Hdt. 9.26.3, of the time of the Heracleidae. On the two battles in 1.82, see above, Ch. I, note 66. The decisive battle is described in only one sentence and is overshadowed by the battle of the three hundred and by the later change of hair style. Cf. in general Schmid-Stählin 1.3.417, note 5.

[21] Cf. Aristagoras' description of Persian fighting (5.49.3), and see Myres, *Herodotus* 210 f.

and of the treatment his body receives from the queen, who puts his head into a wineskin filled with blood (1.214.4-5). In a similar manner, the brief realism of the Spartan siege against Polycrates in Samos is overshadowed by other stories (3.54-56.1). Herodotus had special information about Samos[22] and so knew that the Spartans had first attempted, but without success, to take the tower of the city fortifications nearest the sea, and had then almost entered the city after winning a battle at another tower further inland. His main point, however, is that on the second occasion the Spartans lacked the courage to pursue the enemy inside the walls, and he tells the story of two Spartans who alone did show such courage and died in the city. Because of cowardice (we are to understand) the Spartans achieved nothing at Samos and retired after forty days of siege.

In these accounts, pragmatic action manages to infiltrate accounts basically concerned with symbolic action. With the Ionian Revolt, we begin to get more detailed descriptions; however, it is characteristic of Herodotus that the basic relation between action and symbol remains the same throughout the *Histories*. The two principal battles of the Ionian Revolt are the battle of Salamis in Cyprus and the battle of Lade (5.110 ff. and 6.8 ff.). The battle of Salamis was fought both on land and at sea, the Cypriotes fighting the land battle and the Ionians the naval engagement. This relationship is stressed in the story that precedes the battle, in which the Cypriotes offer the Ionians their choice of fighting the Persians on land or the Phoenicians by sea (5.109). The Ionians answer proudly that they will keep to their ships. In the land battle the main story concerns Onesilas, king of Cyprus, who receives from his Carian squire a promise to subdue the Persian general Artybius by slaying his horse.[23] Then the battle on land and sea is told only briefly: the sea forces are victorious, but the land forces are defeated through the treachery of some of the Cypriote troops (113.1). When the Ionians hear of the results of the land battle, they return home (115). The relation of the land to the sea battle is here similar to the relation of Thermopylae

---

[22] Jacoby, *RE* Suppl. 2.220 ff.

[23] Hdt. 5.111-12. The master with his squire is of course a common folk-tale motif: see K. Reinhardt, "Herodots Persergeschichten," *Vermächtnis der Antike* (1960) 158 ff. (=Marg, *Herodot* 349 ff.). Another group of stories concerns horses: cf. the cavalry motif cited above, Ch. III, note 184, and below, 291. The Persians held horses in special regard (e.g. 1.136.2; 1.189.1 ff.).

to Artemisium in Herodotus' version. In both events the land
battle is decisive for the sea battle, and it is lost through treachery
alone. In the Cypriote battle the decisive factor was the disunity
of the Cypriotes, which is shown up against the relative unity and
courage of the Ionians. Herodotus here contrasts, quite seriously,
the relative strength of the Ionians no longer under tyranny with
the effects of despotism in Cyprus.[24] The motif of disunity is thus
applied to the Cypriotes, compared with whom the Ionians are
relatively more courageous, whereas at Lade they appear disunited and weak: the latter is Herodotus' judgment when he
contrasts the Ionians with the mainland Greeks.

   The battle of Lade is the first in the work on which Herodotus
had full information and for which he gives all the different aspects
of the battle pattern.[25] Its outline is as follows:

6.6:		Persian army and navy collect against Miletus.
	6.7:	Ionian council at Panionium decides to fight a sea battle, but no land battle.
	6.8-9.1:	Battle order of Ionian fleet. Totals for Ionians and Persian ships.
	6.9.1-10:	Persians arrive at Miletus; unsuccessful attempt to have the Ionian tyrants each make his city desert the Ionian cause.
	6.11-13:	a. Council of Ionians; speech of Dionysius.
		b. Ionians dislike drill and give it up.
		c. Samians decide to desert.
		d. Who Aeaces was.
	6.14-15.2:	Battle of Lade: first engagement; Samians desert; Lesbians desert; Chians remain at post.
	6.16-17:	(After the battle:)
		a. Fate of Chians at Ephesus.
		b. Flight of Dionysius to Sicily.
6.18 ff.:		Persian siege and capture of Miletus.

The battle of Lade was an attempt to avert the siege of Miletus;
as a group, the Ionians quickly decided to support their central
city, but when it came to the battle many of them deserted

---

[24] How and Wells on 5.109.3, however, think that Herodotus is sarcastic about
the superiority here assumed by the Ionians.

[25] See Pohlenz, *Herodot* 16 ff.

individually. As we have seen, to Herodotus the Ionian Revolt was a slave revolt, since the Ionians had been under the Persians for so long,[26] and he treats the whole action very critically. The central idea of the battle is therefore that the Ionians were patriotic only up to a point, an idea which complements their relative nobility at the battle of Salamis in Cyprus.[27] As at Salamis, the Ionians decide to fight on the sea only. After the short planning sections (6.6 and 7) we see the arrival of the Ionian and Persian fleets (6.8-9.1 and 9.1-10), but the principal story concerns the Persians who, fearing the size of the Ionian navy, employ the deposed tyrant of each city as an intermediary in an attempt to persuade that city to desert. At this point, the Ionians do not listen:

> But the Ionians to whom these messages came remained firm[28] and did not accept the offer of betrayal; they each thought the Persians were announcing this to them alone. (6.10)

Ionian patriotism had indeed its limitations: the individual cities remained with their brethren only because they did not realize that many of them had received the same message. The council section (6.11-13) describes another aspect of this characterization: when their general Dionysius asks the Ionians to drill, they can stand it for only seven days, and thereafter, preferring slavery to hard work, they take refuge from sunburn in their tents on land.[29] The Samians, seeing the disorganization of their compatriots and fearing the Persian might, then decide to desert—wisely but unheroically.[30]

[26] Above, Ch. V, 232.

[27] E. Howald, "Ionische Geschichtsschreibung," *Hermes* 58 (1923) 116, denied all true patriotism to Herodotus here; this has been well answered by Pohlenz, *Herodot* 17, note 1, who, however, overstresses Herodotus' Panhellenism in the account of the Ionian Revolt.

[28] On the term ἀγνωμοσύνη, used here, see Pohlenz, *loc. cit.* (preceding note).

[29] Dionysius' drill was intended to teach the Ionians the διέκπλους or "breakthrough," on which see How and Wells on 6.12.1. Herodotus, however, is not interested in the maneuver itself, but in the moral implications of discipline. The "unbearable pains" of which the Ionians complain seem to be sunburn (6.12.3). Similarly, Thucydides characterizes Syracusan lack of experience by saying that they withdrew to their tents (6.100.1). Presumably this is jocular; a similar motif occurs in Menander, *Dyscolus* 522 ff.

[30] Herodotus does not forgive the Samians for their betrayal; see above, Ch. V, note 123. It is made plausible by the behavior of the other Ionians.

The battle description falls into a series of statements on the behavior of individual Ionian states, and these statements are at times separated by stories placed in what has been defined in Chapter II as the pause. There is no account of the tactics of the battle beyond the statement that the Chians alone fought bravely, practicing the *diekplous* (15.2). After the announcement of the beginning of the battle Herodotus declares himself unable to record accurately which of the Ionians fought bravely and which did not, owing to the fact that "they accuse one another." Then follows the defection of all but eleven Samian ships, whose captains were later honored by a stele in the market place at Samos. The Lesbians and the majority of other states also defect, and the Chians alone remain, "accomplishing great deeds and not giving up," until they are forced to flee. The section on the aftereffects of the battle shows the tragedy of the only two heroes of the battle, the Chians, who are slaughtered by the Ephesians in error, and Dionysius, who goes west to become a pirate. The battle of Lade stresses symbolic action over tactics because Herodotus wants to show that the Ionians, with their loss of freedom, had lost their strength, both morally and physically, and their regional cohesion.

The battles of Eretria and Marathon, during the expedition of Datis and Artaphernes in 490 B.C., occupy a special position.[31] Marathon is to Herodotus an event that prefigures the Persian Wars proper, without actually being a part of them. He solved the question of the relative importance of the events of 490 and 480 B.C. in two ways: by a careful connection of acts of mutual aggression (*aitiai*) he showed that Marathon was caused by the Athenian participation in the Ionian Revolt and caused, in its turn, the expedition of Xerxes. On the other hand, by isolating it as a separate composition he also showed its lesser importance when compared with the events of 480 and 479 B.C. In so doing, he was probably following the bias of tradition during the years before the Peloponnesian War, since in Aeschylus' *Persians* Marathon likewise plays a very minor role. It would seem that the importance of Marathon was stressed more during the Peloponnesian War, when Athenian patriotism needed a battle where Athens alone (or nearly alone) had won a great victory.[32]

[31] Plutarch, *De Herodoti malignitate* 26-27, shows clearly the dissatisfaction felt by a Greek "patriot" with Herodotus' treatment even of the Athenians at Marathon.
[32] Above, note 8.

We must therefore look at Marathon as an important antecedent of the "Persian Wars," but not as a part of them.

Marathon is a campaign *logos* of medium size, describing one of a series of actions originated by Darius against the Greeks.[33] The account begins with the Persians—despite the fact that the Athenians are the attackers on the field of battle.[34] Thus we hear first of Persian preparations, then of their attack on Naxos and their dealings at Delos; their return is given in equal detail. Greek action is also full, but subordinated to the Persian in the manner of other campaigns before Salamis. The Persians are characterized in two ways. First, their ambivalence appears in the destruction of some sanctuaries (Naxos, Eretria) and the respect shown to others (Delos), as well as in Darius' initial anger against the Eretrians, in contrast with his eventual leniency.[35] Secondly, the Persians are overconfident in the battle. Having managed to capture Eretria through the treachery of a pro-Persian party, they expect the same to happen in Athens—not without good reason, as is shown by the existence of the shield signal flashed to the Persians right after the battle (as Herodotus has it), and by the words of Miltiades to Callimachus: "If we do not fight, I expect a great division will shake the minds of the Athenians, so that they will medize" (6.109.4-5). Both their ambivalence and their overconfidence connect this picture of the Persians with that given in the campaign of Xerxes.

The themes of the Greek sections of this *logos* also foreshadow later Greek accounts. There is first the question of internal disunity exemplified, in Eretria, by the betrayal, and in Athens, by the shield signal and the division among the Athenian generals. External disunity is stressed in the story of the earlier alliance between Plataea and Athens, in which Sparta is shown to be successful in embroiling Athens with Thebes, while the Corinthians vainly attempt to mediate (6.108.2-6), and in the late arrival of the Spartan troops (6.120). Against this stands the great

---

[33] Above, Ch. III, 122 ff. On the "proem to Marathon," see above, Ch. II, 66.

[34] See the outline, Ch. III, 123-24.

[35] The burning of sanctuaries by the Persians has two motivations: (a) vengeance for the burning of Sardis, e.g. 6.101.3, and (b) unlimited conquest (see e.g. 6.96—the capture of Naxos, which had been planned before the Ionian Revolt; cf. 5.34). These motivations parallel the two basic motivations of the Persian Wars as such. Cf. also Ch. IV, note 102. Eretrians: 6.94.2 and 119. On the favorable characteristics of the Persians and their kings, see above, Ch. IV, 173 and 182-83.

friendship of the Plataeans for Athens and the unanimity reached between Miltiades and Callimachus about the decision to fight. In the latter case, Herodotus had to decide between a tradition favorable to Callimachus and another partial to Miltiades.[36] His account favors Miltiades as the planner and executor of the battle, but without slighting the patriotism and heroism of Callimachus.[37] We see here already the tendency to praise the victory of Marathon as a proof of Athenian unity—a meaning which in later authors becomes the central theme of the praises of Marathon.

Another basic idea of Marathon is the relationship between Athenian local patriotism and Panhellenism. Marathon later was often used to support the Athenian claim to Greek leadership, a claim that already appears in the so-called Marathon epigrams, which are nearly contemporary with the battle.[38] In Herodotus the question is raised principally in the speeches of Philippides at Sparta and of Miltiades before Callimachus. In Sparta, Philippides said:

> "Oh Spartans, the Athenians ask you to assist them and not to allow the oldest city among Hellenes to fall into slavery by the hands of barbarians. Just now Eretria has been enslaved and Greece has become weaker by an important city." (6.106.2)

The speech of Miltiades forms a contrast with this Panhellenic argument, for he stresses a purely Athenian, if not actually imperial, viewpoint, when he says that the victory over the Persians

---

[36] Above, note 8.

[37] Myres, *Herodotus* 208, is probably correct in stating that Herodotus, by mentioning Callimachus' election by lot as polemarch, wants to stress the divine chance that resulted in a man with such an auspicious name ("fine fighter") heading the army at the right time. Furthermore, the mention of the lot is part of a cluster of "numerical" observations by Herodotus, such as the voting 5 to 5, with the voice of the polemarch added; the waiting for Miltiades' day of command to start the battle; and the phrase ὡς ἠριθμέοντο αἱ φυλαί, for which see Pritchett, cited below, note 40. These observations may be intended to convey the idea that Callimachus' presence was a stroke of luck, but that Miltiades proceeded rationally, and legally.

[38] The idea that Marathon was fought as a service to Greece appears in the upper of the two epigrams. Unfortunately, their connection with the battle, as well as their date (before or after Salamis), are at present a matter of dispute. See e.g. B. D. Meritt, "Epigrams from the Battle of Marathon," *The Aegean and the Near East: Studies Presented to Hetty Goldman*, ed. by S. S. Weinberg (Locust Valley [N.Y.] 1956) 268-80, esp. 272, and Meritt's article in *AJP* 83 (1962) 294-98, with further bibliography. This Athenian Panhellenic *claim* for Marathon is altogether absent from the Herodotean account, despite the mention in Philippides' speech, as quoted in the text above, of the Panhellenic *importance* of that battle; cf. also the absence of the claim from the speech of the Athenians at Plataea (9.27.5).

will not only guarantee the freedom of Athens, but will also make her the first city in Greece (6.109). It should not be forgotten that Miltiades himself had been a tyrant. Consequently the battle *logos* of Marathon stresses the same contradictory Athenian attitude (the attempt to combine self-interest with the good of Greece) that we have found earlier to be a key factor in Herodotus' description of Athens in the work as a whole.[39]

We turn now to the battle in the narrow sense (6.112-13). There is perhaps no better example than this of Herodotus' symbolic use of tactical situations. Herodotus knew that when Miltiades began the battle two things happened: (a) the Athenians attacked the Persians "on the run," and (b) the Athenian battle line, weakest in the middle, was broken at that point, but the Greek wings turned round and defeated the victorious Persians in the center. In his account these two facts are interpreted as follows. In the Greek battle order (6.111.1) Callimachus led the right wing and the Plataeans the left: that meant, Herodotus implies, that the wings of the formation were particularly strong.[40] That the Persians usually placed themselves in the center seems to have been well known to him and his Greek readers.[41] Herodotus looks at the Greek order of battle from the point of view of the honor it conferred on the participants (see 111.2). Luck, we are to understand, had placed the best troops on the Greek flanks, whereas the Persians occupied their usual positions.

To Herodotus, the attack "on the run" is an expression of Athenian courage and not, as it is e.g. to Myres, a tactical maneuver especially invented by Miltiades,[42] for "the run" was one element in the tradition that correctly pictured Marathon as a great hoplite victory.[43] On the other hand, the tactical scheme

---

[39] Above, Ch. V, 222-23.

[40] As W. K. Pritchett has shown (*CalCA* 4, No. 2 [1960] 147), Herodotus does not make reference to the official order of tribes in the battle. He likewise shows no knowledge of the fame of Callimachus' tribe Aiantis, a fame which was said to be derived from the tribe's position in the line of battle (Toepffer in *RE*, s.v. Aiantis No. 2 [1894]; Pritchett, *op. cit.* 146). Thus the strength of the wings may be simply an inference, on Herodotus' part, from the known valor of Callimachus and of the Plataeans, who occupied them. Herodotus' whole description is pointed toward the praise of hoplite valor, and all other aspects are left obscure—including the Persian attempt at Phaleron.

[41] Cf. Myres, *Herodotus* 210, and How and Wells on 6.113.1. However, this was not true at Plataea.

[42] Myres, *Herodotus* 210-11.

[43] Consequently, after a certain build-up Herodotus drops all reference to the Persian cavalry—a procedure that constitutes a major crux in the interpretations of

was for Herodotus the merest accident:

> And then, when the Athenians were getting into position at
> Marathon, the following happened: when the army was
> extended equally with that of the Medes, its middle contained
> only a few lines and was there weakest, whereas each wing
> was strong in numbers. (6.111.3)

This famous passage has been much misunderstood.[44] Its central
idea is the notion of the equal (*ison*). Now it is a Greek view that
accident accomplishes the wishes of the gods, and, as we saw
earlier, Herodotus emphasizes that Callimachus was present on
the battlefield through choice by lot. Here we find that equalization of the battle lines brings about, *by accident*, a favorable
tactical situation. In any battle, the gods (or "the divine" as
Herodotus has it) must give the combatants an equal chance, as
Miltiades explains to Callimachus before the battle.[45] At this
occasion, the "equal" chance given the Athenians was the result
of the equality of the lines, and this rendered their victory possible.

The battle of Marathon thus uses tactical descriptions in a
symbolic sense. Hence the outline of the battle consists of short
sections not really descriptive of the battle itself. After the mention
of favorable sacrifices, the first section deals with "the run," the
distance to be overcome, its effect upon the Persians, and the initial
fighting (112.1-3, first sentence). To this is added the emphatic
statement that the Athenians were the first Greeks to endure
the sight of the Medes (112.3, end). The bulk of the fighting
is then mentioned in a single formula, and the stratagem of the
central breakthrough and pursuit from the wings is part of
victory and flight (113). The pursuit goes as far as the ships, with
the pursuers "asking for fire"—this last a reminiscence of the

---

the battle now current. See How and Wells 2.353 ff.; Grundy, *Great Pers. War* 183 ff.;
Hammond, *Hist. Greece* 217, note 1; A. W. Gomme, "Herodotus and Marathon,"
Phoenix 6 (1952) 77-83 (=his *More Essays in Greek History and Literature* [Oxford 1962]
29-37); Pritchett, *op. cit.* (above, note 40) 173.

[44] See in general Grundy, *Great Pers. War* 187 ff.; J. A. R. Munro in *CAH* 4, 232 ff.;
Macan, *IV-VI*, Vol. 2,245 ff.; Pritchett, *op. cit.* (above, note 40) 143-45. Stein, on
6.111, line 13, also assumes that the arrangement was accidental.

[45] θεῶν τὰ ἴσα νεμόντων, 6.109.5. The same phrase is used by Dionysius of Phocaea
before the battle of Lade (6.11.3), and the idea recurs in similar form in a remark
Herodotus makes concerning the storm off Magnesia in 480 B.C. (8.13). It is perhaps
taken from contemporary epigrams: see F. Hiller von Gaertringen, *Historische griechische
Epigramme* (1926), No. 55 (413 B.C.). On the idea of the *ison*, see also above, Ch. IV,
note 8.

Iliad.[46] Then comes the list of the fallen, the capture of seven Persian ships, and the march of the Athenians to Athens, i.e. sections that belong properly to the aftereffects of battle (114-16.)[47] The whole is closed off by the numbers of the slain and the story of Epizelus (117): thus the battle in the narrowest sense ends with the arrival at the ships (113.2); in a wider sense it continues to the blinding of Epizelus. The central feature of the battle description is the image of the Athenians advancing "on the run." The moral view here overshadows the tactical.

In the campaign *logos* of Marathon as a whole, the religious element, although stressed less than in the later encomiastic tradition,[48] appears first of all in the destruction and preservation of sanctuaries during the advance of the Persians, as mentioned above. Philippides' meeting with the Arcadian Pan, and the subsequent introduction of that god to Athens, foreshadows the parallel relations of the Athenians with Boreas, the North Wind, ten years later.[49] One might well ask what in particular Pan contributed to the victory at Marathon. We cannot prove that Herodotus connected the occurrence of "panics" in armies with this god, but it is perhaps attractive to speculate that Pan in this battle helped the Athenians to withstand the terror inspired by the enemy.[50] In three places the underlying theme is the terror of the Persian

[46] *Iliad* 15.718; cf. Aly, *Volksmärchen* 150.

[47] The events at Athens and at Phaleron after the battle of Marathon play a large part in modern reconstructions of the whole battle complex; the suggestion has even been made that there was more to the fighting at Phaleron—with the Persians attempting a landing to attack Athens directly—than Herodotus indicates (A. E. Raubitschek, *AJA* 44 [1940] 58; see further, Pritchett, *op. cit.* [above, note 40] 162-63). However that may be, Herodotus did not consider the events at Phaleron a separate battle, but a part of the aftereffects of the victory, which was won on the plain of Marathon alone.

[48] Already in Micon's painting in the Stoa Poecile, Athena, Heracles, the hero Marathon, Echetlaus, and Theseus are present at the battle (Pausanias 1.15.3 and 32.5). See How and Wells, 2.354 ff. Cf. generally A. R. Burn, *Persia and the Greeks* (London 1962) 254-56.

[49] Pan: 6.105.3. Boreas: 7.189.3. Attic vase paintings prove that their cults were introduced in Athens after the Persian Wars: see, for Pan, Brommer in *RE* Suppl. 8.954 ff. (1956), and for Boreas, J. D. Beazley, *Der Panmaler* (Berlin 1931) 11, and H. U. Instinsky in Marg, *Herodot* 492, note 70.

[50] On the connection of Pan with panics, see Brommer in *RE* Suppl. 8.969, lines 49 ff., and cf. 958, lines 14 ff. and 967, lines 38 ff. The Herodotean word for panic is φόβος: see Stein on 7.10e, line 7. At Marathon, Herodotus stresses mostly the fearful aspect of the battle upon the Greeks, whereas later writers (and the painting by Micon) have mythical figures inspiring fear in the Persians. On Pan and panics, cf. also E. R. Dodds, *Euripides: Bacchae*[2] (Oxford 1960) 109-10 (on lines 302-304); C. P. Segal, *HSCP* 66 (1962) 108, note 50.

attack. After the first mention of their movement against Eretria, we hear that there was at that time an earthquake on the island of Delos (6.98.2-3), which is explained as an omen of the terrible troubles which were to befall the Greeks down to Herodotus' own time. The second passage referring to the terror aroused by the Persians is the description of the "run" already discussed, and the third is the story of the blinding of Epizelus, who, it will be recalled, had a vision during the battle in which he saw a figure of terror, which was fighting on the Persian side, pass him by and kill a companion; whereupon Epizelus lost his sight. This story well summarizes the feeling of "panic" on the part of the Athenians, and the help given to them by Pan in their terror (if these speculations are correct).

Other divine elements in the account of Marathon are found primarily in some typical Herodotean correspondences. Two dreams are found on the Persian side: Hippias dreams that he is having intercourse with his mother and interprets this falsely to mean that he will reoccupy Athens (6.107.2-4),[51] while Datis, on his way home, has a dream to the effect that he must return a certain statue to a Greek sanctuary (6.118.1). On the Greek side, a similar correspondence exists between the two waking visions of Philippides in Arcadia and Epizelus at Marathon. There is a third parallel, between the Greek encampment at Marathon at a sanctuary of Heracles, and the return to the city to "another Heracleum in Cynosarges" (6.116).[52] These Athenian contacts with the divine contrast strongly with the Spartan sense of religious obligation, which makes them observe the festival of the Carneia rather than assist the Athenians on time.[53]

III

The five great battles of the invasion of Xerxes are arranged, as has been stressed by Pohlenz and others, in a symmetrical pattern, whereby land and sea battles precede and follow the battle of

[51] The motif identifying the relation of a tyrant with his city as incest with his mother may be a development from the *topos* that a tyrant "rapes women" (3.80.5; cf. Euripides, *Suppl.* 452-55); at any rate this motif recurs in Sophocles, *OT* 980-82, and in Plato, *Rep.* 10.571 c 9.

[52] This resembles the correspondences between sanctuaries which Herodotus notes at Mycale and at Plataea; see below, 288 and note 149.

[53] The Spartans pleaded the full moon (6.106.3), and this may be the full moon of the Carneian festival; see How and Wells *ad loc.*

Salamis in such a way that the land battles are contained, as it were, within the accounts of naval action.[54] The basic outline is as follows:

> 7.179-96: Movement of Persian navy from Therma to Aphetae near Artemisium; engagements preliminary to battle of Artemisium.
> 196-200:   Persian army from Therma to Malis.
> 201-239: Battle of Thermopylae.
> 8.1-26:   Battle of Artemisium.
> 27-39:   Movement of land army to Boeotia and Delphi.

8.40-125: Battle of Salamis.
126-29:   Return of Artabazus to Mardonius.

> 8.130-32: Greek fleet to Delos and Persian fleet to Samos.
> 8.133-9.89: Actions connected with Plataea.
> 9.90-113: Battle of Mycale.

9.114-22:   The Greek navy at Abydos and Sestus.

In this scheme Herodotus judges the divergent Greek traditions about the relative merits of Salamis and Plataea, not by attempting to harmonize accounts, but simply by an arrangement in which Salamis overshadows Plataea.[55] The contrast between land and sea, while helping to establish the same point, has a much larger significance. In the *Persians*, Aeschylus with great skill presents the battle of Salamis as both a sea and a land battle, by the simple expedient of emphasizing the minor engagement on the island of Psyttalia, led by Aristeides, and by placing it on a par with the Themistoclean sea battle.[56] In this way he makes peace between two factions of the Athenian state and intimates that Athens needs its hoplites (who are its farmers) as much as the aggressive new merchant class. However, his meaning is not just political: in fifth-century thought the sea often stands for freedom, wealth, and imperialist expansion, and the land for law, order, and

[54] See above, Ch. III, 137-38. Pohlenz, *Herodot* 162. Myres, *Herodotus* 63-64, 105, and 126.

[55] On the other view (that Plataea was the decisive battle), see above, note 8.

[56] See above, note 8. The account of the fighting at Psyttaleia constitutes one of the three main sections of Aeschylus' messenger speech: see J. de Romilly, *Histoire et raison chez Thucydide* (Paris 1956) 120 ff.; and R. Lattimore, *Classical Studies . . . A. W. Oldfather* (1943) 88. On the contrast between agriculture and maritime commerce, see Ch. V, note 27.

conservatism. Herodotus, in stressing the sea against the land, there-by stresses the progressive forces of the Athenian democracy, despite his great sympathy for certain aspects of Spartan conservatism; a direct line thus leads from his view of Athenian politics and life to the picture developed by Thucydides.[57]

As regards structure, we should distinguish between the direct line of action in the five-battle complex and the symbolic corre-spondences. The action consists of the movements of the Persian navy and army down to Boeotia (8.39), at which point the scheme is abruptly abandoned. The battles of Thermopylae and Artemi-sium are inlaid in this account of Persian aggression. With 8.40, the structure changes radically, and we now follow the movement of the Greeks, first to Salamis and then to Mycale. A short con-necting section (8.126-29) prepares for the battle of Plataea, which is isolated by surrounding naval action. It is interesting to note that the battle of Salamis is actually framed by two short sections dealing with movements on land. The symbolic correspondences within each group—Thermopylae and Artemisium, Plataea and Mycale—will be described later. At this point, it may suffice to mention some correspondences between the two pairs of battles. Plataea is the vengeance for Xerxes' treatment of Leonidas (8.114.2 and 9.79.2), and as a Spartan victory it wipes out the defeat at Thermopylae. Mycale finds Leotychidas repeating a stratagem of Themistocles at Artemisium (he attempts to persuade the Ionians to desert), and as an Athenian victory it wipes out the comparative ill-success of the earlier naval battle.[58]

The five battles cannot be understood without considering certain thematic connections established by the preceding narrative, especially the march of Xerxes and the Greek prepara-tions discussed in Chapter III. The former establishes Persian unified strategy by land and sea. The aim of the Persians through-out is to use army and navy together: this plan is presupposed for Thermopylae and Artemisium, and it is specifically underlined in the conversation between Darius, Demaratus, and a Persian admiral after Thermopylae (7.234-37). Themistocles' scheme for Salamis destroyed this plan, as it destroyed Persian initiative

---

[57] The use of this motif is also an important indication of Herodotus' relation to Pericles, on which see above, Ch. V, note 77.

[58] Leotychidas' stratagem: 9.98.3; cf. 8.22. As stated in Ch. V, note 129, I believe 9.98.4 to be an interpolation, but the comparison of the actions is nevertheless valid.

generally. The Persian march section also establishes the theme of Persian overconfidence, for they expect the Greeks to run away. The story of the Greek preparations, on the other hand, is primarily the story of patriotic versus medizing factions, i.e. the story of Greek disunity.[59] Beside the accounts of medizing Greeks, this story refers to the quarrel of the Hellenic League with Gelo of Syracuse over the hegemony, and to a number of oracles, and it thus raises the question of the help of the gods. It ends, significantly, with the story of the Delphic prayers to the winds. All these themes are central to the five battles.

Herodotus' presentation of the relation between Thermopylae and Artemisium has often been criticized, and modern reconstructions of the events differ widely from his account, with regard both to chronology and to the motives behind Greek strategy. To Herodotus, however, the connection between the battles is not pragmatic, but analogical. His account shows them to be strictly parallel, although his narrative technique does not, as we saw in Chapter II, lend itself to the description of parallel action.[60] Hence the parallel nature of the battles is mentioned only once:

> It so happened that the sea fights (at Artemisium) and the land battles at Thermopylae took place on the same days. (8.15.1)

As Macan rightly points out, this synchronism of the three days' battles must be the starting point of any reconstruction.[61] Now the number three also plays a part in the narrative that precedes the three days' actual fighting. Prior to its arrival at Artemisium, the Persian navy had been buffeted for three days by a violent storm off the coast of Magnesia (7.191.2), and *during the same period* Xerxes was inactive at Thermopylae, hoping the Greeks would flee (7.210.1).[62] Since this parallelism is not expressed directly, it has

---

[59] Above, Ch. V, 225-26.   [60] Above, Ch. II, 59-61.

[61] Macan, *VII-IX*, Vol. 2,272 ff. The present discussion, however, concerns only the meaning of Herodotus, and not the actual course of events. Cf. also Hauvette, *Hérodote* 369 ff., and A. Dascalakis, *Problèmes historiques autour de la bataille des Thermopyles* (Paris 1962) 149 ff.

[62] Of the chronologies proposed, that of Macan (*VII-IX*, Vol. 2,275) alone agrees with Herodotus' narrative, at least for the last seven days (Macan's days 12-18). Myres, *Herodotus* 255, erroneously intrudes an extra day of fighting at Thermopylae (his day XIX). How and Wells, 2.327-73 (Diary A), separate the arrival of the Persians at Aphetae from the first naval battle, and this is a common error. How and Wells further place the arrival of Xerxes at Thermopylae too late by two days, as does also

escaped most commentators, especially because there is no direct connection between Xerxes' voluntary inactivity and the enforced idleness of the fleet. The two events, like the three days of fighting, are simply analogical or coincidental.

The parallelism between the two battles extends further. Thermopylae and Artemisium had been chosen as defensive positions by the "counselors" of the Hellenic League assembled at the Isthmus; some troops, and the navy, had been sent to prevent the Persian "inroad into Greece" by defending the two narrow passes of Thermopylae and the Euripus in positions close enough for an exchange of news (7.175-77). To Herodotus this meant that the pass at Thermopylae and the narrows off Euboea were equivalent topographical elements, and that the encirclement of the Spartans by Ephialtes and the contemplated enclosure of the Greek fleet by the Persians' Euboean squadron were analogical events. As we shall see, Herodotus looked upon these events as differing only in that the naval forces were assisted by a storm and a reinforcement of Athenian ships, whereas the Spartans at Thermopylae were left to their own valor. Also parallel is the initial attitude of the Greek forces. Both at Thermopylae and at Artemisium many of the Greek allies were anxious to give up their positions (just as Xerxes expected them to), and there are consequently a number of parallel council scenes.[63] In the end, however, the Spartans stayed to the death, while the Athenians withdrew.

A certain parallelism between the three days of fighting at

Grundy, *Great Pers. War* 320, note. The crucial question is: How many days before the last day of fighting (which was the same for both Thermopylae and Artemisium) did Xerxes arrive at Thermopylae? Herodotus has two notations on this: (a) Xerxes let four days pass before he attacked the Greeks at Thermopylae (7.210.1), and (b) Xerxes had invaded (Herodotus uses the pluperfect) Malis, i.e. Thermopylae, and had already been there for three days, when the Persian fleet arrived at Aphetae, i.e. near Artemisium (7.196). Since the arrival of the Persian fleet fell on the same day as did the first sea fight, the two notations should refer to the same time-interval. Thus we should count, for (a): the day of arrival, plus three days of inactivity; and, for (b): *not* the day of arrival, but the same three days of inactivity. I disagree, then, with Macan's explanation of 7.196 (Vol. 2,274), as well as with the general reconstruction which the other commentators make. It is the use of the pluperfect that makes possible the identification of the three days with the four. We are not here concerned with whether this Herodotean chronology is historically plausible. On that problem, see now C. Hignett, *Xerxes' Invasion of Greece* (Oxford 1963) 379 ff.

[63] Cf. Hdt. 7.207 and 8.4.1, and also 7.183.1 and 192.1. Further, 7.219 (news of encirclement and council) and 8.8-9.1 (news of first storm, encirclement, and council). The council in 8.18, however, has no correspondent at Thermopylae.

Thermopylae and Artemisium may also be noted. At Thermopylae, Xerxes attacked the Greek position on the first two days (7.210-12), with the battle on the second day a repetition of that on the first. At Artemisium, the Greeks attacked on the first and second days, and again the attack on the second day is seen by Herodotus as a repetition of that on the first (8.9-10 and 14.2).[64] On the third day, Xerxes' army and navy launched what amounted to a two-pronged attack upon the Greeks—at Thermopylae, confident of the arrival of Ephialtes' party, and at Artemisium, because of their fear of Xerxes (8.15.1). The battle at Artemisium began at noon, while that at Thermopylae began a little earlier, in mid-morning (7.223.1), but Ephialtes' party must have arrived on the scene around noon, so that the final effort of the Persians took place contemporaneously in both localities.

The parallelisms not only underline the similarity of the tactical situation, but also serve to bring out the essential difference between the two battles, a difference that exists principally on the moral plane. Characteristically, Herodotus perceives the relation between the two battles as one of similarity and opposition, i.e. in the sense of polarity. Artemisium follows the pattern of Thermopylae, but by this means we perceive the fundamental difference between the realistic behavior of the Athenians and the valor of the Spartans, the two protagonists on sea and land.

The whole complex of the battle of Thermopylae is a circular composition of great power:

A. (7.196-200: March of Xerxes' army from Therma to Malis).[65]
   B. 201-207: The Greeks at Thermopylae.
           201:        Geography.
           202-206: Roster of Greek troops.
           207:       First council of Greeks.
   C. 208-18: Early actions of Xerxes.
           208-209: The Persian spy; *conversation of Xerxes and Demaratus.*
           210-12.1: FIRST DAY OF BATTLE.
           212.1-2: SECOND DAY OF BATTLE
           213-14: Ephialtes' betrayal.

[64] The parallel consists in the time of the engagement, from late afternoon to nightfall; i.e. the two actions are equally inspired by fear. Only on the third day did the Greeks really give battle.

[65] See above, Ch. III, 137.

As Sir John Myres saw, the description of Thermopylae is centered on Section D, the reaction of the Greeks to the news that they had been encircled by the Persians, and in this section the "center-piece" (to speak with Myres) is Leonidas' decision to remain at the pass, a decision based, in Herodotus' opinion, on an earlier oracle, according to which either the king or Sparta must perish.[67] This section is framed by Persian action on the first two days of battle and on the third day, respectively (Sections C and C'). Before and after, we again have sections that concern the Greeks (B and B'), and then again two Persian sections, the march of Xerxes and his second conversation with Demaratus (A and A'). The two Demaratus scenes, although not placed at exactly the same points, further reinforce the circular arrangement. Leonidas is mentioned prominently in four places: first, the roster of Greek troops takes his ancestry back to Heracles; in the center of the composition falls his decision to fight; his death closes the third battle before the encirclement; and the defilement of his body closes the account of Thermopylae as a whole.[68] Here again the first and last stories frame the composition.[69] Circular also is

---

[66] Achaemenes, son of Darius and brother of Xerxes, satrap of Egypt after Xerxes' reconquest (7.7), but now an admiral of the fleet (7.97 and 236 ff.); his death in *ca.* 460 B.C., when still in Egypt, is also mentioned (3.12.4).

[67] Myres, *Herodotus* 111-12 and 129.   [68] Hdt. 7.204; 220; 224.1; 238.

[69] The significance of the name Leonidas, "son of Lion," is emphasized by the alliteration that occurs at the mention of his tomb: ὅκου νῦν ὁ λίθινος λέων ἕστηκε ἐπὶ Λεωνίδῃ (7.225.2). This should be compared with the mention of lions attacking the

the section on the Greek reaction to the encirclement itself, especially in the use made of the seer Megistias.[70] Finally, the stories of the behavior of Thebans and Thespians enclose the central action at Thermopylae.[71]

The account of the battle of Thermopylae thus consists of two superimposed structures moving on two different levels. The first, on the level of pragmatic and dramatic action, is the plot of the battle, with the encirclement under Ephialtes as the decisive factor in the three days of fighting. It shows that the Greeks were successful against the Persians until they were encircled: during the first two days, Xerxes achieved nothing, but lost many troops, and even on the third day the Greeks were undefeated until the arrival of Ephialtes' party. Leonidas died before the arrival of the traitor: his death, a willing sacrifice, preceded the defeat. Hence, Herodotus has divided the action of the third day into two stages: first, the reckless fight of the Spartans against the direct Persian assault, in full knowledge of their approaching doom, and secondly, the final battle on the hill after Ephialtes' arrival. The defeat of the Greeks was not due to Spartan failure to send a full contingent of troops, but entirely to Ephialtes' treachery, without which the Persian attack would have remained ineffective. On the Persian side, the plot structure reveals *hybris* and inferiority. The Persians expected the Greeks to flee with the first onslaught: their resistance was a complete surprise, and Xerxes leaped three times from his throne in fear for his army, in which he had the greatest confidence (7.212.1). The motif of the unexpected reappears in the battle of Artemisium (8.10.1).

Persians at the entrance to Greece (7.125-26), the story of Leo in the sea fights before Artemisium (7.180), and the "lions" mentioned in the oracle given to Sparta before the invasion (7.220.4). On the significance of the lion imagery in Aeschylus and Herodotus, see B. M. W. Knox, *CP* 47 (1952) 17-25, esp. note 15. On Pericles "the lion," see above, Ch. III, note 138.

[70] The section on the Greek reaction to the encirclement (Section D in the outline above) is introduced by Megistias giving the first news of the impending disaster (7.219.1), and near the end we hear of his heroism (221). In the second council the main motif concerns the question of why the allies were sent away, with Herodotus giving three reasons; in the center of this account stands the oracle (220.4). At the end of the section the allies leave, except for the Thespians and Thebans (222), recalling the beginning of the council. Thus (if 222 be excepted) the section is framed by Megistias and has as its central feature the oracle, which is an earlier prediction balancing the prediction of Megistias.

[71] Hdt. 7.233; cf. 227 and 222.

The other type of structure, the circular composition mentioned above, moves on the level of symbolic action. Leonidas decided to remain at Thermopylae in order to gain fame for himself and to safeguard the good fortune (*eudaimoniê*) of Sparta (7.220.2). The combination of personal fame and service to the country shows him to be the typical representative of the citizen soldier of the Greek *polis*,[72] despite the fact that he was a king. He thus died, like a citizen, "as a very brave man" (7.224.1), and the defilement of his body was an insult to the Greek war code.[73] The nobility of Leonidas is the central idea of Thermopylae, if we consider the battle in its symbolic, rather than its pragmatic, sense. Herodotus did not attribute any great strategic importance to the battle, and he therefore isolated it by surrounding it with accounts of fighting at sea. The moral significance, on the other hand, was to him outstanding, a fact which becomes evident from the arrangement of the several sections of the circular composition.

However, in the development of the moral pattern, we again find polarity: the actions of Leonidas constrast with those of both Demaratus and Ephialtes, the latter his antagonist, and this contrast between patriotism and betrayal runs through the whole account. There is first the question of withdrawal: in the first council the Greeks decide against evacuation to the Isthmus, but after the betrayal the allies want to leave and are sent away by Leonidas. The Thespians and Thebans, alone retained by him, again exemplify opposite attitudes: the Thespians are true patriots, the Thebans the vilest of traitors, who are branded by the king as his slaves (7.233.2). In the list of deeds of valor, the same antithetical grouping occurs: the heroism of Deieneces and other Spartans (as well as of two Thespians) is contrasted with the lack of heroism in the case of Aristodemus, who failed to participate in the battle and had to redeem himself at Plataea, a story symbolic of the relation between the two battles.[74] The section on the

[72] For the combination of personal fame and service to one's country, see W. Jaeger, *Paideia: The Ideals of Greek Culture*, tr. by G. Highet, 1² (1945) 92 ff.; B. B. Shefton, *BSA* 45 (1950) 150-52; C. M. Bowra, *Early Greek Elegists* (Cambridge [Mass.] 1938) 65 ff.

[73] ἀνὴρ γενόμενος ἄριστος. For the idea of the ἀνὴρ ἀγαθός, see J. Gerlach, *Anèr Agathos* (Diss. Munich 1932). Xerxes had been warned by Demaratus of the Spartan military code (7.104.4-5; 209.3). In failing to understand the heroism of Leonidas, he seems to have considered him a rival king rather than a citizen of Sparta. His anger against Leonidas (7.238.2) is based upon this misconception.

[74] Hdt. 7.226-32; cf. 9.71 (Aristodemus at Plataea).

valor of the Greek combatants, although written in their honor, thus combines praise with blame.

Within this antithetical scheme, the heroism of Leonidas and his Spartans stands out as an extreme of courage such as exists only in death, and Herodotus adds a few Homeric touches to the narrative, since the Homeric hero is the prime representative of absolute standards of value, exceeding the standards of the *polis* with its requirements of valor. The long genealogy of Leonidas back to Heracles is one such feature; the epic battle over his corpse is another (7.225.1, cf. *Iliad* 17.274 ff.), the latter closely related to the struggle between Greeks and Trojans over the body of Patroclus. As in the Homeric battle, the Greeks are successful in saving the body: Xerxes lays hands on Leonidas only after he has killed every Spartan. The battle over the corpse closes the fighting before the arrival of Ephialtes, showing once more the success of the Greeks before the betrayal.

Although briefer than the account of Thermopylae, that of Artemisium is also extremely well organized. It is necessary, in order to understand the complex structure of this battle, to consider it together with the story of the first storm and the preliminary sea skirmishes before Artemisium, as told in a section preceding the battle of Thermopylae: [75]

> I. (7.179-95:   Movement of Persian navy and *first storm*.)
>
> . . . .
>
> II. 8.1-6:   Roster of Greek forces and First Council.
>> 1.1:   Announcement, connecting with 7.192.2.
>>> 1-2.2: Roster.   Eurybiades   was   general.
>>>
>>> 2.2-3.2: The   question   of   hegemony.
>>
>> 4-6.1:   *First Greek Council* and *bribery of Themistocles*.
>
> III. 8.6.1-7.2:   Arrival of Persians; squadron sent around Euboea; review of Persian navy.
>
> IV. 8.1-9.1:   Greeks informed by Scyllias of effect of first storm: *Second Greek Council*.
>
> V. 8.9.2-11.3: FIRST BATTLE.
>> 11.3:   Desertion of Antidorus.

[75] Cf. above, Ch. II, 72, and Ch. III, 137-38.

VI. 12-14.1:   *Second storm.*
          12.1-2: Effect at Aphetae.
          13-14.1: Destruction of squadron at Euboea.

VII. 14.1-2:   SECOND BATTLE (with Athenian reinforcements).

VIII. 15.1-18.1: THIRD BATTLE.
          17:   *Aristeiai* on both sides: Egyptians and Athenians.

IX. 18-20:   Greeks get ready to withdraw.
          18:   *Third Greek Council.*
          19:   *Stratagem of Themistocles* (Euboean cattle).
          20:   The oracle of Bacis given to Euboeans.

X. 21-22:   Greek withdrawal.
          21:   Announcement of defeat at Thermopylae.
          22:   *Stratagem of Themistocles* (inscriptions for Ionians).

XI. 8.23-25.3:   The Persians after the battle:
          23:   Fleet to Artemisium and Histiaea.
          24-25.3: Viewing of dead at Thermopylae.

This analysis shows that the composition of Artemisium is not circular to the same extent as that of Thermopylae. While it is true that the section dealing with the second storm (Section VI) occupies a central position, the exact correspondences of the other sections found at Thermopylae are here lacking. Circular structure is used only for the two sections surrounding each of the storms. In Chapter II we saw that the account of the first storm is itself a model of circular composition, with an initial Greek defeat balanced by a Greek success at the end.[76] Before the storm, we are told, the fleet at Artemisium had fled to Chalcis in Euboea, but when they heard of the Persian losses, they returned (7.183.1 and 192.2). By reducing the numbers of the Persians, the first storm encouraged the Greeks to face the enemy and gave them limited success. The second storm had exactly the same effect.[77]

[76] Above, Ch. II, 72.
[77] There has been much discussion about the relation between the two storms and their effects. Many scholars claim that there was only one storm, and that Herodotus

It occurred between the first and second day's fighting at Artemisium, and these two days, as we have seen, also balanced each other. Now the first sea fight was a minor action fought late in the day by the Greeks despite their decision to abandon Artemisium once more and to defend Euboea. They had based their decision upon the information that the Persian fleet was still stronger than they had expected, and that a squadron had just been sent around Euboea. By destroying this squadron, the second storm kept the Greeks at Artemisium, and they fought another successful engagement, encouraged also by the unexpected arrival of an Athenian squadron of fifty-three ships. The two storms are thus exactly analogous, and each is central to its own circular composition. The remainder of the *logos*, however, does not have such a structure.

Nevertheless, concentric framing is used here also. The bribery of Themistocles, through which the Greeks remained at Artemisium, corresponds to his two stratagems after the battle and establishes him as the key figure in the battle, although he is not mentioned during the fighting itself, since he was not commander-in-chief. Another framing element consists of the three Greek councils, which deal with the safety of the Isthmus versus the defense of central Greece. Here the navy at Artemisium shows itself more practical and less heroic than the Spartans at Thermopylae, but this does not imply a criticism of the Athenians. Just as the hostility of his sources does not carry over into Herodotus' own evaluation of Themistocles, likewise the picture of the fleet is not fundamentally hostile. Both Themistocles' attitude and that of the Greeks are simply common sense. The main difference between Thermopylae and Artemisium lies in (a) external fortune (the storms), and (b) the contrast of Athenian opportunism and Spartan military virtue. The storms did not give the Greeks victory, but they did allow them to face the Persians' reduced strength. Herodotus apparently believed that the might of the Persian navy was such that without the storms the Greeks would have had no chance at all, especially since their naval complement was not up to full strength, and the open sea was favorable to the enemy. Through the storm, the gods gave the Greeks "an equal

misunderstood his sources; but none of this concerns us here, since Herodotus clearly believed that there were two storms and that the second followed the pattern of the first. See R. Lattimore, "The Second Storm at Artemisium," *CR* 35 (1939) 57-58.

chance,"[78] meaning that external circumstances were favorable. Yet their location and their numbers still left the Persian fleet stronger than the Greek, a fact which is illustrated by the use of the encircling maneuver in the first and third battles.[79] Thus the withdrawal of the fleet was a practical necessity.

Herodotus is modest in his claims for Artemisium, as he also had been for Marathon. Neither victorious nor defeated, the maimed Greek fleet saved itself by withdrawal for Salamis.[80] The movement of the three engagements is thus contrary to the movement of Thermopylae. At Artemisium the Greeks attacked on the first two days, with limited success, while at Thermopylae the Persians attacked twice without success. On the third day, the Greeks were attacked by the Persians at Artemisium and, simultaneously, at Thermopylae; but Herodotus remarks that the Spartans at Thermopylae behaved almost like attackers on that day (7.223.2 and 4). In this last battle, the navy was not defeated, but it decided to withdraw *before the arrival of the news of the disaster on land*—that news merely hastened their flight. This last sequence should be contrasted with the fight for Leonidas' body and the Spartans' final stand on the hill in a noble but ineffectual death.[81] Here again the parallelism of the two battles contributes to an essentially antithetical meaning.

From the Persian point of view, the battles are indeed alike, for they were a strategic success in that they allowed the Persians to continue their combined march farther into Greece, while at the same time they proved to an overconfident Xerxes that Greek

---

[78] See above, note 45. The Greek naval strength at Artemisium was incomplete; cf. 8.42.1. This too may be compared with the lack of troops at Thermopylae. In 8.60b, Themistocles states that the open sea is to the advantage of the enemy, while narrows are advantageous to the Greeks. Both points apply to Artemisium (as well as to Salamis), although neither point is mentioned directly in the narrative there.

[79] The encircling maneuver was executed by the barbarians during the battle of the first day, but the Greeks broke through (8.10.1: ἐκυκλοῦντο αὐτοὺς ἐς μέσον, and see 8.11.1 for the counter-maneuver). The Persians employed it again on the third day (μηνοειδές, 8.16.1), but the excessive number of barbarian ships caused confusion. For a sketch of the maneuvers, see Myres, *Herodotus* 259, fig. 16.

[80] However, Herodotus does not state that the fleet saved itself for Salamis. This implication is made in an important passage in Pindar (fr. 93 Turyn), in which Artemisium is called the "foundation" (κρηπίς) of Greek freedom, i.e. (as I would interpret it) the battle, though not itself a victory, yet led to the victories of Salamis and Plataea.

[81] Decision to leave Artemisium: 8.18. Flight hastened after news of Thermopylae: 8.21.2. That the Spartan stand at Thermopylae was ineffectual is implied by Herodotus himself in 7.139.

hoplite valor and Greek naval skill were greater than expected. This unity of the battles both as victories and as warnings is expressed through the viewing of the dead at Thermopylae by the Asiatic naval contingents, a viewing in which Xerxes had to hide the large number of casualties he had suffered.[82]

IV

The battle of Artemisium looks forward to Salamis, a connection established in the structure of the narrative by multiple specific references. Again, the similarity of the battles is analogical. The figure of Themistocles exemplifying the Athenian ideas of adaptability, self-interest, and patriotism, and the motif of Greek disunity shown in the attempts to desert to the Peloponnesus, are two principal connecting links. Another is the emphasis, in the description of Artemisium, on the decisive nature of the third battle, an urgency expressed by the shouts of the sailors to one another; their words recall the famous lines of encouragement by the Greeks in Aeschylus' description of Salamis.[83]

[82] See Hdt. 8.24-25.

[83] Herodotus describes the third battle in 8.15-16. On the third day, the Persians become impatient with the existing stalemate and attack about noon, παρακελευσάμενοι (**a** P: παρασκευασάμενοι **d**, the latter wrongly accepted by Hude). Powell, *Lexicon*, s.v. παρακελεύομαι, translates παρακελευσάμενοι in the sense of the order being given to attack. As the sequence shows, this is erroneous, for the sentence above is followed by the synchronism of the final battles at Artemisium and Thermopylae (cf. above, 257), and then by the statement that "the whole struggle at sea was over the Euripus, just as for Leonidas' troops it was about the guarding of the pass" (8.15.2). After this, the word παρακελεύομαι is repeated, now clearly in the sense of "encouraging by shouts": "The Greeks shouted to one another not to allow the barbarians into Greece, and the Persians, to destroy the Greek forces and gain the passage." Clearly, the shouting on both sides is mentioned because of the preceding reference to the Euripus (which in turn was comparable to the pass at Thermopylae), and the Persian shouts are here repeated from their previous allusion by means of the participle παρακελευσάμενοι. The wording of the Greek shouts, ὅκως μὴ παρήσουσι ἐς τὴν Ἑλλάδα τοὺς βαρβάρους, is repeated from 7.175.2, where the Greeks formulate their plans for Thermopylae and Artemisium. For the similarities with the famous battle cry in Aeschylus' description of Salamis (*Pers.* 402 ff.), cf. especially πᾶς ὁ ἀγών, Hdt. 8.15.2, and νῦν ὑπὲρ πάντων ἀγών, *Pers.* 405. These shouts, then, concern the main issue of battle, and they are related to generals' speeches as a fixed literary genre. A good example of generals' speeches (παρακλητικοί) and subsequent shouts occurs in Thuc. 7.69.1 (generals' speeches, use of the participle παρακελευσάμενοι) and 7.70.7 (shouts on both sides, ἡ παρακέλευσις; they comprise both tactical and general statements—in Herodotus we have only the latter). On generals' speeches, see Pohlenz, *Herodot* 146, note 3; H. Breitenbach, *Historiographische Anschauungsformen Xenophons* (Diss. Basel 1950) 74; O. Luschnat, *Die Feldherrnreden im Geschichtswerk des Thukydides, Philologus*, Suppl. 34 No. 2 (1942). Incidentally, παρακελεύομαι in 9.102.2 is likely to bear the same meaning

In the description of Salamis, Artemisium is constantly referred to: Herodotus says that there were many more ships at Salamis than had been at Artemisium, that the supreme commander was the same, and that certain states had sent the same number of ships as had taken part in the earlier battle. The Persian forces are reckoned with reference to the navy and army list preceding the storm off Magnesia.[84] For the Persians, Salamis was to be vengeance for the opposition encountered at Artemisium (8.76.2). The behavior of the Ionians at Salamis is contrasted with the expected result of Themistocles' message (8.85.1). The analogy lies partly in the fact that both battles, fought at sea, were illustrative of Athenian character.

The overall structure of the battle of Salamis comprises three groups of stories: (1) the antecedents of the battle (8.40-82), by far the longest and most important section; (2) the battle description proper (8.83-96); and (3) the aftereffects of battle on the Persian and the Greek sides (8.97-125). But the idea of finding in this arrangement a circular composition is largely illusory. It is true that reversal of fortune is expressed in a number of framing stories before and after the battle. Of these the most important, on the Persian side, are the two messages sent by Xerxes to Susa, one announcing the occupation of Athens, the other his defeat at Salamis, and the two council scenes, in which Artemisia, queen of Halicarnassus, surpasses the Persians in wisdom. On the Greek side, the two messages sent by Themistocles to Xerxes, before and after the battle, and the council at Andros corresponding to the great council scenes before Salamis, fulfill the same function.[85] However, the real center of the composition is not the battle description, since it is overshadowed by the great Greek council scenes, which do not in themselves have symmetrical structure. Nor is the whole composition dramatic: that term can be applied perhaps to the first section, but to it alone. The battle description is a simple chain of events with anecdotes inter-

(*pace* Powell, *Lexicon*). The idea of encirclement also furnishes a parallel between the Herodotean description of Artemisium and the Aeschylean description of Salamis (see above, note 79, and *Pers.* 368, 418, 458; cf. 504).

[84] Hdt. 8.42-46; 8.66.1-2; cf. 7.188 ff. and 8.12 f. The storm mentioned in 66.2 is the storm off Magnesia (the first storm); the second storm caused losses which Herodotus considers part of the losses at Artemisium. (The theory proposed in How and Wells, 2.374, seems to me erroneous.)

[85] Messages: 8.54 (for the word εὐπρηξίη, see its only other occurrence in Herodotus, 7.49.4); 8.98-99. Artemisia: 8.68-69; 101-103. Councils: 8.49 ff.; 58.2 ff.; 74; 108 ff.

spersed, and the third section consists of alternating Greek and
Persian accounts. Thus, each of the three parts has its own
structure, while their combination produces two different effects:
the framing elements interpret the battle as a change in fortune,
while the distinction between word and deed (a pattern, it will be
recalled, outlined in Chapter II) emphasizes the verbal battles
before Salamis as the main feature of the composition.[86] Herodotus
sees the importance of the battle not merely in its pragmatic
aspect, but in a complex of meanings resulting from different
relationships.

The first of the three sections uses the principle of "refrain
composition" for a special effect:[87]

I. 8.40.1:　　Greek fleet moves from Artemisium to Salamis
　　　　　　　upon request of the Athenians.
　　40.1-2:　　Athenian reasons: evacuation to Sala-
　　　　　　　mis; necessity for councils since Pel-
　　　　　　　oponnesians had abandoned Boeotia.
　　　　　　　FS

8.41.1:　　Fleet to Salamis, except Athenian ships to Athens.
　　41.1:　　Fleet evacuates Attica.
　　　　　41.2-3: The Salamis oracle and the
　　　　　　　　　story of the snake leaving the
　　　　　　　　　Acropolis.
　　FS

8.42.1:　　When Greek fleet has come to Salamis from
　　　　　　Artemisium, Troezenian contingent joins.
　　42.2-48:　　Roster of Greek fleet.

8.49.1-2:　Generals at Salamis hold COUNCIL I: majority
　　　　　　wants to withdraw to Isthmus.
　　50-54:　　Messenger announces capture of
　　　　　　　Athens by Xerxes.
　　　　　55:　The olive tree on the Acrop-
　　　　　　　olis.
　　　　　FS

8.56:　　Greeks at Salamis ready to flee because of news of
　　　　　capture of Athens.
　　56, end-63: Advice of Mnesiphilus and COUNCIL II
　　　　　　　of Greek generals, at night.
　　　　　FS

[86] Above, Ch. II, 73.
[87] On refrain composition, see above, Ch. II, 57.

64: Preparations for sea fight; dawn; Aeacids called from Aegina.

65: Dicaeus and Demaratus hear the Eleusinian procession.

FS

II. 8.66-70.1: Persian preparations.

66.1-2: Arrival of fleet from Trachis; number of ships restored to original force.

FS

67-69: PERSIAN COUNCIL I: Artemisia's advice.

70.1: Persian fleet moves toward Salamis, but postpones fight till next day.

III. 8.70.2: Greek fear for Peloponnesus.

71-74.1: Building of Isthmus wall. (Persian army moves to Peloponnesus "that night," 8.71.1).

73.1-3: The seven nations of the Peloponnesus.

FS

8.74.1-2: Greek fear resumed: COUNCIL III of generals caused by popular dissatisfaction. Peloponnesians win.

75.1-3: Night message of Themistocles to Xerxes.

FS

76.1-3: Persians, after midnight, encircle Greeks.

FS

77: Bacis' oracle on Salamis.

FS

8.78-82.2: COUNCIL III continued.

79-80: Aristeides and Themistocles.

81-82.2: Greeks apprised of encirclement.

82.1-2: Honor of Tenians; numbers of Greek fleet explained.

The most conspicuous stylistic feature of this composition is the use of framing sentences (marked in the outline as FS) in two specific ways. The gathering of the Greek fleet at Salamis is reiterated, in the manner of refrain composition, with the other events all subordinated to these repeated statements. Pohlenz has noted that the narrative of the councils is influenced by tragedy, in that all events taking place elsewhere are seen through the eyes of the Greeks assembled at Salamis.[88] However, the main stylistic device used to effect this is the undramatic one of refrain composition, with the messenger motif (which had already been used at Thermopylae and Artemisium) used as a secondary motif only.[89]

Secondly, framing sentences are used to isolate not only the subsidiary parts of the story, such as the capture of Athens and the fortification of the Isthmus, but also the true anecdotes. The complicated narrative of the antecedents to Salamis is based on the same principles as the composition of the early books.[90] It consists of three main parts: (1) two Greek councils culminating in the decision to fight; (2) the Persian preparations, including preliminary maneuvers for battle; and (3) a third Greek council ending in the forced decision to fight. In this arrangement the one Persian section is overshadowed by two Greek sections, and the decisive Persian action—the encirclement of the Greeks at Salamis—is subordinated to the message of Themistocles. (Similarly the capture of Athens by the land army is subordinated to the First Greek Council.) This shows that the Persians are losing the initiative and the Greeks are winning the fight.

The elaborate sequence of Greek councils is peculiar and has given rise to much criticism.[91] It is not our purpose to decide whether Herodotus' facts are correct, or whether he has fallen victim to a confusion in his sources. At any rate, he clearly marks the sequence of events: the First Council takes place on what I

---

[88] Pohlenz, *Herodot* 143 ff.

[89] Messenger motif at Thermopylae: 7.208 ff. (the Persian spy); 219.1 (announcement of party of Ephialtes). At Artemisium: 8.8 (Scyllias the diver); 14.2 (news of the second storm); 21.1 (news of Thermopylae); 23 (Persians receive word of Greek withdrawal).

[90] On the alleged difference in style between the early and the late books of the work, see above, Ch. II, note 35.

[91] See e.g. How and Wells, 2.378 ff. G. Smets and A. Dorsinfang-Smets, "La bataille de Salamine. Les sources," *Pankarpia: Mélanges Henri Grégoire; Annuaire de l'Institut de Philologie . . .*, Université libre de Bruxelles (1953) 409-26, have proposed the hypothesis that 8.74-76 is a doublet of the earlier councils of the Greeks (8.49-73), not recognized by Herodotus as such, and taken from Aeschylus' *Persians*. Cf. earlier, C. d'Amico, "La battaglia di Salamina in Eschilo e in Erodoto," *A&R*, n.s. 12 (1931) 231-42. In this argument, Themistocles' speech at 8.83.1 plays a part; however, it is clearly a general's speech addressed to the troops before battle, and not comparable to the earlier speeches; cf. Sophocles, *OC* 1429-30, and van Groningen, *Comp. litt.* 237. On the Herodotean *logos* under discussion, see also above, Ch. V, 218.

shall call the first day, with which the capture of Athens is synchronized—presumably the final capture of the Acropolis is meant.[92] In this day council, the problem is the same as that discussed at Artemisium: the Peloponnesians, including Eurybiades, want to leave, while the Athenians and the other central Greek states insist on remaining.[93] The result is the decision to abandon Salamis, since Athens has been captured. The capture of Athens has frightened the Greeks so much that, like the Greeks in *Iliad* 2, they prepare to flee even before the council has so decided.[94]

Night falls (8.56, end) and the situation changes: Themistocles succeeds in calling a Second Council and manages to reverse the Greek decision. The Peloponnesians bow to the clever ultimatum of a single man and are thus forced to remain. In the morning of the second day (8.64.1) the Greeks decide, after an earthquake, to send for the Aeacid heroes from Aegina.

Now with reference to the Greek councils, Herodotus does not say when the Persian fleet arrived at Salamis, but the sequence of events makes it clear that this occurred on the second day, and therefore the Persian preparations section continues directly after the summoning of the Aeacids.[95] Their council is held in the daytime, and later in the same day the fleet moves out into the open (8.70). Meanwhile nothing is said about the Greeks: we must assume that on the second day they were still debating. The Third Greek Council (the beginning of which is not dated) lasts into the second night and in fact all through it into the morning

---

[92] The capture of the Acropolis took some time, although Herodotus does not say how long (8.52.2: ἐπὶ χρόνον συχνόν; cf. 8.53.1, beginning). Some historians assume a siege of about two weeks: see e.g. G. Busolt, *Griechische Geschichte*[2] 2 (Gotha 1895) 695, note 1; J. A. R. Munro in *CAH* 4.304 assumes three weeks. The messenger who comes to the Greeks at Salamis announces the invasion of Attica (8.50.1), but this statement is resumed in 8.56, where the capture of the Acropolis is mentioned. It is therefore unlikely that Herodotus had in mind a period as long as two weeks. His synchronism is likely to be with the capture of the Acropolis; the story of the olive tree happens on the day after that capture (8.54). On the army and navy logs after Thermopylae and Artemisium, see Macan, *VII-IX*, Vol. 2,291 ff. (cf. 275). The chronological vagueness is due to the shift of the narrative to the Greek side. Cf. also R. Sealey, *Hermes* 91 (1963) 376-77.

[93] Hdt. 8.49: Eurybiades submits to the council the question on where to fight, but rules out Salamis.

[94] *Iliad* 2.149. Cf. Pohlenz, *Herodot* 144, note 1, and 146, note 2.

[95] I.e. Hdt. 8.66.1 would come right after 8.64.2, on the same day. The arrival of the Persian fleet is dated in relation to Artemisium (see Macan: above, note 92), but the arrival of the Greek fleet at Salamis is not dated.

of the third day, the day of the battle.[96] During the second night Themistocles forced the decision by sending a message to Xerxes that the Greeks were about to flee, thus causing the encirclement of the Greek fleet (8.76.1). During the same night, but prior to Themistocles' message, the Persian army had moved toward the Peloponnesus, throwing the Greeks into utter confusion, and this led to Themistocles' action.[97]

Therefore, the Greek councils lasted two days and two nights (while the battle was fought on the third day), and there is an intricate play of the symbolic meaning of day and night.[98] In the daytime the decision is in favor of fleeing, at night of staying: for during the first night Themistocles forced the decision of the Second Council, and during the second night he arranged for the encirclement. Each time, Themistocles, the trickster, shows his ability at night rather than in the daytime.[99]

The central theme of the Greek councils is the disunity of the Greeks, as it appears in the altercations of Themistocles and the Corinthian general Adeimantus, and in particular in the quarrel between the Athenians and the Peloponnesians. Herodotus' belief that such a quarrel took place derived perhaps from the message of Themistocles. The wording of the message as reported in Herodotus differs from the text of the same message in Aeschylus' *Persians* in some small but significant details. In Aeschylus, the message simply stated that the Greeks, at nightfall, would flee to their several homes. In Herodotus, Themistocles adds that the Greeks are quarreling over the question of flight, and thus will not defend themselves against a Persian attack, but may be expected to fight among themselves.[100] Aeschylus, who throughout insists

[96] Cf. Hdt. 8.83.1.

[97] There is thus no difficulty in the notorious passage, 8.71.1: "the land army of the barbarians traveled during the present night toward the Peloponnesus." Some scholars refuse to believe in the accuracy of this statement (see e.g. Pohlenz, *Herodot* 146; Legrand, Budé, Book 8 [1953] 71, note 1). It may of course be invented, but it does not disturb the sequence of events, as seen by Herodotus, if the chronology given in the text is correct.

[98] Cf. the sequence of days and nights at Thermopylae and at Artemisium.

[99] The principal difficulty in the interpretation of Herodotus' chronology outlined above is that he gives us no information about the Greek activities on the second day (we assume that the council was still in progress). This absence of information may be due to Herodotus' view that the Greeks made no substantial preparations for a sea battle (which they did not want) until the third, or final, day. The number three no doubt appealed to him also, after the pattern established for the earlier battles.

[100] Connected with this discrepancy is the difference in the dating of the message

on Greek unity, does not have this last detail, which is central to Herodotus' conception of Salamis, and indeed to his whole understanding of the role of the Greeks in the Persian Wars.[101] The quarrel of the Greeks, so heavily stressed in the story of Salamis, is the reason for the comparison of the councils with battles: before Salamis the Greeks were intent on verbal battles rather than on the real one.[102] Because of these verbal vacillations the battle came to be the decision of a single man, rather than the result of democratic debate. This idea is underlined by the fact that Xerxes makes his decision against the advice of Artemisia, on the grounds that he wants to bow to majority opinion (8.69.2).

The inlaid accounts likewise have a thematic importance. In the first, the Athenians call their allies to Salamis to save their women and children and to hold a council on future plans, since the Peloponnesians had abandoned Boeotia against Athens' expectation. Now Salamis was only one of the places for evacuation, but the motif here stands for Athenian self-interest in general.[103] The second inset deals with the evacuation from Attica and culminates in the story of the sacred snake (and therewith Athena) leaving the Acropolis, whereby the Athenians leave a city already abandoned by their gods.[104] Religious stories, mostly from local Athenian tradition, abound throughout the Salamis narrative. Herodotus uses these as he had used similar religious tales for Marathon and for Artemisium: he does not necessarily commit himself to their truth, but at the same time he shows that the local gods participated in the struggle and the

---

in the two authors. Herodotus has it delivered at night, and after the Persians have already moved (for so he tells us, 8.70.1). In Aeschylus, however, it is delivered in the daytime and causes the first movement of the Persians; hence it is more effective in Aeschylus. Furthermore, in Herodotus, Themistocles deceives both the Persians and the Greeks, whereas Aeschylus at the very least omits the deception of the Greeks (cf. How and Wells, 2.379-81) and may perhaps not even intend it.

[101] An unspoken antagonism between Athens and Sparta runs through the account of the Persian Wars; cf. above, Ch. V, note 103, and see Hdt. 7.139; 7.161 (embassy to Gelo); 9.54.1, etc. (Plataea); 9.106.3 (Ionian Question).

[102] Hdt. 8.78 (ὠθισμὸς λόγων). Further: 8.64.1 (ἀκροβολισάμενοι) and 8.81 (ἀμφισβασίη): on this term, see R. Hirzel, Themis, Dike und Verwandtes [Leipzig 1907] 87, note 2).

[103] On the places to which the Athenians evacuated, see now M. Jameson, Hesperia 29 (1960) 210 ff. Herodotus stresses the surprise of the Athenians when they found Boeotia abandoned by the Peloponnesians (8.40); the motif is repeated before Plataea: cf. 9.6 and 9.48.3.

[104] Hdt. 8.41.2-3. On the snake in the Erechtheum, see How and Wells ad loc.

victory.[105] So we find the stories about the miraculous rebirth of the sacred olive tree, the Eleusinian procession, the earthquake on "the second day," and the stories of oracles. Many of them are particularly connected with Themistocles, for in a speech after the battle he subscribes to a belief in the help given by the local gods:

> "This (victory) has not been accomplished by us, but by the gods and heroes, who were jealous that one man should rule over both Asia and Europe, a man unholy and wicked, who made no distinction between sanctuaries and private possessions, burning and destroying the images of the gods ..." (8.109.3)

Themistocles himself had interpreted the oracle of the wooden walls to the Athenians—correctly, as the event proved. This harmony of Themistocles' practical interpretations and the will of the gods is stressed, one feels, by the local anecdotes. Athena, in leaving the Acropolis, proved his maxim:

> "When people take reasonable counsel, the outcome is usually favorable; when they counsel unreasonably, the god usually does not support human planning." (8.60c)[106]

To Themistocles the gods help those who help themselves. This contrasts with a Spartan piety that often conflicts with self-interest.[107]

The catalogue of ships has several unusual features. We have already mentioned the frequent references to Artemisium. The arrangement of forces differs, however, from the arrangement at Artemisium by size of contingent. Here it is according to geographical order: Peloponnesians, Central Greeks, and Islanders. From the West there is only one ship, that of the famous athlete, Phayllus of Croton. The order shows the area at present defended, part of which the Peloponnesian plan would have abandoned, and stresses the concept of the Greeks as the champions of Europe in their diversity of race and origins.[108]

---

[105] On the difference between the dramatic use of religious stories and Herodotus' own religious beliefs, see below, 299, and Conclusion, 312-13.

[106] This statement does not necessarily reflect Herodotus' own opinion about the relation of counsel and success, although it fits the situation of Salamis well; see *Tat und Geschichte* 520, note 39.

[107] Above, Ch. V, 204.

[108] On the navy list, see Myres, *Herodotus* 262 and 263, note 2.

The Persian attack and capture of the Acropolis, reported, as Pohlenz has stressed, like a messenger speech in tragedy, provides the connection with the earlier march of the Persian land forces, and refers to the medism of the Thebans in their quarrels with other Boeotian cities (8.50.2). The siege of the Acropolis is another story that praises Themistocles indirectly, for the defenders of the Acropolis are shown to have been misled by their interpretation of the oracle of the wooden wall. The Persians, like the Amazons at the time of Theseus, attack from the Areopagus, and the siege is successful only after a passage is discovered through which the Persians can ascend.[109] After the capture, the Persians first commit a number of religious crimes, then repent and ask the surviving Athenians to sacrifice to their gods: at this occasion Athena's olive tree is seen to have sprouted. All this is pure religious legend.[110] The olive is used elsewhere as a typically Greek symbol.[111]

The story of the building of the Isthmian wall continues the emphasis on the divisive and selfish actions by the Peloponnesians.[112] It should be noted that the account of the building of the wall is not strictly relevant to the narrative, since the Peloponnesian desire to withdraw is not based directly on the existence of the wall, but on the movement of the Persian army to the Peloponnesus. The description of the building operation is thus important mainly for the theme of the quarrel between Athens and the Peloponnesians. A short description of the nations inhabiting the Peloponnesus is added, complementing the remarks made in the roster of the Greek navy; this Peloponnesian roster also stresses Greek divisiveness.

The meeting of Themistocles and Aristeides is not inlaid, strictly speaking, but is rather an integral part of the Third Greek

---

[109] Cf. the capture of Sardis, 1.84; Cyrus' capture of Babylon, 1.190 ff.; and Darius' recapture of the city, 3.151 ff.

[110] On these legends, see now Crahay, *Litt. orac.* 299 ff. Xerxes may have been influenced by a dream vision, which no doubt told him to respect Greek sanctuaries (8.54); cf. Datis' dream after Marathon (6.118.1).

[111] Use of olive tree: 4.34.2 (olive tree on Delos); 5.82 ff. (the Epidaurians receive olive wood for their statues from the Athenians, for Athenian olive trees are the most sacred. On this well-known motif, see especially Sophocles, *OC* 694 ff.); 7.19.1 (Xerxes dreams that he is crowned with an olive wreath; cf. Crahay, *Litt. orac.* 223 and 76); 8.26.2 (the olive wreath as the prize for victory at Olympia); 8.124.2 (olive wreaths as prizes for the victory at Salamis).

[112] Above, Ch. V, 205.

Council, just as the advice of Mnesiphilus is connected with the Second. Here also the initiative comes from the other man, and here also Themistocles shows his practical intelligence by listening to him. Aristeides first offers Themistocles peace:

> "At all times, and especially now, our quarrel should be over which of us may confer more benefits on our country." (8.79.3)

The motif of internal disunity is thus converted into the motif of a peaceful strife (*stasis*) operating in favor of victory. Such competition is implicitly accepted by Themistocles. In the quarrel with the Peloponnesians, however, deceit had been necessary:

> "For it was necessary, since the Greeks did not want to fight out of their own free will, to force them against their will." (8.80.1)

Thus a contrast is drawn between real disunity and peaceful competition, a contrast such as will shortly appear in the battle description.

The affairs of the Persians prior to the battle are, as we have seen, secondary to the Greek councils.[113] The Persian Preparations Section is introduced by the account of the movements of the fleet from the vicinity of Thermopylae.[114] The numbers have increased enormously (as have also those of the army), until their original strength at the Hellespont is equalled, for the king forces everyone to fight on his side.[115] After the fleet arrives, Xerxes visits it, asking for counsel from his generals and admirals alike.[116] Artemisia alone counsels against fighting a battle. She accuses Xerxes of rashness and warns him, as Artabanus had done at the Hellespont, not "to be in a hurry":

[113] Above, 256. Herodotus (8.50.2) gives the movement of the army to explain the messenger's report at Salamis. This passage continues the direct march section, which had ended at 8.34, with the Thebans (cf. also 7.132) here having the same function as the Thessalians did in the earlier section.

[114] Hdt. 8.66. See above, note 95.

[115] As in 7.184 ff., the mention of the totals of the combined Persian forces in 8.66 follows the mention of the navy, although the original army and navy lists had been primarily connected with the march of the land forces (7.61 ff.). In the present passage, Herodotus gives no new figures, but simply claims that the original numbers had been re-established: his desire for balance has here obviously gotten the better of his accuracy.

[116] The ἐπιπλέοντες of 8.67.1 must be both sailors and marines (i.e. their commanding officers), despite Stein on 7.184, line 31.

"But if you are in a hurry right now to do battle at sea, I fear
that the navy, worsted, will harm the land army as well."
(8.68c)[117]

Xerxes finds this advice excellent, but as we have seen, he bows,
in a curious attack of democratic feeling, to the advice of the
majority of his generals. The First Persian Council is a typical
adviser scene in the form of a warning.

The further preparations of the Persians are part and parcel
of the Greek accounts: the advance of the land army is told
as the motivation of further Greek vacillation, and the encircling
maneuver of the navy, as the result of the message of Themistocles.
The encircling move has given rise to much speculation, but I
agree with those who think it largely derived from the oracle of
Bacis, which Herodotus considered one of the clearest oracles ever
pronounced.[118] Now (1) the oracle states: The enemy "bridged
with their ships" the sacred shore of Artemis. Herodotus under-
stands this term as an oracular reference to ship maneuvers in
which ships are placed in line.[119] (2) It involves Cynosura,
which Herodotus mentions in connection with Ceos (the latter, it is
true, is not alluded to in the oracle). (3) It refers to the destruction
of Athens as a feat of rash expectation, i.e. a disregard of the

[117] "If you are in a hurry" (ἤν . . . ἐπειχθῇς, twice) is a common reproach by
warners who advise "holding back"; see above, Ch. V, note 90. "The navy . . . will
also harm the army" is a reminiscence of Aeschylus, *Pers.* 728.

[118] Hdt. 8.76.1; cf. 8.77. I agree with H. Grégoire, *EC* 4 (1935) 519-31, and
Myres, *Herodotus* 274-75, at least insofar as to believe that Herodotus thought of
Ceos as the well-known island and located Cynosura near Marathon. See, however,
Ph.-E. Legrand, *REA* 38 (1936) 55-60, and N. G. L. Hammond, *JHS* 76 (1956) 38,
note 22. Generally, see Stein and How and Wells on Hdt. 8.76.1, and W. K. Pritchett,
AJA 63 (1959) 261-62. Grégoire, *loc. cit.*, makes a distinction between the inclusion of
Ceos and that of Cynosura, saying that the former must be historically true, since it is
not in the oracle, while the second was added because of the oracle; this is worth
considering. (He then goes on to justify Cynosura also, but as a previous stop for the
Persian fleet.)

[119] Is it too fanciful to derive from the same oracle the tradition that Xerxes
attempted to build a mole from the mainland to Salamis? Herodotus places this
attempt after Salamis (8.97), but later tradition, from Ctesias on, put it before the
battle (see N. G. L. Hammond, *JHS* 76 [1956] 42 f. and 49). For the Artemisium
mentioned in the oracle, see How and Wells on 8.77 (page 262); but there is no need
to refer the oracle to Artemisium rather than to Salamis. The oracle used the idea of
bridging in a symbolic sense, comparable to Xerxes' bridging of the Hellespont, which
was also mentioned in an oracle (H. Reynen, *Hermes* 83 [1955] 374-77), the latter
used by both Herodotus and Aeschylus. Herodotus himself did not of course connect
the mole with the oracle. Since the oracle (like that about the Hellespont bridge) is
no doubt *post eventum*, we may use it after all as a source for the existence of a plan for
a mole.

still-existing forces of the Greeks. (4) It interprets the defeat of Xerxes as Justice punishing Satiety, the son of *Hybris*, a situation corresponding exactly to Salamis, where Satiety (the possession of Athens) precedes defeat and is the result of *Hybris* (the disregard of the Greek fleet).[120] (5) It describes a battle in which Greece is liberated. The oracle does indeed correspond point by point to the account of Salamis as Herodotus gives it and is in turn a "source" for his account. Whether the mention of Ceos and Cynosura has any reality outside the oracle is hard to say, but one would expect that Herodotus had found some independent evidence. At any rate, the quotation of the oracle right after the encircling maneuver is meant to explain the mention of Cynosura in that maneuver.

The account of the battle is a simple series with anecdotes placed in the pauses:

8.83.1:	Greeks prepare for battle.
83.1-2:	Themistocles' speech to the marines. Arrival of Aeacids.[121]
8.83.2-84.2:	Beginning of battle.
84.1:	The Athenian Ameinias began it.
FSS	
84.2:	The Aeginetan claim.
84.2:	A divine voice urges the Greeks on.
8.85.1:	The battle order.
85.1-3:	Medism of Ionians: the two Samian traitors.
	85.3: What orosangs are.
FS	
8.86:	Persians have a rough time, but try to impress Xerxes.
FS	
	87-88.3: Artemisia saves herself.
	FSS (internal too).
	89.1-2: Persian casualties.
8.89.2:	Beginning of flight.

[120] The more common relation between Satiety and *Hybris* is that *Hybris* is the child of Satiety, although the relation employed in the oracle is not unique: see the passages listed in How and Wells. Further, W. C. Greene, *Moira* (Cambridge [Mass.] 1944) 76, note 157. It is the *triple* association of Justice, Satiety, and *Hybris*, that suggests Salamis.

[121] Note that according to Herodotus' chronology it took a whole day to get the Aeacids from Aegina; see above, 272-73.

90-91, beginning:
> Phoenicians accuse Ionians, but lose their heads.

FSS

8.91:   Pursuit of fleeing barbarians.

91:       *Aristeiai* of Aeginetans and Athenians.

92:       Competition of Themistocles and Polycritus, son of Crius of Aegina. (Saving of Pytheas of Aegina.)

FS

8.92.2:   Persians arrive at Phalerum.

93:       *Aristeiai* of Aegina and Athens.

ibid.: Artemisia not captured.

FS

8.94:   Adeimantus and the mystery boat.

94.4:   Corinthian variant.

FSS

8.95:   Aristeides at Psyttaleia.

8.96.1:   Greeks return to Salamis.

96.2:   The wreckage drifts to Colias: oracles.

(8.97:   Xerxes anxious to flee: the Hellespontine bridges, and the mole to Ṣalamis.)

The stages of battle are almost barren of detail in their mechanical sequence: Greek preparations—beginning of battle—battle order—Persian difficulties and losses—flight and pursuit—return to original stations. No tactical plan whatsoever is mentioned, nor any special maneuver by the Greeks. Yet we know from Aeschylus that the Greeks, encircled by the barbarians, broke out by an encircling maneuver of their own.[122] This counterpoise of encircling maneuvers has for Aeschylus a symbolic value, for to him the unified force of the Greeks was morally the equal of the Persians, and encirclement stands for total annihilation. Herodotus, who had described partial encirclement at Artemisium, does not mention it at Salamis, because for him the principal features of the battle were the disunity of the Greeks and their consequent lack of enthusiasm for battle. The very beginning of the battle is described as an accident, when the Athenian Ameinias rammed a ship, failed to disengage, and the rest of the Greeks came to his assis-

[122] See above, note 83, end.

tance. A female apparition shouted at the Greeks so that the whole fleet could hear it:

"You fools, for how long will you back water?" (8.84.2)[123]

It is clear from Aeschylus' description that the battle of Salamis was famous for the use of the ram by the Greek ships.[124] Herodotus also knew this: he uses the word *emballein* in the meaning "to ram" only at Salamis, and there with frequency.[125] But the symbolic meaning of the Herodotean ramming maneuvers differs greatly from the Aeschylean. Ameinias, in ramming the first ship, did not mean to start the battle (8.84.1). Artemisia, when pursued by an Athenian ship, saved herself by ramming a ship on her own side (8.87.2). While the Phoenicians were accusing the Ionians on their side of treachery, a Samothracian ship was seen ramming an Attic trireme, and being rammed in turn, it captured the ramming vessel (8.90.2). Finally, Polycritus of Aegina, while ramming a Sidonian vessel, chided Themistocles whether he still thought of the Aeginetans as supporters of the Mede (8.92.1-2). Thus, the three major inlaid anecdotes (the stories of Artemisia, the Ionians, and Polycritus) are ramming stories. They are seen, however, as individual happenings, not as the result of a combined strategy, and they illustrate the good fortunes of clever, or lucky, individuals in the confusion of battle. The ramming stories reinforce the themes of disunity and competitive strife to the exclusion of tactical motivations.

The ramming stories are important in other ways. The first two deal with events on the Persian side and take place at the height of the battle. The Greek queen Artemisia not only saves herself from a pursuing ship by ramming one of her own, but also, through a misunderstanding, earns high praise from Xerxes, who says:

"My men are born women, and my women men." (8.88.3)

Artemisia shows that a woman can be superior to men, if she is a

[123] This apparition has had the honor of being incorporated into the Greek strategic plan; see Myres, *Herodotus* 280-81 and 282.
[124] Aeschylus, in the *Persians*, calls the beginning of the battle a "ramming" (ἐμβολή, line 409), and says of the mutual interference of the Persian ships in the narrows of the strait that they were hit by their own bronze-clad rams (415-16). For the invention of the ram (which occurred much earlier than the battle of Salamis), see now L. Casson, *The Ancient Mariners* (New York 1959) 84 and 99.
[125] See Powell, *Lexicon*, s.v. ἐμβάλλω, under II.

Greek and the men are barbarians.[126] In a similar manner, the Ionians save themselves before Xerxes by sinking an enemy ship just when they are being accused, and Xerxes has the Phoenicians decapitated. The third ramming story, placed in the pursuit, shows peaceful competition between the Athenians and the Aeginetans, once bitter enemies (as Aristeides and Themistocles had been): later the prizes for valor show that the Aeginetans had been the bravest in battle, and that the Athenians had achieved only second place.[127]

A general series of antitheses thus runs through the whole account. The Greeks do not want to fight, but are brave; the Aeginetans compete with the Athenians; a woman is superior to men; the Phoenicians quarrel with the Ionians. The Corinthian Adeimantus meets a mysterious boat while attempting to flee,[128] just as a woman's voice had been heard by the Greeks before the battle: this story continues the quarrel of Themistocles and Adeimantus in the council. Aristeides in turn cooperates with Themistocles by occupying Psyttaleia. Adeimantus and Aristeides stand in different antithetical relationships to Themistocles, one as an outright enemy, the other as a peaceful rival.[129] Thus, even where Themistocles is not mentioned, the stories help to bring out his central position in the battle.

Xerxes' attitude in the battle can again be characterized as one of false expectation. Seated on the shore with a full view of the participants, he expects his troops to fight much better at Salamis than at Artemisium, where he was not present (8.69.2). But his supervision is futile, because he misinterprets everything he sees. The account of this battle is punctuated throughout by references to Xerxes as the supervisor who does not see.[130]

---

[126] See above, Ch. IV, note 114.

[127] Competition Athens-Aegina: above, Ch. V, 228. Hdt. 8.64.2 and 83.2 (Aeacids); 8.93 and 122 (prize of valor). The mention of Themistocles at the end of the sea fights, and his address to the troops at the beginning of the battle (8.83.1-2), frame the account. The address is a typical general's speech, such as we know from Thucydides and later authors; see above, notes 83 and 91; differently Smets, *op. cit.* (above, note 91).

[128] So according to the Athenian version, which Herodotus, while probably disbelieving it, tells in full (8.94). Cf. also Ch. V, note 113.

[129] The contrast is stressed by the juxtaposition of the stories about Adeimantus and Aristeides. Otherwise the occupation of Psyttaleia by Aristeides has little importance in Herodotus, who does not emphasize the victory "on land" at Salamis. Cf. above, note 56.

[130] Hdt. 8.86, end; 88.3; 90.4; 97.1. Cf. also above, Ch. IV, 182.

The third part of the Salamis description deals with the after-effects of the battle and consists of alternate Greek and Persian sections:

I. 8.97-107: Xerxes' actions after the battle.

97:                          Ruse of mole and desire to flee.
FS
98-100.1:   Second messenger to Susa: effect on Persians.
                             ibid.: note on *angareion*.
100-103:   Second Persian Council with Artemisia.
103, end-107.2: Departure of Xerxes.
                             104-106: Story of Hermotimus, eunuch of Xerxes.
FS
107.1-2:   Xerxes, accepting Mardonius' offer to continue the war, flees. The navy escapes to Hellespont.

II. 8.108-12: Greeks pursue to Andros.

108.2-110.1:   Fourth Council of Greeks, and Speech of Themistocles to the Athenians.
                             110.2-3: Second message of Themistocles to Xerxes.
                             FSS
                             111-12: Siege of Andros by Themistocles. Carystus and Naxos.
                             FSS

III. 8.113-20: The return of Xerxes' land army.

113.1-3:   Mardonius to winter in Thessaly.
                             114.1-2: The Delphic oracle asks for vengeance for death of Leonidas.
                             FSS
115-20:   Return of Xerxes to Hellespont and Sardis: hunger; plague; chariot of Zeus stolen; the king of the Bisaltians (FSS); crossing of Hellespont.

118-20:   Alternate version of crossing by boat. Xerxes at
Abdera.

FSS

IV. 8.121-25: The Greeks return to Salamis: gifts to gods and
prizes for men.
125:           Anecdote about Themistocles.

After the battle, we first see Xerxes "thinking of running away"—
a phrase used of the Greeks before the battle.[131] Like the Greeks
earlier, he is now filled with fear, but it is fear for his own person.
The second messenger to Susa fills the Persians with a similar fear,
allayed only when the king arrives back in Persia.[132] The same
concern for himself is shown in Xerxes' acceptance of Artemisia's
arguments in favor of leaving Greece:

> "(If Mardonius should die in Greece) it will not be a great
> misfortune so long as you survive and your affairs over there.[133]
> For if you and your house continue, the Greeks will fight many
> more battles on their own behalf." (8.102.2-3)

Thereafter Xerxes sends home those of his illegitimate children
who had accompanied him on the campaign, under the guardian-
ship of Artemisia and in company with his trusted eunuch
Hermotimus. He himself rushes home as fast as he can, and
Herodotus knows a story, which he reports in great detail even
though he does not believe it, that told how in a storm Xerxes had
his Persian nobles jump overboard to save the person of the
king.[134]

In connection with the return of the illegitimate sons, Herodotus
tells the terrible story of the eunuch Hermotimus, a Carian, who
had been castrated by the Greek Panionius of Chios, had risen high
at the Persian court, and when Xerxes was spending the winter in
Sardis prior to his march on Greece, had met Panionius and taken
the most cruel vengeance on record by making him castrate his
own children and having them castrate their father. I believe the
most important connection of this story with the main narrative

---

[131] δρησμὸν ἐβούλευε, 8.97.1 = 100.1; cf. 8.75.2.

[132] Hdt. 8.99.2 and 100.1. In Aeschylus, the Persian elders fear not only for
Xerxes, but also for their country, and they bemoan their dead commanders.

[133] On the text, see Ch. IV, note 94.

[134] Cf. also the story of Xerxes' affair with Artaynta, at the end of the work, and
the resulting destruction of family (9.108-13; above, Ch. IV, 180).

lies in the synchronism with the campaign of Xerxes. Hermotimus is one barbarian who succeeded in taking vengeance on a Greek, as Xerxes decidedly did not. In addition, the motif of the destruction of children is emphasized, at the moment when Xerxes is fearing for his offspring. Finally, the story also casts an unfavorable light on the Ionians: the name Panionius is significant.[135]

Xerxes' return, like the similar but not identical retreat of Xerxes in the *Persians*, is simply a series of symbolic stories stressing the change of fortune caused by the battle.[136] The actual course of Xerxes' route is not emphasized.

The story of the Greeks after the battle is mainly the story of Themistocles, as described in the preceding chapter.[137] The Greeks first expect another battle with Xerxes, but when he has fled they proceed to Andros. There Themistocles' advice to go to the Hellespont is opposed by Eurybiades, who argues that the Persian must be allowed to leave so that the fight may be carried into his own country (8.108.4)—a statement that looks forward to Mycale and the end of the work. Defeated, Themistocles turns the delay to his advantage, and his "cleverness and good counsel" (*sophia kai euboulia*) carry the day once more.[138]

When the Greeks return to Salamis, the section on the awarding of gifts to the gods and of prizes to men has as one guiding idea the premise that Salamis was won with the help of the gods. The Aeginetans are asked by Apollo to give him his due, presumably because their prize of valor was won with his help. The main theme, however, is the envy of the Greeks for one another, an envy that illustrates both the hostile and the peaceful forms of strife. When the Greeks vote for the best man, each votes first for

[135] Castration is mentioned as an Eastern custom also in 3.48.2 ff. (but the tyrant Periander assists). Perversion of sex (as it might be called) is in fact characteristic of tyrants; cf. Peisistratus, 1.61.1, and above, note 51. In the East, perversion of sex appears also in the story of the Pedasian priestess who at times grows a beard: there the motif is connected with misfortune (1.175=8.104), and that may be another connection of the Hermotimus story with the story of Xerxes. Note that the Pedasian priestess (whose story is told by Herodotus twice) reappears precisely in the Hermotimus story. (I believe both passages to be genuine, although written at different times.) Aly, *Volksmärchen* 184, considers the possibility of a foreshadowing of Persian misfortune here, but rejects the idea.

[136] Hdt. 8.115-20; cf. Aesch. *Pers.* 482 ff.

[137] Above, Ch. V, 223-25.

[138] Hdt. 8.110.1; cf. above, Ch. V, 224. The council at Andros and the sieges of the island cities illustrate Themistocles' "pursuit of gain," mentioned at Artemisium (8.5.3); see Ch. V, note 100.

himself, then most vote for Themistocles in second place. Likewise the Spartans, although they honor Themistocles greatly, give the first prize to their commander Eurybiades.[139] Finally, the idea of envy is central to the famous anecdote of Themistocles and Timodemus of Aphidna:

> When (Themistocles) returned to Athens...Timodemus of Aphidna, an enemy of his, but not otherwise a notable person, insane with jealousy, kept taunting him, throwing up to him the trip to Sparta, (saying) it was thanks to Athens that he had the prizes from the Lacedaemonians, and not because of himself. Themistocles, when Timodemus kept on saying this, replied: "This is the way it is: neither would I have been so honored by the Spartiates if I were a Belbinite, nor would you, fellow, though you are an Athenian." (8.125)[140]

Thus the story of Salamis ends in discord, but not without reference to the greatness of both Themistocles and Athens.

The account of Salamis bears a curious relation to the five battles as a whole. Carefully prepared for by the preceding descriptions of naval action, it nevertheless has a number of themes all its own. Instead of merely praising the patriotism of the Greeks, it emphasizes elements of strife and disunity, since these are at the very center of Herodotus' conception of the superiority of the Greeks over the Persians. The trickster Themistocles is superior to the powerful Xerxes, because he can adapt himself to unforeseen circumstances and thus also has the help of the gods. The selfishness of Themistocles in no case conflicts with his patriotism,

[139] As Dr. Hubert Martin, Jr., reminds me, Plutarch, *Themistocles* 17.2, in his paraphrase of the Herodotean statement (8.124.2), says that Eurybiades got the award for valor (ἀνδρείας), and Themistocles the award for wisdom (σοφίας). Following this paraphrase, J. E. Powell, *Herodotus: Book VIII* (Cambridge 1939), after Cobet, has put ⟨ἀνδρηίης⟩ in the text. I believe, however, that ἀνδρείας in Plutarch is an explanatory gloss by Plutarch himself. Thereby Herodotus' statement loses its point, for he meant that the award for valor is the only true ἀριστήιον, and that Themistocles got "second prize."

[140] The meaning of the story comes out clearly if we compare the slightly different version known already to Plato, *Rep.* 329 E, and given by Plutarch, *Themistocles* 18, in which the interlocutor is not an Athenian, but from Seriphus. In this version the envy is between Greeks of different nationalities, while in Herodotus it is an intra-city rivalry. Plutarch characterizes Themistocles as φιλότιμος after Herodotus, and this ambition causes envy (φθόνος); see H. Martin, Jr., "The Character of Plutarch's Themistocles," *TAPA* 92 (1961) 331-39. J. Labarbe, "Timodemos d'Aphidna," *RBP* 36 (1958) 31-50, tries to show that the Herodotean interlocutor was from Aphidna in Laconia, a place otherwise unknown.

and his use of the divine for his own purposes is not irreligious. Themistocles represents the Athenians in their character of a seafaring people who are able, by a naval victory, to injure greatly both the sea and the land forces of an inflexible Xerxes.

V

The connection between Salamis and the battles of Plataea and Mycale is made, on the pragmatic level, through the sections dealing with the return of the Persian army and the pursuit of the Greeks. The Greek council after Salamis looks ahead toward the fight in the homeland of the Persians,[141] and the last Persian council prepares for Plataea by Mardonius' offer to stay behind. On the analogical level, Mardonius' second capture of Athens imitates that by Xerxes, since Mardonius throughout is the king's weaker image. The Athenian request that the Peloponnesians do battle in Boeotia appears as a repetition of an Athenian plan before Salamis.[142] The quarrel between Athens and Sparta, and the problem of the Isthmian wall, also connect Salamis with Plataea. Yet the principal themes of the narrative of the last two battles differ from Salamis, and reveal a closer connection with Thermopylae and Artemisium.[143]

Plataea and Mycale are made parallel to Thermopylae and Artemisium by a number of structural devices, such as the direct references mentioned earlier, but even more by the sustained imagery of land and sea. In both narratives the sea surrounds, as it were, the land. The break between the sea skirmishes and Artemisium is thus paralleled by the break between the first and second Ionian embassies to the Greek fleet.[144] Like Thermopylae, Plataea, placed between these sections, is isolated from the remainder of the action. In this isolation a value judgment is implied: just as Mardonius was inferior to Xerxes, so Plataea (the pride of Sparta and the continental Greeks)[145] was a lesser battle than Salamis. Like the earlier Spartan battle, Plataea has no positive

[141] Hdt. 8.108.4.

[142] Capture of Athens: 8.50-55 and 9.1-3. Battle in Boeotia: 8.40.2 and 9.6; see above, note 103.

[143] See above, 256.

[144] The first Ionian embassy precedes the campaign of Mardonius (8.132), and the second follows it (9.90-91).

[145] See above, note 8.

consequences, whereas the sea battles lead logically toward an increasing strength of Athens and of the naval arm of the Greek League.

The parallelism between Plataea and Mycale in turn presupposes a specific interpretation and evaluation of these battles. In the first place, Herodotus sees both battles as defensive actions. This was true enough of Plataea strategically, but Herodotus has extended this interpretation to the tactical situation also, in which the Greeks forever refuse to engage the enemy. For Mycale, essentially an aggressive battle in the King's own country, the matter was not so simple, but Herodotus defines its immediate aim as the liberation of "the islands and the Hellespont," and correctly marks it further as the preliminary step in the liberation of the Greeks of Asia Minor.[146] Having neglected the tactical connection between Thermopylae and Artemisium, he also represented the two later battles as analogical events,[147] a relationship expressed by three symbolic comparisons: (1) The battles were fought on the same day. (2) Just before the attack at Mycale, a rumor spread that the Greeks had been victorious at Plataea, a miraculous occurrence which Herodotus finds confirmed by the fact that Plataea was fought in the morning and Mycale in the afternoon. In addition, a herald's staff was found washed onto the beach at Mycale.[148] (3) Both battles were fought near a sanctuary of Demeter, and, we may add, sanctuaries of Hera play a part in both accounts, although Herodotus does not stress this last point.[149] In the comparison of the battles there is thus a very strong religious element. Compared with this the factual parallelism of the two battles is minor. It consists primarily of the existence of a wall of wicker shields and a walled camp of the Persians in each

[146] Islands and Hellespont: 9.101.3. Thucydides differs here by adding the Greeks of Asia Minor too (Thuc. 1.89.2), whereas to Herodotus the result of Mycale was the revolt of Ionia (9.105 and 106.2), and the newly-gained allies were all islanders (9.106.4); hence he does not describe the actual liberation of Ionia. Cf. Pohlenz, *Herodot* 176; *Tat und Geschichte* 511, note 23.

[147] A strategic connection is assumed e.g. by How and Wells, 2.390; cf. also Hammond, *Hist. Greece* 251.

[148] Hdt. 9.90.1 and 100.

[149] Hdt. 9.101. Sanctuary of Hera: 9.96.1; cf. 9.69, etc. The watchword of the Greeks at Mycale is given as *Hebe* in the MSS (9.98.3); *Hera* is an attractive conjecture by Roscher, but since there is no compelling need for this change, the matter must remain uncertain.

locality,[150] but the relation of the Athenian and Spartan troops is also very similar in each battle. However, the parallelism of the two battles is something of a *tour de force*, and one is apt to forget that Mycale was not really a sea battle, but was fought by marines on land, and that by Herodotus' own figures it was a much smaller battle than the other four.

The battle of Plataea is notorious for its tactical and structural difficulties. We are not here concerned with its actual course, nor with the reliability of Herodotus' multiple sources of information, but only with the battle account as a literary composition. The problem, in a nutshell, is to find the principal structural idea in a loosely joined series of tactical movements, which, for the most part, are not kept separate by framing sentences or anecdotes. The battle account is introduced by a series of short sections describing the actions of Mardonius in the spring of 479 B.C.: first, after consulting several Greek oracles, he sent an offer of alliance to Athens; next he occupied the city and again asked for alliance; finally, upon receiving reports of the Peloponnesian advance toward Boeotia, he marched from Athens to Thebes.[151] In the first and last of these sections, he is informed by Greeks: in the first, apparently by a Greek oracle (Herodotus could not be sure of it), and in the last, by three messages sent to him by medizing Greeks. Mardonius does not really possess the initiative here.

I would suggest that this pattern (Mardonius goaded into action by Greeks) goes far toward explaining the following arrangement of the narrative, if we add two occasions where Mardonius acts, on his own, against religion. The first of these is his decision to attack at Plataea (9.41 ff.), and the second, his crossing of the river Asopus during the battle (9.58 ff.), both motivated by disregard of oracles and unfavorable sacrifices. They correspond to Mardonius' earlier occupation and burning of Athens, which was motivated by pride and the desire to please Xerxes.[152]

---

[150] The correspondence has been noticed before: see How and Wells, 2.396 (Appendix XXII), and J. A. R. Munro, *CAH* 4.344. Wall of wicker shields: 9.99.3 and 102.2-3; cf. 9.61.3 and 62.2. Fortified camp: 9.96.3 and 102.3-4; cf. 9.15.2-3; 65.1, etc.

[151] See above, Ch. III, 142-43. On the Peloponnesian advance to Plataea, see Macan, *VII-IX*, on 9.19, line 1: in his view, Mardonius begins to evacuate Attica when the Spartans set out from home; he leaves Attica when they are at the Isthmus; and he builds his camp when the Athenians join the Spartans at Eleusis.

[152] Hdt. 9.1-3 and 13.2. Cf. the motivation of Aryandes, 4.166 and 167.3. This is the motif of the underling trying to equal his master; cf. Ch. IV, note 105.

Mardonius thus shows initiative only when he goes against the gods, but otherwise has no independent strategy. With these two exceptions, the account of Plataea and its antecedents consists of a series of sections, each of which begins with Greek initiative and ends with Persian action—mostly in a cavalry skirmish:

I. 9.12-18: Argive message to Mardonius. His movement to Thebes. Banquet of Attaginus. Trial of Phocians by Persian cavalry (*Mock fight*).

II. 9.19-24: Greeks move from Isthmus via Eleusis to foothills of Cithaeron.
Cavalry engagement in which Masistius falls (*Fight I*).[153]

III. 9.25-32: Greeks move forward to Plataea and the spring Gargaphia. Quarrel of Athenians and Tegeans over position on left wing. Greek order of battle. *Persian order of battle.*

IV. 9.33-40: Sacrifices:
a. On Greek side.
  Story of seer Teisamenus.
    Story of seer Melampus.
  The five contests.
b. On Persian side.
  Story of seer Hegesistratus.
Cavalry attack by Persians (*Fight II*), and delay for ten days.

V. 9.41-49: Council of Mardonius; discussion of oracles.
Advice of Alexander to Greeks (at night).
Double shift of Spartan position.
Message of Mardonius taunting the Spartans.
Mardonius attacks Gargaphia with cavalry (*Fight III*).

VI. 9.50-57: Council of Greeks and withdrawal (at night) to "island." Greek center to Heraeum. Stubbornness of Amompharetus. Athenians in the plain. Spartans (at daybreak) move to sanctuary of Demeter. Mardonius' cavalry attacks (*Fight IV*).

---

[153] Sections I and II are not properly part of the battle description, although they follow the same pattern and are thus repeated here; see above, Ch. III, 142-43.

VII. 9.58-65: BATTLE.

        Mardonius' decision to cross the Asopus.

        Attack by Spartans and Tegeans.

        Pausanias prays to Hera of Plataea (61.3).

        Spartan attack on Persians, and victory.

        Death of Mardonius; flight to camp.

            Demeter avenges the defilement of her sanctuary at Eleusis.

VIII. 9.66-75: Last Stages of Battle.

        Flight of Artabazus.

        Athenians defeat medizing Greeks.

        Actions of Greeks at Heraeum.

        Persians slaughtered in camp.

        Aristeiai of Sparta; Athens; Tegea.[154]

IX. 9.76-85: After the Battle.

        Story of Coan concubine; late arrival of Mantineans and Eleans; Lampon's impious request to avenge Leonidas; booty and gifts; Pausanias' banquet; Plataeans find caches of gold.

        Bones of Persians; Mardonius' corpse; Greek burials.

X. 9.86-88: Punishment of Thebes and disbandment of army.

XI. 9.89: Return of Artabazus to Persia.[155]

The principal theme used for the organization of the narrative is the danger to the Greek forces caused by the Persian cavalry, a motif carefully prepared before the battle by the mock attack of the Persian cavalry against the Phocians, and by the preliminary skirmish, in which Masistius, the tallest and most handsome Persian, lost his life.[156] Persian cavalry forced the Greeks to abandon Gargaphia and move toward the "island," and during the retreat the Spartans were heavily pressed by the Persian horse (9.57.3). But this very retreat brought about victory, for it caused Mardonius to attack the Spartans with his infantry, and in this kind of fighting the Spartans were clearly superior.

[154] Section VIII makes the transition from the battle to its aftereffects, and belongs with the next section more closely than with the preceding.

[155] I have not marked the framing sentences in this battle account, since they are used only very sketchily: 9.16.5-17.1; 18.3-19.1; 24-25.1; 31.1; 36; 41.1; 66.1; 70.1; 80.1; 88-89.1. Section IX, a series of anecdotes, uses framing sentences more fully.

[156] Cavalry motif: see above, note 23, and Ch. III, note 184.

The sections preceding the decision on the field begin with Greek action, with the exception of Sections V and VII, which describe Mardonius' folly. These Greek actions, however, are in themselves curiously aimless and weakly motivated. After the Greeks have established themselves in the foothills of Cithaeron, they move forward toward Plataea merely because the neighborhood of the spring Gargaphia is more suitable for encampment (9.25.2). They are prevented from attacking by the fact that the sacrifices are propitious only for defense (9.36), and they subsequently show much fear. The Spartans twice change their position in line to avoid facing the Persians, who eventually force battle upon them during their retreat to the "island." While this treatment admirably expresses the Greek fear of the enemy's cavalry, it has deeper reasons: the battle up to the moment of the final decision is not heroic. Mardonius, whose sacrifices are similarly favorable only for defense (9.37.1), attacks not in a heroic spirit, but as a fool. Human action, both on the Greek and on the Persian sides, is purposely devaluated, because divine rather than human action is at the center of the narrative.

In their speech to the Spartans disclaiming any intention to make common cause with Mardonius, the Athenians had already stated that the war against the Persians was largely a war on behalf of Greek religious institutions and in retaliation for the Persian destruction of Greek sanctuaries (8.144). The later legend that Plataea was fought as vengeance for the destruction of sanctuaries is here already in formation.[157] Another element is the Spartan attitude toward religion: having delayed sending an army, ostensibly because they were celebrating the Hyacinthia, the Spartans take omens both at the Isthmus and at Eleusis, and they continue only when these omens are found to be propitious.[158] The reader meanwhile knows that Delphi had earlier pointed to a battle with Mardonius as the just revenge for the death of

[157] Herodotus considered Plataea, in the first instance, the vengeance exacted for the defilement of Leonidas' body after Thermopylae (9.64 and 78-79; cf. 8.114.2), i.e. a Spartan rather than a purely Panhellenic affair. See L. Solmsen in Marg, *Herodot* 666. Vengeance for the destruction of Greek sanctuaries, mentioned in 8.144, is a secondary motif appearing, e.g. in 9.65.2; this is later stressed in the fictitious "Oath of Plataea," now extant in a fourth-century inscription: see *GHI* 2, No. 204. Recently, C. Habicht, *Hermes* 89 (1961) 11 ff. and 18, has once again argued for its spuriousness, while A. E. Raubitschek, *TAPA* 91 (1960) 178, assumes its genuineness. Cf. also Macan, *VII-IX*, on 8.144, line 9.

[158] Omens: 9.19. Hyacinthia: 9.7.1 and 11.1.

Leonidas.[159] As soon as the Greeks were in position at Plataea they performed the sacrifices previously mentioned, which nullified their initiative. Mardonius in turn shows an ever closer contact with religion. Before leaving Thessaly he consulted Greek oracles: Herodotus tells the story, how at the Ptoum, Apollo even spoke Carian to Mardonius' emissary (8.135). While the Greeks were sacrificing at Plataea, Mardonius also sacrificed *more Graeco* (9.37.1), as did the Greek auxiliaries in his camp (9.38.2). For ten days Mardonius abided by the injunction of Greek sacrifices, but on the eleventh he decided to disregard them (9.41.4). Despite warnings by Artabazus, who advised withdrawal to Thebes and a slow conquest of Greece through bribery (advice already given earlier by the Thebans), Mardonius declared he would fight *more Persico*—i.e. by attacking at once.[160] He asked his generals whether they knew of any oracles predicting the destruction of the Persians in Greece, and he himself erroneously quoted an oracle that seemed to predict the Persians' defeat if they were to plunder Delphi. By avoiding offense of the Greek gods he expected to avoid defeat—but the oracle, Herodotus knew, did not refer to this Persian campaign, and furthermore, we may add, the Persians had attacked Delphi.[161] Mardonius' attack on the Greeks is an act of impiety.

The specific question confronting Mardonius at the moment of decision was the crossing of the Asopus river, which separated the Greek position from the Persian; the battle began with this crossing (9.59.1). Now the crossing of rivers (or such branches of the sea as the Hellespont) is a significant motif in Herodotus, and it is always used to prove the *hybris* of the aggressor.[162] But at Plataea the crossing of the Asopus is specifically linked with the motif of divine intervention. Mardonius, by crossing the river, does not automatically fall victim to the Greeks: his first attacks upon the retreating Spartans appear to be successful. The river

[159] Hdt. 8.114.1; cf. above, note 157. Crahay, *Litt. orac.* 312 ff.

[160] Hdt. 9.41.4: τά τε σφάγια τὰ ʿΗγησιστράτου ἐᾶν χαίρειν . . ., ἀλλὰ νόμῳ τῷ Περσέων χρεωμένους συμβάλλειν. On the *nomos* of the Persians, see below, Conclusion, note 39.

[161] Mardonius' misquotation: 9.42-43. Attack on Delphi: 8.35 ff. Herodotus does not make reference to the latter, although he knew that the gods punish even the intent of wrongdoing (cf. Macan, *VII-IX*, on 9.42, line 9). Plataea as vengeance for the attempted destruction of Delphi would have been a further concession to the Panhellenic view of the battle; see above, note 157.

[162] River motif: see above, Ch. III, note 17, and Ch. IV, note 40.

294 FORM AND THOUGHT IN HERODOTUS

motif is not central to the defeat of Mardonius, but initiates it.[163]

The religious motif complements and overshadows the river motif, as can be seen from the structure of the battle in the narrow sense (Section VII), where Pausanias' prayer occupies a pivotal position. A duel between Persians and Spartans (with assistance only from the Tegeans), the battle turns into a simple matter of attack and counter-attack. The Spartans are unable to withstand the Persians until Pausanias prays to the goddess Hera, who had a temple at Plataea:

> And since the sacrifices did not turn out right for (the Spartans), many fell at that time and many more were wounded. For the Persians formed a wall with their wicker shields and let go numberless arrows, so that when the Spartans were hard pressed and the sacrifices did not turn out (favorably), Pausanias looked toward the Heraeum at Plataea and called upon the goddess, asking her not to forsake them in their hope. And while he was still calling out, the Tegeans, advancing first, attacked the barbarians, and the Spartans, immediately after the prayer of Pausanias, had sacrifices that were favorable. When these (omens) had finally turned out right, they too advanced against the Persians . . . (9.61.3-62.1)

The Spartans now break through the wicker shields and win the greatest victory ever known (9.64.1), but that victory rests upon the help of the local gods. Seen from the religious point of view, the confusion of the battle becomes clear. The battle of Plataea, more than the battle of Salamis, was the work of the Greek gods and heroes, to use Themistocles' words (8.109.3). The intervention of the divine changes a confused series of maneuvers into a great victory. It is significant that the religious element appears here in connection with the Spartans, a religious nation *par excellence*. By their support the gods really give the Greeks "an equal chance," and thus the religious motif adumbrated at Artemisium comes to its full flowering here.

The numerous stories about seers underline this interpretation in typically Herodotean ways. The names of the seers themselves are significant. Teisamenus, "the avenger," served the Greeks,

---

[163] References to the crossing of the river abound in the Plataea narrative: 9.36 (sacrifices tell the Greeks not to cross the Asopus); 9.40 (neither side crosses); 9.43.2 (oracle by Bacis cites rivers); 51.1-2 (the "island"); 57.2 (sanctuary of Demeter is near a river); 59.1 (Mardonius crosses the Asopus).

for the Greeks and their gods were taking vengeance for Persian religious crimes. Hegesistratus, "the leader of the army," served the Persians, who ultimately were the attackers. Hippomachus, "the cavalryman," served the Greeks on the Persian side, who took pride in their cavalry.[164] Lengthy stories about the first two men illustrate the divisiveness among the Greeks, and in particular the attitude of Sparta toward foreigners. Teisamenus, sought out by the Spartans because of an oracle that he would win five "contests," manages to get Spartan citizenship for himself and his brother—he had learnt something from the mythical Melampus, who under similar circumstances had received a part of the kingdom of Argos. Hegesistratus, on the other hand, was a bitter enemy of Sparta, where he had once been imprisoned (he escaped by hacking off his foot). These stories connect the divine level with the human. A third story about seers is told at Mycale (9.92 ff.).

The final victory was won near a sanctuary of Demeter, and Herodotus wondered why no Persians took refuge in it: he thinks the goddess kept them out in revenge for what the Persians had done to her sanctuary at Eleusis (9.65.2). This is the clearest indication that Herodotus himself thought of the local gods as participating in the battle.

The human element, although secondary to the divine, is clearly elaborated according to the themes of the earlier battles. The three main states on the Greek side are the Spartans, the Athenians, and the Tegeans. The divisiveness of the Greeks appears primarily in the quarrel of the Athenians and Tegeans over who shall lead the left flank.[165] The Athenians appear in the battle as the altruistic helpers of the Spartans.[166] Of the latter we get a double picture: before the omens turn in their favor, they are vacillating, even cowardly; calling upon the Athenians for help on various occasions, and afraid to face the Persians, they quarrel during the retreat, when the Spartan captain Amompharetus delays the withdrawal by his stubbornness. This last story shows

[164] Teisamenus: 9.33 ff. Hegesistratus: 9.37 ff. Hippomachus: 9.38.2. Telling names are common for seers: were they hired in part for their names? Cf. also that other Hegesistratus, who "led the Greek navy" from Delos to Samos before Mycale (9.90 ff.): was he chosen as leader of the embassy because of his name?

[165] Above, Ch. V, 215 and 226; the Tegeans stress their hostility to Sparta, the Athenians, the benefits rendered to other nations (including the Heracleidae).

[166] Hdt. 9.21.3; 46.2-3; 54.1-56.2; 60 f.; 67; 70.2.

not only the internal divisiveness of Sparta (it may be compared with the quarrels between the Spartan royal houses), but also reaffirms true Spartan valor against the behavior of Pausanias. Both attitudes can be explained: as a Spartan, Pausanias cannot act courageously in the face of opposition from the gods, while Amompharetus could not be blamed (and was not, since he was cited for valor after the battle) for remaining to face the enemy as the Spartan code demanded.[167] The picture of the Spartans changes after Pausanias' prayer: in direct conflict with the Persians, they show their excellence in fighting ability, and after the battle Pausanias shows his true religious and moderate spirit. This picture agrees with Herodotus' opinion that the Spartans were excellent in battle, but not much good for anything else (7.139.3-4). When the fortified camp of the Persians is attacked, the Athenians show a much greater skill than the Spartans in breaking through the walls (9.70.2). However, the defeat of the Persian infantry was decisive. Therefore:

> Among the Greeks, while the Tegeans and Athenians had been brave men, the Spartans surpassed (all) in valor. (9.71.1).

An interesting sidelight is the evaluation of Oriental valor at Plataea. Throughout the battles Herodotus stresses the superiority of the Persians to the other nations under Persian control, but in this battle alone they are considered truly brave.[168] This contributes considerably to the glorification of the Spartans who defeated them. At the same time, the battle shows the Persians and Mardonius morally in a most unfavorable light, as barbarians. In the course of his work, Herodotus demonstrates the origin of the antithesis between Greeks and barbarians. Originally, "barbarian" was not a word of abuse—it came to be that as the result of the Persian Wars.[169] Hence in the earlier parts of the work, "bar-

---

[167] Amompharetus: 9.53.2 ff. Spartan vacillations: 9.46; cf. the taunts of Mardonius, 9.48, and 58.2. Further: 9.55.2; 60.1. All this precedes Pausanias' prayer.

[168] At Thermopylae Xerxes sent his Persian Immortals when the others had failed (7.211.1), but they fared no better. After Salamis, Mardonius drew a similar distinction between Persians and other troops (8.100.4); cf. Artemisia before Salamis, 8.68c. Bravery of Persians at Plataea: 9.62.3; 68.

[169] On the development of the contrast between Greeks and barbarians, see above, Ch. V, note 1, esp. Jüthner, *op. cit.* 13-21. In the earlier part of the work, Herodotus uses βάρβαρος frequently in a purely ethnographic sense, i.e. =non-Greeks (see Introductory Sentence; 1.57-58; cf. the definition, 2.158.5). In this meaning, the word is connected with the distinction between Asia and Europe (1.4.4), and barbarians

barian" does not have a bad connotation, but in the battle of Plataea the hatred of the Greeks for their would-be conquerors appears in a clear light.

This is particularly true of the sections following the battle description (Sections VIII and IX). No other battle has so many anecdotes closing the battle composition. The section I have called "The Last Stages of Battle" (VIII) is introduced by the flight of Artabazus, whose return to Persia closes off the next two sections (XI).[170] Thus the storming of the Persian camp (the main Athenian achievement) is separated from the Spartan victory and subordinated to the main battle account. Section VIII concludes with a very brief account of Persian and Greek *aristeiai*, in which Aristodemus redeems himself for his cowardice at Thermopylae. Section IX, consisting of a number of anecdotes mostly separated by framing sentences,[171] has two guiding ideas, the magnanimity of Pausanias as a representative of the best in Greek moral behavior, and the treatment of the dead. Pausanias acts as a true gentleman toward a Greek concubine from Cos who had been on the barbarian side; and he rejects the impious request of the Aeginetan Lampon, who suggests dishonoring the body of Mardonius in retaliation for Xerxes' treatment of the body of Leonidas:

> "This action befits barbarians more than Greeks; and we detest it even in barbarians." (9.79.1)

The contrast between barbarians and Greeks is then paramount in Pausanias' preparation of a Persian and a Spartan banquet in order to point the folly of the luxurious Persians, who attack the indigent Greeks (9.82.3). The praise of Pausanias implied in these anecdotes is in glaring contradiction with his later tyrannical behavior at Byzantium, a deterioration of character well known to

---

are considered inferior in a few places (1.58 and 60.3). Later the Persians are often called simply "barbarians" (5.49.3, etc.; see Powell, *Lexicon*, s.v. βάρβαρος), whence stems the unfavorable connotation cited in the text.

[170] The battle account of Plataea likewise has more anecdotes initially than that of any other battle. The Artabazus episodes in particular are used to separate the main *logoi* of the narrative: in 8.126-29, the story of his trip to the Hellespont and his return to Mardonius separates Salamis from the events of 479 B.C. In 9.89 his flight to Asia separates Plataea and Mycale. During the battle of Plataea, Artabazus acts throughout as an antagonist to Mardonius (9.41; 58.3; 66.2-3; 70.5). Note also that the number ten occurs for chronological notations both before and after the battle: see 9.41.1; 86.2; 87.1.

[171] See above, note 155.

Herodotus.[172] In the delineation of individual character (as well as in national behavior) Herodotus admits the possibility of change into the opposite. The picture of Pausanias is deliberate.

The principal feature of the three stories of the dead is the disappearance of the body of Mardonius, who (Herodotus implies) was probably buried secretly. It is as if the gods had made sure no defilement would take place, and the story, paralleling as it does the disappearance of other war heroes,[173] tends to raise our estimation of Mardonius. The problem of the character of Mardonius has been raised recently by Myres, who considers him the hero of the whole account of the Persian Wars.[174] But Myres is here the victim of his theory of circular composition. Xerxes is clearly the hero of the Persian Wars: he acts independently (if foolishly), and as the master of great wealth and a great nation he has the greatness required of a hero. Mardonius, on the other hand, is a derivative figure: his actions parallel those of his master Xerxes, he cites him constantly and tries to impress him. Another feature that reduces our estimate of Mardonius is his dependence, noted above, on Greek oracles and Greek information. Mardonius lacks independence and magnificence. The story of the disappearance of his body and the attempts by Persians to find his grave are meant to increase his stature somewhat, in order to make him a worthy opponent of Pausanias.

The significance of Plataea lies in its balance with Thermopylae quite as much as in its effect on the liberty of mainland Greece. Plataea is primarily vengeance for religious crimes committed by the Persians against gods and men. By being isolated in its effects from the remainder of the narrative, Plataea is clearly devaluated in comparison with Salamis. This judgment may be the reason for Herodotus' failure to include an account of prizes and celebrations, as he did for Salamis. After the punishment of Thebes, we are

[172] See Herodotus' statements, 4.81.3; 5.32 ("if the story is true"); 8.3.2. The conflict of characterizations is notorious; however, it seems to me to be simply a case of incongruity between different *logoi*, noted already for the Persian kings (e.g. above, Ch. IV, note 54). It is easily explained by the Herodotean conception of character, according to which complete changes (*metabolai*) are possible; cf. also Ch. IV, note 3. Cambyses and Croesus both experience similar changes.

[173] Cf. the disappearance of Hamilcar, 7.166-67.1. This story shows a connection with stories of self-immolation (cf. 7.107.2) and with the disappearance of shamanistic types in the Scythian *Logos* (see Hdt. 4.14 and 95). Cf. E. R. Dodds, *The Greeks and the Irrational* (Berkeley 1951) 140 ff.

[174] Above, Ch. IV, note 105.

told abruptly that the army is dismissed, and we hear no more of the affairs of mainland Greece.[175] Internally, the account stresses the differences and the competition between Athens and Sparta, as well as other divisive elements among the Greeks, but these are unified by the emphasis upon the divine, which is seen especially under the guise of local divinities participating in the battle. The dramatic use of local stories about particular divinities does not conflict with Herodotus' own religious beliefs. It is true that when speaking of his convictions, he often refers to his own belief in a general "divine," i.e. in an obscure power not clearly related by him to the gods of Greek tradition. We have seen, however, that when he refers to the sanctuary of Demeter at Plataea he speaks as if he believed in the goddess, and this belief must be accepted. Herodotean religion combines the belief in the divine as a unified power with a limited trust in the stories of tradition.[176]

The battle account of Mycale is shorter and simpler than that of Plataea:

8.130-32:	Persian fleet at Cyme; First Ionian embassy to Greek fleet, which moves to Delos.
(8.133-9.89:	Plataea, etc.)
9.90-92.1:	Second Ionian embassy (Hegesistratus).
	92.2-95: Sacrifices.
	93-95: Story of seer Euenius.
9.96-97:	Greek fleet moves to Samos: the Heraeum. Persians move to Mycale: council.
9.98-99:	Greek landing and Persian countermeasures.
	a. Council and decision to sail to mainland.
	b. Leotychidas calls on Ionians to desert.
	c. Landing on beach.
	d. Persians disarm Samians, remove Milesians, and form wicker wall.
9.100-101:	Rumor about victory at Plataea; the herald's staff. The two Demetria.

[175] Dedications (9.81) are mentioned, but prizes are not; for the latter, Herodotus says that he had no information except in the case of Pausanias (9.81.2), a most remarkable statement. Dismissal of army: 9.88. Herodotus omits the meeting of the allies after Plataea (Plut., *Arist.* 21; Thuc. 2.71), the harsh conditions imposed on Thebes (J. A. R. Munro, *CAH* 4.341), and a probable meeting of the allies at the Isthmus (cf. Macan, *VII-IX*, on 9.88.7), where the prizes would presumably have been conferred.

[176] For Herodotus' religious beliefs and the representation of divinity in his work, see also Conclusion, 312, and note 14.

9.101.3-105: BATTLE.

    a. Athenians and Spartans.

    b. Taking of wicker wall; flight of Persians.

    c. Taking of wall at camp.

    d. The Persian dead.

    e. Further action; arrival of Spartans; Greek dead.

    f. Samian help. Milesian help.

      "Thus Ionia revolted for the second time from the Persians" (9.105).

    g. *Aristeiai:*

      Death of Hermolycus.

9.106:   Greek actions after battle:

    a. Booty and departure to Samos.

    b. Council II, on fate of Ionia. Islands admitted to the League.

    c. Departure to Hellespont.

9.107-13:   Return of Persians:

    a. Quarrel of Masistes and Artayctes.

    b. Return to Sardis.

      Loves of Xerxes and death of Masistes.

      (Return to Susa).[177]

The battle of Mycale is defined in an introductory sentence preceding the Second Ionian Embassy, cited above (Ch. III, 144) as containing the synchronism with the battle of Plataea. The central motif is the fear of the Greeks, which parallels that of the Spartans at Plataea;[178] it is overcome not merely by the repeated entreaties of the Ionians, but also by the omen of the name "Hegesistratus," one of the Ionian ambassadors.[179] In

---

[177] As in the case of Plataea, the first sections of the outline of Mycale need not be taken as parts of the battle *logos* in the narrow sense; cf. above, Ch. III, 144. Framing sentences occur in 9.90.1 and 101.3-102.1.

[178] A major motif in the accounts of the Persian Wars is that of fear: it is used for Marathon (above, 253), for the Greek navy at Artemisium and at Salamis (above, 264 ff. and 281), and at Plataea (the Spartan refusal to face the Persians, 9.46). The Greek attitude toward fear of an enemy is different from ours: so already in the *Iliad*, e.g. when Hector flees from Achilles. In Thucydides, fear is a main principle in the mechanism of power politics; see J. de Romilly, "La Crainte dans l'oeuvre de Thucydide," *C&M* 17 (1956) 119-27. Cf. also her booklet *La Crainte et l'angoisse dans le théâtre d'Eschyle* (Paris 1958) 109 ff.

[179] Hdt. 9.91.1 and 92.2; cf. above, note 164. Leotychidas accepts the omen of the name and has the ambassadors commit themselves to a Samian alliance with the Panhellenic League. What happened thereafter is obscure, as the text seems to be

the same way, the Greek fear of barbarians in the battle itself is allayed by the "rumor" that Plataea has been won, which gives them courage (9.100.2). Thus, the religious motif is strong in the account of Mycale too, but with the difference that the gods are representatives of Panhellenism more than of specific localities.[180]

Before moving from Delos to Samos, the Greeks make sacrifices, which are propitious (9.92 ff.). Their seer is Deiphonus, an unusual name meaning "he who kills in battle." Herodotus tells the story of his father (or supposed father), Euenius of Apollonia, in the third of the great seer anecdotes. Euenius was a noble citizen of Apollonia, whose turn had come to watch over the sacred sheep of the Sun God in a cave every night for a year. Once he fell asleep, and when sixty sheep were killed by wolves, the Apolloniates put out his eyes. Thereupon flocks and crops refused to prosper, and the oracles of Dodona and Delphi declared that the gods themselves (i.e. Zeus and Apollo) had sent the wolves and would not rest until Euenius had received justice. Euenius was to choose his own recompense, and in addition the gods would make him most happy. The Apolloniates tricked Euenius into being satisfied with two portions of land, but the gods conferred the gift of prophecy on him. The story is articulated into three parts, with the divine response in the center, where the gods are seen acting in unison as Zeus and Apollo interfere with Helios' sheep.[181] The central idea of the story lies in the idea of atonement as divine justice, and its contrast with human conduct: the Apolloniates, who are told that they must atone for the blinding, trick Euenius into accepting a lesser reward, but the gods give him what they

---

corrupt; see Macan, *VII-IX*, on 9.92, line 3. The omen may have been intended by the Samians, or it may have been pure chance ($\kappa\alpha\tau\grave{\alpha}$ $\sigma\upsilon\nu\tau\upsilon\chi\acute{\iota}\eta\nu$ $\theta\epsilon o\hat{\upsilon}$ $\pi o\iota\epsilon\hat{\upsilon}\nu\tau o\varsigma$, 9.91.1), i.e. the gods brought it about. The latter view would be that of Leotychidas, and also of Herodotus.

[180] The speech of Hegesistratus is Panhellenic in character: 9.90.2. The gods also have a general Panhellenic, as well as a specific local, role at Mycale: 9.100-101. There is no mention of the particular relations between Athenians and Ionians till after the battle (9.106.2-4).

[181] I would analyze the story as follows: (1) 9.93.1-3 ($\sigma\tau\epsilon\rho\eta\theta\hat{\eta}\nu\alpha\iota$). (2) 93.3-4, end. (3) 94 entire, despite the repeated phrases in that chapter. This puts the divine response in the center. The oracles say that "they themselves" had sent the wolves that caused the trouble for Euenius; the reference must be to Zeus and Apollo, since the oracles are those at Dodona and Delphi. Individual gods are here acting in unison for a common purpose (the creation of a soothsayer). Cf. the action of Apollo at Paros against Miltiades, 6.135.3. In both cases individual gods are named by oracles. See further on this story, Crahay, *Litt. orac.* 82-84.

have promised. We may consider Plataea and Salamis similar
acts of atonement before the gods. This is perhaps the best of the
tales about seers, and it supports the religious element in the
story of the rumor and the sanctuaries of Demeter.

The account of the battle stresses first the contrast of sea and
land, and secondly, the continued competition between Athens
and Sparta. The Greek fleet arrives at Samos expecting a sea
fight, but the Persian navy, in fear of the Greek, prefers to support
the land forces in their fortified camp. The Persians send their
Phoenician contingent away—no doubt for its own safety.[182] The
Persian infantry had been located at Mycale by command of
Xerxes (9.96.2), whose presence as a central figure is thus still felt
in the narrative. The camp is fortified with a wall of ships for both
offensive and defensive action.[183] Thus, the sea battle turns into
a land battle through Persian fear.

The Greek landing and attack upon the Persian camp brings to
the fore the Athenians and the Spartans as two separate forces.
As at Plataea, the Athenians remain in the plain, while the
Spartans advance through hilly country,[184] but at Mycale this is
to the advantage of the Athenians, for they reach the camp earlier
than the Spartans and display in breaking through the wall the
same skill they had shown at Plataea. With all this, Herodotus
does not describe the tactical situation in any detail, nor does he
bother to give the order of battle, although it was known to him.[185]
To Herodotus the battle becomes a competitive effort of Athenians
and Spartans:

> So long as the wicker shields of the Persians remained upright,
> they put up a defense and held their own in the battle; but
> when the Athenians and their neighbors in line, in order that
> the achievement should be theirs and not to the credit of the

---

[182] Hdt. 9.96.1; there is much scholarly speculation as to why the Phoenician navy
was dismissed, and at what time. See Stein on 8.130, line 13; Macan; How and Wells;
Munro, *CAH* 4.341-42. Herodotus' narrative, however, seems to indicate clearly that
they were sent away for their own safety, and just before the battle. Thus the fear
motif is prominent here also. The passage appears to be the last mention of the
Phoenician navy in the work.

[183] Defensive and offensive combined: 9.97, end. This should not be bracketed;
see *Causation* 256, note 28.

[184] Hdt. 9.102.1; cf. 9.56.2.

[185] Athenians' skill at breaking through wall: 9.102.3; cf. 9.70.2. Herodotus knew
something of the order of battle, for he mentions as an afterthought that the Athenians,
Corinthians, Sicyonians, and Troezenians were stationed together (9.102.3).

Lacedaemonians, shouted and exerted themselves more fully, the situation changed. (9.102.2)

At Mycale, the Athenians and not the Spartans won the prize of valor.[186]

Mycale was fought to free the islands, the Hellespont, and Ionia from the Persians, and thus the battle also fits into a line of pragmatic action which begins with the Ionian Revolt and continues through the naval actions of Artemisium, Salamis, and the siege of Andros to the subsequent actions at Sestus. Herodotus avoids stating that the battle of Mycale resulted in the freedom of the Ionians: it rather caused the second revolt of Ionia, and therewith a new series of actions which resulted in the Delian League. Nevertheless, the Ionians are important to the battle description in two respects: two Ionian embassies (by the Chians and the Samians, both islanders) brought the Greeks to the coast of Asia Minor, and in the battle the Ionians showed the first stirrings of freedom. The main heroes of Mycale among the Ionians are the Samians,[187] with the Milesians taking second place. The beginning of the "Second Ionian Revolt," as Herodotus calls it, results in the *de facto* separation of the Spartan and Athenian forces—only the latter continue the war to the Hellespont. The Ionian islands are admitted to the Panhellenic League. Herodotus says nothing of admitting the Ionian mainland cities at this time.[188] The islands having been admitted, there remained the Hellespont; Herodotus ends his work with the account of the actions there.[189]

VI

The five battles against Xerxes' invasion are, as we have seen, a unified complex, with the main decision made by the Athenians at Salamis. This complex, which is followed only by a short account of the aftereffects of Mycale in the fighting at the Hellespont, is thus itself the climax and end of the work. In the

---

[186] According to Jacoby, *RE* Suppl. 2.466-67, the account of Mycale is based primarily on Samian sources, with some Attic additions. But the Samian sources are concerned mainly with facts, whereas the bias of the whole account derives from Athenian sources. Hence the account of Mycale gives the impression of being pro-Athenian. It is true that both Samians and Milesians are also given considerable credit, but that is secondary.

[187] Cf. *Samian Stories* 321.   [188] Above, note 146.   [189] Above, Ch. III, 144-47.

arrangement of the battles with respect to one another, pragmatic action is carried almost entirely through the events at sea. The connections of the land battles are secondary and therefore less fully developed. At the end of the work, we are left with the Athenian navy in Asia Minor. Symbolic action is infinitely more important, both on land and on sea, than pragmatic action, and this has led to a series of static, or near-static pictures, which overshadow, in the reader's mind, the pragmatic movement. Just as at Marathon the picture of the Athenians "on the run" overshadows the strategy of the weakened center, so at Thermopylae the decision of Leonidas is central, with its contrast to the betrayal by Ephialtes. At Artemisium, the storms and the stories of Themistocles' common sense overshadow the sea maneuvers, while at Salamis, the decisions of Themistocles and the competitive ramming of ships have the same central function. At Plataea and Mycale, the central motifs concern, as we have seen, the divine. The Herodotean battle description is both more and less than a proper military account.[190] Its real importance lies in its contribution to our understanding of the Persian defeat and the Greek victory. These battle accounts, like everything else in Herodotus, are what Karl Reinhardt has called significant "gestures," or they are like visible "monuments," from which one may glean significant meaning.[191]

The human element in the battles is primarily a delineation of the divergent traits of Greek regional character, especially the contrast between Athens and Sparta, and the self-destruction of the Persians through folly and bad strategy. The battles give a vivid picture of the conflicts between Greek patriotism and medism, between Panhellenism and self-interest. On the Persian side we are left with the picture of Xerxes destroying members of his own family, and with the early advice by Cyrus to remain simple and strong, an admonition which we feel has not been heeded.[192] In the battle description we see both the decrease of Persian and the growth of Athenian power, and we witness thereby the end of a period in history. Especially during the battle of Plataea, a strong contrast is drawn between Greeks and barbarians.

If the battles thus show the divisiveness of human affairs, these differences are unified, and in a sense overcome, by the emphasis

---

[190] *Action* 18.   [191] Cf. above, 239. *Ergon* 261-75.
[192] Cf. Cambyses, above, Ch. III, 97, and Xerxes, above, Ch. IV, 177.

on the divine. Both Herodotus' own "divine," which is in accordance with "that which has to be," and the local Greek gods, who are taking vengeance on the Persians for specific crimes, give the Greeks the final push, without which they could not have won. At Artemisium the gods saved the Greek fleet, and at Plataea and Mycale they concluded the victories by driving out the remnants of the Persians and completing the liberation of Europe. Framed by these divine actions, Athenian courage and cleverness won the battle of Salamis, and thus the Athenians were almost the equal of the gods in repelling the invader:

> Now if one were to say that the Athenians had been the saviors of Greece, he would not miss the truth: for to whichever side they turned, that side was bound to go down on the scales. By choosing for Greece to be free, they were the ones who awoke all the rest of the Greeks (so far as these did not medize) and next to the gods repelled the Great King (7.139.5).[193]

[193] On this passage, see above, Ch. V, 217-18; *Action* 37; and *Tat und Geschichte* 529, note 59.

Conclusion

HISTORY AND THE ORDER OF NATURE

The work of Herodotus was not produced in a single effort like a modern book, and when its author died it remained somewhat unfinished: yet the study of its structure has shown that it is a highly organized and complex work of art—a single *logos* that has the form of a chain and embodies the single conception of the rise and fall of Asiatic power as the enemy and attacker of the Greeks. A survey of the individual units has further demonstrated the connections of shorter *logoi* with the overall plan, according to the principle of attachment at single points. The arrangement of the Greek *logoi* in particular proves that the Greeks had the function of causing a change of fortune (*metabolê*) in the process of Asiatic history. The work thus encompasses an entire period of Eastern history, a period of expansion, the beginning and end of which were determined by contact with the Greeks. Internally, Eastern history has as its guiding idea the progressive unification of the world under despotic rule: first, Western Asia was unified by the Lydian kings, while Eastern Asia fell under the Medes; then Cyrus combined these two parts, and Cambyses added Egypt (a country *sui generis* on the border of Asia and Africa); finally, Darius was the first to overstep the boundary between Asia and Europe. The Persian aspirations for world domination, however, had only very limited success: Cambyses was foiled on the way to Ethiopia, the troops of Aryandes accomplished little in Africa, and the Scythian Campaign was the first of a series of Persian failures in Europe which reduced Asiatic power once more to Asia and Egypt. The work assumes the existence of a natural order by which Europe and Asia are equal and separate, and it deals with a period which constitutes a disturbance of that order by the unlimited expansionism of the Persians. Another unifying idea of Persian history is the two-generation cycle, by which two pairs, each consisting of a great father and an inferior son, reinforce the understanding of the futility of despotic rule. Thus Cambyses foreshadows Xerxes, but the whole course of absolutism is

306

already summed up in the figure of Croesus. The sequence of *logoi* within the single *logos* of the *Histories* results from a highly articulated total conception of a particular period of world history.

This special history exemplifies the overall pattern of history as such. The organization of the work is based on a simple sequence of action and reaction, by which the cumulative weight of Asiatic activities is crushed in the five-battle complex of Xerxes' invasion, a reaction foreshadowed by the three preceding *logoi* that show Greek initiative and by the multiple failures of earlier Asiatic kings. The result of such counteraction is a balance of world forces achieved through *metabolé*, thus assuring the continuity and indeed the permanence of history. The pattern of rise and fall is tragic only when we confine our point of view to the individual agents of historical action. When we look at the overall pattern, the tragic fate of states and individuals is seen to be a mechanism for the perpetuation of world order. The pattern of such order is neither theological nor moral, but existential. Thus Herodotus establishes the individuality of the great Eastern kings simply by developing in each case a particular aspect of the overall cycle of rise and fall. Croesus' wealth, Cyrus' apparent divinity, Cambyses' legitimacy, Darius' unlimited power, Xerxes' "chosen necessity" at the end of a long development—these features are the causes both of their successes and of their failures. The contrary effects of these elements in the pattern of a king's life are Herodotean applications of the principle of the identity of opposites, and as causative factors of individuation within the pattern of rise and fall they guarantee the unity as well as the diversity of history. Unity and diversity are applied by Herodotus to the East and the West respectively (although strictly speaking each is applicable to both regions), so that the behavior of Eastern monarchs is explained by excessive unification, while European strength is due to the pattern of disunity and strife. Two forms of strife (war and peaceful competition) go far toward explaining the victories in the Persian Wars. In the world as a whole, unity and diversity balance each other, causing ever-recurring irregular patterns of doing and suffering. It is an important Herodotean axiom that despite its vicissitudes human history has remained constant since its inception, and that it is liable neither to overall progress, nor to cataclysmic destruction.

In this study there has been little occasion to discuss many of the ideas commonly associated with Herodotus: ideas of a religious nature, such as the envy of the gods, or ideas that reflect the moral order and by which history teaches the value of moderation. We have also neglected certain parts of the narrative, such as the great moral discourses and parables, and in particular the ethnographic *logoi*. It appears that the study of structure has the effect of isolating the purely historiographical aspects of the work, together with their philosophical foundations, to the detriment of its anthropological, geographical, ethnographic, and generally anecdotal features. While this isolation undoubtedly limits the understanding of Herodotus, yet it is significant that moral, religious, and anthropological ideas appear chiefly in the internal structure of individual *logoi*, whose external structure reveals the pattern of history. It should not be necessary to state that Herodotus is not principally a moralist, a theologian, or an anthropologist, but a historian, if by history we understand a way of comprehending the world of men, and not mere chronicle. Yet Herodotus is often thought of as a storyteller with a religious, moral, and folkloristic bias. It is true, of course, that such elements exist in his work, and the question arises how they are to be assessed in relation to the pattern of history.

Max Pohlenz has rightly stressed the frequency of actual and implied moral judgments in Herodotus.[1] It is not too much to say that all human actions are liable to such judgments, and that the reader must supply them where they are not expressly given. Herodotean morality is based throughout on conventional standards of the Greek city state and therefore need not be constantly reaffirmed by the historian. Characteristically, the word *aretê*, when applied to humans, almost always means military valor, or deed, as it does e.g. in the famous words spoken by Demaratus before Xerxes:

> "In Greece, poverty has always been indigenous, while *aretê* has been acquired, fashioned by skilled practice (*sophiê*) and strong law (*nomos*); by the use of which (valor) Greece wards off both poverty and despotism." (7.102.1)

It is also noteworthy that Herodotus in this passage speaks of military valor as an acquired characteristic, whereas elsewhere

[1] Pohlenz, *Herodot* 91 ff.

he mentions it as an inborn faculty.[2] He is thus not affected by the sophistic problem of inborn vs. acquired *aretê*, but in accepting both ideas as conventionally valid, he combines aristocratic and middle-class morality. In two places *aretê* is used in a non-military sense, but again in the conventional sense of political excellence.[3] Herodotus is far removed from the relativism of Thucydides, to whom *aretê* is largely a question of appearance, i.e. of the reputation of excellence.[4] In Herodotus, *aretê* is an objective characteristic of men.

Nevertheless, since Herodotus did not overburden his work with moral judgments, they appear to be marginal to the historical narrative. We may then ask, what is the function of *aretê* with respect to historical action? Sometimes *aretê* is cited for dramatic effect as conspicuous in unsuccessful actions, notably at Thermopylae (cf. 7.225.1). More significant is the fact that *aretê* is connected with defense rather than attack throughout the accounts of the Persian Wars. This negative aspect of noble actions shows that the historical agent as such is presumptuous and blind, as I have argued elsewhere. At the same time, nearly all the actions in Herodotus' work (with but few exceptions, as for example the attack on the run at Marathon, and the Athenians' refusal to take the command of the Panhellenic League) are morally ambiguous, a fact which becomes particularly clear in the behavior of the Greeks before and during the battle of Salamis.[5] The historical function of *aretê* is therefore ambivalent, and it can lead either to success or to failure. Here we discern yet another application of the principle of the coincidence of opposites.

Even stronger is the delineation of the negative character of the virtue of moderation, which is often considered the virtue most heavily stressed by Herodotus. However, it should give pause for

---

[2] *Aretê* in the military sense, mainly of land fighting, occurs fourteen times; add two occurrences in the plural (deeds of valor). Also related is the use, once only (8.26.3), for athletic contests at Olympia. See Powell, *Lexicon*, s.v. ἀρετή.

[3] 3.82.3: in an oligarchy many practice *aretê*, and thus they come into conflict (speech of Darius in the Debate on Government). 7.237.2: Xerxes, speaking of envy among fellow citizens, says that a citizen will not give honest advice unless he has progressed far in *aretê*, which is rare. (Aristeides would be an example of the kind of person Xerxes has in mind.) These two passages speak of civic virtue, and not, as Powell, *Lexicon*, thinks, of moral goodness.

[4] Cf. Thuc. 1.33.2; this meaning derives from the more general meaning of "civic service"; cf. L. Pearson, *CP* 52 (1957) 242, note 7.

[5] Cf. *Action* 39-40.

thought that Herodotus uses *sôphrosynê* and related terms only rarely, preferring instead a number of more neutral circumlocutions.[6] The idea of moderation is most prominent in the famous warnings of Solon, Amasis, and Artabanus, since it is the fundamental idea in advice given by warners.[7] In these scenes it takes the form of asking the king to "hold back," showing thereby its purely negative character, on which in turn its dramatic function is based.[8] Thus the idea of moderation is used in a special form suitable for a historical context.

Such particular application of moral concepts is characteristic of all moral judgments. Hence, in addition to their absolute value we must also consider them with regard to their historical function. It is this function which is always ambivalent, since success and failure do not depend on morality. We have seen that the idea of justice was detrimental to the growth of Sparta, whereas Athenian injustice was advantageous to the Athenians.[9] Similarly, the cycle of *hybris—koros—atê* (in which destruction overcomes the wrongdoer through his own folly) is used in Herodotus only in an indirect manner, being applied as a historical rather than a moral pattern, for it has the function of furthering growth and decay.[10] Of the terms comprising this famous cycle Herodotus uses only *hybris* with any frequency, since it implies a moral judgment on all aggressive action. The word is of frequent occurrence in speeches and in reasoning about unjust acts; it is best analyzed in the Debate on Government.[11] Its function in history is closely connected with the roles of injustice and vengeance, as in the following passage, in which Herodotus speaks for himself:

> The Corinthians also participated in the (Spartan) expedition against Samos, so as to make it possible, and that eagerly; for an insult (*hybrisma*) had been inflicted on them as well (as on

[6] Powell, *Lexicon*, s.vv. σωφρονέω and σώφρων.
[7] Hdt. 1.32; 3.40; 7.10 and 16; 46 ff.
[8] *Action* 37 ff.; above, Ch. V, note 90.
[9] See above, Ch. V, 213.
[10] The cycle is presupposed in the Croesus *Logos*, but only *atê* appears prominently, in the Atys story. See above, Ch. IV, 158. *Koros* is found only in the oracle 8.77.1 (on which see above, Ch. VI, 278-79), where something like this cycle is alluded to.
[11] 3.81.1 and ff. *Hybris* occurs nine times in speeches, twice in quoted poetry (5.77.4 and 8.77.1), and four times in narrative. Interesting is a parallel from nature, where Cyrus' horse and the river Gyndes commit acts of *hybris* against each other (1.189.1-2). περιυβρίζειν is used three times in speeches and four times in reasoning.

the Spartans) by the Samians, in the generation before this campaign and at the same time as the (aforementioned) seizure of the mixing bowl. (3.48.1)

However, as we read on to find out the nature of the insult, we discover that it was the Corinthians (i.e. their tyrant Periander) rather than the Samians who were in the wrong. Herodotus is not interested in the justice of the case, but only in its historical effect, for he later declares that it was really the present situation rather than the old grudge in itself which made the Corinthians attack the Samians, using the old wrong as a pretext (3.49.1-2).

The world of the gods is more important in the work than morality, since they are, in Greek thought, the guarantors of the workings of nature, as well as the objective correlatives to the functioning of civilization. In Homer and tragedy the world of the gods duplicates on a higher plane the world of men, but in Herodotus it is seen from a greater distance and appears more mysterious. Herodotus treats religion on two levels: in his own belief he rationalizes the gods into a semi-abstract "divine," but at the same time he gives much scope to popular traditions with their world of specific divinities and religious practices.[12] Concerning the latter, Herodotus develops, by means of derivations and comparisons, a species of history of religion, according to which the Egyptians, as practically the first of men, and blessed with divine kings in their first period of existence (2.144), discovered the nature of individual gods and transmitted them to the Pelasgians, who originally had possessed only a generalized conception of the divine (2.52.1). From the Pelasgians the Greeks later got their gods, who were finally systematized by Homer and Hesiod (2.53). Thus religious tradition is of absolute antiquity, since it goes back to the beginnings of mankind, and it has great authority. At the same time, religious beliefs and practices are of considerable diversity, and by comparison (*synkrisis*) the historian brings this diversity to the surface. Hence not all religious belief can be literally true.

Of great importance, as Pohlenz has stressed, is Herodotus'

[12] Above, Ch. VI, 299. On Herodotus' religion, see Pohlenz, *Herodot* 96 ff.; Daniels, *Rel.-hist. Studie*; M. P. Nilsson, *Geschichte der griechischen Religion* 1 [2] (Munich 1955) 760; I. M. Linforth, "Named and Unnamed Gods in Herodotus," *CalCP* 9, No. 7 (1928) 218 ff.; W. Pötscher, "Götter und Gottheit bei Herodot," *WS* 71 (1958) 5-29.

statement that the Pelasgians, while lacking names for individual gods, named them all collectively *theoi*,

> from the fact that (the gods) had arranged all affairs in order (*kosmôi thentes*) and also controlled all divisions (of the world). (2.52.1)[13]

The Pelasgians had perceived a unity of religious forces that Herodotus also detected behind divergent traditions. The importance of the divine in Herodotus is precisely that it guarantees the world order. Therefore the majority of the historical actions in Herodotus are accompanied by some kind of divine causation, which parallels human motivation, but on a higher plane.[14] It would have been in the manner of Greek popular tradition to name specific divinities as causal agents, but Herodotus prefers to hide these (he was no doubt convinced that in each case specific divinities were responsible) under the common abstraction "the divine," or even under phrases that merely point to the existence of a "necessity," without always directly involving the notion of the divine. The reason for this treatment of religious causation is Herodotus' overriding concern for pattern as such. History develops in accordance with principles of order because all nature is ordered by the divine. With regard to the order in the animal kingdom Herodotus states the idea precisely:

> And in some way divine providence, as is natural since it is intelligent (*sophê*), has rendered all cowardly and edible (animals) fertile, in order that they might not become extinct, though eaten, but fierce and harmful (animals) it has rendered unprolific. (3.108.2)

The main concern of the divine is the maintenance of balance;

---

[13] Pohlenz, *Herodot* 100 ff.

[14] *Action* 36; *Causation* 254 ff. (metaphysical causation). On the dual plane, see recently, H. D. F. Kitto, *Form and Meaning in Drama* (London 1956) 71 ff. Pohlenz, *Herodot* 96 ff., has shown that individual divinities occupy a secondary position for Herodotus, and that his belief in "the divine" shows remarkable similarities to the Pelasgian conception of religion (Hdt. 2.52; Pohlenz, *Herodot* 100 f.). Against this theory, Daniels, *Rel.-hist. Studie*, urges that Herodotus is a polytheist (who nevertheless believes in a single moral will of the gods). It seems to me that both views are correct in the sense that Herodotus' belief in "the divine" does not exclude his conventional belief in religious traditions, although he does not believe in such traditions fully, nor blindly. At the same time, the dramatic use of religious stories has a function quite separate from the author's faith, in that it raises the level of the action in the last battles above the rationally comprehensible.

Herodotus has the phrase *theôn ta isa nemontôn* probably from contemporary epigrams.[15] Such balance appears everywhere in nature and therefore also in history; the historian need not cite specific gods, because all gods have the function of preserving it.

Another function of the divine is the function of separation, without which equalization cannot exist. This distributive function of the divine is called by Herodotus, with a popular phrase, "envy" (*phthonos tou theiou*). He has been much ridiculed for this, but what matters here is not the origin of this primitive notion, but its importance for the work. In the warnings of Solon, Amasis, and Artabanus, and in a speech by Themistocles, the notion of divine envy is applied to great kings and tyrants.[16] Only once does Herodotus himself mention a similar concept. Pheretime, queen mother of Cyrene, died a horrible death as punishment for the cruel vengeance she had taken on the citizens of Barca,

> for men's excessive acts of vengeance are abhorred (*epiphthonoi*) by the gods. (4.205)

The emphasis here is on the word "excessive": for Pheretime's punishment was a divine reaction equally excessive (she was eaten alive by worms). The passage guarantees, if this is felt to be necessary, that the great advisers do indeed propound a Herodotean idea. Through *phthonos* the divine preserves first of all the boundary between men and gods; but it also preserves the order of society by preventing conquest and absolute rule.

Envy has a similar function when exercised between men, so that a strict parallel can be drawn between divine and human envy. Otanes in the Debate on Government (3.80.3) states that envy is inborn in men, and that tyrants feel it themselves (3.80.4); they must in turn expect it from others (Periander to his son, 3.52.5).[17] In one of the Demaratus conversations, envy is defined as the basic relation between citizens of the Greek *polis* (7.236.1 and 237.2). The notion that through envy the citizens of a free society prevent the rise of despotism is in fact current in fifth-century

[15] See above, Ch. VI, note 45.

[16] Hdt. 1.32.1; 3.40.2; 7.10e; 46.4; 8.109.3. On the envy of the gods, see e.g. Meyer, *Forschungen* 261, note 1 (=Marg, *Herodot* 20, note 6); Pötscher, *op. cit.* (above, note 12) 23 ff.; K. Nawratil, *Philol. Woch.* 60 (1940) 125-26.

[17] Cf. Fränkel, *Stileigenheit* 67, note 3. The idea is common in Pindar.

political thought,[18] but to Herodotus envy is rather a sign
of that disunity which, as an aspect of diversity in the historical
process, is so essential to his political philosophy. Therefore he
applies it to international relations also. After the battle of Salamis
the Greeks made an effort to award prizes, but they could not
decide who was the best:

> But although the Greeks did not want to decide this matter
> because of envy, and returned without a decision each to his
> own country, nevertheless Themistocles was renowned and
> thought of as by far the wisest Greek in all of Greece. (8.124.1)

There follows the story of Timodemus of Athens and his jealousy
of Themistocles, drawing a perfect parallel between *phthonos* in
international relations and in internal city life (8.125.1).[19]

It is only natural that Herodotus' theory of history should be
in closer agreement with his own notion of "the divine" than
with the manifold legends of gods and heroes told in his work. If
the divine is responsible for maintaining the overall pattern of
history, the local gods (much like Homeric divinities) show great
partiality in their interference. Greek gods defend Greece,
Egyptian gods care for Egypt, and Persian divinities feel a concern
for their country.[20] Only when the order of nature as a whole is
disturbed do the gods act in concert, thereby becoming Herodotus'
"divine." The principal appearance of the local Greek gods is in
the five battles of Xerxes' invasion, in which, as we have seen,
specific divine actions frame the Athenian achievement at
Salamis.[21] Such divine defense of one's own territory is in harmony
with a world order which is based on such diversity.

If we now turn to the natural world, we find that Herodotus
shows an interest in a number of subjects which we today no
longer associate with history in the strict sense. Jacoby felt so

[18] See R. Hirzel, *Themis, Dike und Verwandtes* (Leipzig 1907) 299 ff.; H. Ryffel,
Metabolē Politeiōn (Diss. Bern 1949) 69 and 82; Lang, *Biogr. Patterns* 76 ff.; H. M.
Martin, Jr., *TAPA* 92 (1961) 333.

[19] For the latter story, see above, Ch. VI, note 140. Human envy as a direct
motivation of historical action seems to be rare, but cf. 6.137.2; 6.61.1; 3.146.1.

[20] The Persian divinities are mainly phenomena of nature: see 1.131.1 f.; 7.37.2,
where the Magi declare that the moon prophesies for the Persians, as the sun does for
the Greeks. On the different ethnic gods, see I. M. Linforth, "Greek Gods and
Foreign Gods in Herodotus," *CalCP* 9, No. 1 (1928) 1 ff., and R. Lattimore, "Herodotus
and the Names of Egyptian Gods," *CP* 34 (1939) 357-65.

[21] Above, Ch. VI, 305.

strongly that the combination of ethnography and history in Herodotus is unique that he tried to account for it by the theory of the author's development from anthropologist to historian.[22] However, it must be remembered that to Herodotus *historiē* means investigation, irrespective of subject matter. The "human events" and "great and marvelous deeds of Greeks and barbarians" of the proem are thus not the only subject of his investigations. Man is a part of the world as a whole and cannot be understood without inquiry into the world as it affects him. This (rather than biographical accident) is the real reason for the inclusion of ethnography and geography in the work. Put another way, investigation can be by autopsy and by oral report. In some places Herodotus goes so far as to suggest that visual investigation is superior to oral reporting—a theory that would put geography before history.[23] No better proof can be found for the all-embracing conception of *historiē* in Herodotus.

The basic phenomenon to be observed by such broad investigation is the analogical structure of the world, by which the same laws are seen to govern its three main branches: animal kingdom, world geography, and peoples. (They also govern, as we have seen, the world of the gods.) Herodotus is much interested in animals, which he treats, in the manner of the Greek fable, as analogues to men. The winged snakes of Arabia, for example, keep attacking Egypt, but the ibis stands guard at the border (2.75.3). The winged snake kills its mother, in imitation of Orestes, to take vengeance for the murder of its father (3.109.2). The fabulous phoenix buries its father in an elaborate ceremony (2.73.4: the story is from Hecataeus). The female camel runs fast, "remembering the children she has left behind" (3.105.2). Between horses and camels there exists a natural hostility (1.80.4); a war between snakes and horses prophesied the war of Cyrus and Croesus (1.78).

The geographical picture of the world in Herodotus is based on that developed by Anaximander and Hecataeus, but it also shows important differences. Its outstanding traditional feature is the schematization of parts. Herodotus knows of the conventional view, according to which the river Ocean runs around a circular flat earth (4.8), and of the division of the world into three

---

[22] Jacoby, *RE* Suppl. 2.352 ff.
[23] Cf. the inner proemia of Book 2, Ch. II, 64-65.

continents, with Africa and Asia together of a size equal to that of Europe.[24] He knows that rivers are taken as the boundaries of continents, as he shows in arguing against the Nile as the boundary of Asia and Africa (2.16.2). His characteristic reaction to this world picture is polemic: he corrects it by empirical observation. To put the matter in the most general terms, he believes that the world is much more irregular than had been assumed by his predecessors. He also tries to combine the popular two-continent conception (according to which Africa is a part of Asia) with the scientific three-continent theory.[25] One result of this curious conflation is the description of the shape of Asia as containing two "peninsulas" (*aktai*), i.e. on the one hand Asia Minor, and on the other Arabia, Egypt, and Africa thrown together (4.37 ff.). Europe he considers to be much larger than Asia and Africa (4.36.2 and 42.1), and he is driven thereby to the famous polemic against map-makers and their artificial symmetry, cited in Chapter II.[26] However, the idea of a balanced symmetry is not by any means absent from his picture of the world, as he shows clearly by his repeated comparisons of Danube and Nile, both of which he thinks run from West to East, and then South and North respectively, so that their mouths come to lie directly opposite each other.[27] He admits a similar symmetry for the seasons in the center and at the ends of the world.[28] The concept of rivers as boundaries is of fundamental importance for his whole work, and he transfers this "river motif" (which has been mentioned repeatedly in this study) even to the Hellespont as the boundary between Asia and Europe. Thus the difference between Hecataeus and Herodotus is not merely empirical (in that Herodotus was able to observe the absence of balance in many cases), but also metaphysical, in that he believes not in an open balance in

[24] J. T. Wheeler, *The Geography of Herodotus* (London 1854) 12 ff. E. H. Bunbury, *A History of Ancient Geography* (1883; repr. New York 1960) 1.145 ff. H. F. Tozer, *A History of Ancient Geography*[2], ed. by M. Cary (Cambridge 1935) 57-97 (the fullest account). J. O. Thomson, *History of Ancient Geography* (1948) 61 and 97 ff. C. van Paassen, *The Classical Tradition of Geography* (Groningen 1957), esp. 117 ff. F. Gisinger *RE* Suppl. 4.567 ff. (1924). See also Trüdinger, *Studien* 9. Cf. Hdt. 4.42.1 and 2.16.1.
[25] On the popular theory, see Pohlenz, *Herodot* 203 ff.
[26] Above, Ch. II, 65.
[27] Hdt. 2.26.2; 33.2-34; 4.50.1. On the balance between theory and empiricism in Herodotus, see also K. von Fritz, "Herodotus and the Growth of Greek Historiography," *TAPA* 67 (1936) 326-27.
[28] Hdt. 3.106.1 and 116.3: cited above, Ch. II, 54.

nature, but in a hidden equality of certain features only, an equality more difficult to observe, but not therefore less fundamental than the Hecataean.

This geographical picture is connected with the historical account by an "anthropocentric" interpretation of geography similar to, but more rational than, that observed for the animal kingdom. The fact that it never rains in Egypt caused the disaster of Cambyses' army on the march against Zeus Ammon (3.26.3). The unknown and unlimited nature of Northern Europe, to which Herodotus alludes repeatedly (3.115-16; 4.45), brought about Darius' failure in Scythia. The poverty of Greece (7.102.1) inflicted great harm upon Xerxes (8.115), for his army drank the rivers dry (7.21.1, etc.), and both land and sea were his enemies (Artabanus, 7.49). In several instances Herodotus directly confronts man and nature, as when Darius views the Pontus, or Xerxes the Hellespont and the valley of Thessaly.[29] In such cases, nature furnishes the yardstick by which to measure man.

The importance of the ethnographic *logoi* in the work is already adumbrated in the proem, where we find a number of stories implying travel over the known world. Phoenicians are seen going to Egypt and to Greece, Io is abducted to Egypt, Greeks (i.e. Cretans) travel to Tyre, where they steal Europa, and to Colchis to abduct Medea. Finally Paris traveled to Sparta for the rape of Helen, and the Greeks went to fight before Troy. Io and Medea are famous travelers—the latter founded the race of the Medes (7.62.1). Europa gave her name to a continent. Egypt is particularly prominent in the proem, especially if it is recalled that according to a version accepted by Herodotus Helen also went there (2.112-20).[30] This treatment of geography in the proem would suggest that Herodotus thought of geographic and ethnographic breadth as a necessary element in his work, and that Egypt in particular was to play a major role. But the order of appearance of individual nations in the work was determined by the principle of attachment to an aggressive war, and thus allowed for choice only where several actions against a single country could be recorded. (In that case Herodotus chose the

[29] Darius: see above, Ch. IV, note 81. Xerxes: Hdt. 7.45 and 130.

[30] I am roughly following a suggestion made to me in a letter by Miss E. T. H. Brann.

first occasion, as he did for Babylon and Egypt.) [31] Nevertheless the ethnographic coverage in the work is well-nigh complete, since the Persians and other Eastern powers attacked "all nations"; among these peoples we must count the Greeks with their "ethnographic" *logoi*.[32] In addition, the Lydians and the Persians have their own ethnographic *logoi*. The sequence of the major ethnographic sections (omitting the main body of the Greek material, which is more properly historical) is as follows:

1.56-58:	Origins of Greece: Pelasgians and Dorians.
1.93-94:	Lydia: marvels; *nomoi*; settlement of Etruria.
(1.101:	Median tribes; 110.2: country.)
1.131-40:	Persian customs.
1.142-51:	Ionians, Dorians, Aeolians.
1.171-73:	Carians, Caunians, Lycians.
1.178-87:	Assyrian *Logos* I: Babylon; Queen Nitocris.
1.192-200:	Assyrian *Logos* II: country; marvel; dress; *nomoi*.
1.201-203:	Massagetan *Logos* I: country.
1.215-16:	Massagetan *Logos* II: dress, *nomoi*.
2.2-182:	Egyptian *Logos*: country; *nomoi*; history.
(3.20:	Ethiopians: *nomoi*.)
3.98-101:	Indians.
4.5-82:	Scythian *Logos*: origins; country; *nomoi*.
4.94-96:	The Getae.
4.99-101:	The shape of Scythia.
4.103-17:	The neighbors of the Scythians.
4.145-67:	History of Cyrene.
4.168-99:	Libyan *Logos*.
5.3-10:	Thracian *Logos*.
(5.16.2-4:	Paeonians).
6.56-60:	Spartan kings.[33]

This list, for the majority of items, is at the same time a survey of Persian attempts at conquest: the several regions, with the

[31] For Ionia the second time, but he does not really describe the first—i.e. the Lydian—conquest of Ionia in a *logos*.

[32] See above, Ch. I, 34-35.

[33] The list omits numerous small ethnographic notations worked into the main narrative; these can easily be found, for the most part, in the outline of Herodotus given by Jacoby *RE* Suppl. 2.283 ff. The omission of the Greek *logoi* here gives the false impression that after 5.16 Herodotus lost interest in ethnography. But 8.73 is an example of the geographic style in the later parts of the work, and for this there exist many parallels.

nations possessing different customs, constitute so many obstacles to world domination, and these obstacles are based on the natural order.

Because of the traditional nature of the topics of ethnographic writing that Herodotus took over, the *logoi* show great similarity. The country is always described with regard to its usefulness to man. Thus Ionia has the finest seasons, Babylonia furnishes one third of the wealth of Persia, the Massagetae are protected by the Araxes river, the Nile gives sustenance to the Egyptians, the plains protect the Scythians from invasion. Customs of various peoples are compared throughout with those of others, and especially with Greek customs. Thus Lydian customs agree with Greek, the Persians have acquired many foreign customs in addition to their own, the Ionians have separated out from other Greeks and are (like the Pelasgians) weak, the Egyptians use customs opposed to the rest of mankind (2.35.2), as do also the Ethiopians (3.20.2). The Scythians abhor all foreign customs, especially the Greek (4.76.1), but other nations have adopted those of their neighbors (4.168.1). *Nomos* establishes the identity of a people, but it is not therefore unchangeable: the Carians once lived on the Aegean islands and were called Leleges (1.171), just as the Athenians were originally Pelasgians (1.57.3) and had a number of different names in the course of their history (8.44.2). Change of specific customs (*metabolê*) is of particular interest to Herodotus.[34] But on the whole, *nomos* resists change and thus is an obstacle to foreign conquest. This idea is fully developed in the account of Cambyses' conquest of Egypt.[35]

The Herodotean concept of custom (*nomos*) deserves a fuller investigation than can be presented here. For it is in the analysis of this term that ethnography can be shown to be closely integrated with history. In several places Herodotus emphasizes the ruling character of *nomos* as "king" or "master" (3.38.4 and 7.104.4), i.e. *nomos* preserves ethnic identity. At the same time, *nomos* is the cause of ethnic independence: thus the Scythians fight for the tombs of their fathers (4.127.2-3), and the Athenians for the common customs of the Greeks (*êthea homotropa*: 8.144.2). Hence *nomos* has an important *historical* function, for two reasons. First,

[34] E.g. Spartans and Argives: 1.82.7-8; Lydians after the defeat by Cyrus: 1.155. Cf. Ch. IV, 150.

[35] Above, Ch. III, 97.

as a product of human intelligence *nomos* provides man with the means of solving problems put by his environment. This aspect of *nomos* is emphasized whenever Herodotus judges customs for the practical intelligence (*sophiē*) they embody. Thus the "cleverest" Babylonian *nomos* was one by which marriageable girls were auctioned off, with the proceeds of the handsome going as dowries for the ugly, a custom which, incidentally, no longer obtains, since after the Persian conquest the Babylonians were impoverished; they consequently "invented" as a substitute the prostitution of unmarried daughters (1.196). The cleverest Scythian custom is their nomadic life, which enables them, by drawing advantage from the nature of their country, to escape any attacker (4.46.2).[36] Both stories show *nomos* connected with history: the Babylonian *nomos* became the victim of conquest, while the Scythian saved its nation.

The second aspect of custom important in this context is its diversity. Darius once made a comparison of *nomoi* by asking some Greeks whether they would be willing to eat their dead fathers. When they answered that no amount of money would make them do this, he asked the Callatian Indians (who eat their parents) for how much money they would bury theirs; the Indians were equally shocked (3.38.3-4). This story is prefaced by the following statement:

> For if someone were to give the choice to all men, telling them to select the best *nomoi* from the totality of *nomoi*, they would look thoroughly and then choose their own. Thus each (people) thinks of its own *nomoi* as by far the best. (3.38.1)

The statement shows that Herodotus, in stressing the arbitrary diversity of individual customs, does not thereby deny the objective validity of Custom as such. The notion of a market place in which all goods are spread out, so that a person can make a rational and advantageous choice, has a long history in ancient thought (its most famous use is in the myth of Er in Plato's *Republic*), and Herodotus uses it again in another place:

> But I know this much, that if all men were to bring their own misdeeds into one place, desiring to exchange them with their

---

[36] This is a *nomos*, cf. 4.59.1. σοφίη in Herodotus usually means "skill," "cleverness," or "practical intelligence," and has little, if anything, to do with theoretical or moral "wisdom"; even Solon's σοφίη is eminently practical and empirical: cf. 1.30.2, etc. Of theoretical knowledge, only 2.20.1 and 2.49.2.

neighbors, after examining their neighbors' misdeeds they would gladly carry back what they had brought in. (7.152.2)[37]

Thus the diversity of customs is due to the rational choice of the peoples involved, and while there is an objective standard of comparison by which one can "inspect" them, the ultimate decision shows that men are bound by their *nomoi*. Hence we find in the world a polarity of customs that corresponds to polarity of geographical regions and of historical forces.[38] It is clear that autonomy and physical separation are the best safeguards for the maintainance of this diversity of *nomos*.

However, the principle of the identity of opposites can also be illustrated in the concept of *nomos*. For while its effect is primarily in harmony with world order, there are customs which have a destructive effect upon the peoples that hold them, and on other peoples as well. Dr. J. A. S. Evans has recently pointed out the importance of two passages in which the consistent expansionism of the Persians is called their *nomos*.[39] In the first, Xerxes justifies his planned attack on Greece before the Persian Council:

"Persians, it is not I myself who will introduce the establishment of this *nomos* among you, but I shall use it as it has been transmitted. For as I hear from my elders, we have never yet stood

---

[37] In this passage, κακά are interpreted by Herodotus as *misdeeds* rather than as *evils*, which was no doubt the original meaning of the word in the story. Such adaptation is similar to that of the meaning of *nomos* ("custom," rather than "law") in the quotation from Pindar that follows the Darius story cited just previously in the text, 3.38.4 (cf. Ch. III, note 57). The opposite change in the meaning of κακόν occurs in 7.203.2, where it should mean *evil*, but is interpreted by Herodotus as *misfortune*; cf. H. Ryffel, *op. cit.* (above, note 18) Appendix 5; Soph. *Electra* 1485, with Jebb's comment. Hdt. 7.152 is interpreted differently by Macan, *VII-IX, ad loc.* Cf. also H. Diller in *Fondation Hardt: Entretiens sur l'antiquité classique* 8 (1962) 65, note 1. For the idea of an exchange of goods, which has a long subsequent history as the idea of an exchange of lives, see *Dissoi Logoi*, Chs. 18 and 26 (Diels-Kranz[8], 2.409); Plato, *Rep.* 10, the myth of Er (from Plato on, a divinity arranges the exchange); Menander, *Theophoroumenoi*, fr. 1 Koerte (I owe this reference to Dr. Henry Wood); Horace, *Sat.* 1.1.16 (with the comments of Kiessling-Heinze); and, for other occurrences, J. C. F. Baehr, *Herodoti Halicarnassensis Musae*[2] 3 (Leipzig 1859) 671 f. (on Hdt. 7.152). The earliest occurrence of the motif is perhaps Pindar, fr. 188 Turyn. See also F. Heinimann, *Nomos und Physis* (Basel 1945) 80 ff., and, on Hdt. 3.38, Pohlenz, *Herodot* 185 ff. Cf. also L. Woodbury, in *Studies in Honor of Gilbert Norwood* (=*Phoenix*, Suppl. 1 [Toronto 1952]) 29–30 and note 55.

[38] On polarity of *nomoi*, see Schmid-Stählin 1.2.564, note 1. Cf. also A. Dihle, "Herodot und die Sophistik," *Philologus* 106 (1962) 207 ff.

[39] J. A. S. Evans, "The Dream of Xerxes and the 'Nomoi' of the Persians," *CJ* 57 (1961) 109-11.

still, since the time when we took over this rule from the
Medes, when Cyrus overthrew Astyages; but a god leads us
thus . . ." (7.8a.1)

In the other passage, Mardonius at Plataea decides to disregard
the Greek sacrifices that are unfavorable to an attack, and instead
announces that he will cross the Asopus:

> For he thought that his own army was much superior to the
> Greek, and that one should attack as soon as possible . . . and
> forget about the sacrifices of Hegesistratus rather than insisting
> (on obtaining favorable results), but to attack using the Persian
> *nomos*. (9.41.4)

The last passage draws a contrast between the Greek custom of
sacrifices (cf. 9.37.1) and the Persian custom of aggression, proving
that both Mardonius and Xerxes are speaking of a true *nomos*.
This had been established by a free decision of the Persians, under
the guidance of Cyrus the Great, who showed them how to lead
a life of freedom and rule (1.125-26). Yet Xerxes refers it to a
divine agency, since once chosen it has become a necessity.[40]
Human and divine *nomoi* can be identical, as in the story of the
vengeance of Hermotimus:

> "You thought it would escape the gods what you had at that
> time contrived," [says Hermotimus to Panionius before avenging
> himself on him,] "but they, using a just *nomos*, have brought
> you (who had done unholy deeds) into my hands . . ." (8.106.3)

In these three passages *nomos* is an instrument in the workings of
nature, either through vengeance (as in the Hermotimus passage)
or through self-destruction (as in the Persian *nomos* of expansion).
Nomos can be both creative and destructive.[41]

---

[40] Similarly, the Athenians in the Melian dialogue in Thucydides: "For we surmise
about the divine, and we know for certain about men, that they always rule by necessity
of nature that which they conquer; and we have not made this *nomos*, nor are we the
first to use it as existing, but we have taken it over for use and will leave it behind for
ever . . ." (Thuc. 5.105.2). This passage has been compared with Hdt. 7.8a.1 by
Heinimann, *op. cit.* (above, note 37) 167, note 7. Another possible comparison for the
Melian dialogue is with Themistocles' speech at Andros (Hdt. 8.111); cf. M. Gigante,
Nomos Basileus (Naples 1956) 136, note 1 (= Marg, *Herodot* 273, note 13), and above,
Ch. V, note 29.

[41] For the concept of *nomos* in Herodotus, see Ch. III, note 57, and this chapter,
note 39. In particular, cf. H. E. Stier, "Nomos Basileus," *Philologus* 83 (1927-28)
225-58, who makes the important point that the Herodotean conception of *nomos* is
not sophistic; M. Gigante, *Nomos Basileus* (Naples 1956), of which the chapter on

Just as Herodotus uses aspects of certain geographical concepts in his narrative, so he does also with regard to a number of ethnographic concepts. The connection between ethnography and history is therefore much closer in the work than is often assumed. In the Egyptian *Logos* he uses the method of appending a historical section to the sections on country and customs. In the Lydian *Logos* he describes the tomb of Alyattes and the settlement of Etruria. The Assyrian *Logos* as we have it contains in its first part a selection of material on the city of Babylon, but this material is merely a series of historical sketches (1.178-87). Historical notations occur even in *logoi* of peoples who have no history in the proper sense, such as the Scythians (4.1-4; 5 ff.). In the Libyan *Logos* the history of Cyrene is treated on a par with the ethnography of primitive African tribes. Thus there is a gradual transition from true ethnography to historical *logoi*, and it is here that the Greek *logoi* of the work find their place. The historical *logoi* about Athens and Sparta, in turn, have as their introduction some ethnographic remarks on Pelasgians and Dorians (1.56-58). These patent observations do not take into account the numerous ethnographic notes used in historical narrative throughout the work, e.g. in the Persian army list (7.61 ff.) and the Greek naval roster before Salamis (8.42 ff.). The close connection of individual ethnographic *logoi* with the campaign *logoi* to which they belong has been stressed repeatedly in Chapter III. Thus ethnography and history stand side by side in the finished work: the reason is to be found in the importance of basic ethnographic concepts for the understanding of history. [42]

*   *   *

Morality, theology, natural science, and ethnography must be considered in their relations with the historical patterns developed by Herodotus. Their cohesion consists in the occurrence of the same basic notions in all these fields, which together make up the

---

Herodotus is now available in German translation in Marg, *Herodot* 259-81; Trüdinger, *Studien*; Pohlenz, *Herodot* 53 ff. and *passim*; Heinimann, *op. cit.* (above, note 37). K. Gregoriades, "Begriff und Wirklichkeit des Nomos bei den Griechen," *Platon* 13 (1961) 205-31, does not treat Herodotus. Cf. also A. Dihle, *op. cit.* (above, note 38) 207 ff.

[42] On the relation between ethnography and history in Herodotus, see e.g. the remarks by Regenbogen, *Werk* 215 ff. (=Marg, *Herodot* 73 f.), and J. Vogt, "Herodot in Ägypten" in Marg, *Herodot* 412 ff.

world of nature as Herodotus understood it. Balance and separation, polarity and identity of opposites, permanence in change
(*metabolê*) are found everywhere and serve to bind the world
together in ever-recurring patterns. Disturbances of this order
affect only individual members of the chain, not its totality.
However, the Herodotean conception of order differs from earlier
conceptions in that it is hidden behind seeming irregularity. In
this respect, the Herodotean notion of equality (*to ison*) is of great
interest. The items on either side of the equations established by
this term are often of very different size and duration. The small
Greek states equal the Persian Empire not superficially, in size,
but profoundly, because of their function in the historical process.
The idea of function as the main criterion for equality distinguishes
Herodotus from previous thinkers (as it does also Heracleitus and
Sophocles). Therefore traditional ideas found in Herodotus have
a tendency to be reduced to abstractions considered merely in
relation to their effects in the historical process. Vengeance
(*tisis*) is not considered primarily from the moral point of view,
but as a main cause of historical action. Injustice (*adikiê*) is the
basic law of such action seen in isolation, but the overall pattern
is one of justice (*dikê*), which fulfills itself in the interplay of action
and reaction, no matter how irregular this may appear. Still
more important than these ethical notions are other abstract
ideas, given sometimes in neuter form, such as *to ison*, equality, *to
chreôn* or *to dei genesthai*, necessity, *to theion*, divinity. For these
stress more than others the functional aspect of world forces.

Have we the right to borrow from Heracleitus the term *logos* to
describe the hidden rationality of things in Herodotus, and further,
may we call his *logoi*, i.e. the work, an account of such an order?
As regards the first question it would surely be an error to impute
to Herodotus the severity of abstract philosophical thought. He
knew well enough that it is a mistake for a historian to treat his
subject with an excessive amount of theory, and he goes to some
lengths to avoid even the type of theorizing familiar from Thucydides. His concept of *logos* remains on the surface of things, and
his description of the world is phenomenological rather than
analytic. Only modern analysis reveals the hidden order incorporated in the work in a largely unspoken manner.

As to the second question, it is clear that the work is highly
organized, but again in such a way that its order is not im-

mediately apparent. Both in antiquity and in modern times
readers have thought of it as a fascinating conglomeration of
disparate stories, judgments and insights, based on the excitement
of marvel (*thôma*), and on a love of detail for its own sake. We have
tried to show that this impression, while not erroneous, is only
superficially correct. The work can be read as a coherent sequence
of strictly relevant parts. We then find, instead of an uncontrolled
desire to tell stories, an equally strong will to the limitation of
material and form. In the proem, in addition to the ideas of
balance and separation of Asia and Europe, we find Herodotus'
conscious decision to begin the work only with Croesus, thereby
establishing the beginning of a numerical series, which we feel
must have an end. The concepts of action and reaction are
primarily responsible for the orderly sequence of *logoi*, and they
force omissions and subordination upon the narrative; Herodotus
calls this aspect of his work the "necessity of the *logos*."[43] Each
individual unit is further limited in a number of ways. The Greek
material in the Croesus *Logos* and the ethnographic *logoi* in the
accounts of campaigns establish antithetical pictures that offset
the picture of unlimited Eastern power. By the emphasis on the
contrast between its origins and its end, each dynasty is shown to
be limited in duration and in its successes.

While Herodotus, so far as I see, has no very precise vocabulary
for the idea of *limit*, yet the concept is central to his work, for it
explains the functioning of history and also gives him the necessary
control over his material. If the delimitation of a period reaching
from Croesus' first aggression to the removal of the Hellespontine
cables furnishes him with the outer limits of his work, the idea
also appears internally in well-marked stages. It is prefigured in
the Croesus *Logos* in two distinct ways: first Croesus was engaged
only in a limited conquest of Greece (he refused to conquer the
islands and made an alliance with the Spartans), a moderation
later ignored by the Persian kings; secondly he was warned
by Solon of the end (although he disregarded this advice). But
the idea of a necessary limit in history is most clearly expressed
in the spiritual center of the work: the *logoi* about Darius. In the
antithetical picture of a realm which is surrounded by regions
beyond the king's control, and which is enclosed by the Ends of
the World that have greater treasure (but also greater difficulty)

[43] Cf. Pohlenz, *Herodot* 56 ff.

than Darius can command or manage,[44] Herodotus has given us the final judgment on all historical activity. This picture in turn contrasts with the Scythian campaign, where the unknown (*aphanes*) and unlimited nature of the country and customs of the North impose a check on Darius' desire for conquest. Hence the Darius *logoi* furnish the basic theory by which to understand the defeat of Xerxes, with its emphasis on the re-establishment of the separation between continents. Another application of the same principle is found in the history of Sparta, with its limited success at empire, owing to Greek antagonisms; the symbol of this self-imposed limitation is the Isthmian wall. On Athens no such limitation is imposed in the period covered by the work (except for the Athenian refusal to take over the presidency of the Panhellenic League), and in this lack of restriction lies, we feel, a particular danger for the future.

Both conceptually and artistically the work of Herodotus has its own hidden order. This is achieved on the basis of ideas and stylistic means that we usually associate with the archaic period. Its total effect, however, once this order is perceived, resembles classical form as we know it in fifth-century Attic art and poetry. In all these works the concern for pattern is the overriding consideration.

[44] Enclosed: see Hdt. 3.116.3-117.1, cited above, Ch. II, 103.

NOTE

References to passages of Herodotus are made in the usual way. With regard to this book, however, the following deserves particular mention. In the Index of *Logoi*, Sections, and Passages Cited, the passages actually cited from Herodotus are arranged serially and set below each outline. This is the section labeled "Passages cited," and here the bold numbers indicate passages in Herodotus, while the places in this book where each such passage is cited are arranged in sequential order immediately after each bold number.

The various sections of this book are abbreviated Intro(duction), (Chapter) I, II, III, etc., and Concl(usion). Whenever one of these abbreviations is used, it is followed both by a superscript arabic numeral indicating a footnote in that section, and by an arabic numeral in parentheses, which indicates the actual page where the passage is cited in that footnote. When a passage in Herodotus is cited in the main body of a page in this book, that fact is shown by a simple page-number.

For example, under "Passages cited" just opposite, the boldface 1.1 refers to the very beginning of the *Histories*, while V^{107} (227) means "Chapter V, footnote 107 (found on page 227)," and **1.3–4:** 146 means that Herodotus 1.3–4 is cited on page 146.

The same system of references to various sections of this book is used in both indices.

INDEX OF *LOGOI*, SECTIONS, AND PASSAGES CITED

For more complete outlines, see Jacoby, *RE* Suppl. 2.283–326, and Myres, *Herodotus* 118–34.

(1) 1.1–5 *Proem*:   17–19   43–44   I⁸³ (43)   80–81
       Outline: 80
       Introductory Sentence: 17   VI¹⁶⁹ (296)
       1.1–4 Persian account: 18
       1.5.3–4 Beginning of injustices: 18–19   III⁵ (80)

Passages cited:

1.1: V¹⁰⁷ (227)		**1.4.3:** V⁴⁴ (207)
1.1.4: II³⁹ (58)		**1.4.4:** I⁴ (18) 44 I⁸⁴ (44) 146
1.2.1: IV⁸ (152)		VI¹⁶⁹ (296)
1.3–4: 146		**1.5.1:** I⁴ (18) 52
1.4.1: I⁴ (18)		**1.5.3:** I⁴ (18) II¹⁷ (50)
1.4.2–3: V¹³³ (234)		**1.5.4:** 153

(2) 1.6–94 *Croesus Logos*:   I¹² (20)   I¹³ (20)   20–21   28–30   41   81–88
       154–61
       (a) 1.6–29.1 *History of Mermnadae from Gyges to Croesus'*
              Accession: 27   78   83   149
              1.8.1–13.2 Gyges story: II⁵⁸ (67)   69–70   77
              1.16.2–22.4 and 25.1 Siege of Miletus by
                                              Alyattes: 41   I⁸¹ (41)
              1.23–24 Arion and the Dolphin: 35   II⁶⁹ (70)
                        72   86

Passages cited:

1.6 ff.: I⁴¹ (29)		**1.21:** VI¹⁷ (243)
1.6.1: 20 49 80 82		**1.22:** IV⁷ (151)
1.6.2: 82 V¹¹⁶ (230)		**1.24.1:** II⁷⁷ (73)
1.6.3: 155		**1.25.1:** I⁵ (18) I³⁴ (26)
1.13: 235		**1.26–27.1:** I³⁸ (27)
1.13.2: 77 II⁸⁵ (77) 161 V¹⁷ (195)		**1.26:** V¹¹⁷ (230)
1.14: I⁴¹ (29)		**1.26.1 ff.:** 29 82
1.14.1: 52		**1.26.1:** I³⁴ (26)
1.14.2: V¹¹¹ (228)		**1.27:** 55
1.14.4: I³⁸ (27)		**1.27.1–2:** II⁷⁹ (74)
1.16.2 ff.: I³⁸ (27)		**1.27.5:** IV⁸⁵ (177)
1.17: V¹⁷ (243)		**1.28–29:** 29
1.18.2: I³⁸ (27)		**1.28:** I³⁸ (27) I⁴³ (29) 82
1.18.3: V¹²⁵ (232)		**1.29.1:** 83
1.20: V¹¹⁷ (230)		

(b)   1.29–33 *Solon's Visit*:   83   155–58

Passages cited:

1.30 ff.: 77 II^{85} (77)	**1.32.4:** IV^{24} (157)
1.30.1: IV^{20} (156)	**1.32.5:** IV^{22} (157) 158
1.30.2: IV^{29} (160) Concl.^{36} (320)	**1.32.6:** 158 IV^{25} (158)
1.30.3: IV^{29} (160)	**1.32.7:** IV^{22} (157)
1.31.1 ff.: Concl.^{20} (314)	**1.32.8:** V^{31} (201)
1.32: Concl.^{7} (310)	**1.32.9:** II^{83} (76) IV^{18} (156) 157
1.32.1: IV^{29} (160) Concl.^{16} (313)	IV^{22} (157)

(c)   1.34–45 Tragedy of Atys: 69–71   II^{85} (77)   83   157–58

Passages cited:

1.34 ff.: 77 II^{85} (77)	**1.41.1:** II^{69} (70) IV^{24} (157)
1.34.1: II^{39} (58) 83	**1.42.1:** IV^{24} (157)
1.35.1: II^{69} (70) II^{83} (76) IV^{24} (157)	**1.44.2:** IV^{24} (157) VI^{18} (243)
1.35.4: IV^{24} (157)	**1.45.1:** IV^{24} (157)
1.36.1: II^{69} (70)	**1.45.3:** 52 IV^{24} (157)
1.37.1: II^{69} (70)	

(d)   1.46–70 *Planning and Preparations Section of Croesus' Persian
           Campaign*:   83–84   158–59
        1.56.2–68 *History of Athens and Sparta*:   35–37
            86–88
        1.56.2–58 Origins of Dorian Sparta and
            Pelasgian Athens: 36
            86   199   318   323
        1.59.1–65.1 Peisistratus *Logos*:   36
            86–87   196
        Outline: 86–87
        1.65.1–68.2 Spartan *Logos*:   36
            87–88   200–202
            V^{138} (235)
        Outline: 87

Passages cited:

1.46.1: II^{22} (52) 83 83–84 158	**1.51.3:** V^{111} (228)
V^{44} (207)	**1.54.1:** IV^{20} (156)
1.50–52: IV^{20} (156) IV^{27} (159)	**1.56:** 204
1.50.1: 159	**1.56.1–2:** IV^{109} (186)
1.50.3: V^{111} (228)	**1.56.2:** II^{17} (50) 84

(e) 1.71.2–4 *Advice of Sandanis*:   84

Passages cited:

(f) 1.73–75.1 *Aitiê-Section*:   84

Passages cited:

Passages cited:

1.75.2:	82 III¹¹ (82) 84 IV²⁶ (159)	**1.80.4:**	315	
1.75.3:	82	**1.82:**	V¹⁰⁷ (227) VI²⁰ (244)	
1.76.2:	I⁴⁵ (30)	**1.82.1:**	I⁴³ (30)	
1.76.4:	VI⁵ (240) 241	**1.82.7–8:**	227 Concl.³⁴ (319)	
1.77.1–3:	I⁴³ (30)	**1.84:**	VI¹⁷ (243) VI¹⁰⁹ (276)	
1.78:	315	**1.85:**	159–60	
1.79.1:	73 85	**1.86.1:**	85	
1.80:	III¹⁸⁴ (143) VI⁵ (240)			

(h)   1.86.9–91.6 Croesus on the Pyre and his Inquiry at
Delphi: 85   159   160–61
1.86.2–87.2 Croesus on the pyre: 85
1.87.3–90.4 Conversations of Croesus and
Cyrus: 85
1.91 Answer of Pythia: 85   236
1.92 Croesus' dedications: I⁴¹ (29)   62
II⁴⁹ (62)   78   82
1.93–94 Marvels of Lydia: 62
II⁴⁹ (62)   82   318

Passages cited:

1.86.3–5:	85	**1.90.4:**	159
1.86.3:	III²⁰ (85)	**1.92:**	Intro.³⁴ (14) I⁴¹ (29) IV²⁰ (156)
1.86.4:	III²⁰ (85)		IV²⁷ (159)
1.86.5:	III¹⁵ (83) IV¹⁸ (156) 160	**1.92.1:**	I¹² (20) II³⁷ (57) 82 82–83
	IV³¹ (160)		V¹¹⁶ (230)
1.86.6:	IV⁵⁴ (167)	**1.92.2–4:**	29
1.87.1–2:	159	**1.92.4:**	I⁴¹ (29)
1.88.1:	III²⁰ (85)	**1.94.7:**	I¹² (20) II³⁷ (57) 82

(3)   1.95–140 *Origins of Persia and of Cyrus and Cyrus' Accession*:   21   30
55–56   88–89   161–65
1.95.2–107 History of Median Dynasty: 27–28   78   88
149
1.96–100 Story of Deioces: 77   III⁷¹ (101)
1.101 Median tribes: 318

Passages cited:

1.95:	56	**1.103.2:**	I³⁸ (27) II³⁸ (58)
1.95.1:	Intro.¹⁴ (7) 21 30 55 162	**1.104.2:**	II³⁸ (58)
1.95.2:	25	**1.105.1:**	II³⁸ (58)
1.98.3 ff.:	IV³⁷ (162)	**1.106:**	III³⁷ (91)
1.98.3–99.1:	IV¹¹⁵ (188)	**1.107.1:**	IV³⁷ (162) 163
1.102.2:	II³⁸ (58)		

Passages cited:

Passages cited:

Passages cited:

Passages cited:

(5) 2.1–3.38 *Campaigns of Cambyses*:   21   31   93–98   167–69
               (a)   2.1–3.16 Campaign against Egypt: 78   93–95
                           2.1 Accession of Cambyses: 93
                           Outline: 93
                                2.2–182 *Egyptian Ethnographic Logos*:   62
                                        64–65   67–68   94   96–98
                                        318
                                Outline: 96–97
                                  2.1–4 Introduction: 96
                                  2.5–34 The Country of Egypt: 96
                                  2.35–98 The Customs of Egypt:
                                        96–97
                                  2.99–182 History of Egypt: 26–28
                                        97
                                        2.99–146 Legendary kings
                                                 and chronology
                                                 of gods: 26
                                        2.147–82 Saite dynasty:
                                                 26–27
               3.1–3 *Aitiê*-Section: 94   168
               3.4–9 Preparations and march section: 94
               3.10 Preparations of the Egyptians: 94
               3.11.1–3 Arrival of Persians and battle: 94
                        242
               3.12 Account of the skulls: 94   VI^{13} (242)
               3.13–14 Aftereffects of battle: 94–95

Passages cited:

2.1:	I^{26} (24) 93 94	
2.1.1:	I^{34} (26)	
2.1.2:	97 99	
2.2:	III^{58} (98) IV^{12} (154)	
2.2–3:	64	
2.4:	III^{58} (98)	
2.15.3:	IV^{12} (153)	
2.16.2:	316	
2.16.3:	Intro.^{34} (14)	
2.19.3:	V^{42} (207)	
2.20.1:	Concl.^{36} (320)	
2.26.2:	III^{58} (98) Concl.^{27} (316)	
2.27:	Intro.^{11} (5)	
2.30.3:	II^{76} (73)	
2.31:	II^{47} (61)	
2.33.2:	Intro.^{11} (5)	
2.33.2–34:	III^{58} (98) Concl.^{27} (316)	
2.35–36:	III^{57} (97)	

2.35.1:	Intro.^{34} (14) 64
2.35.2 ff.:	II^{17} (50)
2.35.2:	319
2.49–64:	III^{57} (97)
2.49.2:	Concl.^{36} (320)
2.51–53:	II^{50} (62) 311–12
2.52:	Concl.^{14} (312)
2.52.1:	IV^{37} (162) 311 312
2.53:	311
2.56.1:	Intro.^{11} (6)
2.70.1:	Intro.^{14} (7)
2.73.3:	Intro.^{14} (6)
2.73.4:	315
2.75:	172
2.75.3:	315
2.77.3:	IV^{3} (150)
2.87.3:	V^{42} (207)
2.91:	III^{57} (97)

Passages cited:

(c)   3.27–38 *Cambyses in Egypt*:   95
           3.27–29 Cause of his madness: 95   III^{57} (97)
           3.30–38 Results of his madness: 95
              3.30–32 Crimes against relatives: 95
              3.33–37 Crimes against other persons
                       and against holy places: 95
              3.38 Darius' inquiry into burial
                       customs: II^{50} (62)
                       95

Passages cited:

3.30.3:	I^{51} (32)		**3.36:**	IV^{30} (160)
3.32:	IV^{57} (168)		**3.36.1:**	IV^{57} (168)
3.32.4:	IV^{85} (177)		**3.36.3:**	II^{81} (75)
3.33:	III^{57} (97)		**3.38:**	III^{57} (97)
3.34.2:	IV^{41} (164)		**3.38.1:**	320
3.34.3:	IV^{85} (177)		**3.38.3–4:**	320
3.34.5:	168		**3.38.4:**	319 Concl.^{37} (321)
3.35:	IV^{57} (168)		**3.38.4–39.1:**	61

(6)   3.39–60 *Spartan War against Polycrates of Samos*:   21–22   24   37   59
          98–99   99   191
          3.40–43 Ring of Polycrates: II^{69} (70)   II^{85} (77)
              3.50–53 Periander and Lycophron story: 70–71
              3.54–56.1 Spartan campaign against Samos: 245
              3.57–59 Escape of Samian exiles: III^{36} (91)

Passages cited:

3.39:	77 II^{84} (77)		**3.48.1:**	V^{111} (228) 311
3.39.1:	I^{68} (37)		**3.48.2 ff.:**	VI^{135} (285)
3.39.3:	V^{47} (208)		**3.48.2:**	V^{104} (225)
3.40 ff.:	77 II^{85} (77)		**3.49.1–2:**	311
3.40:	56 II^{82} (75) Concl.^{7} (310)		**3.52.4:**	II^{83} (76)
3.40.2–4:	III^{15} (83)		**3.52.5:**	313
3.40.2:	Concl.^{16} (313)		**3.53.7:**	V^{104} (225)
3.43.2:	II^{22} (52)		**3.56.2:**	98
3.44.1:	III^{46} (94)		**3.59.3–4:**	V^{104} (225) V^{110} (228)
3.44.1–2:	98		**3.60:**	III^{63} (99)
3.47.1:	203 V^{35} (203)		**3.60.1 and 4:**	II^{54} (65)

(8)   3.88–116 *The Power of Darius*:   30–31   99   101–102   171–72
              3.88 Power: 102
              3.89–96 Satrapy list: 48   78   102
              3.97 Peoples bearing gifts: 102
              3.98–105 How the Indians collect gold: 102
                        Outline: III⁷⁴ (102)
                        3.98–101 Ethnographic *logos*:   318
              3.106–16 *Ends of the World*:   54–55   99   102–103   172
                        Outline: III⁷⁵ (102)
                        3.107–13 Arabian wealth and harassment: 103
                                 3.108–109 Divine providence in the animal
                                           kingdom: II⁵⁰ (62)
                                           IV⁸ (152)   172   312

Passages cited:

3.88.1:	31 I⁴⁹ (31) 101			
3.88.3:	32 102 V⁴² (207)			
3.89.3:	IV⁵⁴ (167) 171			
3.91.4:	I⁵¹ (32)			
3.94.2:	102			
3.96.2:	IV²⁰ (156) 171 207			
3.97.1:	I⁵¹ (32)			
3.97.2:	31			
3.97.4:	III⁷³ (102)			
3.97.5:	103–104			
3.101.2:	III⁷³ (102)			
3.102:	II⁶³ (68)			

3.103:	II⁶³ (68)
3.105.2:	II⁴⁷ (61) 315
3.106 ff.:	77 II⁸⁵ (77)
3.106.1:	49 54 Concl.²⁸ (316)
3.107–109:	II⁶³ (68)
3.107.2:	172
3.108.2:	III⁷⁶ (103) 312
3.109.2:	315
3.115–16:	317
3.116.3:,	54 Concl.²⁸ (316)
3.116.3–117.1:	103 Concl.⁴⁴ (326)

(9) 3.117–38 *The Five Anecdotes*:   103–104   173–74
     (a) 3.117 *The Story of the Plain in Asia*:   103–104   171–72
     (b) 3.118–19 *The Death of Intaphernes*:   103–104   173
     (c) 3.120–25 *The Death of Polycrates*:   56   70   103–104   191
     (d) 3.126–28 *The Assassination of Oroetas*:   37   103–104
          IV[78] (174)
     (e) 3.129–38 *The Greek Doctor Democedes*:   II[34] (56)   94
          III[48] (94)   99   103–104
          3.133 ff. Escape of Democedes from Persia:
          III[36] (91)   IV[76] (174)

Passages cited:

3.117.6:	103–104		**3.128:**	V[112] (187)
3.118.1:	III[79] (104)		**3.128.5:**	IV[74] (173)
3.119:	Intro.[15] (7)		**3.129.1:**	38 III[79] (104)
3.119.4:	II[76] (73)		**3.129.3:**	38 III[79] (104)
3.120.1:	37 56 II[76] (73) 98		**3.130.4:**	IV[74] (173)
	III[79] (104)		**3.131:**	V[110] (228)
3.120.3:	IV[105] (183)		**3.131.1–2:**	III[79] (104)
3.120.4:	II[77] (73)		**3.133.1:**	38 III[79] (104)
3.124.1:	II[85] (77)		**3.134:**	I[31] (25) I[69] (38) 174
3.125.4–126.1:	56		**3.134.2:**	179
3.125.4:	II[22] (52) III[15] (83) IV[31] (160)		**3.134.5:**	V[111] (228)
3.126–28:	37		**3.134.6:**	II[76] (73)
3.126.1–2:	I[54] (33)		**3.137.4:**	III[129] (121)
3.126.1:	III[79] (104)		**3.138:**	IV[112] (187)
3.127.1:	32 I[54] (33) II[14] (49) II[76] (73)		**3.138.4:**	II[47] (61) 98 III[129] (121)
3.127.3:	I[54] (33)			

(10) 3.139–6.140 *The Campaigns of Darius*:   22–23   31–33   104–26
         172–73   174–76
     (a)   3.139–49 *Conquest of Samos*:   22   105   113
          3.148 Escape of Maeandrius: III[36] (91)
          105   V[10] (192)   202

Passages cited:

3.139.1:	22 I[26] (24) 104		**3.142.3:**	IV[47] (165)
3.139.2:	32		**3.143.1:**	I[26] (24)
3.140.1:	II[56] (66)		**3.146.1:**	Concl.[19] (314)
3.140.4:	IV[74] (173)		**3.147.1:**	IV[73] (173)

(b)   3.150–60 *Second Conquest of Babylon*:   22   30
105–106   174
Outline: III⁸³ (105)

Passages cited:

3.150: II⁴³ (59)	**3.156.1:** III⁸³ (105)
3.150.1: 105 III⁸⁴ (106)	**3.159.1–2:** IV⁷³ (173)
3.152: III⁸⁴ (106)	**3.159.1:** 106
3.153 ff.: IV⁷⁶ (174) VI¹⁷ (243)	**3.159.2:** IV⁷⁵ (174)
VI¹⁰⁹ (276)	**3.160.1:** IV⁵⁴ (167)
3.153.1–154.1: II⁷⁶ (73)	**3.160.2:** III⁸³ (106) IV⁷⁴ (173)
3.154.2: III⁸³ (105)	IV¹¹⁰ (186)
3.155: III⁸³ (105)	

(c)   4.1–142 *Scythian Campaign*:   22   106–10   111
174–75   178   IV¹⁰³ (183)
Outline: 107
4.1–4 Announcement of campaign and *aitiê-*
section: 108   323
4.5–82 Scythian Ethnographic *Logos*:
62   II⁵⁰ (62)   65   68   175
318   323
4.36.2–45.5 Geography of the
world:
II⁵⁰ (62)

Passages cited:

4.1.1: 107–108	**4.39.1:** I⁵¹ (32)
4.5 ff.: V¹⁵ (195)	**4.42.1:** 65 II⁵⁵ (65) II⁶³ (68) 316
4.5–6: 142	**4.44.1–3:** I⁵⁶ (33)
4.5.1: III⁵⁸ (98)	**4.45:** 317
4.7.3: 108	**4.46:** II⁵⁵ (65) III⁹² (108)
4.8: 315	**4.46.2:** 320
4.14: VI¹⁷³ (298)	**4.48–50:** III⁵⁸ (98)
4.15.1: Intro.¹¹ (5)	**4.50.1:** Concl.²⁷ (316)
4.16: 108 III⁹¹ (108)	**4.56:** I⁶⁶ (37)
4.18.3: III⁹¹ (108)	**4.59:** III⁹² (108)
4.31: III⁹¹ (108)	**4.59.1:** Concl.³⁶ (320)
4.31.1: Intro.¹¹ (6)	**4.63:** II⁴⁷ (61)
4.34.2: VI¹¹¹ (276)	**4.76.1:** 319
4.36.2: 65 316	**4.81.3:** VI¹⁷² (298)
4.37 ff.: 316	**4.82:** Intro.³⁴ (14) II²⁴ (52)

4.83–142 Campaign *Logos*:   107
    4.83–98 March of Darius from
        Susa to Danube: 48
      4.94–96 The Getae:
        318
    4.99–101 The shape of Scythia:
        318
    4.103–17 The neighbors of the
        Scythians: 318
    4.121–42 Outline, campaign *logos*
        proper: III^{96} (109)

Passages cited:

4.83.1–2: IV^{76} (174)
4.83.1: III^{91} (108)
4.84.2: IV^{74} (174)
4.85.1 ff.: IV^{81} (175)
4.87.1: IV^{81} (175)
4.90–91: IV^{81} (175)
4.92: IV^{81} (175)
4.95: VI^{173} (298)
4.97–98: IV^{81} (175)
4.97.2 ff.: IV^{76} (174)
4.97.4: III^{91} (108)
4.102.1: II^{76} (73)
4.118.2: V^{78} (217)
4.121: III^{91} (108)
4.121.1:   109

4.124.2: III^{91} (108)
4.125.5: III^{91} (108)
4.127.2–3:   319
4.128 ff.:   243
4.128.1–2: III^{97} (110)
4.128.3: III^{184} (143)
4.133.1–3: III^{97} (110)
4.134: VI^{16} (243)
4.134.2 ff.: IV^{76} (174)
4.134.2: III^{91} (108) IV^{81} (175)
4.136–39: III^{97} (110)
4.137.2–3: IV^{81} (175)
4.137.2:   232
4.142:   110   232

(d)   4.143–44 and 5.1–27 *European Campaigns of Megabazus*
       and Otanes: 22 II^{50} (62)
       110–11   173
Outline: 110–11
5.3–10 Thracian *Logos*:   318
5.16.2–4 Paeonians: 318

Passages cited:

4.143: V^{92} (222)
4.143.1:   110 III^{129} (121)
4.143.2: IV^{74} (173)
5.1.2–3: VI^{17} (243)
5.11: IV^{74} (173)
5.12.1 ff.: II^{58} (67)
5.12.1: III^{129} (121)
5.13.2: IV^{109} (186)

5.14: I^{66} (37)
5.16:   Concl.^{33} (318)
5.22:   235
5.22.2: V^{107} (227)
5.23.2 ff.: IV^{76} (174)
5.25: IV^{74} (173)
5.25.1:   110
5.26–27:   116

(e) 4.145–205 *Libyan Campaign*: 22 68 111–13 175
Outline: 111–12
4.145–67.2 City history of Cyrene: 112
196 318
4.147–49 Escape of Theras: III^{36} (91)
4.168–99 Ethnographic *Logos*: II^{50} (62)
112–13 318
4.181–85 Geographic section: III^{106} (113)
4.200–205 Campaign: 112

Passages cited:

4.145: V^{30} (200)
4.145.1: III^{103} (111) 112
4.147 ff.: V^{35} (203)
4.150 ff.: 77 II^{84} (77)
4.150.1: II^{54} (65)
4.152.1: III^{107} (113)
4.152.5: III^{107} (113)
4.155.1: V^{15} (194)
4.158.3: III^{107} (113)
4.159.2–3: 236
4.160.4: V^{22} (197)
4.161.1: V^{15} (194)
4.161.2–3: III^{107} (113)
4.161.3: V^{22} (197)

4.162.3: V^{111} (228)
4.163.2: V^{17} (195) V^{22} (197)
4.164.4: IV^{47} (165) V^{22} (197)
4.165.3: 112
4.166: IV^{105} (183) VI^{152} (289)
4.166.2: IV^{74} (174)
4.167.1: III^{107} (113)
4.167.3: 112 VI^{152} (289)
4.168: IV^{13} (154)
4.168.1: 319
4.201.2–3: VI^{17} (243)
4.204: 111
4.205: 25 313

Passages cited:

6.24.1:   IV¹¹² (187)
6.24.2:   IV¹⁸ (156)
6.27:   V¹²⁵ (232)
6.31:   V¹²⁵ (232)
6.32:   III¹⁴ (82)   V¹¹⁶ (230)
6.33:   23   116
6.34 ff.:   192   V⁵⁸ (210)   V⁹² (222)
6.35:   V⁸ (192)
6.36:   V²⁸ (200)
6.36.1:   V¹³⁶ (235)

6.36.2:   V⁹² (222)
6.37.2:   191
6.38.2:   191
6.40.1–41.1:   191
6.41:   IV⁷⁴ (173)
6.41.2–4:   191
6.42 f.:   IV⁷⁵ (174)
6.42:   23   116
6.42.1:   III¹¹⁰ (114)   115   III¹⁸⁸ (145)

(g)   6.43–45 *Mardonius' Expedition Wrecked at Mt. Athos*:
23   120–21   175

Passages cited:

6.43:   III⁷¹ (101)
6.43.1:   I²⁶ (24)   III¹¹⁰ (114)   115

6.43.3:   101   III⁷¹ (101)   V¹⁴² (237)
6.44.1:   III¹⁶⁶ (135)

(h)   6.46–48.1 *Subjugation of Thasos*:   I²¹ (23)   121

Passages cited:

6.46.1:   I²⁶ (24)
6.46.2:   V¹³ (193)

6.48.1:   I²⁶ (24)

(i)   6.48.1–49.1 *Heralds Sent to Greece*:   I²¹ (23)   121

Passage cited:

6.48.2:   I²¹ (23)   66   121   III¹³¹ (121)
III¹⁶⁶ (135)

6.49–93 *Aeginetan Logos*:   38–39   121–22
        212 V^{65} (212)   V^{138} (236)
        Outline: 121–22
        6.56–60 Spartan kings: 318
        6.67–70 Escape of Demaratus:
                III^{36} (91)
        6.86 Speech of Leotychidas: 122
        213–15

Passages cited:

6.48.2–49:   134
6.49 ff.:   V^{59} (210)
6.49:   V^{103} (225)
6.49.1:   38
6.50:   V^{110} (228)
6.50.2–3:   190
6.51 ff.:   77   III^{84} (77)
6.52:   III^{71} (101)
6.52.2 ff.:   197
6.53–55:   V^{57} (209)
6.53:   V^{15} (195)
6.56–60:   V^{57} (209)
6.59:   V^{26} (198)   V^{57} (209)
6.61 ff.:   192   197–98
6.61.1:   Concl.^{19} (314)
6.61.3:   IV^{18} (156)
6.66.2–3:   193
6.70.2:   III^{48} (94)
6.70.3:   V^{136} (235)
6.71.1:   126
6.72:   V^{70} (214)

6.72.2:   V^{106} (226)
6.73:   V^{59} (210)
6.73.2:   190   V^{67} (213)   V^{110} (228)
6.75.3:   193
6.76 ff.:   V^{107} (227)
6.76.2:   I^{66} (37)
6.77.2:   IV^{114} (187)
6.78 ff.:   VI^{19} (244)
6.79–81:   193
6.83:   227
6.84.1–3:   193
6.84.3:   193
6.85:   V^{59} (210)
6.86.1:   V^{67} (213)
6.86a.1:   V^{69} (214)
6.86c: 236
6.87 ff.:   V^{59} (210)
6.87:   V^{109} (227)
6.89:   V^{112} (229)
6.92:   V^{107} (227)
6.93:   66

(k) 6.121–31 *The Defense of the Alcmaeonids*:   39
         124–25   127   III[176] (139)   V[94] (223)
     Outline: 125
     6.125–31 Fame of Alcmaeonids: I[23] (23)

Passages cited:

6.120:	127	**6.126 ff.:**	V[14] (194)
6.121.1:	39	**6.126.2:**	V[136] (235)
6.122:	III[137] (125) V[136] (235)	**6.127.3:**	V[107] (227)
6.125.1:	III[119] (117)	**6.131.2:**	VI[14] (242)
6.125.5:	V[136] (235)		

(l) 6.132–36 *Miltiades' Attempted Conquest of Paros and his Death*:   38   125   127   140

Passages cited:

6.132:	V[29] (200) V[47] (208) V[48] (208)	**6.135.3:**	V[140] (236) VI[181] (301)
6.133 ff.:	192	**6.136:**	191
6.133.1:	V[29] (200)	**6.136.2:**	125

(m) 6.137–40 *Miltiades' Capture of Lemnos*:   I[23] (23)   38
         125   127

Passages cited:

6.137 ff.:	III[8] (81)	**6.140.1:**	125
6.137.2:	Concl.[19] (314)	**6.140.2:**	III[142] (127)

(11)   7–9 *The Greek Campaigns of Xerxes and Mardonius*:   23–24   126–47
            176–84   IV^{103} (183)   V^9 (192)   241
        (a)   7.1–18 *Aitiê- and Planning Section*:   128–29
                    7.1–4 *Legacy of Darius and Succession of Xerxes*:
                            126–28   178–80
                    7.2–3 Advice of Demaratus to Darius:
                            126–27   IV^{55} (167)   178   179
                            IV^{95} (180)   V^{26} (198)
                7.5–6 *Persuasion of Xerxes by Mardonius, the Aleuadae,*
                        and the Peisistratids: 128
                7.7 Egyptian Campaign: 127
                7.8–11 *Council of Persians*:   128–29   181
                        7.12–18 *Dreams of Xerxes and Artabanus*:   129
                                IV^{39} (163)   181

7.1:	I^{22} (23) I^{26} (24) 127 III^{142} (127)	**7.8d.1:**	129
	III^{166} (135)	**7.9a.1:**	V^{42} (207)
7.1.1:	III^{142} (127) V^{59} (210)	**7.9.2:**	I^{56} (33)
7.1.2:	127	**7.10:**	II^{82} (75) 77 II^{85} (77)
7.2.2:	32		Concl.^{7} (310)
7.4:	23 I^{22} (23) I^{34} (26) 28 127 175	**7.10d.2:**	II^{78} (74)
7.5:	IV^{76} (174)	**7.10e:**	Concl.^{16} (313)
7.5.1:	V^{48} (208)	**7.11:**	32 I^{50} (32) IV^{63} (170)
7.6.4:	128	**7.11.1:**	IV^{85} (177)
7.7:	33 127 128 VI^{66} (260)	**7.11.2:**	IV^{63} (170) 178 V^{31} (201)
7.8:	III^{191} (146)	**7.13.2:**	IV^{92} (179)
7.8.1:	128	**7.14:**	178
7.8a.1:	176 321–22 Concl.^{40} (322)	**7.16:**	Concl.^{7} (310)
7.8b.2:	175	**7.16a.1:**	IV^{92} (179)
7.8c.1:	I^{51} (32) IV^{87} (177)	**7.16b.2:**	IV^{92} (179)
7.8c.3:	180–81	**7.18.2:**	IV^{92} (179)

        (b)   7.19–26.2 *Preparations Section*:   78   129–30
                    7.20–21 Internal Proem: 63–64   129   130
                    7.22–24 Digging of Mt. Athos canal: 129
                    7.25 Cables and food depots: 129

Passages cited:

7.19.1:	VI^{111} (276)	**7.24.1:**	Intro.^{11} (5) IV^{86} (177)
7.19.2:	129 III^{148} (129) IV^{101} (182)	**7.25.1:**	IV^{83} (176)
7.20:	V^{133} (234)	**7.26 ff.:**	IV^{83} (176)
7.20.2:	IV^6 (151)	**7.26.1–2:**	129
7.21.1:	IV^{103} (183) 317	**7.26.1:**	II^{43} (59) 129
7.22:	IV^{83} (176)	**7.26.2:**	III^{148} (129) IV^{101} (182)
7.24:	IV^{103} (183)		

(d) 7.131–78 *Greek Preparations Logos*:   39   59   133–37
225–26   256
Outline: 136
7.131–44 Introduction: III¹⁶⁴ (134)   136
7.138–45.1 Athenians consult oracle:
III¹⁶⁸ (135)
7.145 ff. Preparations *Logos* proper: 135–37
7.178 Delphic prayers to the winds: 62   137   140

Passages cited:

7.131:   39   II⁴⁷ (61)   133   134
III¹⁶⁷ (135)
7.132:   VI¹¹³ (277)
7.132.1:   134
7.132.2:   134   V¹⁰⁹ (227)
7.133.1:   III¹³¹ (121)   134   III¹⁶⁶ (135)
III¹⁶⁷ (135)
7.133.2:   V⁷¹ (214)
7.134–37:   134
7.136.2:   IV⁸⁶ (177)
7.137:   V⁷⁸ (217)
7.137.3:   Intro.³⁴ (14)   134   V¹¹³ (229)
7.138.1:   39   134
7.138.2:   III¹³¹ (121)   135
7.139:   135   206   217   VI⁸ (241)
VI⁸¹ (266)   VI¹⁰¹ (274)
7.139.3–4:   III¹⁷⁷ (139)   205   296
7.139.5:   V⁸⁶ (220)   305
7.140–44:   135
7.143–44:   223
7.143.1:   V⁵⁷ (210)
7.143.3:   217
7.144:   212   V⁶⁵ (212)
7.144.1–2:   V⁵⁹ (210)
7.144.3:   III¹⁶⁸ (135)   III¹⁶⁹ (135)
7.145.1:   III¹⁶⁹ (135)   212

7.148 ff.:   227
7.151:   IV⁹⁵ (180)
7.152:   IV⁹⁵ (180)
7.152.2:   320–21
7.152.3:   I⁴⁰ (28)
7.154.3:   V¹¹¹ (228)
7.157.3:   II⁷⁸ (74)
7.159:   V³⁸ (204)
7.161:   V³⁸ (204)   V⁸⁵ (220)   VI¹⁰¹ (274)
7.161.3:   215
7.164.1:   IV³ (150)
7.166–67.1:   VI¹⁷³ (298)
7.166.1:   II⁴⁵ (60)
7.170.2:   IV³ (150)
7.170.3–4:   V¹⁰⁵ (226)
7.171:   V¹³³ (234)
7.171.1:   IV⁷ (152)
7.172 ff.:   205
7.172.1:   III¹⁷⁰ (136)
7.172.2:   III¹⁶² (133)
7.175–77:   258
7.175.2:   VI⁸³ (267)
7.176:   138
7.176.3:   48
7.176.4:   V¹⁰⁴ (225)
7.177:   39   III¹⁶³ (133)   III¹⁶⁹ (135)

Passages cited:

Passages cited:

(g) 8.1–26 *Battle of Artemisium*:   139 257–59 263–67
        Outline: 263–64
          8.24–25 Visit of Persians to Battlefield: 139
              VI⁸² (267)
          8.26 Celebration of Olympic festival: 139

Passages cited:

8.1: 138 V⁸⁷ (221)
8.2.2: V⁸⁷ (221)
8.3: V³⁸ (204) 217 220 V¹⁰³ (225)
8.3.1: V⁸⁶ (220) V⁹⁰ (222)
8.3.2: 220 V⁹⁰ (222) 233–34
        VI¹⁷² (198)
8.4.1: VI⁶³ (258)
8.4.2–8.5: 139
8.4.2–5.3: 224
8.5: V³⁸ (204) V¹¹³ (229)
8.5.3: VI¹³⁸ (285)
8.8–9.1: VI⁶³ (258)
8.8: VI⁸⁹ (271)
8.9–10: 259
8.10.1: 261 VI⁷⁹ (266)
8.11.1: VI⁷⁹ (266)
8.12 f.: VI⁸⁴ (268)
8.12: 137–38
8.13: 52 VI⁴⁵ (252)
8.14.1: V³¹ (201)
8.14.2: 259 VI⁸⁹ (271)

8.15–16: VI⁸³ (267)
8.15: IV¹⁰¹ (182)
8.15.1: 257 259
8.15.2: VI⁸³ (267)
8.16.1: VI⁷⁹ (266)
8.18: VI⁶³ (258) VI⁸¹ (266)
8.19: III¹²¹ (118) 224
8.19.1: 139
8.21: III¹²¹ (118)
8.21.1: VI⁸⁹ (271)
8.21.2: VI⁸¹ (266)
8.22–23.1: 224
8.22: VI⁵⁸ (256)
8.22.2: V⁷⁵ (216) V⁷⁶ (216)
8.23: V⁸⁹ (271)
8.24.1: IV⁸³ (176)
8.24.2: IV⁸⁶ (177)
8.25.3: 140
8.26: 139 235
8.26.2: VI¹¹¹ (276)
8.26.3: Concl.² (309)

(h) 8.27–39 *March of the Land Army from Thermopylae to Boeotia,*
        and to Delphi: 139–40

Passages cited:

8.27 ff.: V¹⁰⁴ (225)
8.28: III¹⁸⁴ (143)
8.30.1: Intro.¹¹ (5)
8.31 ff.: V¹⁰⁴ (225)
8.31: 140
8.33: IV¹⁰² (183)

8.34–35.1: 140
8.34: I²⁴ (23) 140 VI¹¹³ (277)
8.35 ff.: 236 VI¹⁶¹ (293)
8.35–39: IV¹⁰² (183)
8.39: 256

Passages cited:

8.69.2:   IV^{85} (177)   IV^{100} (182)   274   282
8.70:   272
8.70.1:   VI^{97} (273)
8.71–74.1:   205
8.71.1:   VI^{97} (273)
8.72:   V^{113} (229)   V^{135} (235)
8.73:   Concl.^{33} (318)
8.74–76:   VI^{91} (271)
8.74:   VI^{85} (268)
8.74.2:   V^{38} (204)
8.75:   224
8.75.1:   IV^{18} (156)
8.76.1:   273   VI^{118} (278)
8.76.2:   268
8.77:   VI^{118} (278)
8.77.1:   I^{85} (44)   Concl.^{11} (310)
8.78:   VI^{102} (274)
8.79–80:   209–10   224
8.79.1:   V^{57} (210)
8.79.3:   277
8.80.1:   277
8.81:   VI^{102} (274)
8.83:   140   224
8.83.1–2:   III^{157} (131)   VI^{127} (282)
8.83.1:   VI^{91} (271)   VI^{96} (273)
8.83.2:   VI^{127} (282)
8.84.1:   281
8.84.2:   281
8.85.1:   V^{128} (232)   268
8.86:   IV^{100} (182)   IV^{101} (183) VI^{130} (282)
8.87.2:   281
8.88.3:   IV^{114} (187)   281   VI^{130} (282)
8.90.2:   281
8.90.3:   IV^{74} (173)   IV^{101} (183)
8.90.4:   IV^{100} (182)   IV^{101} (182) VI^{130} (282)
8.92:   190   V^{98} (224)   V^{110} (228)
8.92.1–2:   281
8.92.2:   VI^{8} (241)
8.93:   VI^{127} (282)
8.94:   V^{113} (229)   VI^{128} (282)
8.94.4:   V^{113} (229)   VI^{8} (241)
8.95:   V^{57} (210)

8.96.2:   III^{172} (137)
8.97:   VI^{119} (278)
8.97.1:   VI^{130} (282)   VI^{131} (284)
8.98–99:   IV^{104} (183)   VI^{85} (268)
8.98.1:   I^{51} (32)
8.99.1:   I^{51} (32)
8.99.2:   VI^{132} (284)
8.100.1:   VI^{131} (284)   VI^{132} (284)
8.100.4:   VI^{168} (296)
8.101–103:   VI^{85} (268)
8.101.1:   IV^{85} (177)
8.102.2–3:   284
8.102.2:   IV^{94} (179)
8.102.3:   IV^{97} (180)
8.103:   IV^{85} (177)   179   IV^{95} (180)
8.104:   VI^{135} (285)
8.106.3:   322
8.108 ff.:   224   VI^{85} (268)
8.108.2:   V^{38} (204)
8.108.3:   V^{31} (201)
8.108.4:   285   VI^{141} (287)
8.109.3:   275   294   Concl.^{16} (313)
8.110.1:   VI^{138} (285)
8.110.2–3:   224
8.111–12:   V^{29} (200)
8.111:   Concl.^{40} (322)
8.112.1:   V^{29} (200)   224
8.112.3:   224
8.114:   236
8.114.1:   VI^{159} (293)
8.114.2:   256   VI^{157} (292)
8.115–20:   VI^{136} (285)
8.115:   IV^{105} (184)
8.117.2:   IV^{3} (150)
8.118.1 and 4:   III^{129} (121)
8.118.4:   IV^{101} (183)
8.119:   III^{129} (121)   IV^{101} (183)
8.122:   V^{110} (228)   VI^{8} (241)   VI^{127} (282)
8.124:   V^{38} (204)
8.124.1:   314
8.124.2–3:   V^{98} (224)
8.124.2:   VI^{111} (276)   VI^{139} (286)
8.125:   286
8.125.1:   314

(j)   8.126–29 *Return of Artabazus from the Hellespont to Mardonius*:
140–41   141   256   VI^{170} (297)

Passages cited:

8.126.1:   141
8.126.2:   III^{129} (121)

8.129.3:   141

Passages cited:

8.130:   141
8.130.1:   III¹²⁹ (121)
8.131–32:   141
8.131.2–3:   IV⁶³ (170)

8.132:   233   VI¹⁴⁴ (287)
8.132.1:   V⁷⁵ (216)
8.132.2:   V¹²⁵ (232)

Passages cited:

8.134 f.:   V¹⁰⁹ (228)
8.135:   293
8.136–9.11:   217
8.136.1 and 3:   142
8.137 f.:   V¹⁵ (195)
8.137.1:   V¹⁰⁷ (227)
8.140a.2:   V⁸² (219)
8.141.1:   142
8.142.2:   V⁷⁶ (216)
8.142.3:   216
8.142.4:   219
8.143.3:   219
8.144:   292   VI¹⁵⁷ (292)
8.144.2:   216   219   V¹¹⁸ (231)
         V¹³¹ (234)   VI¹⁵⁷ (292)   319
9.1–3:   VI¹⁴² (287)   VI¹⁵² (289)
9.2:   II⁸² (75)   V¹⁰⁹ (228)
9.3.1:   IV¹⁰⁵ (183)
9.4.1:   V⁸² (219)
9.6:   219   VI¹⁰³ (274)   VI¹⁴² (287)
9.7.1:   VI¹⁵⁸ (292)

9.7a.1:   V⁸² (219)
9.7b.2:   V⁸² (219)
9.8.1:   205
9.8.2:   206
9.9:   V¹⁰⁶ (226)
9.9.2:   III¹⁷⁷ (139)   206   V⁸⁴ (220)
9.10:   V²⁵ (198)
9.10.2–3:   205
9.11.1:   VI¹⁵⁸ (292)
9.12:   143   V¹⁰⁸ (227)
9.12.1:   III¹⁸³ (143)
9.13.2:   VI¹⁵² (289)
9.14:   III³² (90)   III¹⁸³ (143)
9.15.1:   III¹⁸³ (143)
9.15.2–3:   VI¹⁵⁰ (289)
9.15.2:   V¹⁰⁹ (228)
9.16:   V¹⁰⁹ (228)
9.16.5–17.1:   VI¹⁵⁵ (291)
9.17.4 ff.:   V¹⁰⁴ (225)
9.18.2:   III¹⁸⁴ (143)
9.18.3–19.1:   VI¹⁵⁵ (291)

(m)   9.19 and 20–24 *March of Greeks to Cithaeron*:   143

Passages cited:

9.19:   VI¹⁵⁸ (292)
9.21.3:   VI¹⁶⁶ (295)

9.24–25.1:   VI¹⁵⁵ (291)

(n)   9.25–89 *Battle of Plataea*:   II⁵⁰ (62)   143–44   287–89
            289–99
      Outline: 290–91
      9.58–65 Battle description: 144   293–97
      9.66–75 Last stages of battle: 297
      9.76–85 After the battle: 297–98

Passages cited:

9.25.2:   292
9.26 ff.:   V¹⁰⁶ (226)
9.26–27:   V³⁸ (204)
9.26:   226
9.26.3:   VI²⁰ (244)
9.27.2–5:   215–16
9.27.4:   V¹³³ (234)
9.27.5:   VI³⁸ (250)
9.31.1:   VI¹⁵⁵ (291)
9.31.2:   V¹⁰⁹ (228)
9.33 ff.:   VI¹⁶⁴ (295)
9.35.2:   V¹⁰⁶ (226)
9.36:   VI¹⁵⁵ (291)   292   VI¹⁶³ (294)
9.37 ff.:   VI¹⁶⁴ (295)
9.37.1:   292   293   322
9.37.3–4:   V¹⁰⁶ (226)
9.37.4:   II⁸³ (77)
9.38.2:   293   VI¹⁶⁴ (295)
9.40:   V¹⁰⁹ (228)   VI¹⁶³ (294)
9.41 ff.:   289
9.41:   II⁸² (75)   VI¹⁷⁰ (297)
9.41.1:   III¹⁸⁸ (145)   VI¹⁵⁵ (291)
            VI¹⁷⁰ (297)
9.41.4:   293   VI¹⁶⁰ (293)   322
9.42–43:   VI¹⁶¹ (293)
9.43.2:   VI¹⁶³ (294)
9.46:   VI¹⁶⁷ (296)
9.46.2–3:   VI¹⁶⁶ (295)
9.47–48:   V³⁸ (204)
9.48:   VI¹⁶⁷ (296)
9.48.3:   VI¹⁰³ (274)
9.51.1–2:   VI¹⁶³ (294)
9.53.2 ff.:   VI¹⁶⁷ (296)

9.54 f.:   II⁴³ (59)
9.54.1–56.2:   VI¹⁶⁶ (295)
9.54.1:   VI¹⁰¹ (274)
9.55.2:   VI¹⁶⁷ (296)
9.56.2:   VI¹⁸⁴ (302)
9.57.2:   VI¹⁶³ (294)
9.57.3:   291
9.58 ff.:   289
9.58.2:   VI¹⁶⁷ (296)
9.58.3:   VI¹⁷⁰ (297)
9.59.1:   293   VI¹⁶³ (294)
9.60 f.:   VI¹⁶⁶ (295)
9.60.1:   VI¹⁶⁷ (296)
9.61.3–62.1:   294
9.61.3:   VI¹⁵⁰ (289)
9.62.2:   VI¹⁵⁰ (289)
9.62.3:   VI¹⁶⁸ (296)
9.64:   VI¹⁵⁷ (292)
9.64.1:   294
9.65.1:   VI¹⁵⁰ (289)
9.65.2:   VI¹⁵⁷ (292)   295
9.66.1:   VI¹⁵⁵ (291)
9.66.2–3:   VI¹⁷⁰ (297)
9.67:   V¹⁰⁹ (228)   VI¹⁶⁶ (295)
9.68:   VI¹⁶⁸ (296)
9.69:   V¹⁰⁹ (228)   VI¹⁴⁹ (288)
9.69.1:   V¹¹³ (229)
9.70.1:   VI¹⁵⁵ (291)
9.70.2:   VI¹⁶⁶ (295)   296   VI¹⁸⁵ (302)
9.70.5:   VI¹⁷⁰ (297)
9.71–72:   V⁴⁰ (205)
9.71:   VI⁷⁴ (262)
9.71.1:   296

Passages cited:

9.106.3: 206 V^{75} (216) 233
VI^{101} (274)
9.106.4: 144 V^{125} (232) VI^{146} (288)
9.107.1: IV^{114} (187)
9.107.1 and 3: III^{32} (90)

9.107.1–3: 144
9.107.3: III^{188} (145)
9.108: IV^{90} (179) IV^{95} (180)
9.109.1 and 2: IV^{85} (177)
9.113.2: III^{32} (90) IV^{101} (183)

(p) 9.114–22 *The Greeks at Abydos and Sestus*: I^{25} (24) 144–47
V^{92} (222)
9.114.2–122 *The Siege of Sestus*: 145

Passages cited:

9.114 ff.: V^{29} (200)
9.114.1: 144
9.114.2: 206
9.115: III^{187} (145)
9.116: 146
9.116.1: V^{133} (234)
9.116.3: I^{84} (44) 146

9.120.4: 222
9.121: I^{25} (24)
9.122: II^{82} (75) III^{190} (146) IV^{54} (167)
186
9.122.3: V^{31} (201)
9.122.4: 50

GENERAL INDEX

Euripus: 258
Europe (see also Asia and Europe):
41 43 107 233 V¹³² (234) 275
305 316
Eurybiades: 204
Evacuation, of Attica: 274
Evans, J. A. S.: 321
Exchange of goods: 320–21
Concl.³⁷ (321)
Expansionism: 25 27–28 31–32 41
43 66 82 84 93 104
111 128 146 149 158
167 175 180–81 191
193 210 VI³⁵ (249)
255 306 321
Expectation, false: see *elpis*-motif

Fable (see also animals): 90 315
Fame: 262
Family: see offspring
Fate (see also *moira*): 154 158
V²² (197) 236
Father and son: 127 IV⁵⁵ (167) 174
178 306
Fear motif: 141 158 181 203
V³⁷ (203) VI⁶⁴ (259) 284
292 300 VI¹⁷⁸ (300) 302
VI¹⁸² (302)
Foreshadowing: II²⁶ (53) 109 121 125
131 158 VI¹³⁵ (285)
306
Formula, Homeric: 11 Intro.²² (11)
Fortune, change of:
I⁶⁶ (37) 72 76 78 III⁴² (93)
98 150 163 164 183 189
190 191 V¹⁰⁵ (226) 229
V¹²⁵ (232) 233 VI⁵ (240) 265
268 269 285 VI¹³⁵ (285)
Fortune, cycle or wheel of:
75 80 150 166 189
V²² (197) 237
Fortune, divine: VI³⁷ (250)
Fortune, height of: 76 77 78 281
Founder's myth: 161–65
Framing sentences: 12 19 24 52–53
II²⁷ (53) 54–58
65–67 70 82 93
102 117 118 132
144 149 269 270
271 279–80 283–84
VI¹⁵⁵ (291) 297
VI¹⁷⁷ (300)

Fränkel, Hermann: 3 Intro.²¹ (11) 46
49
Freedom: 23 III³⁶ (91) III⁷¹ (101)
102 108 132 134 146
III¹⁹⁰ (146) 155 175 181
184 218–19 230–33 248
251 255 VI⁸⁰ (266) 322
Function, idea of historical: 324

γάρ: see *δέ*
Gar-sentences, in Herodotus: III²¹ (86)
Genealogies, of nobility: III¹¹⁹ (117)
Generals' speeches (see also speeches):
VI⁸³ (267) VI⁹¹ (271)
Generations: see father and son
Genetic problem, of work: 3 8
Geography: 315–17
Gephyraeans: III¹¹⁹ (117)
Gifts: 102 159 172 IV¹¹⁰ (186) 285
Glaucus of Sparta: 213–14
Gnomê (opinion, reflection): Intro.¹¹ (5)
75
Gobryas: 178
Gods: see divine
Gods, local: 257 274–75 285 294
299 305 314
Gold: 207
Gorgo, daughter of Cleomenes: V²⁵ (198)
Government, Debate on: III⁷¹ (101)
γράφειν (to write down): Intro.¹⁴ (6–7)
Greece, conception of: 234–35
Greek material, in work:
34–42 59 86–87 94
* III¹⁰⁵ (113) 233–37
Greek states, relations of: 225–30
Greeks, role of in work (see also Hellenes):
233–37
Groningen, B. A. van: 46
Growth and decay, cycle of: 153 189
310
Growth of power: see *αὐξάνεσθαι* and
power

Halys river: 20 25 I⁴³ (29) 30 82
84 155
ἁρπαγή (raid): I⁴³ (30) 41 155
Harpagus: 162–63 165
Hecataeus: II⁷ (47) 47–49 65
II⁶³ (68) III¹⁰⁴ (112)
III¹⁰⁶ (113) III¹¹⁹ (117)
207 315–16

OTHER PUBLICATIONS
OF THE
AMERICAN PHILOLOGICAL ASSOCIATION

The American Philological Association issues three series of publications, *Transactions and Proceedings*, *Philological Monographs*, and *Special Publications*. These are published for the Association by The Press of Western Reserve University, Cleveland, Ohio 44106. All orders should be sent directly to the Press. Members are entitled to a 20% discount, but only if the order is accompanied by the notation, "Member's Discount Applies." *Transactions and Proceedings* is available in cloth and, for some volumes, in paper binding. *Monographs* and *Special Publications* are available in cloth only.

A. TRANSACTIONS AND PROCEEDINGS

The Association's *Transactions and Proceedings* is published annually; 96 volumes have appeared. The history of the separate publication of *Transactions* and *Proceedings*, which has been abandoned, will be found in *Proceedings* 90 (lix), and on the corresponding page in preceding volumes. It is no longer possible to supply complete sets. Volumes 54–96 are available directly from The Press of Western Reserve University. Volumes 1–50 are available at reproduction prices, and without member's discount, directly from Kraus Reprint Corporation, 16 East 46th Street, New York, N.Y. 10017.

B. PHILOLOGICAL MONOGRAPHS

I. The Divinity of the Roman Emperor, by LILY ROSS TAYLOR. 1931. Pp. x + 296. Out of print.

II. NEOI, A Study of Greek Associations, by CLARENCE ALLEN FORBES. 1933. Pp. ix + 75.

III. Index Apuleianus, by WILLIAM ABBOTT OLDFATHER, HOWARD VERNON CANTER, and BEN EDWIN PERRY. 1934. Pp. liii + 490.

IV. The Vatican Plato and Its Relations, by LEVI ARNOLD POST. 1934. Pp. ix + 116.

V. The Critical Edition of the Germania of Tacitus, by RODNEY POTTER ROBINSON. 1935. Pp. xiv + 388.

VI. Criminal Trials and Criminal Legislation under Tiberius, by ROBERT SAMUEL ROGERS. 1935. Pp. ix + 216. Out of print. (Xerox edition available from University Microfilms, Inc., Ann Arbor, Michigan.)

VII. Studies in the Text History of the Life and Fables of Aesop, by BEN EDWIN PERRY. 1936. Pp. xvi + 240; Plates I–VI.

1

VIII. Scholia Platonica, edited with preface and indices by WILLIAM CHASE GREENE. 1938. Pp. xlii + 569.

IX. Written and Unwritten Marriages in Hellenistic and Post-classical Roman Law, by HANS JULIUS WOLFF. 1939. Pp. vi + 129.

X. Philodemus: On Methods of Inference; a Study in Ancient Empiricism, by PHILLIP and ESTELLE DE LACY. 1941. Pp. ix + 200. Out of print.

XI. The Local Historians of Attica, by LIONEL PEARSON. 1942. Pp. xii + 167. Out of print.

XII. Dunchad: Glossae in Martianum, by CORA E. LUTZ. 1944. Pp. xxx + 68.

XIII. Dichtung und Philosophie des fruehen Griechentums, by HERMANN FRAENKEL. 1951. Pp. xii + 680. Out of print.

XIV. The Tradition of the Minor Greek Geographers, by AUBREY DILLER, with a new text of the *Periplus of the Euxine Sea.* 1952. Pp. x + 200.

XV. The Magistrates of the Roman Republic, by T. ROBERT S. BROUGHTON, with the collaboration of MARCIA L. PATTERSON. Volume I, 509 B.C.–100 B.C. 1951. Pp. xix + 578. Volume II, 99 B.C.– 31 B.C. 1952, reprinted with Supplement 1960. Pp. x + 647. (Copies of the Supplement separately in paperback form [pp. v + 92].)

XVI. Subjunctive and Optative: Their Origin as Futures, by E. ADELAIDE HAHN. 1953. Pp. xvi + 167.

XVII. Exclusus Amator: A Study in Latin Love Poetry, by FRANK O. COPLEY. 1956. Pp. ix + 176. Out of print.

XVIII. The Bronze Tables of Iguvium, by JAMES W. POULTNEY. 1959. Pp. xvi + 333.

XIX. Plutarch's Quotations, by WILLIAM C. HELMBOLD and EDWARD N. O'NEIL. 1960. Pp. xiv + 76.

XX. The Lost Histories of Alexander, by LIONEL PEARSON. 1960. Pp. xvi + 276.

XXI. A Critical Concordance of the Tibullan Corpus, by EDWARD N. O'NEIL. 1963. Pp. vi + 361.

XXII. Secundus the Silent Philosopher, by BEN EDWIN PERRY. 1964. Pp. xiv + 342; Plates I–VII.

XXIII. Form and Thought in Herodotus, by HENRY R. IMMERWAHR. 1966. Pp. xv + 374.

XXIV. Menander's Dyscolus, edited by WARREN E. BLAKE. 1966. Pp. vi + 228; Plates I–XXI.

C. SPECIAL PUBLICATIONS

I. Serviani in Aeneidem Commentarii: Editio Harvardiana, by
EDWARD KENNARD RAND, ARTHUR F. STOCKER, ALBERT H. TRAVIS,
AND OTHERS. Volume II (*Aeneid* I–II) 1946. Pp. xxi + 509; Volume III
(*Aeneid* III–V) 1965. Pp. xvii + 590.

II. Ilias Atheniensium: The Athenian Iliad of the Sixth Century B.C., edited by GEORGE M. BOLLING. 1950. Pp. x + 514.